The Praxis of Justice

The Praxis of Justice

Liber Amicorum Ivo Aertsen

Brunilda Pali, Katrien Lauwaert and Stefaan Pleysier
(Eds.)

eleven
international publishing

Published, sold and distributed by Eleven International Publishing
P.O. Box 85576
2508 CG The Hague
The Netherlands
Tel.: +31 70 33 070 33
Fax: +31 70 33 070 30
e-mail: sales@elevenpub.nl
www.elevenpub.com

Sold and distributed in USA and Canada
Independent Publishers Group
814 N. Franklin Street
Chicago, IL 60610
USA
Order Placement: (800) 888-4741
Fax: (312) 337-5985
orders@ipgbook.com
www.ipgbook.com

Eleven International Publishing is an imprint of Boom uitgevers Den Haag.

ISBN 978-94-6236-969-6
ISBN 978-94-6094-000-2 (E-book)

Table of Contents

Introduction

Brunilda Pali, Katrien Lauwaert and Stefaan Pleysier

1 Context

The collection 'The Praxis of Justice' is a Liber Amicorum that brings together contributions that centre on the work of Ivo Aertsen. In October 2019, Ivo Aertsen retired from his position as professor of Criminology in the Faculty of Law at KU Leuven and from his lead function as head of the Restorative Justice and Victimology Research Line at the Leuven Institute of Criminology. As earth-shattering as this event is, instead of despairing, we took this opportunity to celebrate in full his *levenswerk*, a work that has highly influenced not only his beloved country, Belgium, but also the rest of the world. Literally meaning a 'book of friends', a Liber Amicorum (also called a *Festschrift*, literally meaning 'celebratory writing') is meant to honour someone's work and life, 'treating them to some flattery' (Zinsstag, this volume).

We identified quite a large (large is literally an understatement!) group of people as being important in the professional background and history of Ivo Aertsen. Some of them were not able to respond to our extremely tight deadline and expressed their sadness as they really wanted to be a part of this 'celebratory' publication. Others took up the challenge and contributed with a material text. We gave a lot of freedom to the participants in the project, and therefore, the contributions are very diverse and range from fully fledged scholarly reflections to personal anecdotes, memories and letters. It has been a joy for us to read all of them, and each of these texts has contributed to the creation of this wonderful and rich mosaic. For Ivo Aertsen, this will hopefully remain a 'living, breathing testament to friendship, growth, accomplishment and adventure; the recognition of a life well-lived by members of his extended family' (Gustafson, this volume).

Why did we come up with 'The Praxis of Justice'? Originally Dutch-speaking, Ivo Aertsen has reflected during several occasions on how fascinating he finds the Dutch expression *rechtvaardig* which translates as 'righteous' but literally expresses the idea that justice is a skill that one can actually do. This expression which he finds fascinating coincides also with his work, both in content and in modalities. The commitment to 'do justice' (intended especially as in righting a wrong) is a core part of the principles of restorative justice, the field on which the work of Ivo Aertsen is mainly built. But his commitment to restorative justice has not been only scholarly. The commitment has come from an authentic place and has been imbued therefore with passion. It is that passion which has inspired and energised others to pay attention, to take action and to impact change. In other words, it has not been about being the face of it, but the heart of it, and Ivo Aertsen has been the heart of restorative justice, its embodiment. For a scholar as him, who embodies his field in this way, *praxis* seemed to us to be the notion that best captured what we wanted to convey. Praxis is not the same as practice. Praxis refers instead to the process by which a theory, lesson, idea or skill is embodied, exercised, applied or realised. It also refers to actions that are oriented towards changing society. Nothing can better define the work of Ivo Aertsen as the 'Praxis of Justice'.

2 LIFE

Ivo Aertsen (born in 1953) studied psychology at KU Leuven in the mid-1970s, a time of vibrant student activism. In the spirit of this movement, a strong social commitment becomes one of the thriving forces behind his professional career, and also the academic part of it, which is characterised by authentic involvement and often goes against the predominant academic grain, in terms of research themes and his continuous collaborations with researchers, practitioners and policymakers, relentlessly seeking for research to result in concrete societal impact.

His professional career starts in 1978. In twelve years he gains field experience, first as a psychologist working in the central prison of Leuven, then starting up the first victim support scheme in Flanders and finally coordinating a new service integrating early intervention, psychosocial and legal assistance to prisoners and victim support. He combines work and study and obtains a law degree from KU Leuven in 1992.

The late Prof. Tony Peters invites him to start an academic career in 1990, as researcher and teaching assistant in the research group Penology and Victimology at the Leuven Institute of Criminology. The results of a qualitative exploration of the situation and needs of victims of violent crime lead to an action research on the potential of victim-offender mediation for serious crimes, conducted in close collaboration with visionary pioneer Leo Van Garsse. This research subsequently lays the groundwork for the fruitful development of a local victim-offender mediation service in Leuven, the gradual implementation of victim-offender mediation all over Flanders and a robust national legal framework. Ivo is actively involved at every stage of this development.

He finishes his PhD entitled 'Victim-offender mediation: a research on the development of a restorative oriented criminal justice system' in 2001 and is appointed assistant professor. Gradually rising through the ranks he becomes full professor (2015) while being the director of the Leuven Institute of Criminology (2012-2016).

Meanwhile, he teaches courses in penology, victimology, forensic mental health, criminal justice and welfare, and restorative justice. He is invited as guest lecturer in numerous academic institutions in Belgium and abroad and provides training to many professionals outside the academic sphere, such as magistrates and other criminal justice practitioners, mediators and policymakers at the local, national and international level.

At the end of the 1990s Ivo Aertsen's work takes a more European turn. He is member of the Committee of Experts on Mediation in Penal Matters, which elaborates the paramount Council of Europe recommendation on mediation in penal matters (1999). Together with the late Tony Peters he initiates the European Forum for Restorative Justice and becomes its first chair (2000-2004). In the following period he launches the research line 'Restorative Justice and Victimology' which becomes an international and interdisciplinary group of over twenty researchers who have been involved in about 50 research projects at the time of Ivo's retirement.

The initial penological dimension of his own research is continued in projects on, for example, community sanctions, the normalisation principle and the offender's experience of punitiveness.

The victimological pillar of the research line investigates victims' needs, services and legislation in general and specific victim categories in particular, including victims and their relatives in cases of homicide, terrorism, sexual violence, partner violence, child abuse, historical institutional violence, road traffic accidents and corporate crimes. Internationally recognised for his leadership in victimological research, Ivo Aertsen serves as member of the Executive Committee of the World Society of Victimology from 2012 to 2018.

The restorative justice research focuses initially on victim-offender mediation for more serious crimes and then rapidly expands to a much wider range of topics, often tackled in close collaboration with the European Forum for Restorative Justice. Projects explore restorative justice models (such as conferencing and peace-making circles) and the psychosocial dynamics in restorative justice (linked e.g. to procedural justice theory, desistance research and moral foundations theory). These projects tackle delicate fields for implementing restorative justice (such as prisons, terrorism, sexual violence, sexual abuse in the church, corporate violence, hate crime or working with child victims) and address crucial factors for the development of restorative justice (such as the attitude of the judiciary, accessibility and initiation of restorative justice services, the creation of social support, the victim's involvement). They support the development of restorative justice in specific regions (such as Southern Europe, Central and Eastern Europe, China, Turkey) or delve into the potential of restorative justice for dealing with mass victimisation in post-conflict situations (e.g. in South Africa, Columbia, Bosnia-Herzegovina and Serbia). The link of restorative justice with other societal developments, such as radicalisation and a polarising society, and other fields such as conflict resolution in schools, cities and the community building sector, is at the heart of still other projects. The interdisciplinary collaboration moves beyond the 'usual suspects' in the criminological field and includes architecture and arts (in the project called 'Art for social change') and philosophy and theology (hosting the Center for Religion, Ethics and Detention). We reserve a special mention for two memorable projects involving an extensive network of researchers. From 2002 to 2006 Ivo Aertsen coordinates the European COST Action A21 on 'Restorative justice developments in Europe', a collaborative effort of about 70 researchers from 21 European countries working on issues of evaluation, policy, theory and violent state conflict and mass victimisation – an endeavour creating strong bonds and fertile ground for many future collaborations. The FP7 project ALTERNATIVE on 'Developing alternative understandings of security and justice through restorative justice approaches in intercultural settings within democratic societies' (2012-2016) was a major collaboration between seven research institutes from six European countries approaching the main theme from a theoretical, comparative and action research perspective.

Since 2002 Ivo is on the editorial board of the journals *Tijdschrift voor Herstelrecht* and *Panopticon: Tijdschrift voor Strafrecht, Criminologie en Forensisch welzijnswerk*. In 2013 he co-founds and becomes the editor-in-chief of *The International Journal of Restorative Justice.*

It is no surprise that Ivo Aertsen receives in 2010 the European Restorative Justice Award and that he is more than ever invited to act as an expert consultant in Belgium and internationally. He advised, for example, the Belgian Parliamentary Commission on sexual abuse in the church (2010-2011), followed by the membership of the Permanent Arbitration Chamber on sexual abuse (2012-2016) and carries out missions for the United Nations, the Council of Europe, the Organization for Security and Co-operation in Europe (OSCE) and the European Union on a variety of topics related to his research domain.

Along the way, many of us have been baffled by Ivo's inexhaustible energy to explore, discuss, advise, engage in new research adventures, bring people together, find compromise and above all to enjoy working together as soulmates and friends.

3 Structure

It has not been easy to structure this book. We had nevertheless asked for this difficulty. The contributions (or 'offerings' to use the poetic language of David Gustafson), only when read together (and also read with many other imaginary contributions which were not written), can shed some light on the complex tapestry that has been interwoven by Ivo Aertsen. More than a proper structure, therefore, we have worked on that tapestry, highlighting some of its main motives. The motives could have been highlighted in completely different ways, and, therefore, we ask the reader not to pay undue attention to the formality of the structure but, instead, delve into the depths of creation that each of the contributors has offered in this volume.

The book is 'structured' into four parts. In Part I, which we have called *Foundations, extended*, we put together a number of voices that revolve around the centre of Ivo's work, either restorative justice or victimology, but do so creatively, freely, making new links, forging new connections of thought. In Part II, which we have called *Praxis, Belgium, up close*, we have put together contributions which relate very closely to Ivo because they highlight their connection to his work in Belgium or because they come from the field of practice. In Part III, which we have called *European journeys*, we have brought together a few contributions which highlight the impact that Ivo's work has had and continues to have in the European continent. Besides referring to specific contents of his work, the contributions testify to a praxis which is very peculiar to his work. Part IV is called *Global challenges* and takes Ivo's work beyond Europe, highlighting the influence he has had among different scholars, students and colleagues globally not only as geographically intended but also as thematically intended.

The complexity of the tapestry we have here interwoven is evident not only in the themes, areas, world regions he has ventured but also in the forms and styles of action and collaborations. Whether the 'offerings' have been academic, practice-oriented or poetic, we have taken them all to be declarations of friendship. For that reason, we would like to dedicate to Ivo what we think to be amazing words written by C.S. Lewis in *The Problem of Pain*, words that have been quoted by Nils Christie in 'Limits to Pain'.

> You may have noticed that the books you really love are bound together by a secret thread. You know very well what is the common quality that makes you love them, though you cannot put it into words: but most of your friends do not see it at all, and often wonder why, liking this, you should also like that. Again, you have stood before some landscape, which seems to embody what you have been looking for all your life; and then turned to the friend at your side who appears to be seeing what you saw – but at the first words a gulf yawns between you, and you realise that this landscape means something totally different to him, that he is pursuing an alien vision and cares nothing for the ineffable suggestion by which you are transported. Even in your hobbies, has there not always been some secret attraction which the others are curiously ignorant of – something, not to be identified with, but always on the verge of breaking through, the smell of cut wood in the workshop or the clap-clap of water against the boat's side? Are not all lifelong friendships born at the moment when at last you meet another human being who has some inkling (but faint and uncertain even in the best) of that something which you were born desiring, and which, beneath the flux of other desires and in all the momentary silences between the louder passions, night and day, year by year, from childhood to old age, you are looking for, watching for, listening for? You have never had it. All the things that have ever deeply possessed your soul have been but hints of it – tantalising glimpses, promises never quite fulfilled, echoes that died away just as they caught your ear. But if it should really become manifest – if

there ever came an echo that did not die away but swelled into the sound itself – you would know it. Beyond all possibility of doubt you would say 'Here at last is the thing I was made for'. We cannot tell each other about it. It is the secret signature of each soul, the incommunicable and unappeasable want, the thing we desired before we met our wives or made our friends or chose our work, and which we shall still desire on our deathbeds, when the mind no longer knows wife or friend or work. While we are, this is. If we lose this, we lose all.

– C.S. Lewis, The Problem of Pain

Part I
Foundations, expanded

The national, the local and the international: the persuasive levels for restorative justice and victims services

Joanna Shapland

1 Introduction

Historically, criminal justice has developed at the level of the nation state, with the ruler of that state being responsible for criminal law and what is done about infractions of that law. Indeed, it has been a matter of national pride for rulers, and more lately national governments, as to what the crime rate is and how effective the police are. Weber (1919) first described the state as having the exclusive right to use coercive force against residents of its territory and saw it as the definition of that state, in the case of crime normally actioned through the police, courts and penal system. Today, despite the growth of international institutions interested in crime and criminal justice, criminal justice remains primarily a matter for the nation state and national legislation.

The result for victims can often be an ill-fitting match between the demands of criminal justice processing, which concentrates upon the offender, and victims' own needs. Once an offender has been identified and is to be prosecuted, typically criminal justice operates at a number of stages, involving the police (investigation and sometimes charging), prosecution, court and penal system. Cases are passed from one state body to another, alongside the offender. As has been known for over 30 years now, however, victims' needs for information about the case, support and participation reach across the stages of criminal justice (Maguire, 1982; Shapland, Willmore & Duff, 1985). Though it is clearly important for the state (criminal justice system) to keep track of the offender and provide information, even legal assistance and support to the offender, because the victim is rarely a full party to the workings of the system, such imperatives do not apply to the same extent. Hence, any moves to provide victim services, to allow the victim to participate in the system and to encourage restorative justice (where victim and offender are in communication) are not intrinsic to the priorities of state criminal justice. They have had to be fought for in each country, sometimes over a long period of time, and not always successfully.

Ivo Aertsen has been a formidable leader in these regards. His research and personal efforts have been highly instrumental in developing victim services and restorative justice. As Brunilda Pali has commented, Ivo is fascinated by the Dutch idea of 'rechvaardig', that justice is a skill that can be performed – the 'doing of justice', or praxis. Praxis, as she says, refers to the 'process by which a theory, lesson, idea or skill is embodied, exercised, applied or realised', as well as actions that are oriented towards changing society. This is a skill which Ivo has perfected. I wish to argue in this short chapter that, in doing so, *because* he has been working on victims and on restorative justice, he has needed to work at different structural and political levels, and that this will continue to be so for future leaders in this area. It is not sufficient, in order to create change in society in these areas, to work purely locally, or nationally, despite the national essence of criminal justice. I would argue that engaging in the international and regional arenas has also been vital.

2 Change and criminal justice

Why would this be so? In many other areas of research, development and practice, change occurs fairly seamlessly, whether work starts at the local level or more globally. Innovations spread through commercial advertising (in the case of products and services), trade fairs and simple word of mouth. But in these fields of science and technology, innovation confers an advantage on the producer or service deliverer. Markets may be very imperfect, but they tend to embrace the new and the effective.

In the public sector, there is less pressure often to innovate or pursue effectiveness. It is one of the reasons why medicine, despite often indicating it as evidence-based (Sagan, 1987), still tends to continue with accepted practice and not to pursue the new – though the demands of new public management (or new public administration or governance) to embrace efficiency and effectiveness have affected all the public sector.[1] Another reason for the persistence of older methods in medicine may be the overriding principle in medicine to do no harm, with the standard for new techniques being to be better than the previous ones, rather than to do good overall.

Criminal justice, however, perhaps alone in the public sector, has made a virtue out of stability, consistency and the absence of change. The argument has been that the criminal law has to be known and clear. Hence, the old ways may not be ideal, but they are at least fairly certain. The result is that new ways and certainly new actors on the penal stage are both unwelcome and require considerable momentum to effect any change. In addition, the diverse legal systems in Europe and elsewhere, though they seem to be growing more alike (Fennell, Harding, Jorg & Swart, 1995), reflect deep-rooted legal cultures with different principles and values embedded in them. The process of policy transfer, always difficult, seems to be even more resisted in the criminal justice sphere.

And that is why I think that working to create opportunities for restorative justice or victim services needs to be at many different levels, and why Ivo's own work and research

1 See Osborne (2006) for the United Kingdom and Schedler and Proeller (2002) in relation to mainland Europe.

is such an inspiration. We can consider three particular levels: the nation state, local practitioners and international work.

3 The three levels: national, local and international

3.1 Working at the nation state level

As the EU Directive of 2012 points out, victims of crime need to receive appropriate information, support and protection and to be able to participate in criminal proceedings (Art. 1.1). This necessarily means that victim services must be tailored to criminal justice processes, which are set by nation states. Similar imperatives apply to restorative justice services, where the EU defines restorative justice as 'any process whereby the victim and the offender are enabled, if they freely consent, to participate actively in the resolution of matters arising from the criminal offence through the help of an impartial third party' (Art. 2.1(d)). It has become clear in many countries that in order for victims to be offered relevant services, those providing the services need to reach out to victims and make them aware of what is available. Victims themselves, often in some shock because of the offence, will not necessarily know who is providing what, let alone whether in the future they might need that service.

In addition, the Directive puts the onus on nation states to communicate with victims about the progress of their case, including the right to receive information from the very first contact with a competent authority (normally the police). In order to do this, those running information and support services for victims need to know how to contact the victim – the information has to be passed on from the first agency meeting the victim (again, normally the police) to later criminal justice authorities and to victim services which apply throughout the criminal justice system.

If we consider restorative justice, the Directive says that victims who choose to participate in restorative justice processes should have access to safe and competent restorative justice services and that member states should facilitate the referral of cases, including through the establishment of procedures or guidelines on the conditions for such referral (Art. 12). This also will require relevant services to be able to contact victims (and offenders) and obtain information from criminal justice agencies. None of this can be accomplished without clear thought and guidance at the national level as to who should pass on information to whom and when.

Though this is a Directive binding on member states, countries have not been noted for their rush to implement EU (or Council of Europe) instruments concerning victims and criminal justice, or restorative justice. The 2012 Directive itself stemmed from the failure of member states to implement the 2001 Framework Directive. Van Dijk and Groenhuijsen (2018) have set out the results of the monitoring of both Council of Europe and EU instruments. It is clear that, even from the time of the 1985 Council of Europe Recommendation on victims in criminal justice, countries were moving at different paces to start creating reforms to aid victims. Brienen and Hoegen (2000) ranked countries at three levels, with the top tier including Belgium, England and Wales, Ireland, the Netherlands and Norway; the middle tier Austria, Denmark, France, Germany, Scotland, Sweden and Switzerland; and the bottom tier Greece, Iceland, Italy, Luxembourg, Portugal, Spain and Turkey. That was fifteen years after the Recommendation was directed at member states and longer since the first relevant research was available as to victims' reactions to national criminal justice systems (Maguire, 2002; Shapland et al., 1985). Van Dijk and Groenhuijsen (2018) correlated the Brienen-Hoegen score with survey-based outcomes on victim satisfaction with victim assistance from the 2004/2005 International Crime Victimization Survey and obtained a high correlation of 0.60 ($p < 0.05$). The pace of reform in relation to victims' needs has been almost a snail's pace – and if asked today to rate nation states' achievements in implementing clearly agreed objectives in relation to either victim support or restorative justice in relation to criminal justice, almost the same ranking scale is likely to be produced.

Indeed, the EU itself was so disappointed with the performance of its member nation states with the 2001 Framework Decision that it decided to 'have another go' in the 2012 Directive. The EU concluded in its monitoring review that none of the member states had fully implemented the Framework Decision, even at the level of formal implementation into national legislation and even on self-ratings by the member states themselves (Groenhuijsen, 2014). Van Dijk and Groenhuijsen (2018) make the important distinction between formal implementation and actual compliance – formal implementation means the provisions are in place legally, but they may well not be used locally or consistently. In terms of the 2012 Directive, early results show that, though there are some positive indications, particularly in the north and west of Europe (rather than the south and east), there are also vast differences between national victim support mechanisms, with inconsistent coverage and few member states having adopted quality standards for victim support delivery. Unfortunately, there is no international survey or monitoring mechanism currently measuring either formal implementation by nation states or how much or what quality of services are being delivered. We do not know whether the snail is maintaining its pace or has metamorphosed into a slightly faster beast. We have no means to measure victims' satisfaction with the services they are provided with across Europe, given that the 2004/2005 International Crime Victimization Survey was the last one funded. This is convenient for nation states (and frustrating for those concerned with victims' rights and restorative justice).

The pattern of implementation tends to suggest that national change (though slow in pace) comes about after governments are 'shamed' through research results on the ability of victims to access information or obtain support or services in that country, sometimes particularly when the country shows up badly in international comparison. Some of this research has been done by university researchers, some (though increasingly less as austerity cuts have bitten) by government researchers and, more recently, nationally appointed commissioners or 'tsars' have acted as spurs.[2] The patchy extent of even formal implementation means that there will be a task for individual researchers working across countries on comparative research in this respect for many years to come.

In relation to restorative justice, national, systemic change is likely to be even more important. We do not have international results on the monitoring of restorative justice measures and provision in the same way as for victim services. However, the ability to access restorative justice services in relation to a criminal offence is even more closely interlinked with the stages of criminal justice and the allowed 'outcomes' for offenders. Restorative justice services for other than the most trivial offences and youngest offenders will need to be undertaken in parallel with criminal justice – a diversionary outcome will not be possible. It is no accident that restorative justice worldwide has tended first to be established for young offenders (Shapland et al., 2011). A diversionary model is often seen as suitable for young people, with youth justice needing to be in the best interests of the young person and often now to minimise the need for appearances in formal, youth justice settings. Once one is dealing with adult offenders or more serious offences, however, using restorative justice in a community setting can clash with the perceived prerogative of police and prosecution to determine outcomes, as has been clear in Northern Ireland (Shapland, et al., 2017a). The only other way for restorative justice provision for adult offenders or more serious offences is to try to work *with* criminal justice and offer restorative justice alongside criminal justice processes, whether those be diversionary (subject to police or prosecution retaining the ultimate decision-making power on outcome), or pre- or post-sentence.

Any such parallel working will, at least after pilot stages, require national legislative input to permit or encourage such outcomes. England and Wales, as part of the national strategy to implement restorative justice, realised that though judges did have the power to adjourn cases pre-sentence for restorative justice in the adult courts, so that the sentence could reflect any information from the restorative justice process, the courts needed encouragement to do so (Ministry of Justice, 2012). They enacted the legislative provision to allow judges to defer sentence for restorative justice (in the Crime and Courts Act 2013, Schedule 16, Part 2). Similarly, it is now an approved 'outcome' for police to divert cases to a 'community disposal', which can include restorative justice – though unfortunately there is no specific provision for restorative justice, so monitoring to what extent the police use this is impossible (Shapland et al., 2017b). Again, where such provisions are not in place, there is both research work and advisory work necessary from outsiders at the national level. Again, those outsiders can be academic researchers or government-appointed commissioners (see Victims Commissioner, 2018).

2 For example, the Victims Commissioner in England and Wales, see her reports from 2017 at https://victimscommissioner.org.uk/published-reviews/.

3.2 *Working at the local level*

The distinction between formal implementation (the provisions exist legally) and consistent implementation at the local level is an important one. If there are few resources, either services will become capped at one point in the year, or will be made available for victims of only some kinds of crime, or they will be very patchy geographically. If there is no pressure at the national level for local heads of services to provide that service, it will be up to enthusiasts or those more favourable to victims' needs to create them in their locality. Examples of both deficiencies are very prevalent in both victim services and restorative justice provision. So, Van Dijk and Groenhuijsen (2018) comment that in Italy, for example, priority seems to have been given to victims of terrorist offences. In England and Wales, Hall (2017) has shown that Police and Crime Commissioners seem to have different priorities in terms of types of offence and victims for victim services. Restorative justice services and provision have been found to be patchy geographically by both research (Shapland et al., 2017b) and official enquiries (e.g. in terms of police services: Criminal Justice Joint Inspection, 2012; Victims Commissioner, 2018). Even in Belgium, where researchers at the KU Leuven, including Ivo Aertsen, have been at the forefront, there are still differences in the ability to be referred to restorative justice services locally, depending on the wishes of the local public prosecutor (Shapland et al., 2017a).

It will take time to smooth out local variation. Both victim services and restorative justice provision have historically local roots (e.g. in the United States, England and Wales, Germany and Austria). They often depend on local volunteers and the enthusiasm of local criminal justice chiefs. Those cultures are long-lasting, particularly when resources are tight.

Moreover, creating change in criminal justice, as we have seen, is slow and difficult. It implies creating and embedding practices and procedures as well as legislation and then getting local practitioners, who are often overstretched, to undertake those new procedures. There are now a number of research studies in relation to restorative justice which have shown that new referral practices need to be not only simple but also simpler than the accustomed and familiar path to succeed.[3] Both victim services and restorative justice provision suffer from not being the main purpose of most criminal justice personnel (who deal primarily with offenders). They also both require individualised decisions from practitioners (Which victim services or support are needed? Is this case appropriate for restorative justice?). Those practitioners require training and, above all, confidence and practice in order to make referrals. Sometimes the need for decisions on referrals by individual practitioners can be short-circuited by technological solutions (e.g. automatic referral to victim support agencies for victims of certain types of offences) or facilitated by

3 In, for example, Finland (Iivari et al., 2009) and England and Wales (Shapland et al., 2017b).

embedded referral agency personnel or 'champions'. It is never, though, a simple task to create such change, and it is always subject to potential disruption through changes in senior personnel or in national priorities (e.g. for the police). The result is a need for constant researcher and inter-agency input in the local practitioner context, to reinforce and monitor change.

3.3 *Working at the international level*

Working at the international level has two benefits in terms of creating change in criminal justice. One is the potential influence of international bodies and instruments, the other the possibility of policy transfer – that what another nation state has done or another city has achieved may provide a solution to a potentially knotty problem. We have already seen the influence of international instruments in relation to victims and restorative justice in the work of the EU and the Council of Europe. Prior to that there was the United Nations Declaration of Basic Principles of Justice for Victims of Crime and Abuse of Power in 1985. Such instruments potentially influence not only nation states which are members but also other international bodies. UN instruments are rarely binding, but can inspire regional successor instruments, such as those of the EU, which create more pressing requirements on states to turn them into national legislation.

In the victims and restorative justice arenas, there is not only the influence of instruments but also the creation of international associations of practitioners (or sometimes researchers), which through their annual meetings provide for the dissemination of new results and the discussion of good practice. So, in Europe, there is Victim Support Europe, which brings together national victim support and assistance organisations. For restorative justice, there is the European Forum for Restorative Justice, which has always had a close association with the Katholieke Universiteit Leuven and has also welcomed academic members. Founded in the late 1990s, Ivo Aertsen was strongly associated with its development and sought funding from the EU and other sources for its projects, which have played a major role in the development of good practice.

Those projects have normally been of a comparative nature, enabling progress and practice to be mapped in different places, and new initiatives which are created locally to reach a much wider audience. Given the difficulties of creating change, as outlined earlier, such projects are invaluable. Europe includes several different legal systems, with their associated deeply valued legal cultures and criminal justice organisations. If it can be shown that a particular problem has been solved in a system similar to one's own, then it is likely to be seen not as an alien import (e.g. from the common law of the Anglo-Saxon world) but as a helpful and interesting experiment by a familiar neighbour. The trick is then to invite partners from countries representing the different legal systems into the project, so that all can find some element of use in the resulting reports.

Comparative research on criminal justice is always difficult, as Nelken (2017) has shown. There is a fine balance to be struck between respecting legal cultures and being able to compare them all. Experts will know (hopefully) about their own country's legal instruments and criminal justice practices but will not be knowledgeable about the legal instruments and criminal justice practices of other countries. In criminal justice, even the vocabulary is difficult, with similar words having very different meanings, because of the philosophical roots of the legal systems. An example, I found, is the word *community*; when applied to criminal justice, it is seen as a positive element in common law countries with more localised criminal justice provision and traditions but abhorred in more centralised states (such as France), where any intermediate body between the state and the citizen is seen as potentially dangerous (Shapland, 1988). Such cultural differences, which include the role of the prosecution compared to the police, and the extent to which oral evidence is required at court from witnesses (including the victim), are key in developing victim services and restorative justice. Often, however, they can only be understood and their implications taken on board when experts from different countries work together on a project for some time. That is the typical model adopted by the European Forum very successfully.

4 Developing victim services and restorative justice in the future

I have argued earlier that those who are interested in creating change in relation to victim services or restorative justice need to work at the national level, the local level and the international level. Creating change through influencing policy and practice directly is the epitome of 'public criminology' (Loader & Sparks, 2013). It will not be to the taste of all academics, some of whom will prefer to work with local or national government, whilst others will critique what government does. In relation to victims, however, both a reformist and a more challenging stance are helpful. Victims are often powerless, whether in relation to criminal justice authorities or the offender. Adding their view and experiences to the debate is key in creating that change in a system which prioritises what is done with offenders (though often not what offenders themselves would see as important).

As a result, I have argued that working at all three levels is essential. Criminal justice is prescribed nationally, operated locally and influenced internationally. Monitoring, evaluating and suggesting what is happening and might be needed in relation to victims and offenders are required at each of these stages. It is a position which Ivo himself clearly took and made major contributions at all those levels.

References

Brienen, M. & Hoegen, E. (2000). *Victims of crime in 22 European criminal justice systems.* Nijmegen: Wolf.

Council of Europe. (1985). *Council of Europe Committee of Ministers Recommendation No. R(85) 11 to the Member States on the position of the victim in the framework of criminal law and procedure.* Strasbourg: Council of Europe. Retrieved from https://polis.osce.org/node/4651 (last accessed 13 May 2019).

Criminal Justice Joint Inspection. (2012). *Facing up to offending: use of restorative justice in the criminal justice system.* London: Criminal Justice Joint Inspection. Retrieved from www.justiceinspectorates.gov.uk/hmicfrs/media/facing-up-to-offending-20120918.pdf (last accessed 13 May 2019).

European Union. (2012). *Directive 2012/29/EU of the European Parliament and of the Council of 25 October 2012 establishing minimum standards on the rights, supports and protection of victims of crime, and replacing Council Framework Decision 2001/220/JHA.* Strasbourg: European Union. Retrieved from https://eur-lex.europa.eu/legal-content/EN/TXT/?uri=celex%3A32012L0029 (last accessed 13 May 2019).

Fennell, P., Harding, C., Jorg, N. & Swart, B. (1995). *Criminal justice in Europe: a comparative study.* Oxford: Clarendon Press.

Groenhuijsen, M. (2014). The development of international policy in relation to victims of crime, *International Review of Victimology*, 20(1), 31-48. doi:10.1177/0269758013511740.

Hall, M. (2017). *Victims of crime: constructions, governance and policy.* London: Palgrave.

Iivari, J., Sakkinen, S. & Kuoppala, T. (2009). *Mediation in Criminal and Civil Cases 2008.* Helsinki: National Institute for Health and Welfare.

Loader, I. & Sparks, R. (2013). *Public criminology?* London: Routledge.

Maguire, M. (1982). *Burglary in a dwelling.* London: Heinemann.

Ministry of Justice. (2012). *Restorative justice action plan for the criminal justice system. London: Ministry of Justice.* Retrieved from https://assets.publishing.service.gov.uk/government/uploads/system/uploads/attachment_data/file/217311/restorative-justice-action-plan.pdf (last accessed 13 May 2019).

Nelken, D. (2017). Rethinking comparative criminal justice. In A. Liebling, S. Maruna & L. McAra (eds.), *The Oxford handbook of criminology* (6th ed., pp. 416-437). Oxford: Oxford University Press.

Osborne, S. P. (2006). *The new public governance? Public Management Review*, 8(3), 377-387. doi:10.1080/14719030600853022.

Sagan, L. (1987). *The health of nations.* New York: Basic Books.

Schedler, K. & Proeller, I. (2002). The New Public Management: a perspective from mainland Europe. In K. McLaughlin, S.P. Osborne & E. Ferlie (eds.), *New Public Management: current trends and future prospects* (pp. 163-180). London: Routledge.

Shapland, J. (ed.). (1988). *Justice, community and civil society: a contested terrain.* Cullompton: Willan.

Shapland, J., Willmore, J. & Duff, P. (1985). *Victims in the criminal justice system.* Aldershot: Gower.

Shapland, J., Robinson, G. & Sorsby, A. (2011). *Restorative justice in practice.* London: Routledge.

Shapland, J., Crawford, A., Gray, E. & Burn, D. (2017a). *Developing restorative policing: learning lessons from Belgium and Northern Ireland.* Sheffield: Centre for Criminological Research Occasional Paper 7. Retrieved from www.sheffield.ac.uk/polopoly_fs/1.714948!/file/Comparative-report-publication.pdf (last accessed 13 May 2019).

Shapland, J., Crawford, A., Gray, E. & Burn, D. (2017b). *Restorative justice at the level of the police in England: implementing change.* Sheffield: Centre for Criminological Research Occasional Paper 8. Retrieved from www.sheffield.ac.uk/polopoly_fs/1.743733!/file/DevelopingRestorativePolicing3.pdf (last accessed 13 May 2019).

United Nations. (1985). *Declaration of basic principles of justice for victims of crime and abuse of power.* New York: United Nations. Retrieved from http://legal.un.org/avl/ha/dbpjvcap/dbpjvcap.html (last accessed 13 May 2019).

Van Dijk, J. & Groenhuijsen, M. (2018). A glass half full, or half empty? On the implementation of the EU's Victims Directive regarding police reception and specialized support. In S. Walklate (ed.), *Handbook of victims and victimology* (2nd ed., pp. 275-292). Abingdon: Routledge.

Victims Commissioner. (2018). *A question of quality: a review of restorative justice, Part 1 – service providers and Part 2 – victims.* London: Victims Commissioner. Retrieved from https://victimscommissioner.org.uk/published-reviews/a-question-of-quality-a-review-of-restorative-justice-part-1-service-providers/ and https://victimscommissioner.org.uk/published-reviews/a-question-of-quality-a-review-of-restorative-justice-part-2-victims/ (last accessed 13 May 2019).

Weber, M. (1919). *Politics as a vocation ('Politik als Beruf').* Lecture to the University of Munich. Munich: Duncker & Humboldt.

Revisioning restorative justice: critique, accusation and hospitality

George Pavlich

1 Introduction

The etymology of the term *restore* suggests ideas of repair, replacement, return, and also renewal, deriving from the Latin '*re*' again and '*staurare ... to set up, place*' (Skeat, 1961: 473). Equally, the term *justice* implies a 'tribunal, or judge' (Skeat, 1961: 312). Combining etymologies of 'restore' and 'justice', as in 'restorative justice', connotes rituals that involve judgement but always in ways that either reaffirm, replace, or renew broken (or harmful) social relations. Here one encounters an incongruity at the heart of restorative justice meanings; there is a basic tension between images of restoration that seek merely to *reaffirm* past relational orders, to put things back to where they were, as opposed to change-orientated processes that seek to *set up* different (renewed) relations.

Ivo Aertsen's (2006, 2008, 2010, 2017, 2018) larger contributions to the restorative justice arena reflect that basic tension, but stand out for their practical insight, pensiveness and an empirical sense of diverse international (intercultural) programmes. His approach not only highlights flaws in punitive responses to misconduct but also recognises the complexity of institutionalising restorative tribunals in ways that remain loyal to participatory aspirations (e.g. Aertsen et al., 2006). My (admittedly selective) reading of his work has inspired a return to promises and critiques of the late 1970s and 1980s that set the community justice movement on a path designed to replenish ailing criminal justice. Echoes thereof resound in his ideas, and I hear overtones in his inclusive sense that doers and reflectors, as well as practitioners and critical theorists, ought to be part of a 'critical restorative justice' (Aertsen & Pali, 2017). That openness seems to guide his self-reflective analyses of the prospect and limits of restoratively produced social change (Aertsen et al., 2006). But Aertsen does not unreservedly endorse or reject restorative justice programming allied with state administrations. In many ways, he worked past maximalists/minimalist arguments by focusing on how restorative justice could be institutionalised, especially in the wake of large-scale violent conflicts, with states in transition (Aertsen, 2008) – prompting reflectively considered political engagements with local, national, intercultural and international contexts (e.g. Aertsen, 2008, 2010, 2017).

Here, one senses that blind expansions of restorative justice could not be counted as successes if they simply replicate penal justice. Hence, his work variously engages the politics of justice behind the state's dominance over modern criminal and penal practices, and his quest to rescind top-heavy retribution by locally formed restorative processes, especially when the latter takes seriously the concerns of the harmed and unfolds out of local needs following criminal events. Victim requirements are, for him, imperative here, but so too is an onus on panels to help offenders take meaningful responsibility for harms caused (Aertsen, 2017). At times, rational impositions of criminal law may also be recalled, but more generally restorative fields carve out responsive arenas beyond the state's reach. In any event, sheer punitiveness is to be replaced by a paradigm shift that would involve humane (ecclesiastically inspired) visions of restoration in reaction to harmful events (akin to Zehr, 2015). As I read it, such thinking shapes Pali's and his analysis of the possibilities and pitfalls of restorative justice committed to local visions of security rather than simple state-based formulations of social defence and order (Pali & Aertsen, 2018). One might here detect an emphasis on local vernaculars to facilitate restorative tribunals that are dynamically responsive to contingently fashioned victim identities (Aertsen, 2017).

To be sure, Aertsen accepts that catastrophic effects often follow destructive human action, even considering intercultural nuances, and generate qualitatively new subject needs and forms. Destructive wrongdoing alters participants' experiences (whether victim, offender or bystander) in basic ways and calls out for very different relations to decide how to 'be with' others in future – a complex task that efficacious restorative tribunals should embrace rather than spurn. As noted, his recognition of local victims as basic to any such justice environments welcomes flexible processes through which offenders might assume meaningful responsibility for their actions. But such processes also enable historically conceived victims to drive – within constitutional limits – outcomes (Aertsen, 2017). The aim is to secure mutually agreeable ways to move damaging relations beyond what they were and to promise a future that relieves the traumas experienced by local participants.

Through this future-directed emphasis, Aertsen recognises that the aftereffects of damaged social relations require alteration, as do the subjects produced by the harm (Aertsen et al., 2006). It follows then that the complex relations driving detrimental events ought to be transformed, not merely restored. Such transformations imply a spirit of relational revival, with different degrees of success, as we see from his scans of restorative justice programmes (Aertsen, 2017). This work eschews settlements that come at unforgiving costs; especially if they harshly return relations to an imagined past 'order'. In short, restorative justice should insert itself into the complex and often chaotic relational terrains that surface out of harmful events, using fair, responsibility-orientated and victim-centred processes. Such responses aim to move social relations in directions that bring security, peace and relational harmony to collective formations, serving as facilitators for new social horizons.

This admittedly choosy interpretation of Aertsen's work emphasises his pragmatic, though critically inflected, attempts to institutionalise fresh calculations of justice. It provides this reader, at least, with a means to think about the promises of non-punitive, victim-orientated tribunals arranged around and by those involved in crimes – where participants deliberate on relational paths to the future, but with restraints placed on capricious mediation practices. It also challenges the reflex to criminalise and punish individuals (criminal justice) without lauding restorative justice as a stateless panacea – even as it calls for, to borrow from Scott (2014), a local 'vernacular' to deal with destructive social relations and conflict. One might well hear echoes of abolitionist calls for community control (Ruggiero, 2011; Snare & Christie, 1975; Mathiesen, 1974), but not the plea to purge state law's capacity to restrain community excesses (Pavlich, 2001).

I read Aertsen in this way precisely because of my interest in the founding politics through which community mediation emerged around the promises of a justice calculated through non-punitive tribunals and the active participation of local subjects (e.g. Shonholtz, 1984, 1988). Such ideas, no doubt, initially drew many to the field; but such formative discourses are often neglected by those who today define restorative justice. Aertsen's and Pali's (2017) critical restorative justice helps to excavate some of these buried ideas, as indeed does the work of others (Woolford & Ratner, 2008). A basic question appears: has the promise to restore social forms by rescinding criminal justice's focus on individual culpability attributions been forgotten? Reading Aertsen through a legacy of early promises, alongside strands of 'progressive' criticism of the day, we might apprehend the stakes behind a pragmatic, reflective, institutionalist approach to the restorative field as it appears today.

2 Tracing a conceptual lineage: critical restorative justice

In view of what has been said so far, there is value in returning to earlier critiques of restorative justice as it materialised. I would even venture to argue that the latter's foundations were shaped by the effects of three critical discussions: first, community-based critiques that contested criminal justice; second, radical social critiques of community and restorative (informal) justice; and, third, critiques of both the radical social critics and restorative justice advocates. Turning to the first, we might note that alluring promises in the 1970s and 1980s called for alternatives to criminal justice by imagining what legal pluralism might mean — especially in the form of alternative dispute resolution, informal justice and community mediation (see Merry & Milner, 1993). In various ways, these discourses pledged community-based tribunals that empowered local participants to take charge of conflict via future-directed mediations. They aimed for lasting settlements and harmonious relational futures, seemingly unavailable to adversarial processes of criminal law (Braithwaite, 2010; Johnstone, 2011; Johnstone & Van Ness, 2007; Zehr & Toews, 2004). Exemplifying various positions, early restorative advocates thus challenged the efficacy of the state's courtroom justice, with its formal, punitive, abstracted, alienating, bureaucratic, disorientating and officially driven procedures. Some even classed these as criminogenic because they marginalised real people and communities (see Gavrielides & Artinopoulou, 2016; Zehr, 2002).

Even if diluted over time, such critiques expedited the institutionalisation of restorative justice measures, especially as they took root in youth justice contexts. To be sure, however, sharper confrontations with state law dulled as a global restorative movement took shape by promising an alternative kind of justice while relying on state agencies to approve its development (de Lagasnerie, 2018). Here, the state authorised restorative justice programmes within permissible legal limits, okaying limited incursions into (and more usually around) courtroom justice (Pavlich, 2005). As might be expected, restorative justice advocates here directly engaged political contexts where states continued to assert an exclusive claim over criminalisation and justice. Indeed, as Scott (2014) notes, contesting state dominance in such realms is always a complex political matter, and historical lessons suggest that significant changes to state arrangements seldom appear through self-reform. In any event, state-non-state bargains were made, and in conflict resolution arenas, they promised to address wider fiscal and legitimacy crises facing many welfare states (Offe, 1984); they also set the terms for widespread neoliberal infiltrations that would follow (Brown, 2015). Regardless, and to my point, restorative justice expanded out of implicit accords made with the very state-legal institutions that once bore the brunt of 'informal justice' critiques (Pavlich, 2005). These developments had the effect of sapping early community advocates' calls for more stringent diversionary, autochthonous and popular justice goals. Indeed, any early resonances with state abolitionism (see Carrier & Piché, 2015) were surpassed by restorative engagements that sought to humanise state forms (Walgrave, 2003). In parts of Aertsen's work we hear echoes of the call for local vernaculars, for communal visions of justice and autonomous participation (e.g. Aertsen, 2008, 2017); and yet these are also coupled with a pragmatic recognition that ruling modern state justice administrations could be restrained even as they authorised restorative spheres of operation (Walgrave, 2002, 2008; Braithwaite, 2010).

One could surely point to successes in limiting punitive excesses of state justice, but the global expansion of restorative justice has not annulled a centuries-old system based on crime and punishment narratives. Often it even buttresses the legal fiction that offenders can be assigned criminal culpability almost exclusively as individuals who freely chose to commit criminal acts (Fassin, 2018; Davis, 2003). Indeed, early instances of community mediation's stark opposition to criminalisation, and its quest to 'divert' cases out of courtrooms, has ebbed in the wake of restorative justice's state-authorised development. In the process, restorative justice was to become part of new state strategies to thwart a dystopic 'nothing works' syndrome (see Cullen & Gendreau, 2001), without rescinding a growing reliance upon 'get tough on crime' remedies (see Williams, 2000). It echoed decarceration and community-based approaches that called on state agents to embrace private controls, and on 'families' or allied 'communities' to participate in non-state spaces of regulation – even if always under the authorising gaze of state administrators (Christie, 2015; Cohen, 1985). In that climate, too, amorphous calls for community participation in criminal conflict struck a chord across the political spectrum, appealing to liberal, social democratic and conservative bents alike (Pavlich, 2005). Here, courtrooms opened up to potentially more efficient 'alternatives' (see Pavlich, 1996a), especially ill-defined promises heralding community-based solutions to crime (Cohen, 1985). Justice reforms increasingly turned to 'community' or 'informal' initiatives (e.g. conferencing, circles, panels, mediation) institutionally overseen by state or designated legal authorities.

Secondly, in response to such community-state alliances, radical social critics challenged how restorative justice appeared to be ensconcing capitalist exploitation under dubious, contrary pretexts. Echoing strands of neo-Marxist thinking of the day, they worried about the way exploitative state apparatuses were expanding through notions of local, community control – versions of the critique were exemplified by Hofrichter (1987), Baskin (1988) and Santos (1982).

Hofrichter (1987), for instance, questioned what he termed a rising 'neighbourhood justice' and its populist claims to 'empower' people to resolve 'minor' disputes without resorting to state intervention. For him, this justice did little to thwart welfare state expansions into people's private lives; on the contrary, it gave the state another way to penetrate and shape subjects that were required by late capitalist economies. By addressing disputes that previously would have been 'lumped', neighbourhood justice reflected the state's and the capital's attempts to manage historical class conflicts by authorising local groups to deal with disputes that previously would have escaped formal attention. By so managing subjects and local ideologies informally, the state could thereby subdue class opposition by shaping subjects who imagined themselves to be empowered, non-alienated and free individuals capable of resolving neighbourhood conflicts. Furthermore, this justice served crisis-laden capitalist economies by allowing states to claim fiscal restraint without sacrificing ultimate control over ideological and subject formation.

For her part, Baskin (1988) tapped a different strand of neo-Marxist thinking (Bonefeld & Holloway, 1992), arguing that post-Fordist capitalist economies were increasingly organised around modes of consumption (as opposed to production) to absorb untapped capital flows. Along with basic changes of this sort came a demand for flexible modes of regulation to yield passive, consuming subjects that held onto non-disserting ideological frameworks. Through privatised forms of justice, for Baskin, state forms could flexibly (informally) regulate private domains and control people from a relative distance (such as through state-sanctioned 'community' mediations). Although her argument remained within Marxist lexicons, she allowed that community justice could at least potentially contest hegemonic state forms (Merry & Milner, 1993). Discerning such prospects required a careful engagement with the politics behind new modes of regulation, especially since current forms of community justice did not contest the privatised foundations of exploitative capitalist relations, leaving their capacity for resistance to float uneasily on the surface of regulatory tinkering.

Santos' (1982) analysis modulated such ideas by arguing that informal justice allowed states to address protracted monetarist and legitimacy crises facing later 20th Century welfare states — specifically in conflict resolution arenas. For him, community-based forms of justice promised, on the one hand, to reduce state expenditures by authorising the privatised regulation (mediation) of conflict that promised more efficient ways to resolve local disputes. On the other hand, informal initiatives involved local subjects in regulating community disputes, thus reducing the risk of challenges to state legitimacy, which became more frequent as welfare state agencies delved further into social life; that is, by allowing communities to deal with conflicts through approved programming, the state could maintain authority over dispute resolution but simultaneously devolve itself of responsibility when local mediation activities went awry. In effect, embattled welfare states could claim to be doing something about their fiscal predicaments, enlist support for popular and participatory democracy through community justice and alleviate legitimacy crunches by deflecting attention away from any errant activities. Yet, for Santos, these developments concealed a ruse: under the guise of claiming to retract and reduce state control, informal justice actually expanded state rule. That rule increasingly operated through enlarged control nets with finer meshwork that could apprehend more people and deeds.

Thirdly, and finally, while agreeing with the broad outlines of such critiques, others felt that neo-Marxist assessments did not adequately allow that affirmative gains could accrue to vigilant engagements with the politics of informal justice (see Matthews, 1988). Fitzpatrick (1988), for one, analysed the 'rise and rise' of informal justice as reflective of changing political moments and pointed to the potential value of using Foucault's work to engage with and conceptualise its meteoric rise. My early wonderings into the field worked off such ideas (Pavlich, 1996a, 1996b); I particularly liked the way that these approaches evaded academic and practitioner cliques and spurned easy distinctions between critics and advocates of community justice. My sense was that factions claiming to be 'for' or 'against' restorative (or community) justice were as unhelpful as those that lined up behind particular tribunals as unequivocally good or bad. Hence, following Fitzpatrick's lead in referencing Foucault's work (e.g. 1979, 1980a, 1980b, 1982), I focused attention on ideas and intersecting powers that enunciated 'state', 'criminal', 'community' or 'restorative' appellations in fragmenting fields of justice (Pavlich, 1996a).

The aim was not to conceal deep divisions; on the contrary, the intent was to map the uneasy alliances and dynamic political landscapes that yielded historical forms of community and restorative justice (Pavlich, 1996b: 707). Such maps showed how governing through restorative practices (mediation, panels, circles, conferences) drifted seamlessly within or alongside criminal justice arenas, even when they promoted quite different visions of justice (e.g. mediation against 'get tough on crime' measures). Political contexts could do quite different things even as they targeted the same regulatory objects, whether individually forged 'victims' or 'offenders', or amorphously envisaged 'communities'. By examining power-knowledge complexes that helped to create such targets, one could point to emerging intersections of powers that targeted legally defined persons with different aims, including criminalisation, harm-based responsibilisation as well as reconciling individual offenders and victims or afflicted communities. The point was to chart the powers of an emerging politics of 'law and order' that bolstered criminal law through normalising (disciplinary), pastoral and governmental (biopolitical) powers (Pavlich, 1996b). The hybrid formations of power and knowledge resulted in a fragmented (postmodern) justice that signalled changing conflict management technologies and riven (rather than universally agreed to) justice aspirations (Pavlich, 1996a).

In this ethos, flexible and local dispute resolution techniques yielded diverse state-community alliances that coalesced around governmental concepts (crime, harm), subjects (disputing individuals, victims, offenders), practices (restorative tribunals), purposes (community peace, harmony, security) and political effects (participatory democracy, civic republicanism). The aim of this genre of critique was not to argue that one model of power – whether located within or outside of state institutions – was intrinsically good (or bad); rather its point was to recognise that all powers are potentially dangerous. This perpetual danger demanded constant reflective vigilance and a careful diagnosis of the complex ways that dynamic powers emerged. As such, the ongoing critical interpretation of these powers is indispensable, especially when dealing with marginalised subjects rendered as the 'other' by historical institutions, whether under the banner of criminal, restorative or any other justice.

3 Recalibrating criminal and community justice: accusation and hospitality

From this critical arena, one might interpret Aertson's consideration of how to institutionalise restorative and criminal justice as a challenge to older calculations of justice. But there are points of contrast between his institutional analysis and my approach to power that might be instructive for thinking about future calculations of criminal justice. First, we agree on the dangers of juridical punitiveness, but without ignoring the negative social effects of (harmful, criminal) wrongdoing. No doubt, as Aertsen (2017) insists, meaningful responsibility should be assumed by subjects who destructively strike out against people and social forms. But there is more to this: one says little new when discerning (as does Aertsen) that many 'offending' subjects are themselves 'victims' of previous circumstances — thus suggesting different categories of victimhood. In any case, the point is that harm-producing events are always symptomatic of complex social processes and relations; when we individualise responsibility for 'crimes' we underestimate, or even worse, ignore, the significance of basic social and political logics at play (de Lagasnerie, 2018). So, it is certainly laudable to find ways for individual perpetrators of criminal events to face their past actions and to involve them in meaningful relational changes that help to define responsibility in context and not simply through state punishment (as Aertsen's work highlights). But is it enough to assign responsibility through victim-centred processes, especially when responsibility is *exclusively* assigned to individuals?

What I am getting at here is that while there may be good reason to negotiate individual responsibilities in given circumstances, it is *also* essential concurrently to address wider social complexes that generate the destructive subjects and relations of conflict in the first place. This implies, and indeed mandates, giving serious consideration to different kinds of responsibility; that is, restorative justice's potential extends beyond the exclusive assignment of meaningful responsibility to individuals, as is often the case with victim-offender conferences, mediated settlement and even circles. Beyond political mechanisms that determine individualising culpability processes, restorative justice processes might also engage socially inflected stories: what responsibility do given collective relations bear for producing contexts that incubate and shape 'individuals' capable of perpetrating destructive acts? What social relations help to forge beings whose phenomenological outlook has developed in favour of ruinous action? And perhaps, as importantly, what can be done to transform such relations through promises of justice?

The point of contrast indicated by these questions suggests an understated potential promised by early community mediation advocates: the search for tribunals that could divert those who are criminally accused from courtrooms, to avoid – let us recall – an abstracted, criminalisation that attributes exclusive culpability for complex social events to individual 'offenders'. Community mediation and then restorative justice promised new lenses by which to conceptualise such events; but how much change in conceptual vision is possible when counternarratives target the very subjects brought into focus by crime and punishment lenses? Attributing responsibility to individual offenders, for example, or seeking 'reconciliations' between individual victims and offenders, seems to replicate rather than divert subjects from categories of criminal justice. Despite differences between legal and normative, harm-based approaches, both forms of justice transcribe complex social relations and events through lenses of 'individual' responsibility. Might restorative tribunals not pursue categorisations and subjects of a very different order from those of criminal justice?

An affirmative response could involve direct engagement with a politics of criminal accusation to divert subjects away from processes that initiate the state's emphasis on individual criminalisation (Pavlich, 2019). One might recall that both 'crime' and 'accusation' derive etymologically from the Latin *crimen* as in 'calling to account' or Greek ideas of categorisation (Antaki, 2017). But there is nothing in that etymology that fixes accusation to 'crime' or criminal law's ways of calling *individual* offenders to account

– through adversarial criminal procedures – as if they were fully able to bear culpability for all that happened. Restorative tribunals that take seriously a quest to divert conflict from the latter might well reconsider the following questions. What exactly is to be called to restorative account (individuals *and* social processes)? What kind of accusations might be directed towards complex relational structures that generate destructive events (rather than individually accused persons)? What sorts of tribunals are best suited to identifying and responding to accusations so framed (rituals that seek settlement and 'reconciliation' or those that pursue wider social transformations)? Such questions are predicated on other assumptions, but they suggest the value of returning to early promises of community mediation to rethink the terrain at hand.

A second point of contrast rests with Aertsen's (2017) implicit recognition that restorative justice need not shore up communal limits, acknowledging instead that communities are always in flux. Indeed, in a way, his programme scans imply that communities harbour both positive and negative possibilities. Apropos the latter, I have argued that all communities are (and even 'can only be') forged through exclusion – there is, quite simply, no absolutely inclusive, universally consensual, harmonious community (Pavlich, 2001). Force is required to establish and maintain communal limits, even if that force often bathes in murky appeals to (say) 'empowerment', freedom outside the state or the spontaneous association of members. One should, however, never lose sight of the force required to fix communal limits – to border and order always imposes limits by rendering 'others' as somehow different from those imagined as the included. Such exclusion (or perhaps 'inclusion through exclusion', as per Agamben, 2005) provides a foundation from whence a community and its members are differentiated. This places a unique responsibility on restorative tribunals that seek community justice since communities only ever emerge as exclusion-based and unfolding relations 'between' subjects. How might we envisage tribunals that recalibrate how to 'be with others' in future and which recognise a basic and enduring responsibility to the others barred from emerging forms of communality?

Even if such a complex question seems beyond the scope of this discussion (but see Pavlich, 2018), suffice to allude to an idea of hospitality that might help us conceptualise prospects for a transformative version of restorative justice. Such justice implies change-orientated tribunals directly involved with developing new ways to be with others in future. When coupled with ideas of hospitality, tribunals could develop practices around notions of 'welcome', conceiving of dynamic subject identities through relations that negotiate between hosts and 'others' that appear as guests (Derrida, 2000). The advantage of this conception is to allow for models of justice that do not restrict themselves to reconciling individual victims and offenders but enable wider processes to change social relations for promised futures – not restoring fixed community limits of a past or present (Pavlich, 2001). In any case, hospitality allows one to better recognise the co-appearance of those who stand at thresholds of what is to come. It also allows one to recognise that the kinds of responses demanded of subjects have the effect of establishing how responsibility is conceived in context and simultaneously creates particular identities through which responses are offered/accepted. The responsibilities of co-appearing hosts and guests do not require hosts to shed their mastery any more than they demand that guests (others) simply accept the hospitality offered. The idea, impossible though it may be to achieve in practice, places a mutual responsibility on all to fashion ways to be with (to 'co-appear'), to face 'being with others' in ways that are endless in their possibilities (Nancy, 2000).

By way of conclusion, I would like to emphasise the abiding respect that Aertsen's work displays for restorative debate, especially when encountering those with different ideas from his own. It is appealing to me to refuse 'for and against' blackmails and exclusionary cliques that claim to have 'the real take' on insoluble matters of justice. Apart from undermining the inclusionary, non-marginalising spirit of early restorative calculations of justice, such ways of 'being with', of co-appearing, repress the incongruities that plague always moving promises of justice. A different co-appearance – one that is evident in Aertsen's careful discussions and hospitable relations with others – reflects a profound respect for democratic participation in political discourse and for critical debate. This author is certainly among the appreciative beneficiaries of Aertsen's everyday engagement with, academic embrace and personal adoption of such fine restorative practices.

References

Aertsen, I. (2008). *Restoring justice after large-scale violent conflicts: Kosovo, DR Congo and the Israeli-Palestinian case.* Cullompton: Willan.

Aertsen, I. (2017). Recalibrating victimhood through restorative justice: perspectives from Europe. *Restorative Justice: An International Journal*, 5, 352-367. doi:10.1080/20504721.2017.1390997.

Aertsen, I. & Pali, B. (eds.). (2017). *Critical Restorative Justice.* Oxford: Hart Publishing.

Aertsen, I., Daems, T. & Robert, L. (eds.). (2006). *Institutionalizing restorative justice.* Portland: Willan.

Agamben, G. (2005). *State of Exception* (1st ed.). Chicago: University of Chicago Press.

Antaki, M. (2017). Declining Accusation. In G. Pavlich & M. Unger (eds.), *Accusation: creating criminals.* Vancouver: UBC Press.

Baskin, D. (1988). Community mediation and the public/private problem. *Social Justice*, 15, 742-786.

Bonefeld, W. & Holloway, J. (eds.). (1992). *Post-Fordism and social form: a Marxist debate on the post-Fordist state.* Hampshire: Palgrave Macmillan.

Braithwaite, J. (2010). The fundamentals of restorative justice. In S. Dinnen, A. Jowitt & T. Newton (eds.), *A kind of mending: restorative justice in the pacific islands.* Canberra: ANU Press.

Brown, W. (2015). *Undoing the demos: neoliberalism's stealth revolution.* New York: Zone Books.

Carrier, N. & Piché, J. (2015). The state of abolitionism. *Champ Pénal Penal Field,* 12. Retrieved from https://champpenal.revues.org/9164 (last accessed 30 September 2015).

Christie, N. (2015). Widening the net. *Restorative Justice*, 3, 109-113. doi:10.1080/20504721.2015.1049876.

Cohen, S. (1985). *Visions of Social Control.* Cambridge: Polity Press.

Cullen, F. & Gendreau, P. (2001). From nothing works to what works: changing professional ideology in the 21st century. *The Prison Journal*, 81, 313-338. doi:10.1177/0032885501081003002.

Davis, A. (2003). *Are prisons obsolete?* New York: Seven Stories Press.

de Lagasnerie, G. (2018). *Judge and punish: the penal state on trial* (1st ed.). Stanford: Stanford University Press.

Derrida, J. (2000). *Of hospitality.* Stanford: Stanford University Press.

Fassin, D. (2013). *The will to punish.* Oxford: Oxford University Press.

Fitzpatrick, P. (1988). The rise and rise of informalism. In R. Matthews (ed.), *Informal justice?* Sage Contemporary Criminology. London: Sage Publications.

Foucault, M. (1979). *Discipline and punish: The birth of the prison.* New York: Vintage Books.

Foucault, M. (1980a). *Power/knowledge: selected interviews and other writings, 1972-1977.* New York: Vintage Books.

Foucault, M. (1980b). *The history of sexuality, vol. 1: An introduction.* New York: Vintage Books.

Foucault, M. (1982). The subject and power. *Critical Inquiry*, 8, 777-795. doi:10.1086/448181.

Gavrielides, T. & Artinopoulou, V. (2016). *Reconstructing restorative justice philosophy.* Retrieved from https://books.google.ca/books/about/Reconstructing_Restorative_Justice_Philo.html?id=b_vsCwAAQBAJ (last accessed 6 June 2016).

Hofrichter, R. (1987). *Neighborhood justice in capitalist society: the expansion of the informal state.* New York: Greenwood Press.

Johnstone, G. (2011). *Restorative justice* (2nd ed.). New York: Routledge.

Johnstone, G. & Van Ness, D. W. (eds.). (2007). *Handbook of restorative justice.* Portland: Willan.

Mathiesen, T. (1974). *The politics of abolition.* Oslo, Norway: Scandinavian University Books.

Matthews, R. (ed.). (1988). *Informal justice?* London: Sage Publications.

Merry, S. E. & Milner, N. (eds.). (1993). *The possibility of popular justice: case study of community mediation in the United States.* Ann Arbor: University of Michigan Press.

Nancy, J.-L. (2000). *Being singular plural.* Stanford: Stanford University Press.

Offe, C. (1984). *Contradictions of the welfare state.* Cambridge: MIT Press.
Pali, B. & Aertsen, I. (2018). *Restoring justice and security in intercultural Europe.* Oxford: Hart Publishing.
Pavlich, G. (1996a). *Justice fragmented: mediating community disputes under postmodern conditions.* London: Routledge.
Pavlich, G. (1996b). The power of community mediation: government and formation of self-identity. *Law & Society Review*, 30, 707-733. doi:10.2307/3054115.
Pavlich, G. (2001). The force of community. In H. Strang & J. Braithwaite (eds.), *Restorative justice and civil society* (pp. 56-68). Cambridge: Cambridge University Press.
Pavlich, G. (2005). *Governing paradoxes of restorative justice.* London: Glass House Press.
Pavlich, G. (2018). Promised communities and unrestored justice. In I. Aertsen and B. Pali (eds.), *Critical restorative justice* (pp. 297-314). Oxford: Hart Publishing.
Pavlich, G. (2019). *Criminal accusation: political rationales and socio-legal practices* (1st ed.). London: Routledge.
Ruggiero, V. (2011). An abolitionist view of restorative justice. *International Journal of Law Crime and Justice*, 39, 100-110. doi:10.1016/j.ijlcj.2011.03.001.
Santos, B. de S. (1982). Law and community: the changing nature of state power in late capitalism. In R. Abel (ed.), *The politics of informal justice: the American experience.* New York: Academic Press.
Scott, J. C. (2014). *Two cheers for anarchism: six easy pieces on autonomy, dignity, and meaningful work and play.* Oxford: Princeton University Press.
Shonholtz, R. (1984). Neighborhood justice systems: work, structure and guiding principles. *Mediation Quarterly*, 5, 3-30. doi:10.1002/crq.39019840503.
Shonholtz, R. (1988). Community as peacemaker: making neighborhood justice work. *Current Municipal Problems*, 15, 291-330.
Skeat, W. W. (1961). *A concise etymological dictionary of the English language.* Oxford: Clarendon Press.
Snare, A. & Christie, N. (1975). Dialogue with Nils Christie. *Issues in Criminology*, 10, 35-47.
Vanfraechem, I., Aertsen, I. & Willemsens, J. (2010). *Restorative justice realities: empirical research in a European context.* The Hague, the Netherlands: Eleven International Publishing. Retrieved from http://www.gbv.de/dms/spk/sbb/recht/toc/644501383.pdf.
Walgrave, L. (2002). *Restorative justice and the law.* Cullompton: Willan.
Walgrave, L. (2003). *Repositioning restorative justice.* Cullompton: Willan.
Walgrave, L. (2008). *Restorative justice, self-interest and responsible citizenship.* Cullompton: Willan.
Williams, J. (2000). Getting tough on crime: will it win the war? *Agenda: A Journal of Policy Analysis and Reform*, 7, 33-45.
Woolford, A. J. & Ratner, R. (2008). *Informal reckonings: conflict resolution in mediation, restorative justice, and reparations.* New York: Routledge-Cavendish.

Zehr, H. (2002). *The little book of restorative justice.* Intercourse: Good Books.
Zehr, H. (2015). *Changing lenses: restorative justice for our times.* Kitchener: Herald Press.
Zehr, H. & Toews, B. (2004). *Critical issues in restorative justice.* Cullompton: Willan.

Motivational interviewing and restorative justice praxis

*John Braithwaite**

1 Emancipation 'with'

This volume is dedicated to one of many aspects of the inspiring contributions of Ivo Aertsen to restorative justice: justice as a skill we can do. In the professional life of Ivo Aertsen, justice has been a skill of collaboration, of 'doing with', in which he has skillfully 'led from behind'. For Aertsen, justice is also an emancipatory skill: 'justice clearly promotes the emancipated victim image: it offers active victims a chance to actively participate in mediation and conferencing' (Aertsen, et al., 2011: 7). This in turn connects to Ivo Aertsen's empirical oeuvre showing that restorative justice 'enabled offenders to change their perspective, to develop empathy with the victim, or to acknowledge the real impact of their behaviour' (Lauwaert & Aertsen, 2015: 4). Justice in the Aertsen vision is not a matter of imposition on passive stakeholders; rather, stakeholders are actively empowered to grasp justice.

But how, in practical terms, and in an evidence-based way, can restorative justice emancipate stakeholders in the art of doing justice actively. With Brunilda Pali and many others in the final year before his retirement from paid employment at KU Leuven, Ivo Aertsen has been networking on how restorative justice might empower environmental activists and regulators to work with nature rather than against it, rather than do for it or to it. A just art of environmental praxis in this emergent part of the Aertsen vision cannot be accomplished by bullying corporations into complying with environmental law. Punishment of corporate environmental offenders certainly has a role. Yet we can no more bully corporate executives into caring about environmental stewardship than we can bully young people to care about the harm of violence against other citizens.

* Some of the ideas in this chapter were first presented when I gave the Fasken Lecture at the University of British Columbia (Braithwaite, 2011).

2 Motivational interviewing

This chapter explores just one kind of justice praxis that can build motivation to care about non-violence and non-domination of people or ecosystems. This is motivational interviewing. A common strand between the work of Ivo Aertsen and the impressive evaluation literature on motivational interviewing is that to change behaviour we must genuinely listen to narratives of non-compliance. More than that, the listening must lead to agreement on desired outcomes and self-monitoring and/or external monitoring of progress towards them. That commitment is secured in the motivational interviewing method by helping people to find their own motivation to attain an outcome. In the application of Miller and Rollnick's (2012) motivational interviewing to restorative justice, we replace 'clinician' with 'facilitator' and 'client' with 'stakeholder' (which includes offenders, victims and affected members of communal or natural ecosystems):

- The stakeholder, rather than the facilitator, should make the arguments for change
- The facilitator's role is to evoke the stakeholder's own concerns and motivations
- To effect this change in approach:
    1. Listen with empathy
    2. Minimise resistance
    3. Nurture hope and optimism[1]

Meta-analyses that include more than 80 randomised controlled trials show formidable effectiveness of motivational interviewing in changing a wide variety of oppressive behavioural outcomes that range well beyond crime (Rubak et al., 2005; Lundahl et al., 2010). In youth justice restorative conferences, stigmatisation is not needed: loved ones discussing how concerned they are about the consequences of the crime, the suffering of victims and what the family can do to help repair the harm is the way to elicit remorse without defiance. Motivational interviewing of these loved ones can draw this out. If desistance from drug abuse is settled as a motivation in a restorative and responsive process, the motivational interviewer asks the drug user why this aim matters to them and their family, what strategies might follow from this shared reason for wanting to desist and how could the family commit to support them.

The motivational interviewing literature mirrors much of what our RegNet research group at the Australian National University discovered along a different path during the past four decades about the limits of regulators being directional and combative as opposed to empathic and eliciting. Motivational interviewing's three key dimensions of motivation (confidence, importance and readiness) mirrors much of what emerges in Valerie Braithwaite's (2008) work on motivational posturing and regulation, trust and governance (Braithwaite & Levi, 1998), and hope and governance (Braithwaite, 2004).

1 These dot points are adapted from a PowerPoint presentation by Dr Stan Steindl to RegNet colleagues.

Ann Jenkins' (1994) research on our 1988-1991 nursing home regulation data showed the importance of 'confidence' or 'self-efficacy' in regulatory compliance. It is easy to grasp the intuition that we achieve more against our outcomes on those days when we arrive at work with a feeling of confidence that we can tackle them. So clear empirical evidence that self-efficacy of managers predicted future regulatory compliance was not a surprise. In my own most recent work, I have sought to connect micro-self-efficacy to a macrocriminology of collective efficacy that cascades crime prevention (Braithwaite, 2019). I argue that restorative justice can help enable and empower this collective efficacy. 'Importance' as motivational interviewing's second key dimension of motivation has a much longer history of empirical predictive power, for example, in the consistent predictive power of commitment to obeying the law in the hundreds of empirical tests of control theory in criminology. In the motivational posturing literature, 'Readiness' is operationalised by asking clients, 'How ready are you to make these changes?' This is based on the finding that ambivalence is the crucial dilemma individuals and corporations face when they consider change. Because people have the feeling that life is short and there are good and bad sides to everything, they often focus on the bad side and take the lazy path of not making a change they know they should bother to make. Again, this insight arrived early in the criminological literature in the brilliant ethnographic work of David Matza (1964) on *Delinquency and Drift*. Delinquents are not often committed to law breaking; rather, they ambivalently drift between worlds of delinquency and law abidingness. They do not think breaking society's rules is right so much as they drift into 'techniques of neutralisation' that soften the moral bind of law (Sykes & Matza, 1957).

Restorative and responsive regulators are therefore skilled at what the counselling literature conceives as Rogerian reflective listening, listening that reflects back commitment to achieve outcomes grounded in motivations chosen by the speaker. Conversations with reflective listening ask open questions as opposed to rhetorical questions or questions that evoke yes/no answers, questioning that shows respect for the person and active listening that summarises back to speakers narratives that they might choose to use to steer their journey to change. This is a very common human skill that all good parents have. It rolls with resistance rather than arguing combatively, while communicating commitment to stick with the problem until it is sorted. While there is a 'high moral ground' that law enforcers must enforce when faced with exceptional intransigence to ensure that clear messages are delivered to third parties about what is morally unacceptable, in street-level law enforcement taking the high moral ground tends to be counterproductive.

Restorative praxis requires engagement with fairness of those who resist. We must show them respect by construing their resistance as an opportunity to learn how to improve the justice system. Valerie Braithwaite's (2008) research on motivational postures concludes that resistance is a good thing in justice and regulatory systems. It is what creates the best opportunities for improving them. The character with which democratic governance responds to resistance is vital to the quality and resilience of a democracy.

Restorative practitioners can learn adaptation through the skill of rolling with resistance. Empirically in both nursing home care quality and tax compliance, the motivational posture that Valerie Braithwaite labels 'resistance' was comparatively easy to flip into commitment to improvement. The tough nut was 'disengagement'. Offenders who opt out of the regulatory game are much harder to deal with than those who resist the regulator. As with the problem of underperforming employees in workplaces, a starting point is in being interested in what people *are* good at. That provides a point of entry to getting them engaged with projects of continuous improvement that regulator and regulatee can begin to see as shared projects. And that is why we seek first to pick strengths and expand them by moving up the pyramid of supports in restorative and responsive regulatory theory (Burford, Braithwaite & Braithwaite, 2019).

Restorative and responsive regulatory theory is also about the idea that all these empathic attempts at engagement will often fail. That failure is an opportunity too. It provides an opportunity to communicate the message that the justice system will keep innovating with alternative strategies until behaviour that brutally dominates nature or other human beings desists. The justice system must show itself to be resilient at persisting with attempts to fix injustice in collaboration with those caught up in the injustice until they are fixed.

Informal praise of stakeholders who seize active responsibility for fixing injustice is fundamental in the toolkit of the restorative and responsive regulator. No tool is cheaper to implement. For the environmental inspector to pause and say, 'You have done a great job in completely cleaning up that leakage I brought to your attention last month,' does not require an increase in regulatory budgets. No mechanism of justice praxis for reinforcing gains from motivational interviewing is simpler to do. The evidence of the effectiveness of informal praise by inspectors in improving nursing home quality of care outcomes in the two years following an inspection is strong (Makkai & Braithwaite, 1993; Braithwaite, Makkai & Braithwaite, 2007). This is also why 'celebration conferences' after an offender has completed the undertakings made in a restorative justice conference is a good practice. The idea is that while motivation to solve life's problems is a great thing, we can make it a greater thing by simple practices of good restorative justice, good regulation, good parenting and good living like praise that sustain the motivation.

3 Aertsen's 'Good Life'

I have found motivational interviewing to have special appeal for integration into restorative praxis because we should want restorative justice to be evidence based, and the evidence for motivational interviewing is strong. As Ivo Aertsen's friend and mentor Lode Walgrave (2016) put it, there are a variety of ways of shifting lenses from 'what works' in justice to 'what helps' those caught up in justice systems. Walgrave conceives the Good

Lives model as another promising approach to building better offender motivations through social support from offender communities of care. The Good Lives model might not have the heft of empirical support of motivational interviewing's 80+ randomised controlled trials, but it bears the hope of a more normatively rich justice praxis.

The Good Lives model is sympatico with restorative justice in shifting from seeing offenders through the lens of the risks they pose; shifting to helping build offenders' capacities 'to live personally meaningful and fulfilling lives' (Ward, Fox & Garber, 2014: 28). Good Lives is about '"What helps" to support the offender's motivation to find his/her own way towards a satisfying socially integrated life' (Walgrave, 2016: 426). Of course, normatively for Walgrave and me as republican theorists, a good life cannot be a life of domination (or for that matter a life dominated by risk managers). While it is desirable for offenders to learn how to better manage their risk factors, and there is strong evidence that points to responsiveness to needs through cognitive behavioural risk management (risk-need-responsivity), perhaps even more can be achieved by also helping offenders to discover fulfilling ways of living (Ward & Brown, 2004; Willis & Ward, 2013; cf. Andrews et al., 2011).

Fulfilled lives are a better, more helpful thing even if future accumulation of evidence does not support large added value for crime prevention. As Seligman (2002: 7) puts it, 'We need to ask practitioners to recognize that much of the best work they already do in the consulting room is to amplify their clients' strengths rather than repair their weaknesses' (Seligman, 2002: 5). Risk reduction strategies often struggle to motivate and engage participants in rehabilitation processes that often have shockingly high attrition rates; herein lies the appeal of motivational interviewing when it discovers and motivates visions for fulfilling lives, individual or corporate (e.g. Ward & Maruna, 2007). When the evidence is in, it might well show that it is easier to persuade criminal offenders to hang in on projects of living more fulfilling lives than on projects of reducing the risks they pose to others.

As we move from individual to corporate offenders, many now also conclude that while the bread and butter of corporate regulation is 'picking risks and fixing them', the essence of regulatory excellence is 'picking strengths and expanding them' (Braithwaite et al., 2007). When environmental leaders take green stewardship up through new ceilings of excellence, that can also drag laggards above floors of minimum environmental standards. More fundamentally, it is now too late to save our planet just by picking risks and treating them. Our only hope is with environmental leaders who rise to the challenge of inventing new solar and other renewable technologies that displace carbon quickly; innovating fast into new electric cars that are better and cheaper than cars that carbonise; inventing cheaper and more environmentally friendly technologies of desalination to stave off famine; inventing entire new visions and implementation paths to smart cities such as China's hydrogen cities, circular cities, forest cities and sponge cities (Shepard, 2017); inventing new kinds of economies that grow jobs through increased consumption of low-carbon human services as they reduce consumption of consumer durables (Burford, Braithwaite & Braithwaite, 2019); and more.

Unfortunately, the risk management myopia of Western capitalist economies has left it too late to shift gears to Good Corporate Lives that make the investments that might save the earth system. Today, China accounts for half the global capital investment in seizing such opportunities, so I suspect Peter Drahos (2019) is right that Western collaboration with Chinese corporate efforts to seize a survivable future is humankind's best or only hope now. Redemptive corporate ethical transformations to better corporate lives often do happen in the aftermath of corporate criminality, but more commonly do not because firms settle for plugging a few fingers in the dykes of their corporate risks. Even so, corporate compliance professionals rightly say that if you want to find the corporation that is taking new risk management and stewardship policies up through new ceilings of excellence this year, go to the companies that were in deepest legal trouble for non-compliance the previous year. The imperative here is to move beyond risk management mentalities to stewardship mentalities, individual and corporate, to restore natural systems and stem the ecocide of our fellow species.

Perhaps motivational interviewing can be helpful not only for finding motivations for changing bad behaviour but also for finding paths to good behaviour. This means living a Good Life in which crime is not as satisfying as that good way of living that offenders are helped to discover. Honig et al. (2015) argue that awareness of risks, needs and more fulfilling ways of living combined with motivation to seize them is not enough. *Pathways* to risk and need responsivity are also imperative and also pathways to Good Lives. The integrated transformation imperative is for AMP – Awareness, Motivation and Pathways. Help with getting secure housing is one example of an unusually important pathway without which many rehabilitation programmes have been shown to fail (Best et al., 2016). Likewise, pathways to employment and to improved study methods to enhance educational Good Lives are of quite general import to tracking to restored and redemptive lives, just as many more minor pathways are of more contextual import. As ecological crisis recursively cascades into economic crises and security crises, pathways to peace will become of more widespread importance to making Good Lives or the risk-need-responsivity paradigm possible as approaches to crime prevention that work (Braithwaite & d'Costa, 2018; Braithwaite, 2019). When human beings are under bombardment, as many people in the world are, responsivity findings from Western populations currently enjoying peace are unlikely to be relevant. If psychologism fingers people as suffering the risks of anxiety, neurosis, addiction to tobacco or alcohol, they are likely to suffer these afflictions more as they live the bad lives of the rockets raining in.

Ivo Aertsen's Good Life today has turned to helping corporate environmental offenders to discover the possibility that environmental stewardship for circular, renewable, economies is a better way of living that can engender richer, more holistic motivation than making more money. The Leuven network for Restorative Environmental Justice is beginning to lead us to discover transformed justice skills that might deliver corporate Good Lives with the AMP – Awareness, Motivation and Pathways – that might help save our planet. Leading from behind with this kind of work as he enters the late stage of his career is what makes Ivo Aertsen richer in life than the richest corporate magnates. For Ivo and his followers in our generation, it is all hands to the pumps of the climate crisis right now to find better ways of spurring good corporate and personal lives that might lay pathways to prevent collapse of the earth system.

REFERENCES

Aertsen, I., Bolívar, D., De Mesmaecker, V. & Lauwers, N. (2011). Restorative justice and the active victim: exploring the concept of empowerment. *Temida*, 14(1), 5-19. doi:10.2298/tem1101005a.

Andrews, D. A., Bonta, J. & Wormith, J. S. (2011). The risk-need-responsivity (RNR) model: Does adding the good lives model contribute to effective crime prevention? *Criminal Justice and Behavior*, 38(7), 735-755. doi:10.1177/0093854811406356.

Best, D., Beswick, T., Hodgkins, S. & Idle, M. (2016). Recovery, ambitions, and aspirations: an exploratory project to build a recovery community by generating a skilled recovery workforce. *Alcoholism Treatment Quarterly*, 34(1), 3-14. doi:10.1080/07347324.2016.1113105.

Braithwaite, J. (2011). The essence of responsive regulation. *UBC Law Review*, 44(3), 475-520.

Braithwaite, J. (2019). Crime as a cascade phenomenon. *International Journal of Comparative and Applied Criminal Justice* (Submitted).

Braithwaite, J. & d'Costa, B. (2018). *Cascades of violence: war, crime and peacebuilding across South Asia*. Canberra: ANU Press.

Braithwaite, J., Makkai, T. & Braithwaite, V. A. (2007). *Regulating aged care: Ritualism and the new pyramid*. Cheltenham: Edward Elgar Publishing.

Braithwaite, V. (2004). The hope process and social inclusion. *The Annals of the American Academy of Political and Social Science*, 592(1), 128-151. doi:10.1177/0002716203262096.

Braithwaite, V. (2008). *Defiance in taxation and governance*. Cheltenham: Edward Elgar.

Braithwaite, V. & Levi, M. (eds.). (1998). *Trust and governance*. New York: Russell Sage Foundation.

Burford, G., Braithwaite, J. & Braithwaite, V. (eds.). (2019). *Restorative and responsive regulation of human services*. New York: Routledge.

Drahos, P. (Forthcoming). *Survival governance: energy and climate in the Chinese century*.

Honig, M., Petersen, S., Herbstein, T., Roux, S., Nel, D. & Shearing, C. (2015). A conceptual framework to enable the changes required for a one-planet future. *Environmental Values*, 24(5), 663-688. doi:10.3197/096327115x14384223590258.

Jenkins, A. L. (1994). The role of managerial self-efficacy in corporate compliance with the law. *Law and Human Behavior*, 18(1), 71-88. doi:10.1007/bf01499145.

Lauwaert, K. & Aertsen, I. (2015). Executive summary. In K. Lauwaert & I. Aertsen (eds.), *Desistance and restorative justice Mechanisms for desisting from crime within restorative justice practices.* Leuven: European Forum for Restorative Justice.

Lundahl, B. W., Kunz, C., Brownell, C., Tollefson, D. & Burke, B. L. (2010). A meta-analysis of motivational interviewing: twenty-five years of empirical studies. *Research on Social Work Practice*, 20(2), 137-160. doi:10.1177/1049731509347850.

Makkai, T. & Braithwaite, J. (1993). Praise, pride and corporate compliance. *International Journal of the Sociology of Law*, 21, 73-73.

Matza, D. (1964). *Delinquency and drift.* New York: Wiley.

Miller, W. R. & Rollnick, S. (2012). *Motivational interviewing: helping people change.* New York: Guilford press.

Rubak, S., Sandbæk, A., Lauritzen, T. & Christensen, B. (2005). Motivational interviewing: a systematic review and meta-analysis. *British Journal of General Practice*, 55 (513), 305-312.

Seligman, M. E. P. (2002). Positive psychology, positive prevention, and positive therapy. In C. R. Snyder & S. J. Lopez (eds.), *Handbook of positive psychology* (pp. 3-9). New York: Oxford University Press.

Shepard, W. (2017, September 1). No joke: China is building 285 eco-cities, here's why. *Forbes.* Retrieved from https://www.forbes.com/sites/wadeshepard/2017/09/01/no-joke-china-is-building-285-eco-cities-heres-why/#291b0ed82fe8.

Sykes, G. M. & Matza, D. (1957). Techniques of neutralization: a theory of delinquency. *American Sociological Review*, 22(6), 664-670. doi:10.2307/2089195.

Walgrave, L. (2016). Positive criminology, criminology of trust and restorative justice. *Restorative Justice*, 4(3), 424-434. doi:10.1080/20504721.2016.1243858.

Ward, T. & Brown, M. (2004). The good lives model and conceptual issues in offender rehabilitation. *Psychology, Crime & Law*, 10(3), 243-257. doi:10.1080/106831604 10001662744.

Ward, T. & Maruna, S. (2007). *Rehabilitation: beyond the risk assessment paradigm.* London: Routledge.

Ward, T., Fox, K. J. & Garber, M. (2014). Restorative justice, offender rehabilitation and desistance. *Restorative Justice*, 2(1), 24-42. doi:10.5235/20504721.2.1.24.

Willis, G. M. & Ward, T. (2013). The good lives model: does it work? Preliminary evidence. In L. A. Craig, L. Dixon & T. A. Gannon (eds.), *What works in offender rehabilitation. An evidence-based approach to assessment and treatment* (pp. 305-318). Chichester: Wiley-Blackwell.

Radical pragmatism: the promise of restorative justice for institutions and cities

Albert W. Dzur

1 Introduction

One of the first things I noticed about Ivo is that he is a fast walker. I am frequently told, 'Slow down, we are not in a rush!'; so when I call Ivo a fast walker this means he is, peripatetically speaking, Olympic class. It is possible he cultivated this superpower to break free of mere mortals and escape pedestrian conversation, but I think the reason has to do with the number of projects he always has going. There is much to do and so the pace must quicken.

As on the sidewalks of Leuven, Ivo has sped ahead in many research areas related to restorative justice. In this brief chapter, I focus on two issues he has raised that are crucial for its future development. The first is the question of how restorative justice can be part of criminal justice institutions in ways that sustain and amplify rather than negate the paradigm's guiding values. The second has to do with the question of whether a broad networking of practices throughout a civic ecosystem can lead to a 'restorative city'. Though he has keen awareness of other countries, Ivo has focused his research on Belgium's experience as a way of facilitating practical growth and change. Thus, these two issues touch on other aspects of Ivo's larger research programme: action research and the need to lower boundaries between professionalised domains and the public, not to mention loosening disciplinary rigidities separating justice from government, social services and education.

2 Institutionalising restorative justice

Restorative justice may have abolitionist strands, but three of the most important early thinkers – Zehr, Braithwaite and Christie – stressed how dysfunctional criminal justice institutions had to be transformed, not eliminated. Lenses needed to be changed, not smashed; the punitive shifted to the re-probative and re-integrative, not dissolved; conflicts shared, not monopolised or eliminated. Yes, they had to leave conventional punishment behind and move to new ways of organising social responses to harm-doing, but this did not mean the institutions had no work to do. Rather, they had a different kind of work to do: facilitating horizontal dialogue that could heal, shift relationships from conflictual to cordial and collaborative, foster responsibility for harmful actions, creatively hatch modes of repair and achieve greater community accountability for people on the margins. Indeed, one of the great strengths of restorative justice as a reform movement was the new lease of life it gave to people working within the system – they could become constructive rather than repressive forces, and by fostering restorative practices they were not becoming redundant, abolishing the grounds for their employment; rather, they were becoming newly relevant.

Ivo has documented how Belgium has institutionalised restorative justice to a degree matched by few other countries. Elsewhere, restorative programmes are generally situated in the juvenile justice system, expanding outwards only hesitatingly to include low-level adult offenders. Belgium, by contrast, pushed forward with restorative justice practices designed for adult offenders, including some serious offences. Starting in 1991, victim-offender mediation practices have been incorporated at all the major stages of adult criminal justice through 'penal mediation', 'mediation for redress', 'mediation at the police level' and 'mediation in the prison' (Aertsen, 2006: 70).

> Belgium is on its way to applying restorative justice in a generalized manner, both in the field of juvenile delinquency and adult criminal law. The service of victim-offender mediation will be available from the beginning of 2006 onwards over the whole territory, and this for different types of crime, varying degrees of seriousness and at all stages of the criminal justice process. This perspective positions restorative justice not just in a diversionary context, but makes it an integral part of criminal justice. (Aertsen, 2006: 73-74)

While such institutionalisation holds great promise to transform criminal justice, it also risks dulling the critical edge of restorative justice. As Ivo notes, 'Whether this can be done without giving up some of the core values and principles of restorative justice remains an open question and an enormous challenge' (Aertsen, 2006: 74).

The promise of institutionalisation includes greater stability and reach of ideas and practices that can wither and fade away if kept external to institutions – as has been the experience with many social justice movements that have been kept on the outside of institutions. Such movements can have a 'fugitive' quality, as the democratic theorist Sheldon Wolin pointed out, as the people involved have to return to their everyday lives after the protests are over (Wolin, 2004). Reform efforts that are able to gain ground from within institutions and are able to shift routine practices can thus have sustained impact over time as ideas that were once seen as radical become part of routine business as usual.[1]

The prison poses a special problem for restorative justice adherents because of its punitive history, coercive tendencies, stigmatising potential and non-transparency. Yet beginning in 2000, in all Belgian prisons, restorative practices were promoted by dedicated staff members appointed as restorative justice advisers. Advisers held full-time positions charged with developing 'a culture, skills and programmes which give room to the victims' needs and restorative answers' (Aertsen, 2006: 73). Working in coordination with staff members at the Ministry of Justice, advisers were to educate and assist corrections staff while also building connections to 'specific programmes with external agencies such as victim support and mediation services' (Ibid.).

Their concrete objectives were as follows: developing consultation structures between the various departments of the prison; raising the awareness of prison staff with regard to restorative justice; setting up consultation structures between internal and external services; raising the awareness of prisoners regarding victims' issues and restorative justice; and raising the awareness of victims and the community regarding detention and restorative justice (Aertsen, 2012: 268). Ideally, advisers were to think of their roles in prisons as facilitators and catalysts rather than restorative justice service providers. 'Sensitising' staff and inmates and community members to restorative justice was to be done dialogically through conversations and reading groups that share responsibility for thinking through the consequences of harmful actions (Aertsen, 2012: 269).

Programmes making aspects of restorative justice a concrete reality in Belgian prisons include victim awareness education, victim-offender mediation efforts and redress fund compensation. With the latter, prisoners may apply to do some community-oriented work for an external organisation and in return receive an amount of money up to 1,250 Euros to hand over to victims. The funds have been established, sponsored and administered by external NGOs (Aertsen, 2015: 68).

Though the Belgian experience with restorative justice in prisons is impressive by global standards, it also exemplifies two significant dangers that coexist alongside the promise of institutionalisation. The first danger is co-optation, either indirectly from steady acquiescence to the norms and routine patterns of an institution that was meant to be transformed or indirectly from budget elimination and staff reallocation. In Belgium, restorative justice advisers were able to form a cohort across different prisons, thus generating an autonomous support network that could help buttress against daily pressures to 'go with the flow'. This network, however, was not sufficient to build a more

1 Change from within was a strategy of the 1960s civil rights and 1970s women's movements in the United States. It is evident today in what I've called *democracy inside* efforts in a number of institutions. In primary education, for example, democratic school reformers empower young people within primary schools to resolve conflicts, shape administrative policies and influence school curricula (see Dzur, 2018).

permanent base of support for their ongoing work. In 2008, central prison administration decided, without consultation with the advisers, to eliminate their special restorative justice mandate and fold them into the general management of the prisons. Officials claimed that the restorative justice mission had been accomplished, though they provided no evidence that this was so (Aertsen, 2012: 275; 2015: 51-52).

A second danger of institutionalising restorative justice is the failure to engage citizen participation. This comes when the transformative force of a critical paradigm gets narrowly channelled, taken up by specialists and representatives and fails to significantly expand in the broader social sphere.[2] Despite the best intentions of restorative advisers to resist becoming experts in restorative justice, to facilitate dialogue and build linkages rather than simply delivering restorative services, public engagement outside the prison did not occur. Restorative justice theory idealises community roots – from the expectation that new lenses will be picked up by lay citizens, reintegration will be done by community members themselves and conflicts will be taken up in informal settings by those with the most at stake – but these roots have been very difficult to nurture in most countries.[3] Conflicts may have been stolen by the professionals, but few communities want them back! Thus, even though Belgium has a robust civil society and its NGOs put in efforts to initiate and sustain programmes like the redress fund, nevertheless, as is common around the world, there is little widespread participation of the broader community (Aertsen, 2015: 81). 'Victim-offender mediation in Belgium is an exclusively professional activity,' Ivo notes (Aertsen, 2000: 174). 'No volunteers or community representatives are directly active in mediation or conferencing practices' (Aertsen, 2006: 78).

Ivo is clear on the civic consequences of a narrowly institutionalised form of restorative justice: a loss of citizen awareness, community engagement and public dialogue over the meaning and purposes of criminal law.

> Participation is no longer seen as an intrinsic goal or a societal value to be realised for its own sake or for its emancipatory potential, but rather as a condition for receiving a service or for justice to be administered. Participation, in this restricted meaning, for those directly involved – victims, offenders and their surroundings – does not refer to a practical and manageable normative perspective which surmounts a rule-conforming approach of morality. So stated, restorative justice practices are losing their potential to restore or revalorize the law as a cultural and communicative phenomenon with its potential for 'de-

2 This is not, of course, a problem limited to criminal justice reform. For example, the bioethics movement of the 1970s, which entered hospitals and clinics to empower patients and to open these professionalized sites up to greater dialogue and participation, has in the past two decades become increasingly professionalised and estranged from broader social networks (see Dzur, 2008).

3 As Rosenblatt notes in her richly detailed study of the role of community in restorative justice, 'despite the great theoretical emphasis placed on community involvement in youth offender panels, I have found that, on the ground, they appeared quite professional, standardised, bureaucratic and formal' (2015: 185).

reification' of dominant meanings around criminality through the active involvement of those seeking justice. (Aertsen, 2006: 80)

The key phrase here is 'emancipatory potential', which Ivo spells out as citizens outside *and* officials inside the justice system taking shared responsibility and discarding 'a unilateral top-down institutional perspective of crime control' in favour of a 'bottom-up perspective of justice-seeking at various levels: the individual, the relational, the informal community, the societal-structural and the cultural' (Aertsen, 2006: 82).

These are in my view some of the most important questions for our current period, in which restorative justice has become institutionally entrenched in some countries' systems and still struggles in others, as in my country, the United States, to head in that direction. What are the best ways to institutionalise? How can the radical anti-punishment spirit of restorative justice persist over time in a setting historically committed to punishment? Does restorative justice require a base outside the institutions to keep it honest on the inside? If so, how do outsiders put effective pressure on the insiders? Addressing these questions will be crucial for restorative justice advocates seeking to gain ground and, thanks to Ivo's pioneering research, we have greater ability to do so.

What I admire most about Ivo's work on institutionalising restorative justice is its radical pragmatism: let's not give up on the emancipatory potential of restorative justice within criminal justice institutions, he suggests, let's hold reforms to very high standards, absorb setbacks and try again. In this, Ivo's perspective reminds me of the 'real utopias' research on efforts pushing participatory and egalitarian norms and practices as far as they can go within conventional institutions (Fung & Wright, 2003). Real utopias are created not in the spirit of ideological opposition but of humanistic innovation taken up by insiders motivated to collaborate with outsiders by their shared refusal to reproduce a dysfunctional status quo. And this is no boring middle ground: Ivo's radical pragmatism refuses strict abolition and do-it-yourself communitarianism, yet it also resists complacent institutionalisation. The goal, he writes, is a 'necessary balance between co-ordination and regulation on the one hand, and informalisation and de-regulation on the other hand'; 'a space in between the positions of, on the one hand, the formal criminal justice system and, on the other hand, the informal and community-oriented ways of conflict handling'; a 'neutral space [that] should allow and even promote at its crossroads the development of its own rationale for dealing with crime' (Aertsen, 2000: 188, 2006: 89).

3 Restorative cities

Cultivating semi-autonomous neutral spaces to a degree where they can make a difference in peoples' lives is a core mission among the advocates of the restorative city. From

Bristol and Hull in England, to Como, Sassari, Montana and Palermo in Italy, Utrecht in the Netherlands, Whanganui in New Zealand, Canberra in Australia and in Ivo's Leuven, reform-minded professionals, citizens and NGOs have joined together to further this mission. It can be an ambitious undertaking, as commentators on the Hull experience note:

> The aim has been to generate a common restorative language through which all children and young people experience education, criminal justice, social services, and so on. Through these types of services, this language is also intended to stretch into the families and communities from which these children and young people come. This restorative language is aimed at providing children and young people with the tools and confidence to resolve their own problems and generate their own sense of purpose and destiny. Hull's vision for a restorative city is, therefore, an emancipatory vision. It is a vision where the adoption of restorative values, principles, and language inspires its young to grow into forward-looking, articulate, and empowered adults who will shape the future of their city. (Green, Johnstone & Lambert, 2013: 447)

Individual practitioners and organisations deliberately integrate restorative justice values and practices in domains outside criminal justice institutions to strengthen a locality's civic capacity to handle conflicts, assume responsibility for articulating social problems and gather information about issues even before they become conflicts or problems. Thus, primary schools, NGOs, businesses, public sector agencies unrelated to criminal justice and even universities all present opportunities for cultivating neutral spaces.

The theory of the restorative city has yet to be fully developed, but it begins with two main claims. First, and reflecting the issues raised with institutionalisation mentioned previously, advocates argue that restorative justice is underused in contemporary criminal justice systems not only because of insufficient commitment from professionals inside, though that is a factor, but also because of inadequate embeddedness in society. Thus, as Ivo states, 'Building societal support and developing models and tools to better embed and anchor restorative justice within (civil) society became an important objective' (Aertsen, 2018b:1).

Anchors outside the criminal justice domain are needed to keep pressure on institutions and officials and staff members to keep the momentum going with restorative justice reforms inside. Civil society provides support, too, such as funding for NGOs and help with integrating former inmates back into ordinary routines. Restorative city theory also builds on social capital research and the sociology of 'justice in many rooms', which suggests that the functional capacity of the formal system is dependent on healthy social relations and a wide range of informal practices (often unnoticed or discounted by officials and professionals) in conflict resolution, harm reduction and social ordering (Galanter, 1981). Restorative city advocates suggest there is underutilised practical capacity outside, not to mention considerable local knowledge to be tapped regarding what is and is not working.

> Civil society organisations have an important role to play in stimulating a climate of dialogue: by strengthening relationships on the one hand (preventative side) and by creating specific contexts where restorative ways to handle tensions, conflicts and even crime are encouraged on the other hand (curative side). In doing so, society's problem solving capacity is maximized. In this perspective, formal justice will have more societal support for its essential role in the restoration of social peace. (Aertsen, 2018a: 9)

In a restorative city, professionals and specialists coordinate their efforts and communicate with each other, but they also seek to learn from already existing informal practices of community organisations, neighbourhoods and citizens involved in problem solving.

The second main claim of restorative city theory is in some ways the mirror image of the first. While it is true that cities offer underutilised resources and capabilities, these must be identified, structured and better organised to confront pressing contemporary social problems. Civil society organisations, neighbourhoods and individual lay citizens have much to learn, and there is a growing need for neutral spaces for them to learn in. Far from the wishful communitarianism of some restorative justice narratives, restorative city advocates have a sober awareness of looming dysfunctional tendencies such as distrust of officials and fellow citizens alike, lack of participation in public affairs, polarisation and the seeking of easy answers provided by people 'like us' and fear of others, whether of different races, sexual identification, religious affiliation or nationality.

Ivo is frank about the double-edged vision of the restorative city, both supportive and critical of the social context ready to hand:

> Leuven's civil society witnesses the polarising and alienating tendencies which impact citizens and society at large. However, rather than just undergoing, the willingness is expressed to counter the downward spiral. They want to engage in creating an environment of encounter, respect, dialogue and working on a climate in which preventative competences and attitudes are developed to respond to daily conflict. (Aertsen, 2018a: 9)

Restorative justice is rooted in the lifeworld, to be sure, but it is no mere expression of traditional forms of dialogue and social action; it is a critical intervention. 'In the current climate of alienation, fear and polarising tensions', Ivo writes, 'restorative justice can have a social role and be a counter movement.' Restorative practices offer a horizontal learning process: 'They are about respect and inclusion, countering stereotypes, non-violence, responsibility, voice and participation.' In the restorative city, such practices 'contribute to social cohesion: the art of living together' (Aertsen, 2018a: 9). They can help to rebuild connections frayed over time, lower barriers and create constructive pressures for people who have avoided proximity to come together. People trained in restorative justice provide guidance and facilitate this kind of civic capacity building and social learning that can then be fed back into a larger process of assessing, critiquing and contributing to formal institutional practice.[4]

Through action research, Ivo and colleagues at KU Leuven have begun horizontal inquiries into how to make restorative city theory a reality. Starting at the ground level, they have looked into the civic resources already available, identifying 'organisational settings' and 'social interactive settings' with the following characteristics:

- where people can be active citizens;
- where there is a high probability of adopting a 'RJ discourse': through talking, thinking, acting;
- where common (RJ) values, principles and skills can be shared or developed;
- where some types and degrees of (internal) regulation exist (formal or informal) and can be discussed;
- where independence can be guaranteed, and inequality and discrimination combatted;
- where various degrees of involvement can be considered (in a direct way, through learning by doing, or in an indirect way, by supporting other or related conflict resolution mechanisms);
- where there is room for surprises. (Aertsen, 2018b: 4-5)

Ivo and his colleagues have found a range of such settings already available in Leuven – schools, sports clubs, private companies, government agencies and neighbourhood organisations, among others. Collaborating with working groups made up with stakeholders in each setting, they developed case studies of real-life events in which people took restorative approaches to dealing with conflict. These have become part of an ongoing learning process that should continue to bear fruit.

4 Conclusion: room for surprises

Ivo's work is inspiring a multidisciplinary, action-oriented research agenda that will shape restorative justice for many years to come. His radical pragmatist picture of re-

4 Restorative city theory has many affinities, worth exploring, with the growing body of research on collaborative governance. This research suggests that city governments across the world are drawn to greater public engagement and power-sharing to build trust and shore up legitimacy, achieve greater efficacy and take on chronic patterns of injustice. See, for example, Dzur (2018) and Fung (2015).

storative justice presents it, rightly in my view, as an evolving set of core ideas and practices that cannot be owned by one specialised field or profession. To have an impact on institutions, restorative justice needs to be part of professional cultures, to be sure, but to have a sustained emancipatory impact it must be embedded and anchored outside in the lifeworld. Who does this anchoring and embedding, exactly? Collaboration-minded professionals and officials, neighbourhood groups, lay citizens, all working together.

No owning but much responsibility – this is the message conveyed by Ivo's research. There is civic capacity in the lifeworld, but it may not emerge without some help. Kay Pranis, once an institutional insider as an official restorative justice planner for the Minnesota Department of Corrections, now works outside as an active practitioner and proponent of restorative circles. For her, restorative justice is inherently rooted in communities, but these are never perfect settings, and long-standing patterns of inequality and historical injustices can nurture angry grievances. Restorative practices, for Pranis, are ways of organising community reactions to crime while also guiding, focusing and drawing upon citizen capabilities for healing and rebuilding. 'If there is a robbery in your neighborhood', says Pranis, 'there is a whole bunch of energy around that. This is initially negative energy. The restorative processes – particularly circles because they can engage more people – give you a way to transform the negative energy that arises naturally into positive community-building energy' (Dzur, 2016: 5). This is only to say that the semi-autonomous neutral spaces we have been talking about here as the objectives of a radically pragmatic restorative justice are going to take constant work to maintain, will involve charged and messy dialogues, but can ultimately usher forth transformative change.

To walk in Ivo's long-spanning footsteps, we restorative justice researchers and advocates would do well to act locally, connect globally and think big while doing so. Though an uphill struggle in many countries facing an eerie resurgence of punitive and neo-authoritarian rhetoric, restorative justice practices inside institutions and throughout city-wide networks are exactly what are needed for renewed hope. So many allies are ready and willing to shape a public world that is more humane than the one we were born into. We should not be afraid to keep kindling the emancipatory energies that brought so many of us to share this long-term project. These will embolden the next generation of thinkers, practitioners and reformers who know they do not want to reproduce the dysfunctional patterns they see around them in civil society and in the worlds of business and government. They are ready to experiment, to make room for the greatest surprise: that human kindness and understanding can emerge out of conflict and suffering.

References

Aertsen, I. (2000). Victim-offender mediation in Belgium. In The European Forum for Victim-Offender Mediation and Restorative Justice (ed.), *Victim-offender mediation in Europe: making restorative justice work* (pp. 153-192). Leuven: Leuven University Press.

Aertsen, I. (2006). The intermediate position of restorative justice: the case of Belgium. In I Aertsen, T. Daems & L. Robert (eds.), *Institutionalizing restorative justice* (pp. 68-92). Devon: Willan Publishing.

Aertsen, I. (2012). Restorative prisons: where are we heading? In T. Barabás, B. Fellegi & S. Windt (eds.), *Responsibility-taking, relationship-building and restoration in prisons* (pp. 263-276). Budapest: P-T Muhely.

Aertsen, I. (2015). Belgium. In F. Dünkel, J. Grzywa-Holten & P. Horsfield (eds.), *Restorative justice and mediation in penal matters: a stock-taking of legal issues, implementation strategies and outcomes in 36 European countries* (Vol. 1; pp. 45-87). Mönchengladbach: Forum Verlag Godesberg GmbH.

Aertsen, I. (2018a). *Leuven restorative city: towards effective integration. Grant proposal, research line in restorative justice and victimology.* Leuven: KU Leuven.

Aertsen, I. (2018b). *Leuven restorative city.* Presented at the Building Restorative Cities seminar, Como.

Dzur, A. (2008). *Democratic professionalism: citizen participation and the reconstruction of professional ethics, identity, and practice.* University Park: Penn State University Press.

Dzur, A. (2016). Conversations on restorative justice: a talk with Kay Pranis. *Restorative Justice: An International Journal,* 4(2), 257-270. doi:10.1080/20504721.2016.1197535.

Dzur, A. (2018). *Democracy inside: participatory innovation in unlikely places.* New York: Oxford University Press.

Fung, A. (2015). Putting the public back into governance: the challenges of citizen participation and its future. *Public Administration Review,* 75(4), 513-522. doi:10.1111/puar.12361.

Fung, A. & Wright, E. O. (eds.). (2003). *Deepening democracy: institutional innovation in empowered participatory governance.* London: Verso.

Galanter, M. (1981). Justice in many rooms: courts, private ordering, and indigenous law. *Journal of Legal Pluralism,* 13(1), 1-47. doi:10.1080/07329113.1981.10756257.

Green, S., Johnstone G. & Lambert C. (2013). What harm, whose justice? Excavating the restorative movement. *Contemporary Justice Review,* 16(4), 445-460. doi:10.1080/10282580.2013.857071.

Rosenblatt, F. F. (2015). *The role of community in restorative justice.* Abingdon: Routledge.

Wolin, S. (2004). *Politics and vision: continuity and innovation in western political thought, expanded edition.* Princeton: Princeton University Press.

How do we 'walk the talk'? Some reflections on restorative justice's (perhaps not so?) hidden values

Fernanda Fonseca Rosenblatt

This is the first time that I am invited to contribute to a *Liber Amicorum*. In the invitation email, the editors say that they have identified me as '**important in the professional background and history** of Ivo Aertsen' (emphasis not only in the original but also in my memory). I had to read this sentence a few times before the 'coin dropped', as we say in Brazil (referring to coin-operated public telephones). That is, it took me a few minutes before I could make sense of what I was reading. 'It is actually Ivo that is important in my professional background and "history" (perhaps, in my case, still a "story"?) and not the other way around!', I immediately thought. And then, my less modest self came to the fore, along with a big smile: '*Amai!*[1] Look how far I've come!' Indeed, I feel very honoured (and proud) to be included in this project.

The second feeling that drives my writing here is that of freedom. One of the things that I most like about contemporary art (and envy contemporary artists for) is that these artists seem free of any constraints equivalent to Harvard or Oxford referencing styles or, more generally, academic writing rules and conventions. They can communicate their 'findings' as they wish and feel, and they probably end up touching more people than we (academics) do. There seems to be no limits placed on top of (or around) their inspiration, no right or best ways to 'do it', no style boxes in which to fit their art – by the way, I once stood for minutes, contemplating an empty box in the middle of an empty room during a memorable exhibition at Tate Modern ... Well, I was told that for a *Liber Amicorum* we are free to write as we wish – even 'personal anecdotes and memories' are welcome, as per the editors' invitation email. So, I can finally write about restorative justice without having to stop at every other sentence to find that page of that chapter in that book where I have read that certain idea, which, in truth, I have often read in so many different places. I can 'put on paper' the exclamations that have always been in my mind and use ellipses even when I am not omitting people's words (but just trying to find my own). I can be emotional and not only talk about the important role of emotions. I can use the subject pronoun 'I' instead of hiding myself behind impersonal writing. I can also introduce this text before writing it, like we pretend to do (but never do) in academic

1 The Flemish word for 'wow', I have learned.

writing and, therefore, allow myself to find out what this will be about while I write and you ('the reader') read(s).

Although there is plenty of disagreement between 'restorative justice people' (this is how my mother refers to 'us'); indeed, 'Ask two restorativists, get three opinions' is just as applicable here – 'we' have come to some agreements. One of restorative justice's main undisputed attributes is that it sees crime as a violation against 'real' people (rather than just a violation against the abstract interests of the State or against abstract legal rules) and, in turn, restorative justice involves returning conflicts to whom they belong, that is, to victims, offenders and the community (sorry, Christie, although this is an easy one to reference, I have decided to exercise my own version of 'contemporary academic writing'). Alright, it remains true that we have not come to an agreement on the use of the singular or plural tense to refer to this third stakeholder (the community or communities). And it is also true that, on the ground, many restorative justice programmes, particularly those implemented within criminal justice systems, have been 'orchestrated' (idealised, coordinated and even led) by criminal justice professionals and not by the parties themselves (e.g. in Brazil, by judges in what has been termed 'judicial restorative justice'). But, having said that, no restorativist would disagree with what I said: restorative justice is about the State (in fact, its representatives) relinquishing power and 'giving power to the people', more precisely, to those (most directly) affected by a particular offence.

We have not yet agreed if restorative justice is more about the process or the outcome, but we all agree that the restorative label should only be placed on processes that are inclusive, that is, where the active participation of all parties involved is encouraged and facilitated. In fact, 'label' is not the right word as restorativists generally (but, again, not unanimously) aim to get rid of those ... but this is another topic ... Restorative justice's call for inclusiveness arises directly from the idea that conflicts should be handed back to the parties most directly affected by crime, or, juggling the words around a bit, the idea of handing conflicts back to their owners can only go ahead if the process of restorative justice is indeed inclusive. Ideally, thus, restorative justice practices should involve a 'live' meeting between the key stakeholders so that chances are given to all of them to express their feelings and to share their ideas on how to deal with the aftermath of a particular offence. Indeed, we all agree that a face-to-face encounter is only the 'ideal' (but by no means the only!) way of 'doing restorative justice' – although there is still fierce disagreement on how far we can stretch the restorative justice 'umbrella' to cover practices where there is no encounter.

So, restorative justice is a collaborative endeavour where key stakeholders share responsibility to 'make things right' (and no, I do not like the term *right*, but we can do with a bit of restorative justice 'jargon' here and there ...) as they engage in a process of discovery, where equal opportunity is given for all voices to be heard, for all views to be represented, for feelings of belonging and interconnectedness to arise. In this context, informality is another value enthusiastically related to restorative justice processes. Restorative justice advocates – researchers and practitioners alike – cannot agree on the right 'amount' of informality, but it is by now 'common restorative sense' that restorative justice processes should be as informal as possible to enable a non-threatening and non-stigmatising environment whereby participants can feel comfortable and able to speak for themselves. Hence, restorative justice practices usually take place in non-courtroom settings, with participants sitting in a circle, with no one wearing wigs or gowns, with participants 'breaking bread' together at the end of the restorative meeting and so on. And I do not know of any restorative justice advocate who promotes 'informality without borders' – in fact, restorativists of all kinds agree that we need a 'pinch' of formality (and, of course, recipes differ) to avoid re-victimisation and so that human rights and legal safeguards are fully respected.

The term *empowerment* has also been unarguably added to the restorative vocabulary. It is seen as a crucial restorative outcome by some, as a welcome side-effect by others, as a strong indicator of 'success' yet by others; that is, we are not unanimous about where we should place 'empowerment' in restorative justice's 'organogram', but none of us, while explaining restorative justice, would leave this term unspoken. Indeed, to fight a mind-set that thinks that conflicts are better dealt with by professionals (or over-professionalised procedures), victims need empowerment to 'own their conflict' and, therefore, they should be empowered to have a say on how they think their own case should be handled. They should also leave the process feeling stronger and not revictimised. On the other hand, in order to overcome a long-standing tradition of passively 'taking' punishment, offenders should be empowered to 'own' their behaviour, to face the consequences of their actions by making amends to individuals and relationships and to seek reintegration into their communities by taking every opportunity they can to demonstrate trustworthiness. Finally, community members should be empowered to inquire into the local sources of crime, to resolve a community's own conflicts and to help determine a plan of action through which repentant offenders are reaccepted into their community (and victims too).

Finally (and only because we have a word limit to obey!), among the 'things we all know' about restorative justice – that is, another of its uncontested features – is that restorative justice is aimed at reparation. Indeed, we may give 'reparation' a different status within the restorative list of priorities (e.g. some would argue that a restorative process is enough of an outcome even if it does not lead to any actual reparative outcomes), but we all agree that reparation should be there, at least as a goal, at least in the horizon. Indeed, restorative justice processes should create opportunities for making amends, for (re)building relationships, for the healing of harms. An offender making financial restitution to the victim is maybe the most obvious and concrete form of direct reparation to victims, but direct reparation can also take the form of practical work (material reparation) or apology (symbolic reparation). The offender can, for example, fix the victim's fence that he or she has broken (material reparation) or write a letter of apology (symbolic reparation). The reparation to victims can also be indirect; for example, the offender can carry out unpaid work at a charity chosen by the victim. Finally, reparation to the 'victimised community' is usually achieved symbolically through community service. That is, to compensate for the harm they have caused to the community, offenders are often required to complete a period of unpaid work for the benefit of the community or its institutions, such as cleaning and repairing trails in a city park. Of course, we can problematise (and we have been criticising!) all the examples given here. How reparative are apologies in domestic violence cases, where the victim has often heard so many 'I'm-sorries' (and, sometimes, has actually forgiven so many times!) throughout the cycle of violence which he or she was (or still is) submitted to? How restorative are 'one-size-fits-all' community service 'packages' (e.g. where an offender, regardless of the offence, his or her personal involvement or his or her own community's context, and regardless of the victim's needs or inputs and the harms caused, is subjected to a few hours of randomly assigned 'litter picking' somewhere in the city)? How restorative is the exercise of writing letters of apology or explanation or empathy (and the list of nicknames is extensive!) when they will not be sent to the victim (as has often been found to be the case)? Controversies apart, 'because crime hurts, justice should heal' is the mantra that we, restorativists, are very familiar with and repeat.

These are all clear, obvious – as I said, undisputable (although, as we can see, surrounded by disputed details!) – restorative justice features, attributes, principles, elements, goals, appeals, topics or what have you. But I would like to turn the second bit of this text towards more hidden, less obvious values. Indeed, whereas 'returning conflict', 'participation', 'informality', 'empowerment', 'reparation' and so on appear in every attempt at explaining what restorative justice is (or is not), there are other values, of course very interrelated with those already mentioned (or perhaps synonymous to some?), that we (well, I) have not read much about. I would like to bring some of them forward.

Restorative justice also involves an ability to see what is not in the room. Some will call this empathy, others will talk about compassionate or active listening, yet others will focus on the potential of 'empowerment'. I want to highlight the restorative value of seeing beyond reach. I am referring to the ability that facilitators or mediators have to see in an at-first-sceptical victim her future willingness to take part in a restorative encounter. The ability that facilitators or mediators have to see future repentance in sometimes-cynical offenders. The ability that victims have to see another victim sitting in 'his or her' offender's chair. The ability that offenders have to see 'community' in the narratives of strangers. The ability that community members have to represent what they cannot see and sometimes have never experienced. This ability to see what is not (yet) in the room leads facilitators to put a lot of time and energy on (sometimes very) long preparatory processes; leads victims to empathise with those who have (sometimes irreversibly) harmed them; leads offenders to take responsibility in front of people with whom they would (probably) choose to not even interact throughout their existence; leads community representatives serve as volunteers in yet another meeting, even when the last meeting seemed a waste of their time (yes, some restorative meetings do go wrong ...). Maybe this ability to see what is not in the room is, in truth and perhaps paradoxically, an ability to see the entirety of what is in the room. The ability to see the whole person. The ability to see the worth of the individual, sometimes even when he or she cannot see it themselves.

Another hidden restorative justice value is that of 'letting people go' or the ability to give people 'wings'. This, again, has definitely to do with empowerment and community (re)building and other unhidden restorative values, but there is something special, altruistic and all at once subtle about being able to spend so much time and energy working with people whom you may never see again. Indeed, on the ground, more often than not, restorative justice initiatives end up building 'aesthetic communities' (thank you, Bauman) and that is all, where the bonds between participants are only experienced 'on the spot' and 'not taken home' to be enjoyed in their daily lives. That is, the restorative ideal of 'community building', in perhaps more practical and non-romantic (or pessimistic?) terms, more often than not, means helping to (re)build other people's communities, communities that will not impact one's own life – besides, of course, the good feeling of having contributed to what will be happily experienced by others. And, yes, I do believe that we can be genuinely happy for others. But, no, I do not believe that a win-win situation is always among restorative justice's possibilities. On the floor, restorative justice may be about 'not losing' instead of winning, and that would already be a paradigm shift ... but that is another topic ...

A third hidden restorative justice value has to do with coherence. With, as stamped on the title, 'walking the talk'. Restorative justice 'teaches' dialogue through dialogue, includes through participation, gives people voice by learning how to listen. Restorative justice classes in postgraduate courses or trainings or restorative justice seminars of all sorts and formats are taught (or should be taught) in dialogue with the students, who (should feel free to) teach as they are taught (and here I feel uncontrollably tempted to suggest Paulo Freire's *Pedagogy of the Oppressed*, and I do so in an admittedly proud tone, for what comes from the Global South, in his case Brazil; is not very often globally known and cited). Indeed, 'restorative justice people' (Lu, my mum, since 2000-and-something) have to 'walk the talk' and apply restorative justice principles to the design and delivery of their courses; they have to adopt a teaching style that is inclusive, that is informal (or flexible) and respectful, that allows 'teachers' and 'learners' to engage not only academically but also interpersonally, just as restorative practices are supposed to be or do. Being restorative while you 'do' or 'think' restorative justice entails being able to admit new voices and perspectives, being able to step back and see things differently in a 'process of discovery' of self and others. And this is not an easy journey, not even for us, those convinced of the potential and 'superiority' of the restorative justice approach to crime (please read Kathleen Daly to avoid using such simplistic terms as superiority).

By no means am I saying that restorative justice has the monopoly on such participatory and peace-promoting values actually shared by (many) other social 'movements' and disciplines or that values and restorative justice are the same thing (I was also Lode Walgrave's student, by the way!). But there is 'lots' in the restorative justice's values box to be unpacked. And the previously mentioned (perhaps not so?) hidden restorative values have not been chosen randomly to fill in the pages of this 'chapter'. They have been highlighted, well, I have highlighted them – now dropping the impersonal tone – because they help to explain what Ivo Aertsen means to me ...

When we first met, I had never experienced research or (actual) academic writing before. I had nothing published, I had never heard about restorative justice and my English was even more imperfect than it is today. I had only my dreams to offer – and that of course he could not see (nor have I offered!). But he saw what, I am sure, was still not there: he saw the researcher and the academic in me when so many people (including myself!) could not (yet) see. After completing my masters at the Katholieke University of Leuven, he (and others!) encouraged me to apply for a PhD, but I ended up 'deciding' to 'disappear' into Brazil's academic 'working market'. I flew with the wings that he (and others!) had given me back in Leuven. And he could not possibly know that I would want to fly back. But I did. One day, some five years later, he got an email 'informing' that I had finally decided to do my PhD abroad, but not in Leuven – 'I want to experience other schools of thought,' I said. And with the courage that maybe the age rips off, I also asked him where, in his opinion, should I go. In other words, I said: 'I do not want to go back to Leuven, but, by the way, where should I go?' And I not only got a reply, but a world map of possibilities formatted into an email. He basically listed all universities in the English- and Portuguese-speaking academic world where I could be supervised by someone 'big' in the restorative justice field. I then 'victimised' him (and others!) by asking for a few dozen recommendation letters until I finally got accepted into Oxford.

My returning to Europe (well, it was for sure Europe at that time ...) meant a return also to Leuven, where I have been on several occasions. Indeed, soon I was again landing under KU Leuven's restorative justice 'shelter', an Ivo-run (and, of course, collaboratively so!) shelter. He has since introduced or e-introduced me to so many 'restorative justice people' (and other human kinds) – including people in my own country! He has given me opportunities to present my loose ideas, even way before I had any research findings to show (or even proper research questions to share). He has helped me to open so many of the doors that I thought could only be opened in my dreams, as well as those that we are not even able to notice when we are pressing the 'starting' button of our academic careers. In other words, Ivo, for me, you have been an example of someone who managed to 'walk the talk' – someone who studies and 'does' restorative justice restoratively.

Thank you for your ability to see what did not exist when you first met me, and for your endless ability to see what is still not there (or here). Thank you for providing me with so many of my current academic wings, for 'letting me go' into a world of possibilities that you have helped to create. Thank you for giving me voice and seeing relevance in what I have to say. While doing so, thank you for teaching me, empirically, what a restorative relationship with students may look like ... In fact, you may not be aware, but you are, in my day-by-day practice as a professor, one of the examples I try to follow. In my academic walk, I have been very lucky to meet people like you, who can 'walk the talk', but overall academia has been a hard experience for me. It has been rewarding at times, but sometimes also lonely and not even partially restorative. You are thus very important in my professional background (and not the other way around as I was flattered to read in the invitation to this book) ... and if one day I get to the point of 'building' a history, you can be sure that you already have a very important role therein. '*Dank u wel*', my dear professor and friend!

Restorative justice and the challenge of Aristotelian anger

Pieter De Witte and Geertjan Zuijdwegt

1 Introduction

Gratitude is the appropriate emotion on the occasion of the retirement of Ivo Aertsen. There are many reasons to look back gratefully at the career of Ivo, and only a volume like the present one can reveal how innumerable these reasons are. As prison chaplains and researchers at the Centre for Religion, Ethics and Detention (CRED) we too have our reasons to be thankful to Ivo. Ivo played a significant role in the establishment of CRED and made sure that the Leuven Institute for Criminology - more particularly, the research line Restorative Justice and Victimology - could be its home.

Ivo's openness and, indeed, eagerness to collaborate with practitioners and scholars from various academic disciplines undoubtedly reflects his attempt to broaden the scope of restorative justice research and to promote a more interdisciplinary take on restorative justice. On a more fundamental level, his engagement with people outside the realm of academic criminology demonstrates an awareness of the fact that certain fundamental issues in the field of restorative justice cannot be grasped within the confines of a single scholarly discipline. One way to clarify this fact is to make the seemingly tautological statement that restorative justice is about *justice*. Once we put it like that, we realise how elusive the concept is that we are trying to qualify. *Justice* is a notion that is so familiar and so internal to our acting and thinking that we cannot grasp it simply and immediately. For what is justice? 'If no one asks me, I know; if I wish to explain to him who asks, I know not', as St Augustine put it in a different context. Justice seems to be some sort of 'regulative idea' that guides the most basic convictions of restorative justice advocates, especially the beliefs undergirding their criticism of the existing criminal justice system. This system is not criticised for being just at the expense of individual and communal well-being, but rather for its failure to realise *justice*. A good instance is Herman Bianchi's insistence that, for centuries, the Western criminal justice system has pursued the wrong ('Greek') concept of justice and that a more victim-oriented response to wrongdoing can only be developed when we rediscover a more adequate (in his case: 'Hebrew') notion of justice (Bianchi, 1994). Everyone assumes that justice is the ultimate criterion. And yet, the question 'What is justice?' keeps troubling us, like a gadfly buzzing around our heads.

The inevitability and elusiveness of the question of justice prevent restorative justice from being a self-contained field of academic inquiry and programme management. The 'field' of restorative justice will always be a space of dialogue with history, law, philosophy, art, religion and so on revolving around the issue of justice. This situation makes us, two theologians and prison chaplains, potential fellow travellers of what Ivo frequently calls 'the Movement'. We gladly accept this role because we are convinced that the religious and philosophical traditions that constitute our academic and personal background can provide resources for the much-needed transformation of our criminal justice system. In this contribution, we will not delve into these traditions to shed a *direct* light on the notion of justice. Instead, we opt for an indirect approach that focusses on *anger*. Analysing this emotion and the way it is dealt with in classical moral philosophy will allow us to better understand some of the dilemmas and aporias of restorative justice as an approach that promises a more just reaction to wrongdoing than conventional criminal justice systems.

The restorative justice movement is committed to a profound transformation of existing criminal justice practices. At times it even indulges in a revolutionary rhetoric. Although the nature of the transformation that is sought can be grasped intuitively by most non-specialists, it is in fact complex. There are at least two ways to describe restorative justice's fundamental 'change of lenses'. First, it seeks the transition from a centralised, state-controlled and law-oriented criminal justice system to a participatory approach, in which stakeholders are granted ownership of the conflict that has manifested itself. One could say that this is a shift in the *locus* of justice. The response to the offence is not decided upon by anonymous laws and bureaucratic procedures, but in an interpersonal encounter of those closest to the harmful events that have occurred. Second, restorative justice seeks a change in the *quality* of justice. It has a certain view on how justice should be brought about and what an appropriate outcome looks like. The desirable transition can be described in different ways: from an oppositional to a collaborative attitude, from a vengeful focus on the past to a constructive imagining of the future, from violence and counter-violence to some form of pacification.

Both aspects of the transformation envisioned by restorative justice are, of course, connected. One way to link them is to show how top-down responses to crime fail to pacify the parties involved in the conflict and how the active participation of stakeholders is more likely to yield agreeable and sustainable outcomes. Another connecting element is the idea that restorative justice is a fundamentally democratic approach to conflict. The notion of democratic government unites the ideas of participation and nonviolent negotiation. Undoubtedly, there are numerous other ways to connect both aspects of restorative justice. Still, it is crucial to see how they are logically independent from one another. We can well imagine a society in which conflicts are fully owned by those involved and where this ownership is expressed in what we would interpret as a cruel and disproportionate retaliation for even the slightest offense. We can also imagine a purely top-down approach to offences, administered by a Solomon-like wise judge, that would settle all conflicts in society in a satisfactory way. Imagining non-pacifying participation and non-participatory pacification may be considered counterfactual, but it suffices as a reminder that both aspects do not *necessarily* belong together.

The question of anger is relevant for a fundamental reflection on restorative justice because it reveals the gap between the two aspects of the restorative transition. As an emotion, it is properly predicated of individuals who, by the very fact of their being angry, show that they are personally affected by a wrong that has been committed. Thus, anger is situated right at the heart of restorative justice's *locus* of justice: the people who are personally involved and who therefore are the central agents in the restorative justice process. Anger is one of the things that will occur when the participatory transition takes place and conflicts are given back to the people. At the same time, anger seems to run counter to the second restorative transformation, that of collaborative and nonviolent conflict resolution. Because anger is an emotion that tends to retaliatory action, it does not seem to provide the right *quality* of justice. To the extent that emotions contain moral and intellectual judgements, anger itself implies a view on justice that claims the moral legitimacy and even necessity of retaliation. This constitutes a challenge to restorative justice. Restorative justice needs to explain to the stakeholders, who are kindly invited to participate in the restorative dialogue and to bring along all their desires, concerns, feelings, experiences and judgements (including their anger), to what extent and on what grounds certain aspects of this anger stand in need of transformation. To rephrase this challenge with reference to the work of Nils Christie: anger will manifest itself when one begins to see 'conflicts as property', but it seems to have an inclination to inflict pain rather than to set 'limits to pain'.

Because of its somewhat ambiguous relation to the objectives of restorative justice, anger may turn out to be an important topic of reflection if one is to find out what restorative justice is all about. In this chapter, we will offer a modest contribution to the study of anger in relation to restorative justice. We will first present a traditional definition of anger that might form a plausible point of departure in a contemporary discussion of anger. Second, we will explore some consequences from this definition for the role of anger in restorative justice.

2 ARISTOTLE ON ANGER

Since we have all been angry, we all have some basic discursive understanding of the emotion. But defining it in a precise way is not so easy. Rather than synthesising the mass of current anger research, we take a rather more anachronistic point of departure. Our no doubt controversial, but for that reason thought-provoking definition was formulated over two millennia ago by Aristotle (384-322 bc), one of the great sages of ancient Greece. Aristotle primarily discusses anger in two of his main works, the *Rhetoric* and the *Nicomachean Ethics*. The former deals with the art of persuasion, the latter with pursuing the good life. Anger is relevant in the context of the *Rhetoric* – our main focus here – because emotions play a massive role in persuasion. To be successful, an orator in, say, politics or the justice system, needs to know how to arouse and to assuage the anger (or the fear, shame, pity or indignation) of a populace or jury, because emotions impact people's judgements. And thus, it is key to know what these emotions are and how they are triggered. For the sake of brevity and clarity, our sketch of Aristotle's view is rather basic, sidestepping several complex philological and philosophical issues. Still, it is meaty enough to show that Aristotle can help us to reflect on anger today, particularly where it concerns its vindictive thrust, its character as a response to belittlement, its rational or discursive dimension and its relation to hatred.

In book II of the *Rhetoric*, Aristotle defines anger – in the translation of Robert Sokolowski – as 'a desire accompanied by pain for a manifested retribution for a manifested belittlement of things affecting oneself or one's own, done by someone who has no business to belittle them' (Sokolowski, 2014: 233; *Rhetoric* II.2, 1378a31-33). This is a relatively complex definition of what psychologists would call state (rather than trait) anger, and it needs to be unpacked carefully. First, Aristotle understands anger as a 'desire' (or drive, or thrust) accompanied by pain. It is what modern research calls 'a negative (aversive) emotion, but one that involves active approach' (Potegal & Stemmler, 2010: 4). In contrast to sadness or fear, anger is out to get something from someone. But what it is out to get, and why, Aristotle defines much more precisely than most contemporary scholarship, and that is one reason why his view is so interesting. For Aristotle, anger is after retribution (or even revenge) in answer to belittlement. It is unequivocally about returning some kind of pain for a particular type of pain sustained. This specific kind of pain is *belittlement* – a term that is of more extensive application than the common translation 'slight' (for the Greek *oligōria*). Aristotle lucidly defines the act of belittling as 'the actualising [or expressing] of an opinion about something that shows up as being worth nothing' (Sokolowski, 2014: 234; *Rhetoric* II.2, 1378b10-11). Thus, belittling is a very specific type of value judgement. When we view things as good or bad, or people as friends or enemies, we take them seriously; they merit our serious consideration. But if we belittle someone, we show that we simply do not care about him or her; he or she is not worth our notice. If we feel treated like that, Aristotle argues, we become angry.

Anger, then, is a response to more than goal blockage alone – a popular contemporary view. A simple, even trite, example can make this clear. Imagine you are in a university library studying for an exam; on restorative justice, say. You came there in the expectation to study intensively and quietly. Instead, two guys next to you are loudly talking and chuckling about their party exploits over the weekend. You ostentatiously raise your eyebrows, cough once or twice, throw meaningful looks in their direction, but you get zero response. Chances are you are getting annoyed. Anger is on the rise. Now your anger is not just about goal blockage – the fact that you cannot study as quietly as you wanted. To see this, imagine the same situation, but now in a coffee bar. If people are talking there – even if you expected the place to be quiet – you will probably not get angry, because you know that people have every right to talk there. In the library, the situation is quite different. The two guys' behaviour will feel like a disregard for your right, that is, your *legitimate* expectation to study in quiet in a place designated for that purpose. Accordingly, you read their behaviour as showing disrespect, spite or belittlement, and that is why you get angry.

According to Aristotle, such belittlement elicits anger not just when it concerns us personally, but whenever it concerns something or someone with whom we identify. We will get angry if someone expresses contempt for a friend, but also for a cause we espouse, or even for a line of study we pursue. Thus, eager philosophers get angry with people who show contempt for philosophy (see *Rhetoric* II.2, 1379a32-35). Such reasons for anger can be quite minimal. Even having your name forgotten is a cause of anger, because 'forgetfulness seems a sign of belittlement; it is due to indifference, and indifference is belittling' (*Rhetoric* II.2, 1379b34-37). The final element of the definition – that the belittling is done by someone who has no business to do so – is key too. What Aristotle gets at here is the idea that the kind of belittlement that causes anger is largely gratuitous. Thus, the belittlement cannot be itself retributive or retaliatory. If we perceive a slight or insult as well deserved, it will not anger us. Consider an instance. Imagine you are driving through town, and nearly knock a cyclist of his bike, because you are looking at your phone. The cyclist gets angry and starts to shout insulting things at you. Chances are that you will not feel much anger in return. You will realise that the near-accident was your fault and that the cyclist has every right to react angrily. Shame or guilt, rather than anger, will be your dominant emotion.

This is just one example of how dynamic and multifaceted anger is as a social emotion. And there is a good reason for that fact. The interpretative judgement on which the eliciting of anger depends – the judgement that a particular act constitutes an unwarranted belittlement – is always dependent on social context. Even outrageous insults do not necessarily cause anger. Just think of the popular format of 'roasts' – the organised insult of an individual for comic purposes – aired on networks like Comedy Central. Similarly, the eliciting of anger is impacted by differences in personal or social relationships. Thus, Aristotle argues that we get angrier with friends than with others. Friendship, after all, means to desire good things for someone, not for your own sake, but for his or hers. So, when friends belittle us, we get all the angrier, because they have the least business to do so (see *Rhetoric* II.2, 1379b2-4, 13-17; II.4, 1380b36-37). Status and power are factors as well; more so in an honour culture like Aristotle's, where social inferiors could never be justified in slighting their betters, but it applies to our day too – just think of the vast imbalance in many professor-student relationships. Finally, audience matters. Aristotle points out that people get especially angry if they are belittled in front of 'their rivals, those whom they admire, those by whom they would like to be admired, those whom they respect, or those who respect them' (*Rhetoric* II.2, 1379b25-27). It is a different thing to be insulted in private, or before total strangers, than to be insulted in front of esteemed colleagues, where a carefully crafted reputation might be at stake.

Aristotle does not just treat of things that make us angry, he also deals with what calms us once we are angry (see *Rhetoric* II.3). Again, this is important information for the orator, who must not only know how to whip up a crowd or jury but also know how to quiet it down. Our anger tends to abate if we come to realise that someone did not belittle us on purpose, that he or she simply knew no better or was in a state of anger him- or herself. Our anger also ceases towards those 'who admit their fault and are sorry'. This seems obvious enough, but the reason Aristotle provides is interesting: 'we accept their grief [or pain] at what they have done as satisfaction' (*Rhetoric* II.3, 1380a14-15). Recall that Aristotelian anger is about retribution. What the angry person wants is to get even. This example shows that getting even does not entail extravagant exercises of vengeance. Often enough, merely witnessing an expression of remorse is evidence of sufficient pain in the person who belittled us to satisfy our craving for revenge. To modern ears, this interpretation of the practice of apologising might sound far-fetched. We might argue that what matters in an apology is not the pain suffered by the person apologising but the fact that his or her apology shows that he acknowledges our pain, which means that he or she no longer belittles us but takes us seriously. But perhaps there is more to it. Few people would be satisfied with a merely formal apology after an egregious insult. Most would want to see that the person who insulted them is somehow pained by the knowledge that he or she wronged them. It is hard to imagine a satisfactory acknowledgement of having wronged another person unaccompanied by at least some unpleasant emotion.

It should be clear by now that Aristotelian anger is far from an irrational emotion. In at least two ways, it is tied up with forms of reasoning. First, the eliciting of anger always depends on an interpretative judgement. For anger to arise, some act directed at us must be perceived as contempt, slight, spite or insult. If a branch falls on my head in the forest, I will not get angry with the tree. But I will get angry with my wife, if she, for no apparent reason, decides to hit me over the head with that same branch. The hurt might be similar, but I only become angry if she does it, and not just if she does it, but if she does it on purpose and to spite me. My anger will quickly disappear if it turns out she wanted to toss the stick to the dog but misjudged her throw, or if by hitting me, she tried to kill a giant hornet about to sting. In the one case, I might chide her for carelessness, and in the other, for picking such a rough remedy, but neither will occasion the marital crisis that would occur when she got into the habit of randomly whacking my head with sticks. Second, and as a corollary to the first, Aristotelian anger is always subject to rational evaluation. Of any instance of Aristotelian anger, one can ask: is it right? This question not only pertains to the interpretative judgement on which anger is based but also to the intensity of the emotion and the extent of the desired or enacted retribution. Anger is about proportion, about finding the right response, and assessing proportion is a task of reason. Of course, Aristotle acknowledges that anger often tends to extend reasonable bounds. In the *Nicomachean Ethics*, he notes that anger 'seems to listen to reason to some extent, but to mishear it, as do hasty servants who run out before they have heard the whole of what one says, and then muddle the order'. Thus, 'anger, by reason of the warmth and hastiness of its nature, though it hears, does not hear an order, and springs to take revenge' (*Nicomachean Ethics* VII.6, 1149a25-31). Nevertheless, it is also possible to lack in anger or to be not exacting enough in taking revenge. Hence, it is a person's duty not to stamp out anger but to regulate it such that he or she is 'angry at the right things and with the right people, and, further, as he ought, when he ought, and as long as he ought' (*Nicomachean Ethics* IV.5, 1125b37-38).

To better grasp Aristotle's view, it is helpful to look at his comparison between anger and hatred. Although Aristotle admits that anger is a prime occasion for the development of hatred, he distinguishes the two emotions in terms of their cause, object and end. First, Aristotle argues that anger arises out of 'offences against oneself', that is, as we have seen, the belittling of us or of what we identify with. Hatred, by contrast, can arise without anything that concerns us personally: 'we may hate people merely because of what we take to be their character' (*Rhetoric* II.4, 1382a3-5). The sense of Aristotle's Greek is that, for hate to arise, it is enough to invest (groups of) people with certain (detestable) attributes or characteristics – an eerily familiar theme in times of a widely exploited fear of migrants and Islam. This explains why, second, the objects of anger and hatred differ. For Aristotle, anger 'is always concerned with individuals – Callias or Socrates – whereas hatred is directed also against classes: we all hate any thief and any informer' (*Rhetoric* II.4, 1382a4-6). The first stipulation is entailed by Aristotle's definition of anger as a desire to avenge an unwarranted belittlement. Because anger responds to perceived acts, it is only elicited by specific agents: 'some particular individual, e.g. Cleon, and not man in general' (*Rhetoric* II.2, 1378a34). Hatred, on the other hand, is a response to certain perceived characteristics (e.g. a proneness to act in certain loathsome ways – for the thief, to steal). Accordingly, one can become an object of hate simply by belonging to a class that is perceived to possess certain attributes, even though one's own behaviour happens to be unobjectionable (think of the Jews or other victims of genocide).

Finally, anger and hatred pursue different ends, or goals. Anger is aimed at 'giving pain to its object', whereas hatred is aimed 'at doing him harm [or evil]'. This might seem a merely theoretical distinction, until we consider Aristotle's explanation: 'the angry man wants his victims to feel; the hater does not mind whether they feel or not' (*Rhetoric* II.4, 1328b8-10). A person who is angry is hurt. This is part of the definition – 'a desire accompanied by pain'. In return, he or she wants to inflict some pain him- or herself. To satisfy this desire, there is no point in doing harm, or evil, without pain. For, as Aristotle reminds us, not every harm or evil is painful. He provides the instance of madness. There are forms of mental illness that constitute evil or harm for the patient, but do not necessarily involve pain. Or think of Alzheimer's disease. It is certainly an evil, but not therefore always painful for the sufferer. Such evil without pain is what an angry person would never want to inflict on the object of their anger, but the hater would. The reason is simple. The angry person 'would have the offenders suffer for what they have done'; the hater, by contrast, 'would have them cease to exist' (*Rhetoric* II.4, 1382b15-16). The ultimate end of hatred is annihilation. And thus, the hater is not moved by pity, whereas a lot 'may happen to make the angry man pity those who offend him' (*Rhetoric* II.4, 1382b13).

3 Aristotelian anger and restorative justice

Philosophers since Aristotle have held very different views on the legitimacy of anger in our moral lives. Seneca (4 bc-65 ad) sees it as a form of madness that leads to no good (Seneca, 1970). In his Stoic view, the morally sound reaction to anger is to develop strategies that prevent anger from having us in its grip. Leading a good life requires anger prevention and, if that does not work, anger management that stops us from acting upon the anger that does arise. At the other end of the evaluative spectrum, we find Thomas Aquinas (1225-1274 ad), who tells us that anger can be worthy of praise (*laudabile*) if it is 'in accordance with right reason' (*Summa Theologiae*, IIaIIae, Q. 158 Art. 1). The remarkable thing about these diverging assessments is that neither of them fundamentally disagrees with Aristotle's definition of anger. Both Seneca and Aquinas would agree that anger is a reaction to a perceived injustice done to us and that it is an emotion that inclines us to take revenge. Both would also say that anger has a tendency to go wrong and that the ultimate criterion to determine whether this happens is its being in accordance or in conflict with reason. The main difference, then, is that Seneca dismisses anger as a state of mind that by definition subverts reasonable judgement, whereas Aquinas appreciates the rationality that potentially belongs to anger.

This brief sketch of two opposing and seemingly clear-cut positions should not conceal the fact that offering a moral evaluation of anger is a complex affair that requires clarity regarding fundamental moral principles, philosophical anthropology and the relationship between reason and emotions – issues which we cannot even begin to address here. We would like to focus on the way the Senecan and Thomistic attitudes to Aristotelian anger encapsulate the tension between the two aspects of the transformation of justice envisioned by restorative justice. The Senecan model, with its explicit rejection of anger's violent potential, fits restorative justice's commitment to nonviolent resolutions of conflict. The Thomistic model, with its more positive take on anger, fits restorative justice's commitment to fully engage stakeholders' moral emotions and desires. In the remainder of this chapter, we offer a three-step argument in favour of restorative justice's adoption of a Thomistic model. First, we argue that anger is not solely responsible for the increase in popular punitive desires. Second, we show that even contemporary moral philosophers have to acknowledge the potency of anger as signalling wrongdoing and instigating action. Finally, we argue that the retributive character of anger can and should be integrated into a restorative justice framework.

A first point to consider is the perceived dominance of anger in the public sphere. Anger is not only an emotion felt by individual stakeholders in a conflict. It also seems to be the dominant passion of an infuriated populace, whose outrage about spectacular crime cases fuels penal populism and upholds a non-restorative and prison-centred criminal justice system. Restorative justice practitioners will feel that this anger-based system does not satisfy the needs of actual victims. Victimological research may show significant discrepancies between political convictions about criminal justice furiously expressed 'in the name of the victims' and the attitudes and opinions of the victims themselves. But before such empirical data can be assessed, Aristotle's definition of anger obliges us to raise a conceptual issue. Is 'anger' really the emotion behind penal populism? At least two other emotions may energise tough-on-crime policies: fear and hatred. The current preoccupation with security and the use of a utopian imaginary of a risk-free society suggest that penal populism is triggered by an awareness of being threatened rather than being wronged. The popular fury vis-à-vis offenders, therefore, might at least to some extent be inspired by a form of fear. Second, in the Aristotelian framework, the emotional motive for the harsh treatment of offenders in present-day criminal justice systems resembles hatred more than anger. The mass of people who demand ruthless punishment seem to speak of whole classes of people (criminals in general, or more specific subgroups, such as paedophiles), of whom they have no personal experience and to whom certain monstrous characteristics are attributed. The endlessness of proposed punishments seems to reflect a desire for annihilation, rather than the wish to inflict a just amount of pain. All this typifies hatred, Aristotle would say. None of this is to say that the populace cannot really be angry. Large groups of people in society may truly and personally feel wronged by the criminal conduct of perfect strangers and thus feel Aristotelian anger towards offenders. In all probability, the populace has 'mixed emotions' towards offenders, that is, a concoction of hatred, fear and anger. But it is certainly misleading to identify anger as the emotion *par excellence* of penal populism. In fact, because fear relates to future events and hatred to assumed attributes, they are more indeterminate emotions than anger and thus more suited as emotional supports for impersonal and depersonalising policies. Anger, by contrast, is always primarily about a particular person having done a particular thing to another particular person.

It is one thing to say that anger is not the sole driving emotion behind penal populism, but quite another to argue that it can lead to good in interpersonal contexts. Let us begin to explore this question by consulting the contemporary moral philosopher Martha Nussbaum, who offers a balanced assessment of anger in her book *Anger and Forgiveness* (Nussbaum, 2016). Nussbaum does not fundamentally question the Aristotelian definition of anger and she accepts that the perception of belittlement ('down-ranking' as she renders it) and the inclination to vengeance are part and parcel of the emotion. At the same time, she largely subscribes to the Stoic verdict on anger as unreasonable. Still, she coins the concept of 'transition-anger' to preserve two aspects of Aristotelian anger as valuable for human relations: anger signals that 'some' serious problem has occurred and that 'something' needs to be done. She retains, in other words, the interpretative judgement implied in anger and its push towards action, but strips both of their specific Aristotelian content (belittlement and retribution). By speaking of 'transition-anger', she hopes to preserve the limited positive effects of anger – signalling a moral problem and calling for action – while indicating that anger ought to be stopped before it becomes harmful. At the decisive moment of action, transition-anger will 'head for the Transition', she says. This means that we opt for a constructive, future-oriented course of action, rather than for fruitless and hurtful attempts to 'get even'. Thus, as a second step in our defence of anger, we note that even contemporary thinkers who are critical of the emotion may have to admit that at least some aspects of Aristotelian anger are worth preserving. Before moving to our final step, which considers anger's impulse to retributive action, we will analyse Nussbaum's transitory take on anger in more depth.

Nussbaum would not call transition-anger morally praiseworthy. Instead, she upholds its *utility* as signalling conflict and instigating action. Even if one would agree with this understanding of the function of anger, one could wonder whether such a utilitarian approach captures the moral significance of transition-anger. Imagine, as a thought experiment, that our transition-anger would be replaced by a machine that through complex algorithms permanently monitors human relations, signals potential moral problems and proposes solutions to these problems that are optimally satisfying and least harmful to individuals and to society. Such a machine would make transition-anger less necessary and perhaps even wholly dispensable. It would definitely be safer than any form of anger, for no 'transition' would be required. The signalling of problems would not be left to a human emotion that always runs the risk of turning into violent action. Instead, it would be in the safe hands of a device that is programmed to be forward-looking and welfare-oriented. And yet, it seems that if such a 'rational' machine would successfully take over our dealings with moral conflicts and expel the emotion of anger from human interaction, we would end up in a morally cold and inhuman universe. For if anger would simply be absent and if all moral evil inflicted upon us would simply be brought to our attention only to become an object of rational, utilitarian reflection (with or without the imagined machine) we would be lacking the emotional responsiveness to others that makes our interaction properly human. In other words, there may be reasons to believe that, even apart from the question about retributive or non-retributive action, anger (or transition-anger) has an *intrinsic* value that cannot be reduced to its usefulness as indicator and instigator.

Our third and most crucial step turns on the issue of retribution. Is Nussbaum right in saying that anger, after having warned us that something is wrong and having called for action, should vanish as soon as possible in order to clear the way for a constructive, non-retributive response to the conflict? Restorative justice advocates may feel that there is some affinity between their most fundamental values and intuitions and Nussbaum's position. The notion of transition-anger seems to give a plausible and appealing account of the role of anger in relation to the double restorative justice transformation we have described in the introduction. The process of conflict resolution is primarily initiated by a stakeholder, whose anger may reveal that a wrong has been committed and that something needs to be done about it, rather than by a procedural system whose only question is whether or not the criminal law has been breached. Once the decision is made to act upon this initial feeling of being wronged, the anger subsides, and the transition is made towards a process that focusses on the needs of the stakeholders and their future well-being. In this way, transition-anger seems to do justice to restorative justice's concern for both participation and pacification.

The question is, however, whether the notion of transition-anger really contains all the aspects of Aristotelian anger that are valuable in our quest for justice after wrongdoing. Despite the appeal Nussbaum's theory of anger might have for restorative justice supporters, there is an alternative way to conceive the relationship between anger and restorative justice, which takes into account the potential rationality of anger's desire for retribution. This account of justice-seeking after wrongdoing starts from Aristotle's claim that some form of belittlement is what really angers people. It asserts that the human sensitivity for belittlement is rooted in an accurate sense of justice, for injustice can rightly be defined in terms of treating human beings below their worthiness or dignity. In Kantian terms, people are wronged when they are regarded merely as a means to an end, not also as ends in themselves, or if they are treated as objects, not as persons. Restorative justice may deal with harm and organise communication between the stakeholders in a conflict in order to facilitate the reparation of this harm. But it will also have to deal with an irreparable wrong that has been committed: that a human being has been reduced to a mere object. It is a legitimate desire of the persons who have been wronged to see the wrongdoer recognise the full humanity of his or her victims *and* admit his or her past failure to give this recognition. What is desired from the offender is, in other words, some form of remorse, which may be defined as the painful remembrance of an action one has undertaken which one now considers wrong. As we have seen, Aristotle believed that observing an expression of remorse on the part of the offender can alleviate our anger, precisely because anger somehow achieves its retributive aim in the intrinsically painful emotion of remorse. It should be noted that this desired pain is not just a form of counter-humiliation to make up for the initial belittlement. Rather, it is the only credible testimony to the fact that the wrongdoer did not acknowledge, but now acknowledges, his or her victims in their full humanity.

Here we have an account of anger that can make sense of its retributive desire to inflict pain even within a restorative justice framework. Of course, anger's retributive thrust can go wrong in a number of ways. It can obscure issues of harm and reparation of harm. It can lead to disproportionate punitive reactions to wrongdoing. It can engage people in pathological attempts to humiliate the humiliator. But none of this means that retribution has no legitimate place in the practices of justice envisioned by the restorative justice movement. It could even have a central place in it; precisely, retributive anger is about a wrong that cannot be undone, except 'symbolically' (i.e. in the sphere of human interaction) by the offender's painful tribute to the victim's humanity.

4 Conclusion

Let us conclude by briefly pointing out two advantages of an approach to restorative justice that has a fundamentally positive attitude towards anger and its retributive impetus. First, anger is taken seriously as a moral emotion that contains a certain wisdom and rationality. At the same time, and precisely for that reason, anger can and should be evaluated and criticised by reason, as Thomas Aquinas would say. Anger may in some cases be exaggerated and its tendency to retaliation is often unreasonable. Conversely, some people may be too apathetic and lenient when being wronged. All of this is open to rational discussion and reflection. Emotions are not just brute facts that we can only throw in each other's faces in our conversations. Nor are they to be dismissed in an *a priori* fashion because of some Stoic ideal of tranquillity. People who participate in restorative justice practices are invited not only to listen to their emotions, for they are sources of rational insight, but also to judge them and to be self-critical about them.

This leads to a second point. There is no extrinsic authority that can legitimately decide upon the morality of our desire for retribution. Traditional formulae like 'an eye for an eye' vaguely communicate the idea of proportionality without giving us a clue about concrete ways of organising retribution. There is no consensus in society about the appropriate amount of pain that has to be inflicted when a crime is committed. Restorative justice invites people to enter into dialogue with each other about what is to be done in the wake of wrongdoing. If retribution is part of this dialogue, it becomes the object of democratic deliberation. Perhaps this is one of the great opportunities for restorative justice today: that it is able to set up a participatory dialogue on the rightful infliction of pain on offenders, at the very moment when the state, with its 'monopoly on violence', is losing its credibility in the eyes of large swaths of the population.

References

Bianchi, H. (1994). *Justice as sanctuary: toward a new system of crime control.* Bloomington: Indiana University Press.

Nussbaum, M. (2016). *Anger and forgiveness: resentment, generosity, and justice.* Oxford: Oxford University Press.

Potegal, M. & Stemmler, G. (2010). Cross-disciplinary views of anger: consensus and controversy. In M. Potegal, G. Stemmler & C. Spielberger (eds.), *International handbook of anger: constituent and concomitant biological, psychological, and social processes* (pp. 3-7). New York: Springer.

Seneca, L. (1970). *Moral essays.* Cambridge: Harvard University Press.

Sokolowski, R. (2014). Honor, anger, and belittlement in Aristotle's Ethics. *Studia Gilsoniana*, 3, 221-240.

Does restorative justice have a future?

Ezzat A. Fattah

It is an honour and a pleasure to be asked to contribute to the liber amicorum of my dear colleague and friend Prof. Ivo Aertsen with whom I worked closely for many years in Leuven and elsewhere. I still remember with nostalgia the nice time we had in Strasbourg when both of us were attending the sessions of the Council of Europe's Committee of Experts on mediation in Penal Matters, chaired by our Austrian colleague, Prof. Christa Pelikan. My wife Jenny and I also have very fond memories of the time Charlotte and Ivo and their kids Eva and Jannes were in Vancouver when he was at UBC on a study leave.

I could have chosen one of various topics for my contribution in view of Ivo's multiple and diversified scholarly interests. I finally decided on restorative justice, a topic that is not only dear to Ivo's heart but is also a field to which he has made enormous contributions. Predicting the future is surely not an easy task, so I hope Ivo will agree with my reasoning and will not judge my conclusions too harshly, and I will therefore anxiously wait for his critical comments.

I would also like to use this opportunity to express my sincere wishes to him for a healthy, happy and active retirement.

1 Prologue

Does restorative justice have a future? This is undoubtedly a complex and bold question, especially for someone like me who does not have a crystal ball. To try to provide a credible non-speculative answer to this rather challenging question I will use a combination of history and logic. The lessons of history are among the most useful tools when thinking about and trying to predict the future. Logic, on the other hand, helps us understand where things may be going and why they are moving in this or that direction.

A series of interrogations will hopefully show whether the current punitive criminal law is achieving its primary goals; whether it is in tune with the Geist of the times, whether it is compatible with the norms, values, realities of post-industrial society; and whether the underlining paradigm has become obsolete and thus there is an urgent need for a new paradigm. Hopefully, interrogations will also show whether our present criminal justice system is successful and sustainable or whether it is failing to achieve its fundamental objectives of deterrence and prevention.

Underlining my predictive endeavour is the assumption, which hopefully is true, that human beings are rational beings who will ultimately let their best social and economic interests prevail over their emotional feelings, traditional beliefs and instinctive responses.

2 How and why did criminal law emerge as a distinctive type of law?

To understand society's response to crime one needs to trace the origins of criminal law and to explore how it emerged as a distinctive type of law. The origins of criminal law can be easily traced to the attempts by the kings and the feudal lords to consolidate their authority, to enhance their powers and to generate revenue for themselves and their estates by imposing fines and by seizing the lands and property of convicted persons. Here is how the process is described by the *Law Reform Commission of Canada* (1974c:8-9) in Working Papers 5 and 6:

> In Anglo-Saxon England there was no criminal law as we know it. Disputes were dealt with by a process greatly resembling our civil law. When an individual felt that he had suffered damage because of another's wrongful conduct he was permitted either to settle the matter by agreement or proceed before a tribunal. Restitution was the order of the day and other sanctions, including imprisonment, were rarely used.
>
> As the common law developed, criminal law became a distinct branch of law. Numerous anti-social acts were seen to be 'offences against the state' or 'crimes' rather than personal wrongs or torts. This tendency to characterize some wrongs as 'crimes' was encouraged by the practice under which the lands and property of convicted persons were forfeited to the king or feudal lord. Fines, as well, became payable to feudal lords and not to the victim. The natural practice of compensating the victim or his relatives was discouraged by making it an offence to conceal the commission of a felony or to convert the crime into a source of profit. In time, fines and property that would have gone in satisfaction of the victim's claims were diverted to the state. Compounding an offence (that is, accepting an economic benefit in satisfaction of the wrong done without the consent of the court or in a manner that is contrary to the public interest) still remains a crime under the Canadian Criminal Code and discourages private settlement or restitution. (sec.141:1)
>
> It would now seem that historical developments, however well intentioned, effectively removed the victim from sentencing policy and obscured the view that crime was social conflict. (Law Reform Commission of Canada, 1974c: 8-9)

This is precisely what Nils Christie meant when explaining in his seminal article 'Conflicts as Property' how the conflicts were stolen by the State from their legitimate and rightful owners, the parties involved.

Christie (1977) lamented the fact that victims who used to be entitled to wergild/restitution were now left with nothing. Civil remedies were not only too costly and too complicated for most victims but the majority of offenders were destitute and once they were imprisoned the victim's chances of any compensation were nil. And to add insult to injury when offenders were sentenced to a penal fine it went not to the victim but to the State's coffers.

Answer: An analysis of the emergence and the historical evolution of criminal law clearly indicates that it happened for political and financial reasons rather than a specific need for such type of law.

3 Is crime a unique type of behaviour? Is crime qualitatively different from tort?

The emergence of criminal law as a distinctive branch of law, dispensing sanctions of different kind than civil remedies, suggests that acts and behaviours subjected to those punishments have their own particular characteristics that justify them being defined as crimes. This begs a series of questions: is crime a unique type of behaviour? Is crime qualitatively different from tort? Is the distinction between the two based on sound criteria? (see Fattah, 1992).

Any objective analysis and comparison of crimes and torts/civil wrongs is bound to lead to the conclusion that the distinction between the two is both artificial and arbitrary and that the demarcation line separating them is blurred. Thus, a comparison of acts made illegal by the criminal code or by statutes with similar behaviours that are unregulated by criminal law suggests that there is no qualitative difference between criminal and non-criminal behaviour. This reality indicates that the rationale for, and the raison d'être of, having a criminal law and a criminal justice system with its own arsenal of sanctions is neither logical nor rationally justified.

Answer: It seems an undisputable fact that acts and behaviour defined as crime by the criminal code are not unique, that there is no qualitative difference, for example, between crime and tort; hence, there is no logical rationale for having a distinct criminal code or criminal justice system that dispenses a different type of sanctions.

4 Are the classical concepts/notions of retributive justice obsolete?

The *Canadian Criminal Code* (enacted in 1892), as well as many others dating back to the 19th century, are historical documents that mirror the mentality of the era in which they were promulgated. Most of them have undergone some piecemeal changes, but they have neither been overhauled nor have been replaced by new, modern ones that are in tune with the times that we live in. This is yet another proof, if one is needed, that the criminal law is the branch of law that is most resistant to modernisation and change.

No century has witnessed more scientific and technological advances, more political changes, or more social upheavals than the 20th century. Unfortunately, the criminal code has not kept pace with social and scientific evolution and remains in most countries as a relic from the past, as a vestige from a bygone era. It is surprising that in this age of science and technology, we continue to have and to accept a criminal law and a criminal justice system based upon concepts, principles, premises and paradigms dating from the Age of Reason and the Age of Enlightenment.

Strangely enough, we do not seem to find anything wrong in having an archaic and antiquated criminal justice system that tries hard to dispense justice not according to earthly criteria but according to divine criteria. That all the fundamental principles, all the basic notions of the criminal law today have been borrowed from the theology and philosophy of the 18th and 19th centuries is simply hard to believe. Notions such as evil, wickedness, malice, guilt, culpability, retribution, expiation, atonement, redemption, to name but a few. Is it not about time to ask whether metaphysical notions such as 'free will', moral responsibility, criminal intent, *mens rea*, premeditation, malice aforethought, as well as many others, do have a place in a modern, secular criminal law? The time has come to ask whether abstract concepts such as those listed previously, as well as several others, do have a place in a modern, secular, socially oriented criminal law that caters to the realities of the 21st century. Shouldn't it be time in this age of technology to ask whether legal concepts such as insanity, diminished responsibility and so on could withstand the test of science? Shouldn't we be asking whether notions such as retribution, punishment, just deserts and redemption are fitting concepts in an evidence-based and secular criminal policy? (see Fattah, 1993).

Answer: The ever-growing secularisation of society has rendered the theological concepts and the religious dictates of the Enlightenment anachronistic and largely obsolete. They are no longer adequate nor compatible with the new realities of the highly technological society of the 21st century. There is therefore an urgent need for Western nations to rethink, reassess and modernise the archaic and antiquated criminal codes they have in place to bring them to the standards of the space age and to make them capable of meeting the challenges of today's society.

5 Is there a need for a paradigm shift in criminal law?

Criminal codes promulgated in the post-French revolution eras have become exceedingly inadequate to deal with rapidly changing social realities. Technological discoveries of the industrial revolution brought about rapid urbanisation, increased mobilisation, mounting communications and so on. Early on, it became abundantly clear that strict adherence to philosophical and abstract notions such as *mens rea*, 'free will', 'moral responsibility' makes it impossible to effectively control, sanction and curb a wide variety of socially harmful and dangerous behaviours. These include criminality of negligence, the vast majority of traffic offences, white collar crime, corporate deviance, crimes against the environment, status offences, offences committed under the influence of alcohol or drugs, and, lately, we may add cybercrime. Legalists, particularly criminalists faced with those challenges, were forced to do some mental acrobatics in order to come up with acceptable deviations, exceptions and exemptions from the metaphysical, yet fundamental, principles of *mens rea* and 'free will'.

As it was necessary in the 19th century to come up with legal presumptions and subterfuges that are outright contradictory to the classical notions of 'criminal intent' and 'moral responsibility' (such as dolus eventualis, irresistible impulse, ignorance of the law is no excuse etc.), contemporary legal scholars had to invent concepts such as technical guilt, strict liability, absolute liability, vicarious liability, corporate liability, preventive detention and so on to make it possible to charge, convict and punish those who are responsible for these harmful, injurious and dangerous behaviours (see Fattah, 1992).

Most people do not realise the extent of offences to which these new types of criminal responsibility apply. Already in 1963 Lady Barbara Wooton stated that the majority of cases dealt with by the criminal courts in England are cases of strict liability in which proof of a guilty mind is not necessary for conviction. A decade later, the *Law Reform Commission of Canada* (1974a) reported that Canadian federal laws contain about 20,000 regulatory offences, the laws of the average province another 20,000 and of the combined total 90 per cent are offences of strict liability. The situation is the same in other Western societies as was shown by Greve (1990).

Answer: The problems created by the obsolete notions of *mens rea*, moral guilt and moral responsibility dictated that they be abandoned in a large number of cases in favour of other concepts such as strict liability. But this is not the only problem with a retributive/punitive criminal law that desperately, yet unsuccessfully, tries to find a punishment that fits the crime! The major failing of the criminal law is undoubtedly its inability to curb crime or to deal with the plight of crime victims. This is because current criminal law is geared towards punishment, not prevention, and reflects a naive and exaggerated faith in the common-sense assumption that punishment deters. In addition, the punitive/retributive nature of current criminal law sadly means that crime victims are left without any redress, without adequate financial remedy to the harm, loss or injury they have suffered. All this has created a host of empirical problems that can only be dealt with effectively through a paradigm shift.

6 Some of the visible problems of the punishment paradigm

- Empirical research findings supporting the ever-growing scepticism about the deterrent effect of punishment.
- Disillusionment with the medical model and growing scepticism about the efficacy of treatment and rehabilitation programmes.
- Enhanced awareness of the pressing need to secularise and sociologise the criminal law and to bring it up to the scientific standards of the computer and space age.
- Growing realisation and concern about a wide variety of extremely harmful actions that cannot be dealt with effectively through adherence to the philosophical and abstract notions of *mens rea*, moral guilt and moral responsibility.
- Realisation that certain behaviours associated with, or using modern technologies, can cause such extensive and irreparable harm and damage (nuclear disasters, oil spills, to name a few) that no penalty, not even the death penalty, can be made to fit the crime. Meting out the same punishment to someone who is responsible for the death of one individual and another who is responsible for the death of say half-a-million shakes the foundations of retributive justice and highlights once again the absolute impossibility of making the punishment fit the crime.
- Growing concern about the plight of crime victims and enhanced awareness of the historical injustice done to them when they were unfairly deprived of the compensation to which they were entitled.

7 Is there a need for a modern criminal policy?

Present criminal policy, based as it is, on punishment as a means of retribution and as an instrument of deterrence, has been a dismal failure; despite this it has been pushed to its absolute limits (see Fattah, 1997a, 1997b). In both traditionally repressive countries such as the United Kingdom and the United States, as well as in tolerant societies such as Holland, Denmark and so on, the prison population has grown, sometimes to historical levels. Despite this increasingly punitive response, none of the salutary results promised by right-wing politicians who supported and implemented such oppressive and regressive policies has materialised. The manifest bankruptcy of these punitive and highly expensive (financially and socially) policies can no longer be denied or ignored. Right-wing political slogans such as 'war on crime', despite being popular with an exasperated public, proved to be hollow. Modest initiatives to help crime victims either through compensation or victim impact statements proved to be nothing more than political placebos or mere palliatives. All this clearly suggests that there is a major policy problem in the hands of those in power, a problem to which a new paradigm can offer a solution.

Enumerating the theoretical, legal and practical problems of current criminal policy, its deficiencies and inconsistencies would require a whole volume! What follows is simply a handful of the most obvious ones:

- Extremely high non-reporting rates shown by victimisation surveys indicate that a high percentage, sometimes a majority of cases, are handled outside the official criminal justice system.
- Ridiculously low clearance rates and the usual attrition in the criminal justice process mean that only a tiny minority of those who commit crime face charges before the courts and even a smaller minority end up being punished. Estimates range between 5 per cent and 10 per cent depending on the offence.
- As a result of the widespread practice of plea bargaining (common in Anglo-Saxon countries) most of those who are punished are punished for offences other than the ones they have committed or are offered a lenient sentence in exchange of a guilty plea.
- A criminal law system that uses the 'ability to distinguish right from wrong' as a prerequisite for being held criminally responsible must rely on psychiatric evidence and has to call on forensic psychiatrists to play an important role in the justice process. It is the psychiatrist who supposedly enlightens the court on issues such as insanity, partial or diminished responsibility, mental disorder, psychiatric disability, dangerousness and so on. And yet, psychiatry is in fact one of the least developed branches of medicine. This explains in part the frequency of conflicting psychiatric testimonies. The distinguished Australian psychiatrist, Bartholomew (1986), had this to say about psychiatric evidence: 'Psychiatrists are unreliable in diagnosis, uncertain as to how to treat those conditions diagnosed, and often unable to measure any change that the treatment prescribed may have produced. Finally, they more often than not are unable to make worthwhile predictions.'

Answer: Hopefully, this succinct summary of the woes of present criminal law and the countless theoretical and practical problems of current criminal policy has provided the needed answers to the two questions posed earlier. Hopefully, it has shown that the current paradigm underlining the criminal law is antiquated and obsolete and in need of urgent modernisation and change. Hopefully, it has also shown that the current criminal policy is not only archaic, ineffective and costly but also incompatible with the social realities of the 21st century.

8 What justice paradigm would be appropriate for the present times?

The deficiencies, shortcomings, inadequacies of the current paradigm and inefficiencies and failures of the present criminal justice system should by themselves indicate the major elements of an alternative paradigm to replace the obsolete one that has governed criminal justice for centuries (see Fattah, 2002, 2007).

Were I to be consulted or asked to propose a replacement paradigm, here are the *seven major elements* I would suggest as the basic foundations for the new one. As the following brief explanation will show, it is rather misleading to describe the proposed paradigm as a 'new' one since most of those elements are by no means new and can be traced to how 'justice' has been practised in non-industrial, non-urbanised societies, societies that were not influenced by the abstract, theological, moral and philosophical notions of the dominant religions in Western societies. The proposed paradigm is neither a novel invention nor a radical, revolutionary innovation. It is historically and sociologically inspired. It is meant to adapt justice practices of societies that are as close to nature as possible to the complex realities of modern societies. It is based on the indisputable fact that the roots of human behaviour have not changed. While society itself has undergone radical and fundamental changes over the centuries, the instincts, needs, impulses and urges that motivate human behaviour remain basically the same. The differences between what we observe in those simple societies and what we see in our own are the variations in the means of shaping, controlling, modifying and preventing undesirable behaviours, the list of which enormously varies according to culture and over time. What is subject to historical and cultural evolution are not the behaviours themselves but society's attitudes and definitions of, and response to, those behaviours.

What follows is a brief description of the seven pillars of the proposed alternative justice paradigm (see Fattah, 1993).

8.1 From a guilt orientation to a consequence orientation

As already mentioned, the vast majority of cases dealt with by the criminal courts are offences of strict liability, negligence, omission and so on. Why did this come about and why was it necessary to abandon, at such a large scale, the traditional and deeply anchored notions of criminal intent, moral guilt and moral responsibility? The obvious answer is that the social consequences of these behaviours were judged to be more important than strict adherence to the philosophical and religious considerations requiring that wickedness, malice or evil intent be a prerequisite for criminal punishment. The pressing need to regulate those behaviours, because of their actual and potential social harm, overrode the requirement of moral guilt. The growing complexity of society and its ever-growing technologisation led to ever-declining emphasis on *mens rea* and to a growing emphasis being placed on the consequences of the behaviours. It goes without saying that this tendency was more pronounced in certain sectors of life than in others.

That harm is slowly becoming the primary criterion for criminalisation can be seen in the report of *the Finnish Criminal Law Committee*, quoted by Lahti (1975). The first task the Committee performed was to try to locate those forms of behaviour that appear to be most harmful when judged in the light of specific goals of each sphere in life. The notion of harm was the yardstick the Committee used in order to judge whether a given behaviour should or should not be criminalised.

A good example of current practice where consequence takes precedence over guilt in determining punishment is that of attempted crime which is punished less severely than completed crime. The same criminal intent (*mens rea*) is present whether the crime is completed or remained at the stage of attempt due to factors external to the offender's will. The lesser punishment is therefore due not to a lesser guilt but to a lesser seriousness of consequences.

As criterion for criminalisation, the notion of harm is in perfect harmony with the generally accepted goals of modern criminal law, namely to prevent the occurrence of socially harmful, socially injurious actions. It is only logical, therefore, that the eligibility of any given behaviour for inclusion in the criminal code (as well as the seriousness assigned to various actions) be judged according to their actual and potential harm and not according to the degree of wickedness or malice of the perpetrator. To use as a criterion, choosing consequence, guilt and harm instead of intent is the best way of correcting the fundamental empirical error of current criminal law, namely, the futile attempt to quantify the unquantifiable (degrees of moral responsibility) and to measure the unmeasurable (degree of freedom of the will, degree of moral guilt etc.).

8.2 *A switch from moral responsibility to social responsibility*

According to Parker (1977), contemporary criminal law is based on the concept of blameworthiness which has its foundations in the Judeo-Christian ethic and the notion of free will. It is rather surprising that although malicious intent at present applies only to a small minority of the workload of criminal courts, there has been no attempt in recent years to discard it and replace it with a new concept that is compatible with behavioural science research and with a different notion that is more in tune with the times. There are, I believe, two compelling reasons that call for abandoning moral responsibility as the fundamental concept of criminal law: one is scientific, the other is pragmatic:

1. Moral responsibility is based on the notion of free will which is incompatible with science as it is the negation of causality.
2. Moral responsibility has been a major hurdle in the way of dealing effectively with a large number of socially harmful and injurious behaviours.

The fact that we live in a society and share the physical environment with others places several restrictions on our freedom to act and dictates that we respect and obey certain rules of conduct and standards of behaviour. It is our social responsibility to refrain from causing harm or injury to others, to society at large and to the global environment, either wilfully, by recklessness or by negligence, whether by commission or by omission. It is also our social responsibility not to infringe upon the rights of other members of society.

8.3 *A move from legal fiction to social reality*

The metaphysical and religious notions underlying current criminal law are far removed from social reality. Many, including the fundamental notion of *free will*, are philosophical abstractions that are not susceptible to any scientific or empirical validation, let alone measurement. The fact that most of the criminal codes today were enacted in the 19th century means that they were neither inspired nor influenced by social and behavioural science. The result is a hiatus between the criminal law and the disciplines of psychology, sociology, criminology and victimology. The anachronism of the principles, concepts and notions according to which the criminal law operates and their incompatibility with the realities of modern society necessitated the invention of many legal assumptions and presumptions. Scholars had to perform legal gymnastics in a desperate attempt to adapt an archaic criminal law to the social realities and the exigencies of the 21stcentury. As a result, the criminal law today is governed by what may be rightly described as 'legal fiction'. Most of this legal fiction is dictated by the need to find some acceptable rational justification for the infliction or the exemption of punishment.

Many of the theoretical distinctions that were invented over the decades to deal with scientific findings are indicative of the quagmire of present criminal law. And yet, in many cases, the destiny of the accused depends solely on these hair-splitting decisions because the distinction often means the difference between conviction and acquittal, and in some cases between life and death! The list is much too long, but here are just a few examples of those legal distinctions: distinction between general intent and specific intent; constructive intention and real intention; voluntary acts, involuntary acts and not-voluntary acts; purpose, intent, and desired result; loss of control, automatism; insane automatism and non-insane automatism; psychiatric disability and diminished responsibility; mental disorder and psychopathic (character) disorder; guilty and sane, guilty but insane, and not guilty by reason of insanity; fully responsible, partially responsible, not at all responsible.

The new paradigm puts an end to all the practical (and theoretical) problems created by arbitrary, artificial and rather meaningless legal distinctions. Replacing the notion of guilt by the notion of harm and replacing moral responsibility by social responsibility will remove any need for legal fiction.

8.4 *A switch from penal repression to administrative regulation*

The criminal law has traditionally served a repressive function. In addition to its use as an instrument of power, its theological and philosophical origins led to its use as a means of enforcing religious commands and moral standards. As Norval Morris (1973) pointed out, by tradition, America (and the same is true for most Western societies) has relied on the criminal code not only to protect persons and property but also to lead men away from vice and sin, including those vices and sins that injure only the sinner. Morris reports that half of all arrests in the United States are for crimes without direct victims, crimes which bring no complainant to the station-house, no call to the police switch board.

The lucid arguments made by Jerome Hall (1982) for excluding negligence from penal liability and for narrowing punishable guilt to voluntary harm-doing are equally valid for excluding acts that are considered 'strict liability offences'. And if morality offences, negligent offences and strict liability offences are excluded and removed, what then remains of the criminal law as we know it today?

There is hardly any doubt that the trend towards legalisation, decriminalisation and depenalisation will become more pronounced with every passing decade.One needs only to look at the legalisation of abortion, gambling, prostitution, marihuana, to mention but a few. And once the paradigm shift takes hold, there will be a much stronger move from repression to regulation.

8.5 *A move from reliance on deterrence and the threat of punishment to active social prevention*

Despite overwhelming empirical evidence accumulated over several decades, present criminal legislation continues to be based on a common-sense assumption that punishment deters as well as on an exaggerated faith in the criminal law's ability to influence people's behaviour. Surprisingly, this uncritical reliance on punishment as a powerful deterrent remains the cornerstone of our crime policy despite the lack of empirical support. As a result, our approach to crime prevention is a totally passive one as if the mere existence of penalties is sufficient by itself to steer people away from committing crime. It is essentially the same conviction as the theological belief that fear of hell will prevent people from committing sin!

But contrary to popular belief and common-sense wisdom, punishment and prevention do not go hand in hand. They are two alternative strategies. Placing the emphasis on punishment detracts from the need for active social prevention. And because too much money is being spent on punishment, there is very little available for effective evidence-based prevention. But since it is much easier to punish than prevent, politicians and the general public have always opted for the former over the latter. For politicians, punishment is an easy alibi because it gives the impression that something is being done about acts that are a source of fear and anxiety to the public. And when years later it becomes evident that the problem has not been solved or has become worse, the typical response is to increase the punishment!

The overconfidence in the intimidation effect of punishment is both misguided and misplaced. It is misguided because there is ample empirical evidence attesting to the severe limitations of deterrence policy. It is misplaced because it puts the stick ahead of, and above, the carrot.

Criminological research has shown that crime rates are closely linked to the available opportunities and are not the least influenced by variations or fluctuations in punishment. All this suggests that abandoning punishment would likely lead to greater emphasis on social prevention. It should also be noted that the efficacy of punishment as a deterrent for negligent, careless or inadvertent actions has been the object of great scepticism.

8.6 A switch from intimidation to mediation, from segregation to reconciliation

Christie (1977) has observed that the key element in a criminal proceeding is that the proceeding has been converted from something between the concrete parties into a conflict between one of the parties and the State. In this scenario, the victim is a double loser, first vis-à-vis the offender and often in a more crippling manner by being denied the right to full participation in what might have been one of the more important ritual encounters in life. The victim has lost the case to the State.

The criminal law which does not cease to broaden its mandate and extend its boundaries has declared a monopoly on every conflict and dispute falling under its jurisdiction. And yet private dispute settlement and conflict resolution through mediators and third parties have several advantages over criminal court proceedings which simply end in the punishment of the offender.

Since criminal law is centred upon punishment and retribution and because of its avidity to extract revenue from the wrongdoers (in the form of fines) it naturally shuns any initiative for settling disputes especially when it is done outside the system. As a result, the criminal justice system has missed a golden opportunity to reduce its caseload and to stop the repetition of certain offences through the reconciliation of the feuding parties.

8.7 A switch from retribution to restitution

One major drawback of retributive sanctions is that they do nothing to heal the injury suffered by the victim or the harm done to the offended party. What they do is to double the pain by inflicting deliberate suffering on the offender. One of the pillars of the new paradigm is a switch from retribution to restitution, a switch aimed at achieving justice through means and methods other than punishment. The emphasis in the new paradigm is not on the infliction of pain but on helping the offended party achieve healing and closure and becoming whole again.

Barnett (1977), one of the many critics of retributive punishment, maintains that the alleged absolute justice of repaying evil with evil is really an empty sophism since Christian moralists have always preached that an evil is to be put right by doing good. Barnett insists that crime is an offence by one individual against another. 'The armed robber did not rob society, he robbed the victim' (Barnett, 1977: 287-288). His debt, therefore, is not to society but to the victim, and he has an obligation to make things right to the one who has been injured or harmed.

One big advantage of a system of justice centred on restitution is that it would enjoy the unqualified support of most victims. There is, in fact, overwhelming empirical evidence indicating that victims prefer reparative sanctions (such as restitution) to punitive sanctions such as incarceration or fines.

9 DOES RESTORATIVE JUSTICE HAVE ADVANTAGES OVER RETRIBUTIVE JUSTICE?

Answer: This is an easy question. The advantages of restorative justice are many. What follows are a few positive and achievable objectives of restorative justice (see Fattah, 1995, 2004):

1. Restorative justice avoids the inherent arbitrariness of retributive punishment and the enormous disparities in its application.
2. By settling conflicts through a process and outcomes somewhat similar to that of civil courts, restorative justice offers a remedy to the arbitrary and often blurred distinctions between civil and criminal conflicts.
3. Restorative justice avoids the vagaries and inherent injustice of punitive systems.
4. Restorative justice avoids or at least minimises the inherent bias of punitive justice.
5. Restorative justice would put an end to the unfair and shameful practice of plea bargaining.
6. Restorative justice encourages and enhances victim reporting.
7. Restorative justice minimises the chances of retaliation and the risks of repeat victimisation and by so doing offers more protection to the victims.

8. Restorative justice is the only possible way of dealing effectively with the new blood feuds in modern society such as gang wars and sectarian conflicts.
9. Restorative justice personalises the response, returns the conflict to its legitimate owners and provides injured or harmed parties a central role in the justice process.
10. Restorative justice offers some remedy to victims whose offenders have not been identified, arrested, convicted and punished.
11. Restorative justice is the most appropriate model for cases of undisputed harm.

10 Can the history of social reaction to harmful, injurious acts give any hints about the future? Do prisons have a future?

Regardless of how imaginative they may be, most people simply cannot conceive of a society that does not hold persons captive behind bars in cage-like cells! Hence, the question I am constantly being asked: 'so, what is the alternative?'

Having studied thoroughly and extensively the tragic and painful history of penal sanctions, I came to the conclusion that no punishment is transcendental, permanent or immutable. Social change is inevitable and unstoppable. All punishments appear only to disappear when they become incompatible with the new mentalities, the modern views and attitudes of the time and once suitable and acceptable alternatives, in harmony with the Geist of the era, have been developed. This is why I deeply believe that the future of incarceration is no different. Imprisonment, like other antiquated, medieval and abandoned punishments of the past, will eventually decline and ultimately disappear. I know this will not happen in my lifetime or any time soon, but I am utterly convinced that it is inevitable and unavoidable. Yes, I am convinced that deprivation of liberty will eventually join other cruel and unusual punishments and will eventually be abandoned. Prisons will become only a historic relic like the gallows. Like the fate of medieval castle dungeons, many prisons will undoubtedly be converted into horror museums.

Answer: The fact is, modern-day technology provides sophisticated tools and instruments making it possible to control the behaviour and movements of dangerous individuals without having to lock them up or to deprive them of the most valuable asset to humans (and animals alike), namely, their liberty. Two major hindrances are delaying the inevitable abolition of prisons and penitentiaries: (a) The first stems from the general public's religious beliefs and punitive attitudes, their mistaken conviction that prisons are indispensable and irreplaceable and their firm insistence that punishment is the proper response to crime. (b) The second stems from the ideology of powerful conservative and right-wing politicians combined with the lucrative economic interests of a thriving and highly profitable prison industry.

11 Does restorative justice offer a viable alternative and a feasible replacement to the current justice model?

Answer: What is restorative justice? A simple answer: it is a rational, peaceful and constructive way of restoring harmony and order that were disrupted by the harmful or injurious act.

Restorative justice offers a great promise. It offers to remove us from the medieval system of punishment that has been in place for centuries and help us move to a new era of social reaction to harmful, injurious behaviours. It provides amicable, less antagonistic means of solving personal conflicts and disputes. It promises a less onerous, less costly, less wasteful and less painful way of dealing with those who offend. It offers justice without caging those responsible. It promotes forgiveness, not revenge. It restores harmony while ensuring redress to the victim. It promises to put an end to the big penal mess we are in right now (see Fattah, 1998a, 1998b).

Unfortunately, there is a widespread, yet mistaken, belief that punishment is indispensable and irreplaceable. Another erroneous belief is that an institutionalised restorative justice system is neither feasible nor viable. Both those beliefs suggest that there is a huge need for education through massive information and effective communication.

Not only is there widespread ignorance about what restorative justice is, there is also a great deal of confusion about its modalities and what does qualify as restorative justice and what does not. This means there is a pressing need for an accurate definition of restorative justice and a detailed explanation of its practices. In an attempt to gain support for restorative justice and to counter or minimise the perception that it is lenient or soft on criminals, there has been a tendency to sell it as a harsh mode of dealing with offenders. Even the *Supreme Court of Canada* in the Gladue decision maintained that when combined with appropriate probationary conditions restorative justice may impose a greater burden on the offender than a custodial sanction.

There is no denying that restorative justice is a more humane mode of doing justice than retributive sanctions. But my favouring of restorative justice over punishment is not merely a humanitarian stance. It is based on a deep conviction that it is a better, viable, constructive and more effective response to harm than punishment.

In my personal opinion, restorative justice, in its true form, has nothing in common with punishment. There is a basic difference between the goals being pursued by both. I see punishment's primary aim as the deliberate infliction of pain on a wrongdoer, a sinner or a criminal offender. Punishment was invented to create on earth a fireless equivalent to hell, and it survived because prisons admirably succeed in doing that.

This, however, is not one of the goals of restorative justice. Restorative justice rejects the notions of retribution, expiation and atonement which are often offered as the moral justification for making the criminal/sinner suffer. It preaches tolerance and forgiveness, not harshness and vindictiveness. Unlike punishment, restorative justice does not deal with or respond to some moral fault or some theological concept of guilt. It responds to the actual injury or harm done and attempts at healing the injury and repairing the loss. Punishment has abstract and unattainable goals. Restorative justice has realistic and achievable objectives.

A stark difference between deprivation of liberty as a penal sanction and restorative justice is the inevitable arbitrariness of the former compared with the latter. In fact, arbitrariness is a structural, innate and irremediable defect in retributive systems that try to follow the Mikado's light-hearted verse in Gilbert and Sullivan's operetta: 'My goal is all sublime; I shall achieve in time; to make the punishment fit the crime.' To maintain that a given number of days, months or years in prison is a fair and equitable punishment for offences such as assault, rape, kidnapping, robbery or something else strikes me as the height of arbitrariness (Fattah, 1982). It is difficult for me to understand how intelligent people such as lawyers, scholars, academics and others could believe and maintain that pain can be measured and dispensed according to some kind of mathematical formula. How could they believe it is possible to create some kind of equation that would make a prison sentence fit a crime that has caused physical or psychological injury, material harm or loss? That a seriously flawed concept and a fundamentally defective sentencing model like 'just deserts' could be accepted and implemented for so long is a mystery. Except in a purely theological perspective, retribution is not, and can never be, an instrument of justice. To speak, therefore, of retributive 'justice' is a contradiction in terms since it is impossible to establish a fair equation between the punishment and the crime, between the pain to be inflicted upon the offender and the pain caused by the offence to the victim and his or her family, associates and friends.

Despite these obvious and glaring defects and shortcomings, it is very difficult to convince the majority of people, who were born and raised under a punitive justice system, to accept a desirable switch to a non-arbitrary mode of doing justice. Punishment is inculcated in people's minds since a very young age. They are repeatedly told, 'if you lie you will be punished; if you hit your sister you will be spanked; if you steal you will go to prison and so on.' This creates in their minds a strong association between punishment and wrongdoing that is much too difficult to abandon when they grow up. This, in turn, creates an almost insurmountable obstacle in the way of replacing the existing punitive system with a fundamentally different one, a system that has its own philosophy, its own goals, and its own modalities. Hence, the piecemeal attempts we are witnessing to introduce restorative justice practices here and there.

Let me repeat here what I have always maintained when promoting restorative justice, namely, that creating a restorative justice system parallel to the existing punitive one will not work, that it will doom restorative justice to eternally remain a peripheral system and a secondary option. I argued that we have to convince the public that the present system, despite its enormous human, social and material costs, is not working, is not achieving its avowed goals and thus has to be replaced by a different and superior system.

Unfortunately, as realist as I am, I know that the chances of this happening in the near future are quite remote. It will take a revolution like the one that made the French people storm the Bastille to achieve this radical yet necessary change.

12 CONCLUSION

The deep dissatisfaction with the punitive/retributive justice system is universal. Offenders complain that it is cruel and inhuman. They deplore the flagrant disparities in sentencing. They point out to the countless errors the system makes even when a human life is at stake. They decry the fact that the punishments inflicted, whether prison or fines, are never personal but inevitably extend to and affect innocent family members, work associates and friends. Victims' dissatisfaction stems largely from the fact that they were excluded from the justice process, have very little say in the outcome and whether the punishment at the end of the trial is prison or fine they get no restitution and hardly any compensation from the State. The general public, the taxpayers, are distressed by the system's inefficiency, ineffectiveness and failure to prevent crime despite its huge costs both socially and financially. For those with vindictive attitudes and punitive inclinations the system is never harsh enough. To those with a humanitarian bend and those who do not believe punishment is the right answer, the system is on the wrong track and its sentences are much too severe. Objective assessments and empirical evaluations tend to confirm the validity of all those complaints. Scholarly criticism of the current system tends to focus on a couple of questions:

(a) If punishment is not an effective deterrent (and there is ample empirical research showing itis not) and if it is not an effective means of prevention (and the record number of offenders incarcerated proves it is not), what useful purpose does it serve? (b) What is society getting in return for the billions of dollars being wasted on punishing wrongdoers? The conclusion is inevitably the same: 'there has to be another and better way of dealing with those who break the law.'

Yes, I believe there is, and to the countless students and others who always asked me what the alternative is, my answer is *Restorative Justice*. Hopefully, this brief chapter will give them a good idea of the compelling reasons for my deeply held and unshakeable faith in restorative justice.

REFERENCES

Barnett, R. E. (1977). Restitution: a new paradigm of criminal justice. *ETHICS: An International Journal of Social, Political and Legal Philosophy*, 87(1), 279-301. doi:10.1086/292043.

Bartholomew, A. A. (1986). Psychiatry, the criminal law and corrections: An exercise in sciolism. Bundalong, Vic: Wileman Publications.

Christie, N. (1977). Conflicts as property. *British Journal of Criminology*, 17(1), 1-19. doi:10.1093/oxfordjournals.bjc.a046783.

Fattah, E. A. (1982). Making the punishment fit the crime: the case of imprisonment. Problems inherent in the use of imprisonment as a retributive sanction. *Canadian Journal of Criminology*, 24 (1), 1-12.

Fattah, E. A. (1992). Beyond Metaphysics: The Need for a New Paradigm. On Actual and Potential Contributions of Criminology and the Social Sciences to the Reform of the Criminal Law. In R. Lahti & K. Nuotio (eds.) *Criminal Law Theory in Transition* (pp. 64-101). Helsinki: Finnish Lawyers Publishing Company.

Fattah, E. A. (1993). From a Guilt Orientation to a Consequence Orientation. In Wilfried Kueper & Juergen Welp (eds.) *Beiträge zur Rechtswissenschaft* (pp. 771-792). Heidelberg. C.F. Muller.

Fattah, E. A. (1995). Restorative and Retributive Justice Models: A Comparison. In H-H. Kühne (ed.) *Festschrift für Koichi Miyazawa* (pp. 305-15). Baden-Baden: Nomos Verlagsgesellschaft.

Fattah, E. A. (1997a). From Crime Policy to Victim Policy: The Need for a Fundamental Policy Change. In M. McShane & F. Williams III (eds.) *Victims of Crime and the Victimization Process* (pp. 75-92). N.Y: Garland Publishing.

Fattah, E. A. (1997b). Toward a Victim Policy Aimed at Healing not Suffering. In R.C. Davis, A.J. Lurigio and W.G. Skogan (eds.) *Victims of Crime* (second edition) (pp. 257-72). Thousand Oaks: Sage Publications.

Fattah, E. A. (1998a). Restorative and Retributive Justice Models: A Comparison. In E.A. Fattah & T. Peters (eds.), *Support for Crime Victims in a Comparative Perspective* (pp. 99-110). Leuven: Leuven Universal Press, Belgium.

Fattah, E. A. (1998b). Some Reflections on the Paradigm of Restorative Justice and its Viability for Juvenile Justice. In L. Walgrave (ed.) *Restorative Justice for Juveniles: Potentialities, Risks and Problems* (pp. 389-401). Leuven: Leuven University Press.

Fattah, E. A. (2002). From Philosophical Abstraction to Restorative Action - From Senseless Retribution to Meaningful Restitution. Just Desert and Restorative Justice revisited. In H.J. Kerner & E. Weitekanp (eds.) *Restorative Justice, Theoretical Foundations* (pp. 308-21). Willan Publishing, Culmcott House, Devon, U.K.

Fattah, E. A. (2004). Gearing Justice Action to Victim Satisfaction. Contrasting Two Justice Philosophies: Retribution and Redress. In H. Kaptein & M. Malsch (eds.) *Crime, Victims and Justice - Essays on Principles and Practice.* Burlington, VT: Ashgate Publishing Company.

Fattah, E. A. (2007). Is punishment the appropriate response to gross human rights violations? Is a non-punitive justice system feasible? In E. van der Spuy, S. Parmentier, A. Dissel (eds.) *Restorative Justice: Politics, Policies and Prospects.* Published under

the auspices of the Faculty of Law, University of Cape Town. (JUTA and Co). Reprinted in *ACTA JURIDICA* (Cape Town) (2007) pp. 209-227.
Greve, V. (1990). *Negligence in Danish Law.* Helsinki. (mimeographed).
Hall, J. (1982). *Social science and criminal theory.* New York: Rothman & Co.
Lahti, R. (1975). The utilization of criminological research in Finnish criminal law reform. Paper presented at the *9th International Congress of Criminology*, Vienna (mimeographed).
Law Reform Commission of Canada. (1974a). *Working paper no. 2: the meaning of guilt-strict liability.* Ottawa: Information Canada.
Law Reform Commission of Canada. (1974b). *Working paper no. 3: the principles of sentencing and dispositions.* Ottawa: Information Canada.
Law Reform Commission of Canada. (1974c). *Working papers nos. 5&6: restitution and compensation-fines.* Ottawa: Information Canada.
Morris, N. (1973). The law is a busy body. *The New York Times* (reprinted by the World Correctional Service Centre).
Parker, G. (1977). *An Introduction to criminal law.* Toronto: Methuen.
Wooton, B. (1953). *Crime and the criminal law: reflections of a magistrate and social scientist.* London: Steven and Sons.

Victimology as a phronetic social science

Antony Pemberton

1 Introduction

It is a great honour for me to contribute this chapter to this volume. Ivo Aertsen has been an example and an inspiration throughout my career, and I consider myself fortunate to have been afforded many opportunities to collaborate with him at venues all over the globe. Our first meeting might have been in a somewhat unassuming venue in the Hague in 2003, at the 'Begeleidingscommissie Herstelbemiddeling', but rapidly expanded to include many European projects, conferences and seminars, from Leuven, to Lisbon, to Onati in the Basque country and even to Santiago in Chile.

We have many shared interests; indeed, I am somewhat at a loss to think of someone whose research profile is more similar to mine. It is therefore also with great pride that I was recently offered the opportunity to follow in Ivo's footsteps in the position as professor in restorative justice at the Leuven Institute of Criminology. And it is a happy thought that over the time of our collaboration, two of our main topics of study – restorative justice and victimology – have shown a marked growth, increasingly moving from the fringe of academic research and policy interest towards the centre.

That is not to say that I consider myself to be an unequivocal cheerleader for the state-of-the-art in victimological research and restorative justice scholarship (see also Pemberton, 2019). In fact, I have similar qualms with both, and my hesitations centre on the topic of the current volume: the lack of sufficient recognition of the importance of practice, as well as context and lived first-person experience. For me the heart of the matter concerns the fundamental approach social science tends to take towards its topics of study, which I believe to be mistaken.

There are different ways to develop this criticism. In a recent article, my colleagues Pauline Aarten, Eva Mulder and myself referred to Pepper's root metaphors of metaphysical systems (see Pemberton, Mulder & Aarten, 2018; Pepper, 1942). The key distinction, relevant for the present chapter, is that between *mechanism* and *contextualism*. As psychologist Theodore Sarbin (1986: 6) explained, the former

> sees events in nature as the products of the transmittal of forces. Modern science has taken this worldview as its metaphysical foundation – a view that supports the scientist's search for causes. Efficient causality description is the

> goal for scientists working with one or another paradigm within the mechanist world view.

The root metaphor for contextualism by contrast is the historical event; rather than focusing on distilling universal and context-independent causes and effects, the metaphor elicits an imagery

> of an ongoing texture of multiple elaborated events, each leading to others, each being influenced by collateral episodes, and by the efforts of multiple agents who engage in actions to satisfy their needs and meet their obligations. (Sarbin, 1986: 6)

Social science research has the tendency to unreflectively adopt the mechanist metaphor, following the example of the natural sciences, also as a means to seem more 'objective'. This is particularly true of criminology and in its wake victimology, given the suspicion that the primary subjects of study, those involved in the commission of crime and/or experiencing its consequences are believed to be less than fully trustworthy. However, this comes at the cost of denying the reality of the manner in which the experience of crime and victimisation is experienced in these subjects' lives (see also Pemberton et al., 2018).

In this chapter, I would like to adopt a line of thinking from philosopher of science and professor of management Bent Flyvbjerg (2001). In many of his works, but in particular in the call-to-arms *Making Social Science Matter: Why Social Inquiry Fails and How It Succeeds Again*, Flyvbjerg criticises much social science research for being irrelevant or even counterproductive in its real-life applications. According to Flyvbjerg, it is because social science mistakenly retains the virtues central to the natural sciences. He makes this point with reference to the three intellectual virtues Aristotle described in the *Nicomachean Ethics*. Natural sciences work on the basis of *episteme* and *techne*. The former concerns universals and the production of knowledge which is invariable in time and space and which is achieved with the aid of analytical rationality (know why, scientific knowledge). The latter is the application of technical knowledge and skills according to a pragmatic instrumental rationality (know how).

For Aristotle, social and political issues should instead rely on *phronesis*, which translates as prudence or *practical wisdom*. There are different ways of describing the characteristics of *phronesis*. In any case, it *emphasises practical knowledge* and *practical ethics*. Phronesis focuses, but also requires experience. It is *pragmatic, variable* and *context-dependent*. It emphasises what is variable, not encapsulated by universal rules, on differences between cases. It is *oriented towards action, based on practical-value rationality*. What must we do in a particular social and political situation to achieve ends we find important? According to Flyvbjerg, therefore, 'Phronesis thus concerns the analysis of values – things that are good or bad for man – as a point of departure for action' (Flyvbjerg, 2001: 57).

Flyvbjerg argues for a full-blown reorientation of social sciences towards a phronetic approach. It is not necessary here to weigh the merits of this full-scale overhaul, and instead I will more modestly insist that phronetic approaches are apt to enlighten particular fields of enquiry into the human condition more than others. In my view, this applies in particular to victimological phenomena, given that they are defined through their normative load and the particular meaning they have in victim's lives. The myriad interactions between intra-psychic and inter-personal aspects in victims' experiences moreover speak against the possibility of usefully and fully unravelling universal causal mechanisms. This is true of the study of victimisation in general, but is particularly true of those domains that study the aspects of ethics and injustice in victims' lives as well as focus on the avenues for victims to take action, both of which are true and even defining for restorative justice. Such an approach not only cleaves more closely to victims' lived experiences but also enhances the emancipatory potential of victimology and restorative justice. The issue with current approaches, as McGarry and Walklate (2015) point out, is 'there is little scope here for an appreciative stance towards the victim as an individual, or a group, who has choices and makes choices' (2015: 11).

In this short contribution, I will sketch some of the features of victimology as a phronetic social science and, in particular, refer to the phenomenon of restorative justice to make the case for this. I do so in a brief discussion of five central issues related to *phronesis*: meaning and narrative (Section 2); morality/ethics (Section 3); power/conflict (Section 4); context/culture (Section 5) and practice (Section 6).

2 Meaning and narrative

The heart of the experience of victimisation lies in its meaning. The aftermath of victimisation, including processes of justice, can be viewed in the light of the victim's attempts to make sense and give meaning to what happened. Doing so invariably involves questions concerning one's identity and the manner in which one's self fits into the world.

In a recent work, my colleagues and I (Pemberton, 2019; Pemberton et al., 2018) have started to refer to the experience of victims in this regard as an *ontological assault* (see also Pellegrino, 1979). Victimisation can be conceived as damage to/diminishment of/destruction of a sense of self. It exposes implicit, but nevertheless fundamental, characteristics of the self, in what it damages. The term *ontological assault* is therefore two-fold: victimisation presents as a threat to existence and in doing so reveals features of being.

In developing this view, we drew heavily on Susan Brison's (2002) phenomenological account of her own experience of rape and attempted murder. In this, she describes the experience in terms of its damage to her embodied self, her self as narrative and her autonomous self. Each of these features share that they concern aspects of her self, which are at the same time inherently social. The extent to which Brison exists as an embodied, temporal, relational and social being-in-the-world became apparent in precisely the moment that this taken-for-granted manner of being was imperilled by the attack. The centrality of meaning-making in the aftermath of victimisation is then located in the diminished experience of being able to connect to sources of meaning, in what we have come to describe as 'radical loneliness'.

In her account, victimisation comprises an experience of truth about the self, albeit an often wholly unwanted one. As Brison found,

> It's been hard for me, as a philosopher, to learn the lesson that knowledge isn't always desirable, that the truth doesn't always set you free. Sometimes, it fills you with incapacitating terror and, then, uncontrollable rage. (Brison, 2002: 20)

The often enduring nature of the experience of victimisation can be located in this feature: it is not merely an event that plagues the victim through the memory of its occurrence, but it has exposed a reality with which the victim will have to come to terms. Alice Sebold, another victim of rape, described this existential shift as follows: 'I was now on the other side of something they could not understand' and to which she added, 'I could not understand it myself' (Sebold, 1999: 27).

As Brison found, this twin damage to the self, and to its sense of communion to the world, requires a remaking of this self. It is not a return to the self that existed before the victimisation. Instead, it is a self that is fundamentally changed by living through the experience, a self in which the victimisation and its aftermath and the manner in which it was situated in time become part of the fabric of existence. Perhaps more apt than restoration, I would think that *re-storying* describes the victims' process (see Pemberton, 2019). A self remade in narrative.

This emphasises the importance of narrative approaches in victimology, both in research methods and in perspectives on victims' experiences, including those with justice processes. As my colleagues and I noted elsewhere,

> narrative victimology would move from defining victimological experience in the terms of justice institutions, to understanding (criminal) justice processes in the way they are encountered by victims as an element of their unfolding narrative. (Pemberton et al., 2018: 11)

This also applies to processes of restorative justice, with this approach serving to highlight the advantages of restorative justice over formal criminal justice processes. There is much more room for the inclusion of crucial elements of the victim's narrative in restorative justice than in criminal proceedings, while the interaction with the offender can offer further assistance in the process of re-storying.

However, restorative justice's potential in this regard can be diminished if and when the process seeks to impose a particular narrative on the experience of the participants (see Pemberton et al., 2018). The kind of 'positive' and 'beneficial' tale of resolved conflict and emotional healing or growth is a heart-warming staple of much restorative justice literature, but it sits uneasily with the reality that many victims experience. The narrative potential of restorative justice is then liable to be spent on the belief that the 'ideal victim of restorative justice' (van Dijk, 2006) is open to victims of all shapes and hues. Instead, I would argue that the greatest potential of restorative justice resides in the situations where the process of re-storying seems to be much more difficult. The issue is then that it might be difficult to see a straightforward process in mediation or conferencing towards a beneficial outcome, but that this is also true, with greater force, of the formal criminal process. The promise of restorative justice is then not so much that it offers a simple solution that is applicable across cases but that it privileges the requirements of the reality of the situation, however messy, over the assumption that a tidy resolution is possible.

3 Morality/ethics

Flyvbjerg points to the importance of an intimate understanding of values and norms in social science. Recently my colleagues and I, those busying themselves with empirical research in victimology, were criticised for rushing to judgement on the basis of our surveys and studies (see Geeraets & Veraart, 2017). To be honest, I was a bit annoyed by this criticism. In my inaugural lecture in Tilburg (Pemberton, 2015), I had made a similar point myself. Referring to Nietzsche's *The Gay Science* I had emphasised the necessity of taking heed of *the magnificent tension of the spirit* that between the *will to truth* and the *will to value* and had argued my misgivings about the widespread emphasis on an 'objective' and 'value-free' social science. Instead I maintained that

> victimologists need to be fully aware of the value component of any attempt to get to the truth. Their subject will often not allow universalisation and will defy general laws, and the victimologist needs to fully understand the perspective (s)he draws from philosophy, rather than pretend to operate under an ethical viewpoint from nowhere, and to separate the will to truth from the will to value. (Pemberton, 2015: 12)

However, I have come to realise that the subject of study in victimology can easily lead us astray as to what the key issues concerning norms and values are. Victimology can be described as the study of the experience of wrongful suffering (see also Pemberton, 2015).

This can lead to the view that what is central in normative terms is the fact that suffering should be resisted. This observation can then quickly be followed by proposals of a plethora of well-meaning instruments and provisions in our justice processes that seek to counter or undo the suffering victimisation has caused. However, our processes of justice, and indeed social institutions in general, are highly limited in the extent to which they can in fact counter or undo suffering. In turn, this view then contains the risk of a never-ending but still unsuccessful attempt to bend processes of justice to this end and/or the type of aspirational but unrealistic language that often accompanies new bodies of victims' rights.

In addition, the focus on suffering as such clouds out the, in my view more relevant, normative issues with which victimology should concern itself. In different publications, I have referred to Avishai Margalit and Bernard Williams, who use the availability of near-synonyms *morality* and *ethics* in the English language to stake out two different normative realms (Margalit, 2002; Williams, 1985, 1993). According to Margalit, the first should be applied to the 'thin' relationship with others, with whom identity, history, familiarity and actual real-life ties are irrelevant. For those with whom we actually have a 'real' relationship – our children, loved ones, friends and the like – a framework in which they are approached as strangers does not suffice. Margalit therefore proposes to use the term 'ethics' to apply to such 'thick' relationships. Recently I followed Williams' view that Margalit's ethics of thick relationships can also be conceptualised in terms of identity questions (Pemberton, 2019). Where Margalit notes that the relationship with oneself is also a thick relationship, I argued instead that other thick relationships should also be understood in terms of the self. Ethics then is not primarily related to justified expectations that my thick relationships might have of myself and my actions but rather concerns the ethical relevance of questions that concern the manner in which I, in my actions and experiences, maintain my own identity.

As is apparent from the previous section, I find a key issue in the experience of victimisation to be the damage/diminishment/destruction of one's sense of self. In turn, this points to the ethical relevance of identity questions in the aftermath of victimisation. This is also in line with a point that can be derived from Williams' (1993) *Shame and Necessity*: formal criminal justice processes narrow issues of crime and victimisation to an examination of guilt and blame, of 'what happened here,' and, subsequently, 'who is responsible.'

However, these questions only gain full meaning in the lives of victims (and of offenders as well) when they are connected to issues of ethics, of 'who am I?' This is typically something that is a staple of restorative justice processes (Pemberton, 2019; see also van Stokkom, 2002). Where Williams criticises our systems of morality – and this criticism can be extended to our justice systems – for pretending that people should be seen as 'characterless moral selves', restorative justice practices concern encounters between real, full-fledged human beings. In restorative justice practices, the questions of 'what happened here' and 'who is responsible' also have their relevance, but they are intimately connected to, rather than artificially separated from, the identity, including the lived and idiosyncratic experience, of the participants. This cautions against the unreflective imposition of standards from outside of the direct experience and of the assumption that restorative justice practices are best understood as repeatable mechanisms.

4 POWER/CONFLICT

The latter point of the previous section can also be read as an issue of power and/or conflict. Conflict is of course a staple of the restorative justice literature (Christie, 1977), while I side with Flyvbjerg (2001) in his Foucauldian interpretation of power, as being an inevitable corollary of relationships rather than something that is affixed to a particular position and/or person. Such a relational perspective on power, I think, is relevant to restorative justice in and of itself, but I will not pursue this subject here.

Instead and more in line with the previous sections, I would like to point to the issues concerning power and conflict that victimology as a phronetic social science can rectify in comparison to current social science approaches. Although the latter maintain the pretence of objectivity and value neutrality, I am inclined to perceive them in terms of something that might amount to (an abuse of) power. In this hegemonic narrative (Polletta, 2006), the status quo of the order that systems of justice are intended to provide is epistemically privileged over victims' lived experience. I can clarify this with reference to Miranda Fricker's (2007) concept of *epistemic injustice*. This term refers to situations in which someone is wronged in his or her capacity as a knower. It can apply both to the weight given to a person's evidence, to 'certain speakers', as a type of *testimonial* epistemic injustice, as well as to the situation in which a societal institution or society *tout court* lacks the interpretative resources to make sense of the meaning a person of a particular social group or in a particular situation gives to his or her predicament, or *hermeneutical* epistemic injustice.

In my view, the latter phenomenon is also visible in the way processes of justices and the social science approaches to the experience of direct participants are conceived (see also Pemberton et al., 2018). Most of what is ethically relevant to victims is not considered in processes of justice: the personal details of what it felt like; the victim's story past, present and future and the manner in which the experience might factor within this story; the imprints of the act on the body and the mind; and the concrete, personal and idiosyncratic meaning of the victimisation in the victim's life. Instead, processes of justice insist on privileging broken rules, over this experience of broken bodies and ruined lives. This is subsequently reinforced and reified by a social science that understands knowledge in abstraction from these situations through general rules and mechanisms. As Elizabeth Anscombe (1958) has pointed out, the former should be understood as a remnant of our theological history, of which the application without reference to its divine heritage is gravely in doubt; the latter is again an example of the transplant of natural science approaches to the social realm, where they can run roughshod over our understanding of empirical reality. Where part of the experience of victimisation can be conceived as the learning of (unwanted) truths – as Susan Brison found, see section 2 –, the experience of secondary victimisation can subsequently also be viewed as the denial of what the victim might experience as central to these truths (see also Pemberton et al., 2018).

Such hermeneutical epistemic injustice can also reside in the denial of the reality of conflict in processes of justice. That might seem odd in reference to restorative justice, in which conflicts have always been afforded central stage. However, like Nils Christie (2013), I have become increasingly concerned with the connotations of the inclusion of the word *justice* in restorative justice. Some of the most vexing but thereby most important situations in the aftermath of crime and victimisation hinge on having to make a – sometimes tragic – choice between incommensurable goods and/or which evils are to be avoided (see also Tessman, 2014). Justice, in particular in liberal 'ideal theories' (e.g. Stemplowska & Swift, 2012), however contains the pretence that a right decision in these cases is possible and that any residing disagreement with this outcome is to certain degree misguided or irrational. This denies the truly political nature of different conflicts, in which the necessity of coming to a resolution or a decision should not be taken to mean automatically that this decision somehow pronounces on what was the right thing to do in these situations. As again Williams (2005: 13) argued,

> A very important reason for thinking in terms of the political is that a political decision – the conclusion of a political deliberation which brings all sorts of considerations, considerations of principle along with others, to one focus of decision – is that such a decision does not in itself announce that the other party was morally wrong or, indeed wrong at all. What it immediately announces is that they have lost.

Choosing to allow the general principles of justice to take precedence over the requirements of the aftermath of a given lived situation of conflict and harm is surely defensible, but it does not mean that those experiencing the drawbacks of this political choice – as is the experience of many victims – should also have to be told their misgivings are misguided and/or inevitable. In recent publications, I have argued that a solution to this issue lies in a clearer understanding of the difference between *doing justice* and *countering injustice* (Pemberton, 2019). In reality, restorative practices already focus on the latter and thereby relax the requirement of the primacy of the virtue of justice over other concerns, including the lived reality of participants. Victimology as a phronetic social science would assist restorative practice in its examination of these truly political conflicts of value.

5 CONTEXT/CULTURE

Part of the antidote to an all-too-positivist victimology can be found in the movement towards cultural victimology[1] Like its counterpart, cultural criminology, this entails placing victimisation and the reaction to victimisation in the context of culture, that is, seeing victimisation and the reaction to victimisation as at least partly cultural products. The knowledge base of victimology is highly skewed towards the experience of particular groups of victims, in particular areas of the world, while the portability of findings to other contexts and cultures is by no means certain. Even in those areas of victim research that hew more closely to clinical and medical psychology, the reality is dawning that universality and generalisability of findings has been too easily assumed. Cultural approaches to and limitations of posttraumatic stress disorder (PTSD) are for instance increasingly recognised (Hinton & Good, 2016).

Such cultural diversity is also evident in the linguistics of central terms in victimology. The connotations of the term *victim* itself already bare evidence of this. In languages based in Latin, this comes packaged with particular etymological history: the 'vitima' label carries with it connotations of sacrifice, which in other languages of the world is absent. Van Dijk (2009) has argued that this meaning – perhaps more obscure to English-language speakers than to those in my home country, the Netherlands, where 'slacht-offer' literally translates as butchered-sacrifice – is not innocent, but, for instance, influences the position victims may or may not have in criminal justice processes. And what applies to 'victim' is also true, perhaps in a somewhat different manner of 'justice'. In translating this term to Dutch an ambivalence emerges (see van Roermund, 2016), which would necessitate precise attention if I were to attempt a translation of the current contribution to the Dutch language.

Sometimes, the answer to these kinds of difficulties is perceived to be some measure of holding the context constant; for instance, finding a linguistic construct that would mean the same thing in different languages/countries. But, in honesty, this is a fool's errand. As Flyvbjerg (2001: 45) writes,

> the problem for social studies [is] that the background conditions change without the researcher being able to state in advance which aspects one should hold in constant in order for predictions to continue to operate. As the background conditions are not facts – as is temperature for the ecological theories in biol-

1 This is the topic of the COST-action CA18121 Cultures of Victimology. See www.cost.eu/actions/CA18121/#tabs|Name:overview.

> ogy – but context-dependent interpretations, even those social sciences which build upon second-order interpretations are incomplete and unstable.

The importance of context in restorative practices, and in particular their relationship to historical and cultural traditions, has a long pedigree, which I will not repeat here. An issue of which I have only more recently become aware is that this means that victimology as a phronetic social science should by necessity be polyglot. A point more generally made by the former director of UNESCO, Bokova, is that the current emphasis on English as the lingua franca of academic life presents a

> missed opportunity to explore perspectives and paradigms that are embedded in other cultural and linguistic traditions. A more culturally and linguistically diverse approach by the social sciences would be of tremendous value to organizations such as UNESCO in our efforts to foster mutual understanding and intercultural dialogue. (cited in Albarillo, 2014: 79)

There is surely something of an irony of an Englishman making this argument in English, but this should not detract from its force. A victimology that is too heavily focused on what can and cannot be expressed in the English language will likely miss much of value: that which is truly *lost in translation*.

6 PRACTICE

The previous sections have already offered many examples of the pre-eminence of practice in restorative justice and the manner in which victimology as a phronetic social science would seek to contribute to these practices. In this regard, I have found it useful to consider the parallels with Pellegrino's approach to the ethics of the medical practitioner (Pemberton, 2019). Pellegrino (1979) coined the term *ontological assault* to describe the sudden sense of disunity and disintegration between the self and the body. He connects this to the practice of medicine by distinguishing *disease* from the *fact of illness*. The latter is the subjective state of the individual experiencing the ontological assault and as such can be distinguished from *disease*, which refers instead to a quantifiable disorder of biologic function objectively located in the body (Davis, 1997). For Pellegrino, the ultimate *telos* of medicine is the former rather than the latter, healing illness over curing disease. In this, healing illness focuses on 'a return to the unity of self and body, although this unity may represent a renegotiation, a newly struck balance, between the self's hopes and the body's capacities'.

This overlaps to a large degree with what I have suggested to be *re-storying* in the aftermath of victimisation, in which the social nature of victimisation, and the experience of being radically alone as consequence of victimisation, emphasises the importance of reconnecting to the social surroundings, also in ways anew (Pemberton, 2019). Practices in the aftermath of victimisation should be alive to their narrative potential and their contribution to rebuilding (the sense of) communion between the victim and his or her social surroundings. Indeed, the practices themselves are part of re-establishing this sense of communion. That is particularly clear in restorative processes that involve members of the community, and similarly to processes of support or mutual aid, which involve peers in the same or similar positions.

In the manner in which this process unfolds, including the choices and actions of those directly involved, I believe David Graeber's analysis of the distinction between *play* and *games* to be important (Graeber, 2015; see also Pemberton, 2015). According to Graeber (2015: 192),

> A game is a bounded specific way of problem solving. Play is more cosmic and open-ended. A game has a predictable resolution, play may not. Play allows for emergence, novelty, surprise.

Processes of justice are typically game-like, while I think restorative practices can and should offer more leeway for playfulness.

Elsewhere, I have contrasted the two in more detail (Pemberton, 2015, 2019). Here, I would just like to stress the use of playfulness in relaxing the emphasis on rules, in stressing the open-endedness of countering injustice and the importance of imagination in coming to terms with the experience of injustice. Playfulness has a 'make it up as you go along' quality, which coheres with the idiosyncrasy and intimacy of coming to terms with an experience of victimisation. The comparison between games and playing and the former's connection to processes of justice also offers the potential to criticise the idea of a resolution of experience of injustice. Justice processes seek an outcome, a decision. The reality of the experience of injustice is instead that it is unclear when, and if ever, the matter can be said to be resolved. An expectation that this is possible, and indeed possible in all cases, is rather a remnant of justice thinking than an adequate reflection of the experience of many victims. Finally, acknowledging the importance of imagination can offer new vistas for victimological research. Much of what a victim might need to express about his or her experience escapes speech, and part of the complexity of coming to terms with victimisation is finding modes of expression that can more adequately capture the victim's ordeal. This often involves going beyond factual truth, involving metaphor and a variety of forms of artistic expression. A particular challenge for victimology as a phronetic social science then lies in finding avenues of academic communication that embrace these forms of expression, rather than having to resort to a reduction back to written language, which speaks against the experience it is attempting to capture.

It also coincides with the way that Flyvbjerg (2001), in line with Dreyfus and Dreyfus (1988), outlines the characteristics of practical expertise: intuitive, holistic and synchronic. It involves a 'qualitative jump', which 'implies an abandonment of rule-based thinking as the most important basis for action, and its replacement by context and intuition' (Flyvbjerg, 2001: 21). This also explains why many 'professionals have a difficult time explaining ... what they are doing in terms of specific procedures and rules' (2001: 20). Trying to capture practical expertise in rules and procedures is step down and backward rather than an adequate reflection that could serve as a model for others to follow. It is something that is undoubtedly familiar for many practitioners working in restorative justice and/or victim support: a move to rules and principles always loses something and will in cases actively work against, rather than support, practice in achieving the best outcomes.

7 Final remarks

In sum, victimology as a phronetic social science emphasises narrative, meaning-making approaches to the study of victimisation; seeks to query the ethics of victimology, pointing to the relevance of questions of identity in understanding victimisation's normative relevance; seeks to critically engage with issues of power and conflict, also where they currently remain implicit; maintains a clear focus on true context dependency, also by intimately involving culture; and, also by doing all these things, seeks to forge a fully interactive relationship with practice, in which the expertise of those immersed in the reality of victimisation is a primary source of knowledge and understanding. Each of these dimensions can contribute to an understanding of practices of restorative justice, whatever misgiving I may have with the term itself. Indeed, I believe the potential of restorative justice to lie in its close coherence to phronesis as a virtue of social and political life.

I would be hard-pressed to think of a scholar who is a better example of what doing phronesis in victimology and the study of restorative justice entails than Ivo Aertsen. The manner in which he has successfully navigated academia, policy and practice in developing restorative justice throughout Europe and the globe can serve as a clear case study in the value and importance of the type of transdisciplinarity to which we should all aspire. I very much hope that we can rely on his guidance in continuing this work for many years to come, and I already look forward to our further collaboration.

References

Albarillo, F. (2014). Language in social science databases: English versus non-English articles in JSTOR and Scopus. *Behavioral & Social Sciences Librarian*, 33(2), 77-90. doi:10.1080/01639269.2014.904693.

Anscombe, G. E. M. (1958). Modern moral philosophy, *Philosophy*, 33, 1-19. doi:10.1017/s0031819100037943.

Brison S. (2002). *Aftermath: violence and the remaking of the self.* Princeton: Princeton University Press.

Christie, N. (1977). Conflicts as property. *British Journal of Criminology*, 17, 1-17. doi:10.1093/oxfordjournals.bjc.a046783.

Christie, N. (2013). Words on words. *Restorative Justice: An International Journal*, 1(1), 15-19. doi:10.5235/20504721.1.1.15.

Davis, F. D. (1997). Phronesis, clinical reasoning and Pellegrino's philosophy of medicine. *Theoretical Medicine*, 18, 173-195. doi:10.1007/978-94-017-3364-9_13.

Dreyfus, H. L. & Dreyfus, S. E. (1988). *Mind over machine. The power of human intention and expertise in the era of the computer* (2nd ed.). New York: Free Press.

Flyvbjerg, B. (2001). *Making social science matter. Why social inquiry fails and how it can succeed again.* Cambridge: Cambridge University Press.

Fricker, M. (2007). *Epistemic injustice: power and the ethics of knowing.* Oxford: Clarendon Press.

Geeraets, V. & Veraart, W. (2017). Over verplichte excuses en spreekrecht: wat is er mis met empirisch-juridisch onderzoek naar slachtoffers? *Netherlands Journal of Legal Philosophy*, 46(2), 137-159. doi:10.5553/njlp/221307132017046002003.

Graeber, D. (2015). *The utopia of rules: on technology, stupidity and the secret joys of bureaucracy* London: Melville.

Hinton D. E. & Good. B. J. (2016). *Culture and PTSD: trauma in global and historical perspective.* Philadelphia: University of Pennsylvania Press.

Margalit A. (2002). *The ethics of memory.* Cambridge: Harvard University Press.

McGarry R. & Walklate S. (2015). *Victims: trauma, testimony and justice.* Oxon: Routledge.

Pellegrino, E. D. (1979). Toward a reconstruction of medical morality: the primacy of the act of profession and the fact of illness. *Journal of Medicine and Philosophy*, 4, 32-56. doi:10.1093/jmp/4.1.32.

Pemberton A. (2015). *Victimology with a hammer. The challenge of victimology.* Tilburg: Prismaprint

Pemberton A. (2019). Time for a rethink: victims and restorative justice. *International Journal of Restorative Justice*, 2(1), 13-33. doi:10.5553/ijrj/258908912019002001002.

Pemberton, A. Mulder, E. & Aarten. P.G.M. (2018). Stories of Injustice: towards a narrative victimology. *European Journal of Criminology.* doi:10.1177/1477370818770843.

Pepper S. (1942). *World hypotheses.* Berkeley: University of California Press.
Polletta F. (2006). *It was like a fever. Storytelling in protest and politics.* Chicago: University of Chicago Press.
Roermund, G.C.G.J. van (2016). Bespreking A. Pemberton, Victimology with a Hammer: The Challenge of Victimology (oratie Tilburg). *Delikt en delinkwent,* 46(5), 324-329.
Sarbin T.R. (1986). The narrative as a root metaphor for psychology. In T. R. Sarbin (ed.), *Narrative psychology: the storied nature of human conduct.* New York: Praeger.
Sebold, A. (1999) *Lucky.* New York: Scribner.
Stemplowska, Z & Swift, A. (2012). Ideal and nonideal theory. In D. Estlund (ed.), *The Oxford handbook of political philosophy.* Oxford: Oxford University Press.
Stokkom, B.A.M. van (2002). Moral emotions in restorative justice conferences: managing shame, designing empathy, *Theoretical Criminology,* 6(3), 339-360.
Tessman L (2014). *Moral failure.* Oxford: Oxford University Press.
Van Dijk, J. J. M. (2006). *The mark of Abel. Reflecting on the social labelling of victims of crime.* Inaugural lecture, Tilburg University, Tilburg.
Van Dijk J. J. M. (2009). Free the victim: a critique of the western conception of victimhood. *International Journal of Victimology* 16, 1-33. doi:10.1177/026975800901600101.
Williams, B. (1985). *Ethics and the Limits of philosophy.* Oxon: Routledge.
Williams, B. (1993). *Shame and necessity.* Berkeley: University of California Press.
Williams, B. (2005). *In the beginning was the deed: realism and moralism in political argument.* Princeton: Princeton University Press.

Part II
Praxis, Belgium, up close

On the border regions between research, experience, belief and commitment

Reflections on a search for restorative justice

Leo Van Garsse

1 Nostalgia

It must have been early 1978. As students in social pedagogy, my girlfriend (today my wife) and I got involved with an NGO facilitating social reintegration of ex-offenders. There was a close collaborating with members of the criminology department of the Catholic University of Leuven, including the late professor Tony Peters. We decided to engage as volunteers in co-housing with ex-offenders in a half-way house linked to this initiative. This included regular visits to Leuven's Central Prison to discuss potential collaboration with prisoners as well as staff members. Among the prison staff we noticed a young, ambitious psychologist with a remarkably critical view on the prison environment as well as on punishment as a whole. It was Ivo. I still remember the discussions with Ivo at the time as inspiring, respectful and mutually encouraging.

Nevertheless, for a couple of years we lost sight of each other. Ivo and the prison system were not exactly two of a kind. After some troubles, Ivo left the prison, to engage in a university spin-off focusing on non-residential aftercare for offenders and for victims alike, strictly separating the former from the latter. Ivo got intrigued by the victim's perspective and engaged in building on practice and theory in the context of the very first Belgian service for victim assistance in 1984.

After graduating from the university, I got engaged in the start-up of a small half-way house for young, homeless offenders after release from detention. The challenging battlefield on the frontiers of criminal justice and juvenile protection, as well as of punishment and education, didn't leave much space for a broader focus on the impact of crime and justice on society in general, let alone the victims. This changed gradually from 1987 onwards. Professor Lieven Dupont, a Leuven scholar in penal justice, contaminated us with fascination for the abolitionist writings of Herman Bianchi and Louk Hulsman. We were searching for ideas and ways to surmount the exhausting dilemma between punishment and juvenile protection through assistance and education. The idea of 'making amends' as an alternative way of dealing with deviant behaviour, was at least worth considering. From 1987 onwards, stimulated by Dupont, me and my former, late colleague Mon Vandekeybus experimented with setting up meetings between, on the one hand, the young offender and his or her parents, and on the other hand, the victims themselves. Although quite promising from the start, this small-scale project provoked suspicion and resistance. It was informally stigmatised for being naive, elitist and lacking legal safeguards for both victims and offenders. We felt insufficiently equipped to defend and justify our practice convincingly (Van Garsse, 2001b).

During the spring of 1993, at the verge of the abolishment of the whole experiment, we got invited to participate in a steering committee of the action research of the Leuven criminologists on setting up, in a more systematic way, an offer of victim-offender mediation for adults involved in serious crime. As a member of the criminology research group, Ivo was actively involved in conceptualising this research, but mediation practice still had to be started up. Indisputably, the confrontation of conceptual thought with pragmatic and factual findings based on our experience on a related domain was most promising for both sides.

No longer than a couple of weeks later, I found myself at the university as a half-time 'mediator-for-redress', with Ivo as my scientific counterpart. It was the starting point of an exciting period of intensive collaboration between 'science' and 'practice' (Aertsen & Van Garsse, 1996; Aertsen, Van Garsse & Peters, 1994). It was also the start of Belgian restorative justice, in practice, in law and even as a matter of formal scholarship (Aertsen, 2004; Lauwaert, 2008; Van Garsse, 2001a).

2 A slight feeling of ambivalence

The sudden relevance of our practice for an ambitious academic study was an overwhelming experience. We felt liberated from our isolated position in the field of juvenile justice and youth care, At the time the actors on this field were focussing on strengthening the legal rights positions of juveniles and appeared to be firmly resistant to taking into account the victims' perspective. Moreover, our collaboration with the university provided us with an extremely challenging and inspiring international helicopter view of the field we had been working in. At the same time, our brand new status as (part of) scientific 'research' appeared to be a real boost for our credibility towards all sorts of institutional stakeholders, such as the judiciary and the public funders. Our growing insight into the complex field we were operating in enlarged our capacity to maintain ourselves in critical debates with all sorts of partners. All of a sudden, we had words for what we had been doing. This new vocabulary appeared to be a key that opened the door to the rest of the world, the keywords by excellence being 'mediation' and 'restorative justice'.

However, as 'practitioners' we had some doubts in using a common language with people working in institutional, legal and sociopolitical contexts differing profoundly from ours. Was our 'mediation practice' really the same as theirs? Part of the ambivalence had to do with a sobering feeling of being cast away from a somewhat heroic position of being the first and only ones to discover brand new ideas and valid practices on human capacities in a field as delicate and relevant as 'doing justice' in cases of transgression of the social rule. Our 'discoveries' appeared to be already a matter of common sense, at least in specific circles of progressive criminologists and practitioners worldwide. How narcissist as it appeared to be, we were eager not to give in too much of our 'particularity'. It was a relief to notice that, all over Europe, colleagues lived a comparable internal struggle.

At the same time, it was obvious for all of us that being discovered by a militant critical group of criminal justice scholars was extremely promising for the future, a miracle as it were, we could only be grateful for. From our side, we were gladly prepared to expose our practice to open critical reflection, even if this included getting used to hear one or another scholar referring to mediation cases he couldn't possibly have been actively involved in: 'I once had a case ... '

People like Tony Peters, Ivo Aertsen and Wilfried Meyvis were far from prototypical for 'the academy'. On the contrary, compared to other scholars we met, the Leuven group used to be deeply embedded in all sorts of forensic practices, confronting themselves with the facts on the floor rather than merely the theories in the book. This allowed for a very direct, personal and open working relationship. As a practitioner, I was involved in almost every aspect of the initial action research. The research team used every opportunity to give the floor to practical experience, and this even on quite formal occasions, where our poor English and our intuitive wording was in absolute contrast with the fluent and well-elaborated speech of others. As a scientific mentor, Tony Peters above all was a pedagogue, eager to push his collaborators' knowledge, their capacities and their self-confidence, far beyond the limits they were likely to see for themselves. These years were one big, extremely intense learning process.

3 Towards institutionalising mediating 'fora'

In 1997, the Belgian Minister of Justice challenged us to extend our Leuven practice all over Flanders. In this perspective, we had to sharpen our view on the nature of what we saw as 'a mediation service'. It seemed logical to integrate scientific research as a constitutive element of mediation service, as we wanted it to further develop. At the same time, our academic partners considered it self-evident to engage in the first steps of the institutionalisation of the promising practice resulting from our common effort. The mediation practice and scientific reflection were not seen separately. In my view as a mediator, mediation was not just an outcome of action research; it was action research itself and should have been institutionalised as such.

Discussing this with Ivo, we elaborated the idea of expanding the research format in every district. In this case, mediation for redress had to be institutionalised in every district as an open forum, not just between victims and offenders but also between the sometime-contradictory reasoning and discourses involved in 'doing criminal justice'. Furthermore, installing a mediation service consisted of negotiating a formal contract, a partnership as it were between the prosecutors, judges, bar association, police, social services both for victims and offenders, and an academic adviser. They would all have to officially engage in the establishment of a common steering committee meeting at least six times a year. This committee would have to focus not just on mediation as such but also on an internal learning process in doing justice in a (more) restorative way. The local mediators would submit their cases (anonymously) to a process of reflection of this group, in order to enable the gradual elaboration and refinement of a proper policy adapted to local circumstances and judicial 'culture' (Van Garsse, 2008, 2013).

The underlying idea was that the relevance of an offer of mediation in the criminal context should be seen from an ethical, political and social-pedagogical angle, rather than from a technical or methodological one. It should be no fabric of agreements, but a process of common learning on the structural and case levels alike, not 'apart' from the institutional contexts and closely and respectfully involving them all (see Fitzpatrick & Joyce, 2007; Foqué & 't Hart, 1990; Gutwirth, 1993; Van Gerven, 1993).

4 What about restorative justice?

This view also reflected on the nature of the organisation we established in 1999 to start up a long-term project where our offer was expanded all over Flanders. The NGO 'Suggnomè' (ancient Greek word literally meaning 'understanding together the same reality') was a paradoxical and utopian attempt to institutionalise 'neutrality' into a common in-depth understanding. In composing a suitable group of 'founders', we carefully tried to balance the presence of the judiciary, social services (private and public), bar association, police and so on. This effort in balancing also applied to the initial board.

As far as the scientific 'wing' of our efforts was concerned, we considered it hardly defendable to limit our partnership to the Leuven criminologists. On the contrary, we deliberately invited criminologists and social scientists from other universities to join us as partners on this forum. Some of them did. We got partners from all Flemish criminology departments, all of them quite eager to contribute to the debate on the relevance of offering mediation in cases of crime.

As a subtitle of our organisation, we chose 'Forum voor herstelrecht en bemiddeling' ('Forum for restorative justice and mediation'). With the explicit referral to the notion of 'restorative justice' ('herstelrecht'), we wanted to connect our project from the start with what we presumed to be a wide movement of people reflecting and practising in a similar way on similar problems and challenges. Given the fragility and the ambitious nature of the whole enterprise, a new isolation was something we absolutely hoped to avoid.

In the meantime, inspired by similar developments in the United States, our Leuven partners of criminology got intensely engaged in building international networks focusing on restorative justice. Tony Peters and Ivo Aertsen took the lead in composing an international expert committee, a mixture of practitioners and researchers familiar with mediation in justice-related contexts, gradually preparing the establishment of a formal European 'Forum'. During the challenging preparatory debates, consensus was easily reached on the definition of mediation as a method of facilitating communication, maximally respecting fundamental principles such as neutrality, voluntary participation of all involved as well as confidentiality. A far more difficult task appeared to be defining the normative notion of restorative justice, as it touched the underlying motives and ambitions of the practitioners and the researchers involved. It was likely to reveal differences in cultural contexts as well as in ideological presumptions. Particularly striking was the problem of a French colleague, who desperately searched for a suitable translation of the term 'restorative justice' and was often seen at the verge of giving up the whole debate.

We had many questions. How far could you go in 'motivating' the parties to come to an agreement? What are the limits in accepting some pressure or in negotiating with prosecutors or judges? How closely could you let mediation be used as a preventative instrument or as an alternative sanction? To what extent, and on what kind of grounds, could we justify not just providing but 'promoting' mediation? What kind of risks could we justify in setting up experimental practices?

By the end of October 1999, the first conference of the European Forum for Victim-Offender Mediation and Restorative Justice took place. It was held in Leuven and chaired by Tony Peters. There were 140 participants, and 24 European countries were represented, demonstrating the common attraction of the development of restorative justice worldwide. However, when we were asked to draw some conclusive remarks at the end of the conference, me and my Austrian colleague Bernd Gläser couldn't but refer somewhat ironically to the underlying differences in everything we had been witnessing. I remember us summarising our concluding intervention with the quote: 'We're still confused, but on a higher level!'

In his contribution, Martin Wright distinguished 'unilateral', 'authoritarian' and 'democratic' ways of applying restorative justice methods (Wright, 2000), categories that are indeed ideological and normative rather than 'scientific'. Tony Peters stated:

> ... the attractiveness of mediation and restorative justice stems from the multitude of aims... It is highly desirable to keep an open mind when discussing restorative justice and victim-offender mediation. The greatest danger is the illusion of the existence of a common language in this field. (Peters, 2000: 15)

Nevertheless, for Tony Peters this was no reason for despair. He used to state that he considered mediation and restorative justice as the most 'criminological' research field he ever got involved in. Beyond any doubt, he strongly welcomed restorative justice as the most interesting meeting point of all sorts of criminal justice-related discourses, particularly the ones on the 'function' of punishment (Peters, 1996). But I still wonder if this meant that he shared a radical identification with some scholars who had a paradigmatic conviction about *the notion* of restorative justice or with those who promoted the idea of restorative justice as being about a bunch of effective methods that could produce a 'brand new' kind of 'justice'.

5 A commitment to engage in learning

From 1998 onwards, we started negotiating the establishment of mediation services in other Flemish districts. Our view explicitly defined a mediation service as a partnership between the rationales of 'justice', 'social order' and 'individual well-being of victim and offender'. In this approach, the notion of 'restorative justice' was seen as an attractive open space, a meeting point for the multiplicity of defendable 'aims' on doing justice in the context of social deviance and crime. The notion of 'restorative justice' hereby was projected not as just another 'aim', another 'method' or as the launching of an 'alternative' system but as a common challenge for all involved in confronting themselves with a multitude of viewpoints on tangible cases. Comparable with the offer of 'mediation' to victims and offenders involved in each particular case, 'restorative justice' was the name of a learning process for all engaged on a daily basis to define and redefine their way of 'doing justice'.

This approach engaged us in a demanding yet fascinating period of meetings with all sorts of professionals. Our 'offer' seemed to consist in bringing together circles of interest absolutely not used to mutually communicate in a respectful way. It was an exhausting, sometimes lonely job, but it was also an extremely enriching process.

I remember promoting the method of mediation, with reference to promising research in many countries. I also referred to our 'own' research on 'mediation for redress' and to our fruitful partnership with the University of Leuven. We didn't have a lot of experience to present other than the proof that setting up the communication between victim and offender was more than an elusive, risky and time-consuming enterprise. This provided our 'mission' with an entry, since all stakeholders were given an 'alibi' to at least make an effort to listen to us. This even was the case for the officials of the prosecutor general as well as for the Flemish 'Union of Lawyers'.

However, our approach raised more questions than it offered answers. It also focused on the notion of 'justice' as a matter of social interdependency, as an ever-ongoing social process of balancing and (de-/re-)codification as it were (Foqué & 't Hart, 1990). The only requirement, the only 'rule' we could bring in, was the principle of 'respect': justice could just not afford to neglect this specific viewpoint on 'doing justice'. Our approach triggered the degree of maturity of each of our stakeholders. It questioned the extent of their capacity and readiness to expose themselves to be openly questioned by other viewpoints on the legitimacy of their policies. I was surprised to experience openness in sectors I first presumed to be rigid and largely self-referential.

6 Who's that mediator?

The respect we tried to give implied the obligation to take other viewpoints seriously ourselves. Mediation seemed to imply a constant, fluid repositioning, always questioning our own standards and principles, sometimes even case by case. But this approach also questioned ourselves as an organisation. Who were we to do this? Who were we to invest in seducing prosecutors, judges, police officers, social workers into a culture of self-reflexivity as a contribution to a local criminal policy?

Even in everyday case work, victims and offenders unmasked the 'drive' of their mediators as not just 'neutral'. I remember people asking me: 'But, tell me honestly, why are you guys doing all this? Who are you exactly?' An answer based upon scientific research would not suffice.

In exactly the same manner, during a few crucial occasions we got confronted with the firm position of some judges and prosecutors who stated that as professionals they would never ever sign any 'agreement' with a private person, let alone engage structurally in a collaboration with one or another NGO. An investigating judge during our meeting expressed himself this way: 'I could as well sign a contract with a local club of pigeon-holders!' Mediation could be scientifically proved to be fruitful and promising, but this did not suffice to justify what they saw as compromising the fundamentals of the legal state. In their view, mediation should be kept out of the public sphere (Gutwirth & De Hert, 2002).

Who were we exactly? A private service ready to assist the judiciary in cases they considered suitable? Or should we opt to embrace the 'movement' of promoters of 'restorative justice' as a radical alternative in doing justice? Rather intuitively, we explored a third option, positioning restorative justice in the sphere of an ambitious concept of democracy and citizenship, however rigorously respecting the prerogatives of the legal state. We acknowledged this option to be a matter of a shared 'felt sense', of a 'practice wisdom' maybe, rather than of 'evidence'. The mediator we had in mind was to be above all a reflective person, ready to engage in deliberately exposing himself or herself to being openly questioned, first of all by his or her own colleagues. The organisation we had in mind would have to constantly mirror the heterogeneity of the local steering committees we were building on, inviting complexity instead of 'solving' problems, stimulating debate instead of concluding it, mistrusting consensus instead of applauding it.

We could easily understand that the figure of a private NGO wasn't exactly an ideal structural operationalisation of the ambitious political aim we had in mind. But frankly, in a certain way we felt it was the government's responsibility to provide this approach with a juridical personality suiting its democratic potential. The mediator wasn't but a challenger of this process, eager to confront traditional policies with demonstrations of precious but unaddressed capacities of real people in real and often very hard circumstances.

7 A (selective) taste of Flemish criminological debate

This slightly paradoxical approach on the further institutionalisation of our practice was doomed to be perceived somewhat hostile to the clear distinctions and working relationships so carefully explained and established during the previous years of social work in the forensic sphere.

As other countries, from the late 1950s onwards, Belgium engaged in building up a welfare state, investing in meeting all sorts of social needs. Only gradually and rather hesitantly this needs-based approach was broadened to the delicate domain of citizens involved in criminal justice proceedings. During this development, state politics and ideology were never far away.

Those were the years of the first steps in the state reform, which put Belgium on the road to becoming a progressive, federalising state, composed with 'communities' based upon 'sociocultural' and linguistic distinctions. In this political context, in the late 1970s, a group of criminologists in the University of Leuven allowed themselves to adopt a critical standpoint towards the state-driven criminal justice system; they were supposed to be supporting and facilitating its aims to be effective. Inspired by insights of critical sociology and developments in the United States and elsewhere, they discovered the notions of crime and punishment to be deeply politically determined.

As students in pedagogy, we felt we were in good company. I remember my fascination attending a controversial lecture of the Dutch scholar Herman Bianchi. His plea was for justice as a space of free speech open to all involved (Bianchi, 1980, 1985). Those ideas seemed to fit the radicalness of authors we were used to read with enthusiasm, like Paolo Freire and Ivan Illich.

Later on, we became familiar with the ideas of Louk Hulsman (1972, 1975), who argued for the need to study criminology with an open eye to carry out critical sociopolitical 'action' while also looking out for the legitimately creative aspects often present in acts of 'deviance'. Academic promoters of this line of thought were prominently present among our teachers in social pedagogy as well as in the boards of the organisations we wanted to work with. Of course, on the other hand, there was practice to confront these ideas with the complexity of daily facts and events and with institutional and juridical requirements alike.

As far as we were concerned, the Leuven criminologists were far from a left-wing revolutionary movement. People like Tony Peters rather seemed to have the ambition to excel in realism. A continuous and close collaboration with Lieven Dupont, philosopher and professor in criminal law, guaranteed an open mind for the fundamentals and prerogatives of 'justice' in its factual dynamics. They weren't likely to oppose the authority of the state *as such*, but they radically distrusted the obvious dominance of any rationale. They strongly opposed the self-evidence of 'logics' masking and silencing underlying facts. This realism had no boundaries and even embarked on criticising the critiques. But 'facts' were to be taken seriously. 'Experience' was to be valorised, even more if the source was a particular person rather than a group, a 'movement' or an institute (be it academic or political). The experience of the individual practitioner all of a sudden found itself in the focus of academic interest.

At first, the echoes on the development of mediation and restorative justice abroad were more a stimulus for observing rather than for practising. Mediation, as developing in the States,was seen as a new method in dealing with minor cases or in 'conflict-management' Clearly interesting from a merely pragmatic standpoint, but too much a product of the Anglo-Saxon criminal justice culture to challenge prosecutors and judges working in the Belgian continental tradition of doing justice (Staelens, 1987). There was of course also awareness of the abolitionist standpoint of Bianchi and Hulsman, positioning the dialogue between victim and offender in the heart of any search for (criminal) justice. However challenging the works of both were considered too ideologically loaded to be useful in building a credible criminological theory.

By the end of the 1970s, there was a wave of disappointment about the firm, and only vane promises about a fundamental criminal justice reform were made by a succession of Ministers of Justice (Dupont, 1980b). Dupont (1987) observed a lack of courage to fundamentally question traditional positions of authority. Looking for a way out of this impasse, he suggested that the abolitionist standpoint could be seen as nothing more than the radicalisation of an historical, but almost forgotten, principle of modern criminal justice: the principle of subsidiarity ('subsidiarité'). His plea was for criminal justice to finally open itself to problem-solving capacity from the outside society, not just by pragmatic opportunity, but systematically and by fundamental juridical principle. The other way round, Dupont urged that social work enlarge investment in the public sphere of criminal justice proceedings, not just on the basis of individual case work in answering private needs but openly claiming a fundamental contribution in doing (criminal) justice and in empowering citizens to do the same (Dupont, 1980a, 1986).

8 The political and the social: science, social work and Belgian state reform

This firm appeal on the (re)politicisation of both criminal justice and criminal justice-related social work was certainly heard and discussed in many circles. But the circumstances were complicated. Internationally, there was the rise of pleas for a 'new realism' in criminal policy, calling for a pragmatic rather than an ideological approach. Thinking on principles was nice, but justice should above all be effective in solving the social problem of crime (Eliaerts, 1984).

In 1980, a first step in Belgian state reform was taken, putting Belgium on the long road towards gradual federalisation into 'Communities'. From the very start, the Flemish community was given authority upon all sorts of person-related matters, including social assistance to citizens involved in criminal proceedings. The departments of training and education would soon follow. On the other hand, the successive steps in state reform time after time strongly reaffirmed criminal justice, including public punishment, as a strictly federal matter. All of this transformed the area of Flemish forensics to a real battlefield of political competences.

The new Flemish community appeared to be ready to invest in social work in the forensic sphere, but understandably all the more if this wouldn't come down to a servile service provided to the authorities at the federal level. Gradually, the community expanded its authority to gain increased competence to carry out action on the social level. The focus of Flemish social politics consisted in promoting an equal distribution of high-quality services to people needing them. The proof of existence of a certain need was key to justify social action. The proof of quality of service and readiness to professionalise was key to get access to 'clients' and to a corresponding degree of public financing. Service providing was urged to emancipate from being an instrument of federal criminal justice policy. Instead, it had to be 'need-focused'.

From that point on, criminological departments seemed to be increasingly questioned about, and financed more frequently for, research oriented to circumscribe certain 'needs' as well as to identify the groups they wanted to study in order to determine 'best practices' and contribute in making services to people involved in criminal proceedings more need-effective or to organise evidence in distributive 'equality' in service provision and in public financing of such service provision. And from the standpoint of the practitioner, being the object of research was likely to be a key to public financing for providing services with an 'evidence-based' quality label.

In this context, Flanders (re)discovered the victim as 'a person in need', in great risk of suffering revictimisation while in contact with state justice and its one-sided focus on guilt and punishment. In the second half of the 1980s, victim services seemed to spring up like mushrooms. The Leuven group around Tony Peters was again fascinated by the new viewpoint their practices pointed at, addressing it as 'the back-side of crime'. At the same time Peters explicitly urged not to over-identify with presupposed victim needs or not to reduce the victim's status to merely 'a client' in need of highly specialised care. Instead, he pointed at the political status of both victim and offender as citizens provided with equal rights (Peters, 1993).

9 Back to restorative justice

How would mediation and restorative justice respond to the dominant requirement to prove its effectiveness? How would it relate to the criterion of need satisfaction as a standard of quality? How would it respond to the new prominence of the victim? And, if not with 'effectiveness', what other kind of quality standards did we have in mind? These were the questions tabled during the first conference of the European Forum in 1999, appropriately titled 'Making restorative justice work'. And quite obviously, 'evidence' through research was the main product academics seemed to point at as the crucial 'need'. This was the need they were preparing to respond to in their contribution to 'making restorative justice work' (Weitekamp, 2000). In this reasoning, the main problem of restorative justice was identified as its lack of credibility as an alternative for the kind of justice people were used to. The observable 'unit' of restorative justice was not 'justice' but one or another 'restorative practice' to be evaluated as such. A logical consequence was the discovery of another urgent 'need': to identify a tangible, objective way to achieve the underlying aim: if not 'justice', then let it be 'restoration'.

One of the frontline arguments in this fight between State and the 'Community' was raised in the context of juvenile justice. The execution of the 'measures' (since 1980 under authority of the communities as 'person-related' matters) ordered by a juvenile judge as a public response to juvenile delinquency (authority of the federal state) seemed to miss a proper status. Should they be considered a modality of education, rehabilitation, 'protection' or rather one of repression, punishment and retribution? Scholars like Lode Walgrave had, for quite some years, invested in searching a way out of this exhausting debate. Walgrave (1992; 2000) was very critical about any formal justice procedure, pointing at it as a source of alienation and stigmatisation. He was of the view that state justice was likely to represent a risk to be avoided, rather than it being a constructive contribution to either the person or the community involved (Vettenburg & Walgrave, 2002; Walgrave & Vettenburg, 2006). Looking for a constructive 'third way', he hoped for community to become a space for more informal processes of education to (mutual) responsibility. His search was not only relevant for the dynamics of the ongoing state reform but had also gradually become more suited to the international discourse on 'Restorative Justice' seen as a radical and fully fledged alternative to the state system of criminal justice as a whole (Walgrave, 2003; 2008; 2010). The effectiveness of restorative method had to be improved. Practitioners had to be better trained in order to offer their clients the 'best'.

Restorative policies had to be developed focusing on selecting the type of client fitting one or another kind of specific restorative approach.

This point of view was quite seductive at first sight. It provided struggling restorative practices with a formal status as 'pioneers' in building a society focused on the well-being of persons rather than on imposing social order by means of repression. It also was a motivating factor for scholars and practitioners to explore, condition and train and instil 'effective' restorative justice knowledge and potential in all sorts of social fields: restorative justice in schools, within prisons and factories, in social housing policy and so on. Restoration seemed to be the logo of a new cultural enterprise of constructing a brand new fabric of justice. But indisputably, this whole effort was likely to assist the communities in further socialising in a field traditionally and conceptually located in the hard nucleus of the democratic state (Foqué, 1992; Dupont, 2001; Gutwirth & De Hert, 2002). 'Agreement', 'peace' and 'equal right on satisfaction' seemed to become the new criteria of a 'justice' freed from the prerogatives of a fading national state. The virtue to be promoted was 'reponsible citizenship' in a society aiming at peace and restoration. In this view, criminology was seen as an science with the utopian mission of a society freed from punishment (Walgrave, 2008).

10 What kind of practice? What kind of science? For what kind of society?

It wasn't easy to see clearly what are the pros and cons of this development, carrying a strong smell of neo-liberalism. There was the dominance of a definition of 'quality' to be proved in facts and figures. Moreover, this development manifested itself in discourses on human rights, social justice and 'distributive fairness' (Mouffe, 2005; similar reasoning in Donzelot, 1994; Dean, 2004). Moreover, a rational, evidence-based social practice certainly has its credentials. Who could blame any government to try to guarantee quality of the services publicly financed? Who could blame the researcher measuring what can be measured on service providing, even in the delicate sphere of forensics? Wasn't it a matter of public responsibility to sharpen procedures for selecting the proper client and the proper case for the proper method in order to promote 'success' and avoid secondary victimisation? Who could blame the 'client' to require full information in order to be able to go for 'the best'? Who could oppose the sudden popping-up of all kinds of mediation services, some specialised for youngsters, some for cases involving severe psychological impact or sex offences and some related to neighbourhood conflicts at the level of the police? Who could deny all these practices the label of 'restorative justice' they were likely to apply for?

We saw it all happen, trying to make the best out of it. But we couldn't convince our colleagues and scholars in juvenile justice not to develop a distinctive set of services and special mediators, which eventually led to creating a separate legal framework. As mediators working in a continuous but sometimes fragile interaction with the judiciary, we often wondered whether we should enlarge our scope from crimes to 'conflicts'. On the other hand, some mediators felt a pressure to 'specialise' in this or that 'type' of crime or clients to gain self-confidence. We indeed heard of mediation services (for juveniles) with an alarming 'success-rate' of more than 70 per cent! We discussed with colleagues and scholars abroad the desirability and ethical questions related to an evidence-based selection of clients before even allowing them in mediation. Others claimed the need for disallowing any agreement without the 'quality check' of a specialised lawyer (or judge). Some suggested the providing of 'safe' standard agreements. I sometimes got the impression of a 'restorative justice' on the road of decontextualising itself from 'justice', an approach in service of a democratic society seen as a 'societé de restoration', with citizens ready to avoid conflict, with specialised mediators trained in evidence-based methods to address any problem, to solve any conflict and to eventually skip any need for criminal justice and punishment. For some, this seemed a democratic utopia. But what about the old insights of Nils Christie (1977) and Thomas Matthiessen (1974)? Could democracy really culminate into collective contentment based on 'the right to be served' or even 'the right to be satisfied' (Van Garsse, 2017; a similar reasoning was made in Mouffe, 2005; Dean, 2004)?

My own experience taught me how much the notions of crime and punishment influenced the informal sphere of mediation, rarely representing a threat or an obstacle but rather functioning as a framing of the private dialogue by situating it in public perspective (Van Garsse, 2001a; 2017; Duff, 2001: 88; Blad, 2012). Furthermore, I couldn't remember victims or offenders investing in a mediation process but ambitious *not* to obtain something particular, something exceptional and unforeseen, rather than just the average, safe and predictable. And, by the way, I couldn't remember meeting many victims or offenders 'in need of mediation'. Instead, the offering of mediation *as such* appeared to imply a challenge, to some extent even a burden (Duff, 2001): an unchosen pedagogical as well as political appeal on a postmodern kind of democratic citizenship, a certain stimulus – even for victims – to be 'responsible' and 'answerable', meaning 'capable and ready to respond' (Duff, 2001: 180). However, quite a few scholars would formulate the same in term of rights: the right of claiming particularity and actorship in front of the law, the right of democratic sovereignty as a precondition for 'doing (criminal) justice' in the context of a refined project of democracy (Derrida, 2001, 2003; Mouffe, 1989; Fitzpatrick & Joyce, 2007; Biesta, 2009).

11 From here…

Within these political viewpoints, and given the current political context in Belgium as elsewhere, the mission is clear: don't let us focus too much on restorative justice as if it were a bunch of methods and techniques 'proved useful' in many contexts. Let's not focus on marginalising criminal justice and its punishment but rather on 'de-infantilising' (infantilising meaning literally: incapable of speech) both. Let's not invest in defining restoration, but let's rather leave this definition case by case to parties involved and on providing them with spaces to speak, privately as well as publicly. Let us work on a legal guarantee that their voice will be of significance, not just for their case, but for (the rule of) society as a whole (Blad, 2012. Also see: Reggio, 2017). And above all, let us restart reflecting on the positioning and the mandate of the mediator, taking into account the underlying political message of his or her offering.

Ivo, you will have to admit, reaching a certain age can hardly suffice as an alibi for not going for this! The past years we often were each other's reflective sparring partner. I cannot imagine anything else but for this to continue. And I am looking forward to it, with both gratitude and impatience.

References

Aertsen, I. (2004) *Slachtoffer-dader bemiddeling; Een onderzoek naar de ontwikkeling van een herstelgerichte strafrechtsbedeling.* Leuven: Universitaire Pers Leuven.

Aertsen, I. & Van Garsse, L. (1996). *Tussen dader en slachtoffer: Bemiddeling in de praktijk. Onderzoeksrapport herstelbemiddeling periode 1/11/1994-31/12/1995.* Onuitg. Rapport. Leuven: KU-Leuven, Faculteit Rechtsgeleerdheid Afdeling Strafrecht, Strafvordering en Criminologie, Onderzoeksgroep Penologie en Victimologie.

Aertsen, I., Van Garsse, L. & Peters T. (1994). *Herstelbemiddeling. Onderzoeksrapport periode 1/1/1993-31/10/1994.* Onuitg. Rapport. Leuven: KU-Leuven, Faculteit Rechtsgeleerdheid Afdeling Strafrecht, Strafvordering en Criminologie, Onderzoeksgroep Penologie en Victimologie.

Bianchi, H. (1980). *Basismodellen in de criminologie.* Deventer: Van Loghum Slaterus.

Bianchi, H. (1985). *Gerechtigheid als vrijplaats: de terugkeer van het slachtoffer in ons recht.* Baarn: Ten Have.

Biesta, G. (2009). Deconstruction, justice and the vocation of education. In M. Peters & G. Biesta (eds.), *Derrida, deconstruction and the politics of pedagogy* (pp. 15-38). New York: Peter Lang Publishing.

Blad, J. (2012). Herstelrecht en de civilisering van de strafrechtspleging. In M. C. Foblets, M. Hildebrandt & R. Foqué. (eds.), *Liber amicorum René Foqué* (pp. 169-188). Gent: Larcier.

Christie, N. (1977). Conflicts as Property. *British Journal of Criminology*, 1, 1-15. doi:10.1093/oxfordjournals.bjc.a046783.

Dean, H. (2004). Human rights and welfare rights: contextualising dependency and responsibility. In H. Dean (ed.), *The ethics of welfare* (pp. 7-27). Bristol: Policy Press.

Derrida, J. (2001). *Kracht van de wet; het 'mystieke fundament van het gezag'*. Baarn: Agora.

Derrida, J. (2003). La raison du plus fort. In J. Derrida (ed.), *Voyous* (pp. 19-160). Paris: Galilée.

Donzelot, J. (1994). *L'invention du social. Essai sur le déclin des passions politiques*. Paris: Editions du Seuil.

Duff, R. A. (2001). *Punishment, communication and community*. Oxford: Oxford University Press.

Dupont, L. (1980a). Toespraak van L. Dupont, voorzitter redactie Panopticon. *Panopticon*, 1(2), 103-106.

Dupont, L. (1980b). Waarover men niet (meer) spreekt. Een eentonig verhaal over strafrechtelijke hervormingspogingen in België. *Panopticon*, 1, 445-449.

Dupont, L. (1986). *Welzijnswerk in de schaduw van het strafrecht*. Leuven: Acco.

Dupont, L. (1987). Polemische bespiegelingen over strafrechtshervorming. *Panopticon*, 8(5-6), 385-398.

Dupont, L. (2001). Herstelrecht, afscheid van een vergeldend strafrecht? In L. Dupont & F. Hutsebaut (eds.), *Herstelrecht tussen toekomst en verleden. Liber Amicorum Tony Peters* (pp. 209-224). Leuven: Universitaire Pers Leuven.

Eliaerts, C. (1984). Het Nieuwe Realisme in het strafrecht en de criminele politiek. *Panopticon*, 5(1), 1-9.

Fitzpatrick, P. & Joyce, R. (2007). The normality and the exception in Democracy's Empire. *Journal of Law and Society* 34(1), 65-76. doi:10.1111/j.1467-6478.2007.00382.x.

Foqué, R. (1992). *De ruimte van het recht*. Arnhem: Gouda Quint.

Foqué, R. & 't Hart, A.C. (1990). *Instrumentaliteit en rechtsbescherming*. Antwerpen: Kluwer/Gouda Quint.

Gutwirth, S. (1993). *Waarheidsaanspraken in recht en wetenschap*. Brussels: VUBpress/Maklu.

Gutwirth, S. & De Hert, P (2002). Grondslagentheoretische variaties op de grens tussen het strafrecht en het burgerlijk recht. Perspectieven op schuld- risico- en strafrechtelijke aansprakelijkheid, slachtofferclaims,buitengerechtelijke afdoening en restorative justice. In K. Boonen, C. P. M. Cleiren, R. Foqué & Th. de Roos (eds.), *De Weging van 't Hart. Idealen, waarden en taken van het strafrecht* (pp. 121-170). Deventer: Kluwer.

Gutwirth, S. & De Hert, P. (2011). Punir ou réparer? Une fausse alternative. In F. Tulkens, Y. Cartuyvels & C. Guillain (eds.), *La peine dans tous ces états* (pp. 67-88). Brussels: Larcier.

Hulsman, L. (1972). Kriteria voor strafbaarstelling. In E. de la Porte, C. de Boer, H. de Doelder, W. van Gelder, M. Mulder, F. Orie, H. de Ruijter, L. Smoor-van Son & P. Veling (eds.), *Strafrecht te-recht? Over dekriminalisering en depenalisering* (pp. 80-92). Baarn, The Netherlands: In den Toren.

Hulsman, L. (1975, December). Justitie en welzijn. *Delikt en delinkwent*, 5, 599-605.

Lauwaert, K. (2008). *Herstelrecht en procedurele waarborgen.* Apeldoorn: Maklu.

Matthiesen, T. (1974). *The politics of abolition.* London: Martin Robertson.

Mouffe, C. (1989). Radical democracy: modern or postmodern? In A. Ross (ed.), *Universal abandon? The politics of postmodernism* (pp. 31-45). Durham: Duke University Press.

Mouffe, C. (2005). *Over het politieke.* Kampen: Klement/Pelckmans.

Peters, T. (1993). Slachtofferschap: probleemanalyse, sociale en penale reacties. In T. Peters & J. Goethals (eds.). *De achterkant van de criminaliteit* (pp. 5-90). Deurne: Kluwer Rechtswetenschappen.

Peters, T. (1996). Probleemoplossing en herstel als functies van de straf. *Panopticon*, 16, 555-569.

Peters, T. (2000). Victim-offender mediation: reality and challenges. In The European Forum for Victim-Offender Mediation and Restorative Justice (ed.), *Victim-offender mediation in Europe. Making restorative justice work* (pp. 9-15). Leuven: University Press Leuven.

Reggio, T. (2017). The broken tablets of Moses and the exodus from (post-) modernity. On rethinking the role and the rule of law in a dialogical way. In I. Aertsen & B. Pali. (eds.), *Critical restorative justice* (pp. 257-281). Oxford: Hart Publishing.

Staelens, M. (1987). Mediation: een alternatieve vorm van conflictbeslechting. *Panopticon*, 8(4), 321-334.

Van Garsse, L. (2001a) Op zoek naar herstelrecht: Overwegingen na jaren bemiddelingswerk. *Panopticon*, 22(5), 423-446.

Van Garsse, L. (2001b). Praktijk en wetenschap. Drie bedrijven uit de ontwikkelingsgeschiedenis van een bemiddelingspraktijk. In L. Dupont & F. Hutsebaut (eds.), *Herstelrecht tussen toekomst en verleden* (pp. 515-530). Leuven: Universitaire Pers Leuven.

Van Garsse, L. (2008). De implementatie van de herstelbemiddeling: veranderingsmanagement in samenspraak. *Panopticon*, 29(5), 14-31.

Van Garsse, L. (2011). (Herstel)recht en criminologie: toelichting bij een herstelgerichte dagvaarding. In I. Aertsen, T. Daems, A. Haaren, F. Hutsebaut & J. Maesschalck (eds.), *Deviante wetenschap; Het domein van de criminologie* (pp. 249-260). Leuven: Acco.

Van Garsse, L. (2013). Zwischen Zynismus und Nostalgie. Die Umsetzung von Restorative Justice in Strafsachen in Belgien. *Infodienst. Rundbrief zum Täter-Opfer-Ausgleich*, 46, 43-50.

Van Garsse, L. (2017). Restorative justice and democratic citizenship: al new social pedagogy or back to 'social defence'? In I. Aertsen & B. Pali (eds.), *Critical restorative Justice* (pp. 127-141). Oxford: Hart Publishing.

Van Gerven, W. (1973). *Het beleid van de rechter.* Antwerpen: Standaard uitgeverij.

Vettenburg, N. & Walgrave, L. (2002). Een integratie van theorieën over persisterende delinquentie: maatschappelijke kwetsbaarheid. In P. Goris & L. Walgrave (eds.), *Van kattenkwaad en erger. Actuele thema's uit de jeugdcriminologie* (pp. 81-100). Leuven: Garant.

Walgrave, L. (1992). Herstelrecht, een derde weg in het gerechtelijk antwoord op jeugddelinquentie. *Panopticon*, 13(1), 24-42.

Walgrave, L. (2000). *Met het oog op herstel.* Leuven, Belgium: Universitaire Pers Leuven.

Walgrave, L. (2003). Introduction. In L. Walgrave (ed.), *Repositioning restorative justice* (pp. VII-XII). Cullompton: Willan.

Walgrave, L. (2008). *Restorative justice, self-interest and responsible citizenship.* Cullompton: Willan Publishing.

Walgrave, L. (2010). Een maximalistische visie op herstelrecht. *Tijdschrift voor Herstelrecht*, 10(1), 21-35.

Walgrave, L. & Vettenburg, N. (eds.). (2006). *Herstelgericht groepsoverleg. Nieuwe wegen in de aanpak van jeugddelinquentie en tuchtproblemen.* Leuven: Lannoo.

Weitekamp, E. (2000). Research on victim-offender mediation. Findings and needs for the future. In The European Forum for Victim-Offender Mediation and Restorative Justice (ed.), *Victim-Offender Mediation in Europe. Making Restorative Justice Work* (pp. 99-119). Leuven: University Press Leuven.

Wright, M. (2000). Restorative justice, for whose benefit? In The European Forum for Victim-Offender Mediation and Restorative Justice (ed.), *Victim-offender mediation in Europe. Making restorative justice work* (pp. 19-38). Leuven: University Press Leuven.

The restorative pyramid: a framework for change towards a restorative prison

Johan Deklerck

1 Introduction

Prof. Dr Ivo Aertsen worked as a psychologist in prison for many years until he started working in the early 1990s with Prof. Tony Peters in the then 'Penology and Victimology' research group. A few years later I could also become a part of this research group. Starting from the perspective of victimology and the concern for the victim, this research group increasingly started focusing on restorative justice and restorative practices. A connection between the prison and restorative justice was also self-evident as it formed one of the common threads in the very extensive research work of Prof. Ivo Aertsen. With this he continued the life's work of his predecessor Prof. Tony Peters. With a lot of warmth I remember the enthusiasm, imagination, high ethical standards, and passion that I experienced over the years while working in collaboration with Tony, Ivo and a proficient group of colleagues: a unique island in a very tough, competitive and mostly ego-driven scientific world. Ivo Aertsen submitted his doctorate in 2001. When I defended my doctoral research in 2005, I also included a part about a restorative prison. This perfectly matched the great ambitions and the work of Prof. Ivo Aertsen. Looking back, I feel like a modest 'partner in crime'. In this contribution, I talk about restorative justice in prison at one of the intersections of Ivo's life's work.

It remains a curious fact that we *deprive someone's freedom* as a punishment but that, subsequently, we do not systematically include working on *restoring this freedom* as the core function of the detention process. This should logically be a core task: gradually restoring freedom around the offence and towards the victim and the society. Committing crime is often connected with a mental loss of freedom. This loss of freedom was already present, sometimes long before someone was convicted and imprisoned. With passionate murder, corruption, addiction and drug-related crimes, escalating conflicts, violence, pedosexuality, terrorism, perpetrators gradually become more and more mentally trapped in a compulsive experience of reality and rob themselves of their inner freedom. They are ruled by obsessive thoughts and strong emotions and see criminal acts often as the only way out: an expression of mental loss of freedom, an inner captivity. In this sense, the deprivation of liberty, detention, is an expression of what was already present before the offence. The detention perpetuates and seals an existing reality institutionally. It is a 'frozen' end situation of a psychological and social reality confirmed by the conviction.

However, this *end situation* should at the same time be the *start* of a major order to restore the lost freedom. This expresses itself in redress towards the victim and the wider society, which cannot be done without inner redress. Becoming free from 'destructive entitlement' (Boszormenyi-Nagy, 1987) and own victimhood and guilt experiences is a condition for taking responsibility for the past and building a fulfilling life. Prisoners have proven through their offence and their broader life story of being hurt and continued hurting to such an extent that they cannot bear their freedom in society without damaging themselves and others. 'Freedom' must be learned and restored. This also applies to their victim and the circle of parents, family, children, friends, stakeholders and the wider society. They are also held hostage by the offence and suffer material, emotional and existential loss of freedom. Prison is the context for the perpetrator to work intentionally and systematically on restoring this freedom.

In my thinking, 'freedom loss' and 'freedom redress' are central. In order to broaden the narrow view on redress (such as paying debts, mediation, a letter to the victim), I developed the model of the *restorative pyramid* in my doctoral research (2005). This is not to be confused with the 'prevention pyramid' (Deklerck, 2011), another scientific idea that I have developed. It is important to really take care of the prisoner and the inseparably linked victim and the wider society. If prison is the context for this, then it must look different from the way it looks now. There is a need for a penitentiary reform with a restorative justice orientation. Only then can prison be a supporting context that facilitates and activates redress in its different aspects. The restorative pyramid offers a conceptual framework to achieve this. It proves to be a useful, scientifically based instrument for rethinking the prison as restorative detention. It broadens, gives direction, organises and integrates.

In the following, I elaborate the model for structural and cultural changes towards a restorative prison culture, bridging prison and redress, two major pillars in the life's work of Prof. Ivo Aertsen. First, I discuss the notion of 'loss of freedom" for perpetrator and the victim. Then, I focus on the prison with the restoration of inner and relational freedom as a goal. Restoration of freedom starts with the facts but should be extended to fully master the basic skills of life itself, in order to earn a place in society. I conclude by describing the restorative pyramid as a helpful instrument to achieve this.

2 From 'the deprivation of freedom' to the 'restoration of freedom'

Victims of serious conflicts, long-term painful experiences during childhood, violence and crimes are held hostage because of these experiences. What they suffered determines their lives and their struggles. Traumatic experiences prevent them from living an open, free and flourishing life. In other words, their flow of life is 'blocked' to a greater or lesser extent (Deklerck, 2005). Pain experiences keep revolving in their thoughts and feelings, both consciously and unconsciously directing their lives. They end up living increasingly in a 'mental prison'. The main result is loss of freedom. This loss of freedom prevents them from taking control of their lives, freely choosing and doing the things that give joy, going on with their lives in full power and fulfilling themselves and developing their future. The full life is strongly curtailed by their mental prison. This prevents them from psychologically integrating their past as 'food' or an opportunity for the future. Feelings such as permanent overload, panic attacks, stress, fear of others, the telephone, the doorbell, certain images and smells, being home alone, and going out determine their actions.

Loss of freedom is the most fundamental damage caused by an offence, which in turn is often an expression of a broader life story of reduced freedom. Consequently, the restoration of freedom becomes the central task. This applies to the perpetrator, the victim and the wider social network. The journey from 'loss of freedom' to 'restoration of freedom' thus becomes a foundation for a restorative detention. What is already being done about restoration, compensation, paying the debt, a letter to the victim and so on is given a place within this much broader 'restoration of freedom'. These are no longer separate elements but part of a more fundamental perspective. Returning to the reality that was there before the offence that is now part of one's life is impossible. But what has happened can lose its hostage-taking power and simply become part of a wider life story, as many other small and big experiences. The perpetrator, victim and their environment can regain their freedom, 'close a chapter' and start over again. Whoever works on redress will regain freedom. In my doctoral research (2005) I defined this notion as:

> Redress is a multi-layered concept that means that any damage caused by an offence is undone to such an extent that the persons involved must be able to lead the same qualitative life (see below) as before the facts. The damage or suffering as a result of the facts can be considered as multi-layered, whereby the material-physical, psycho-emotional and ethical-existential component can be represented to a greater or lesser extent. This damage can be found in the personal functioning of the victim, the perpetrator and in the functioning of (them in) their environment in decreasing involvement. It expresses itself in a reduced freedom ... Redress is expressed in an increasing material, psychological and existential freedom that may have been reduced by the parties involved to varying degrees, as a result of the offence. Fundamental redress also means that possible factors that have led to the offence, such as victim experiences of the perpetrator, aggression-provoking attitudes of the victim or criminogenetic factors in the environment are also taken into account, and contribute to a

> deeper, existential redress which means again fully being connected with one's flow of life. (Deklerck, 2005: 241-242)

Restoration of freedom is central to this definition. The life story, social fabric and environmental factors are partly constituent for the run-up to the offence and for redress. Redress around the facts is thus supported by a much broader fundamental redress.

3 Restorative justice and the unruly prison reality

The idea of redress as a basic goal is not self-evident within the current prison reality. Dupont and Foqué (1998: 145) speak of the 'almost complete absence of a restorative dimension, both within the current penal regulations and within the penal praxis'. The structural framework of the prisons is outdated and leaves little room for fundamental renewal (Snacken, 2002: 131-134). Prisons are very cumbersome structures. Even small changes have to be guided through complex procedures and often take a lot of effort. The strong focus on external and internal security and the stereotypical image in the media constitute additional obstacles for a humanising prison policy, let alone a policy of fundamental redress. The current prison regime now stands in the way of this and thus hinders the chances of prisoners, victims and society.

It is not evident that prisoners spontaneously reflect on their offence and the consequences for the parties directly involved, their families, the victim and his environment and society. After all, the strict penitentiary system can mean that the involvement with the outside world and therefore also with the victim decreases steadily during their prison stay. Detainees hereby become estranged from their offence and use a variety of neutralisation mechanisms (Vandeurzen, Verhoeven, Verstraete, Willemsens & Peters, 1999: 31). It often happens that a prisoner wishes to accept his or her sentence in the first phase of his or her detention and is also willing to settle his or her debt to his victim, but he or she is soon overwhelmed by the numerous secondary effects of his or her deprivation of liberty. For many detainees, the detention conditions and the 'actual regime constellation are a breeding ground to justify or rationalise their detention situation and to experience themselves, together with their fellow sufferers, as victims of an unjust or at least nonsense system' (Neys, 2001: 412).

Redress, however, could be the common thread and the core task of the detention. This would benefit the perpetrator, the victim and the wider society and be central to the ambitions that we have with detainees, but which are not being realised now.

> The prisoner must be given the opportunity to be able to express problems, failures, including his feelings in relation to the committed acts (feelings of guilt or lack thereof). An imprisonment that shields or makes this confrontation

> impossible, alienates the detainee from his personal and social history and offers a substitute world in which institutional-subcultural values and meanings prevail. (Peters, 1991: 293)

Reforming prisons into places where meaningful work is being done on restorative processes is a major challenge. For this we need a goal and a conceptual framework that provides tools that can guide the process of change. The goal would be the 'redress of freedom' described previously (see also Deklerck, 2005). As a conceptual framework, I propose the 'restorative pyramid' which I describe as follows.

4 The restorative pyramid

4.1 *The model*

'Redress of freedom', as described earlier, is understood broadly and comprehensively. Redress is first and foremost about the offence, but it is also about the life course, the perpetrator, his or her social context and all that went wrong there. Redress is further about acquiring all kinds of specific skills that are often lacking in perpetrators. It is ultimately also about *learning to live* as a basic skill itself. Redress of someone's material, emotional-psychic and existential freedom thus encompasses a broad spectrum of interrelated elements. These elements are initially centred on the facts, but they become wider and increasingly more indirect in relation to the offence. Redress is therefore a multi-layered concept, visually presented as follows in the restorative pyramid (Deklerck, 2005: 277-294).

Fig. 1. Restorative pyramid (Deklerck, 2005)

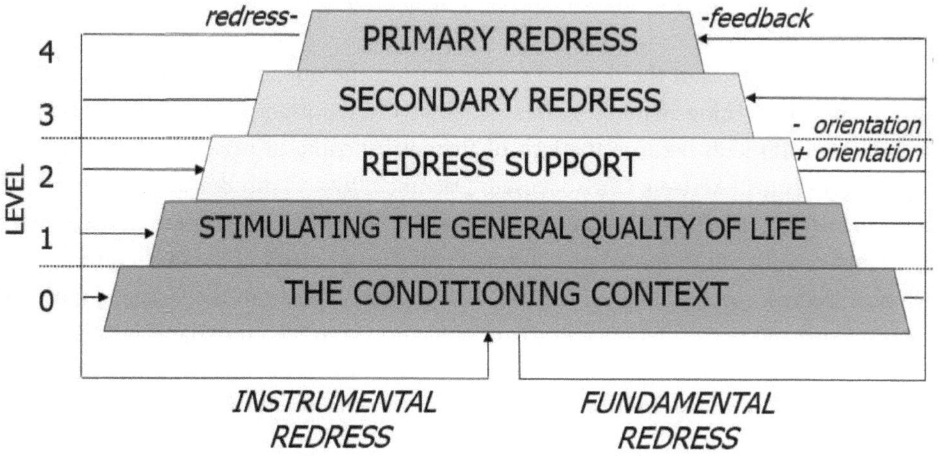

The restorative pyramid is structured in five levels: 4-0. Level 4 is about 'primary redress' which relates directly to the facts and circumstances. Level 3 is about 'secondary redress' which deals with the direct contextual aspects of the offence, such as elements from the life course of the perpetrator and of the victim, which have contributed to an increasing loss of freedom and to the offence. Level 2 is about 'redress support' which contextualises the redress levels 4 and 3. This level is about positive learning elements. Working on these elements increases the chances of success for the higher levels. For example, someone who is not proficient in language and, therefore, quickly becomes angry can learn communication skills. Level 1 is about stimulating the general quality of life. It is the general (detention) framework that does not focus specifically on redress but on 'learning to live' itself. This seems obvious but is often not acquired by detainees within their former home situation or the time they spent in institutions. This level is the foundation and is part of an integral and fundamental redress. Action levels 1 to 4 take place within a broader social context or the 0 level. In the following, I provide a brief description of the levels and some of the main characteristics of the pyramid.

4.2 *Level 4: primary redress*

This level stands for 'redress of the offence' in the narrow sense. Every offence brings direct damage, especially for the victim. However, the damage is usually not limited to this. There is also damage to the family, partners, parents and children of the victim. They also suffer the process of destruction, material loss, pain, sadness, powerlessness, mourning, fear of moving freely and spend sleepless nights. Material, emotional and existential damage takes an endless number of forms, but it has the common feature of 'loss of freedom'. The damage that results from an offence is also present in those who are close to the perpetrator, such as a parent, partner, child or friend. Often they also feel harmed, disappointed and sad. Feelings of failure, co-responsibility, guilt and shame, fear and uncertainty for the future, the search for understanding and compassion, and fear of loss occupy their lives.

The actual redress of the damage resulting from the offence is most obvious in the agreements concerning material redress, such as the reimbursement of the civil party. This is often difficult because the lack of financial income in prison makes it hard to repay larger sums (Aertsen, Christiaensen, Daeninck, Van Camp & Van Win, 2001: 19-26). Other forms of damage repair are also possible. They are sometimes imposed by the court, but can also result from a mediation. It concerns a variety of possible issues such as symbolic redress, practical agreements such as staying away from the victim, conditions for residence and work, therapy and so on. Mediation with regard to damage and redress is important for both the victim and the perpetrator. It helps to place the offence better in their life story. This can contribute to an existential integration of the offence into their flow of life. If the victim is not open to mediation, the confrontation with victimhood experiences of others can also be of importance for the offender. The experiences teach the offender to empathise with the other party and to experience the depth of the damage from much closer. The prison must play an important role in facilitating this, developing 'structural options/channels so that they [perpetrators] can gain insight into their actions and the consequences thereof for the victim, for their own family and society' (Vandeurzen et al., 1999: 24).

4.3 *Level 3: secondary redress*

At level 3, we are concerned with 'secondary redress', which tackles the problematic side of the prisoner as a person. The offence can only be understood if it is placed in a broader context, such as the 'problematic life course' of the offender and his or her personality development in a broad sense. Often, for example, personal victim experiences in a broad sense, such as problems with growing up, may be directly related to the offence. If problems at this level are not resolved in substance, then the unfortunate life of the offender is continued (Neys, 2001: 410). Problems due to existential injury, including recidivism, then continue. For offenders with a hard past that mainly consists of debris and chaos, working on redress is a basic task. It can help them to acquire a basic orientation in their life and to focus on their future in a more positive way. Fundamental issues can be discussed here, such as learning to deal with loss, neglect, being rejected, existential pain, anger and aggression, fears, powerlessness, iniquity and other big questions of life.

Various forms of therapy such as psychotherapy, talk therapy, trauma processing, social-emotional bodywork, psychiatric counselling and so on belong at this level. Open conversation and evenings of encounter between detainees, victims, staff and others are possibilities. They bring together experiences about the course of life, damage, detention experience and redress in an open and authentic way. They increase self-insight, problem awareness and a sense of responsibility. They contribute to a growing awareness about the relationship between life course, lifestyle and criminal career. In prisons, there is generally very little commitment to such goals. We can even speak of 'the absence and/or chronic understaffing of a professional counseling and supporting framework' (Neys, 1994: 301). The psychosocial services mainly work on evaluation reports for conditional release, and '(this) has the consequence that there is not much time left for crisis support, pre-therapeutic programs and other accompanying tasks' (Casselman, 2001: 111). Furthermore, problems can rarely be reduced exclusively to the person of the offender but must be understood from the 'perpetrator in his wider context'. The system of therapeutic approaches becomes important to consider. The person-centred approach is then opened up: the perpetrator as part of complex, often broken, networks over generations can be taken into account for redress.

4.4 *Level 2: redress support*

Level 2 is about redress support. The special situation and the individuality of the prisoner are taken as the starting point for a range of different initiatives and interventions. These again take into consideration common factors such as the background and life history of the prisoner as a basis for planning interventions with a *positive* orientation. Such interventions do not have a therapeutic purpose but contribute to increasing the basic skills and insights into (daily) life, raising the quality of life and responding to the special individuality of the prisoner. Such 'redress support' activities, by strengthening the person and his or her environment, increases the chances of redress at higher levels. Redress support activities can be, for example, about training social skills, work competencies, learning to function in structured environments, relaxation exercises or mindfulness. Likewise, working on communication skills or relationship building, gaining insight into differences between men and women, learning to deal with sexuality belong at this level. Working on health, on the basic physical and psychological condition where the path of life has caused damage can also support redress. Learning daily skills, such as cleaning up the cell, learning a day and night rhythm, learning to cook, learning to apply for a job, using a library, speaking for a group, being able to deal with multiculturalism, learning to handle money, using medication properly and assertiveness training, contribute to an integral redress process (Brouckmans, De Jaegher, Vandeurzen, Verhoeven & Verstraete, 1998: 17-18). The creation of the basic conditions for functional reintegration in society, such as arranging the various administrative procedures (sickness fund, identity documents, social services etc.), finding accommodation and debt repayment, also belong at this level of redress. These skills make a person grow as a person and make a social (re)integration possible.

4.5 *Level 1: Stimulating the general quality of life*

Level 1 stands for stimulating the general quality of life. The prison can be a living environment that promotes fundamental human qualities. The 'learning to live' is central to this objective. 'Creating a humane prison environment' starts with the organisation of daily life within the walls that is as normal as possible and that resembles the life outside the prison as much as possible (Dupont & Foqué, 1998). This can be further enhanced with the introduction of a small-scale detention. In 1977, Wim Ter Horst wrote a book addressed to remedial educationalists in the care of the disabled, titled *The Restoration of Normal Life* (Ter Horst, 1988). His ambition was to draw attention to a forgotten dimension within institutions for children with disabilities. He described what he called 'dialogal basic forms' as the foundations of daily life. He distinguishes ten such forms: 'eating, drinking, caring, playing, celebrating, touching, going out, working, learning, talking.'

These 'dialogal basic forms' form the basis for our lives, and (all the more) for living in special situations, such as people in detention. They form a fundamental language with which people relate to each other. It is about fundamental, not specifically therapeutic, qualities. At first glance, they seem banal, but are far more significant than we think. Anyone who has properly integrated these basic forms into his or her life acquires a high-quality social life. Anyone who is able to talk, touch, work, care for, celebrate, learn, go out and so on has made a whole evolution on a personal level and has developed a good basis for his or her personal existential development. The 'dialogal basic forms' can play a key role in redress. Daily life is a permanent concatenation of these basic forms.

For the penitentiary context, they can form a strong foundation for stimulating the general quality of life. They are an agogic interpretation of life in detention. What or how one eats, drinks, touches, cares, talks, plays, expresses a fundamental life skill. For many prisoners, these seemingly obvious 'dialogal forms' are problematic. Eating, drinking, learning, playing, touching are areas where things often go wrong. Many prisoners have acquired few such skills from childhood, and this 'deficiency' is only perpetuated within the prison regime. Disrupted relationships with food, for example, might express themselves in a drinking problem or the choice for unhealthy food. Things like taking care of oneself, but also being able to touch or being touched, are often disturbed. For many, the need for touching transforms into physical violence or sexual aggression. Many cannot lose or fail to be absorbed in a relaxed way in a game process. For many detainees, working is not obvious. Many have had a very irregular working career, partly due to the lack of meaningful work in the labor market but also to personal inability. For some, having an open talk, especially if this has to do with feelings, can lead to major problems, and they might lack listening skills or might not be able to express themselves without rough language.

The basic forms are not spontaneously realised, let alone being structurally built into the prison regime. Often the problems faced by detainees in this area are exacerbated by the prison regime and the prison culture. Dervaux (1993: 233) points to this problem:

> Restoring the ordinary also means that the custodian brings up the politeness again. The wider and freer the regime, the more important this factor becomes. E.g. around the showers, and also e.g. where this occurs during the joint meals. 'Restoring the ordinary' also means that people can talk again and think about other things than just the immediate detention data.

These basic forms are the foundation on which more specific redress can be grafted. They have therefore an intrinsically restorative purpose. A prison structure could promote a restorative culture based on this purpose. The current focus on small-scale prisons with communities offers an incredible opportunity to reach this objective. Level 1 is a basis for more focused redress at the higher levels of the pyramid. It is the context that is as normal as possible through which prisoners learn to live together.

4.6 *Level 0: the conditioning context*

Level 0 occupies a separate place relative to the four other action levels. Level 1 to 4 are inside, whereas level 0 is outside the walls. This level is therefore about the broader social context. It is also about social changes and political decisions and policies that have an impact on what is happening inside prison, about the security discourse in politics and the media, about evolutions in crime figures and about other external factors that have an impact on prison life. For example, there is the wider restorative justice movement viewed as an alternative to traditional punishment. By contrast, there is a call for a more repressive, harsh approach to crime, tougher penalties, longer detention and a reluctance for alternative sanctions. This has a direct repercussion on the development of a restorative detention. Social developments have a direct impact on what happens inside the walls, making sometimes certain choices very difficult.

5 Elaborating further concepts

5.1 *Hierarchy*

There is a hierarchical relationship between the different levels. The higher levels are supported by the broader levels below. They support and stimulate the concrete redress after the offence, the individual redress process, which is at level 3 (the perpetrator) and 4 (the act). The process of redress after the offence and individual redress (higher levels) is the ultimate goal of restorative detention. It is of course much better achieved if it is bathed in a climate of integral and fundamental redress (lower levels) as a rich breeding ground. The restorative pyramid is about broadening and strengthening redress to a basic quality of life itself. The levels must all be expanded in their full width. If the lower levels have not been sufficiently developed, the individual restorative process will only receive little support. Restoring freedom then becomes more difficult to achieve.

5.2 *Positive - negative orientation*

Levels 1 and 2 focus on positive qualities, specific constructive elements and daily life. They are the supporting context for redress. They are not problem-oriented, such as the higher levels 3 and 4 that focus on problems, repair of the damage and personal redress. The two orientations, the negative one at levels 3 and 4 and the positive one at levels 1 and 2 are complementary. A balance is necessary. Problems and therapeutic needs deserve the necessary attention, but a one-sided problem-oriented attention makes an overall positive outcome difficult. Attention to positive qualities must therefore be proportionately present. It is about the life behind the damage and redress itself.

5.3 *Instrumental and fundamental redress*

At the bottom of the pyramid there is a split between instrumental and fundamental redress. This division divides all levels vertically into instrumental and fundamental redress. *Instrumental* redress refers to functional and practical skills such as practicing a profession, dealing with money, being technically competent, reading, writing, administration, housework and paying debts. These skills enable and support a person to continue with everyday life. *Fundamental* redress refers to the personal development path of the convict: working on inner processes, increasing inner freedom, connectedness and autonomy. Deeper existential questions, which can easily come up in case of serious problems, are discussed here. Necessary care must be given to both poles of redress. The fundamental redress, the existential dimension, is often undervalued or forgotten, but 'creating and keeping open the room for self-redress for this category of convicts will mean that they are made aware of the dignity of their own human existence' (Neys, 2001: 409).

5.4 *Redress feedback*

This concept refers to the arrows on the side of the pyramid, which connect all levels. A lot can be learned from one level for the others. For example, mediation (level 4) may show that withdrawal for drugs is needed or aggression therapy (level 3) or mindfulness and non-violent resilience (level 2). An institution's past challenges the person concerned to gain positive experiences and learn from them. The signals at the levels of personal and damage redress, levels 3 and 4, can serve as a continuous adjustment at the levels of redress support and life skills (levels 2 and 1). Permanent feedback between all levels can promote holistic and integral redress. The individual restorative process is a dynamic process. Redress feedback can be used to respond in a very direct way to developments, changes and needs for an integrated process of regaining freedom.

6 Conclusion

At the interface between restorative justice and prison, an interesting and creative field can arise for an integral redress, in spite of the social reality of prison. Those who love living together in freedom cannot do without thinking for an alternative and restorative settlement after the offence. Prisons are currently places of 'custody' until prisoners are released after their sentence, without actually being able to bear the freedom. But freedom must be acquired by intentionally and systematically working on redress.

In this contribution, freedom is the core of what it is all about. The offence itself is already a logical consequence of a loss of inner freedom. Imprisonment after the conviction is the institutional seal of an already existing psychological and social loss of freedom on a material, emotional-psychological and existential level. It is a reality for all involved in an offence, including the perpetrator and the victim in their social context.

Loss of freedom should therefore include the invitation to redress freedom, including material restitution and all elements that involve a classical restorative process. But there's more. Redress is a multi-layered concept that also includes underlying redress levels into the level of learning to live itself. It is this integral and fundamental redress that can form the basis of a restorative detention, with the redress of freedom as a focus, and the restorative pyramid as a framework. This can provide an operational framework for prisons that take up the challenge of a restorative detention. The 'restorative pyramid' framework is currently used in various practices in Belgium as a framework that leads towards restorative prisons. In this way, it hopefully contributes to expand the importance of the work of Prof. Ivo Aertsen, the core of which has been the implementation of restorative justice in a socially committed and scientific way.

References

Aertsen, I. (2001). *Slachtoffer-daderbemiddeling: een onderzoek naar de ontwikkeling van een herstelgerichte strafrechtsbedeling* (Diss. Doct. in de Criminologische Wetenschappen). Faculteit Rechtsgeleerdheid, Afdeling Strafrecht, Strafvordering en Criminologie, KULeuven, Leuven.

Aertsen, I., Christiaensen, S., Daeninck, P., Van Camp, T. & Van Win, T. (2001). *Wetenschappelijke ondersteuning van het project herstelgerichte detentie.* Brussel: Ministerie van Justitie.

Boszormenyi-Nagy, I. (1987). *Foundations of contextual therapy.* New York: Brunner Mazel.

Brouckmans, P., De Jaegher, K., Vandeurzen, I., Verhoeven, H. & Verstraete, A. (1998). *Vrijheidsstraf en herstelrecht: kan dat?* Leuven: KULeuven, Faculteit rechtsgeleerdheid, Afdeling strafrecht, strafvordering en criminologie.

Casselman, J. (2001). De gevangenis als psychisch ongezond leefmilieu. In L. Dupont & F. Hutsebaut (eds.), *Herstelrecht tussen toekomst en verleden: liber amicorum Tony Peters* (pp. 99-114). Leuven: Universitaire pers.

Deklerck, J. (2005). *Delinquentie en haar context bekeken vanuit een cyclisch model van 'integratie-desintegratie'* (Diss. doct. KU Leuven in de Criminologische Wetenschappen). Afd. Strafrecht, Strafvordering en Criminologie, Leuven.

Deklerck, J. (2011). *De preventiepiramide. Preventie van probleemgedrag in het onderwijs.* Leuven: Acco.

Derveaux, W. (1994). Het werk van de gevangenisbewaarder. In A. Neys, T. Peters, et al. (eds.), *Tralies in de weg: het Belgische gevangeniswezen: historiek, balans en perspectieven* (pp. 211-225). Leuven: Universitaire pers.

Dupont, L. & Foqué, R. (1998). *Op weg naar een beginselenwet gevangeniswezen: proeve van voorontwerp van wet gevangeniswezen en tenuitvoerlegging van vrijheidsstraffen,* Leuven: Universitaire pers.

Neys, A. (1994). Pastorale en levensbeschouwelijke begeleiding. In A. Neys, T. Peters, et al. (eds.), *Tralies in de weg: het Belgische gevangeniswezen: historiek, balans en perspectieven* (pp. 297-332). Leuven: Universitaire pers.

Neys, A. (2001). Over de 'herstelgerichtheid' van het gevangenispastoraat. In: L. Dupont & F. Hutsebaut (eds.), *Herstelrecht tussen toekomst en verleden: liber amicorum Tony Peters* (pp. 399-424). Leuven: Universitaire pers.

Peters, T. (1991). Waarheen met de uitvoering van de vrijheidsstraf. *Panopticon*, 293-301.

Snacken, S. (ed.) (2002). *Strafrechtelijk beleid in beweging.* Brussel: VUB Press.

Ter Horst, W. (1988). *Het herstel van het gewone leven.* Orthovisies 5. Groningen: Wolters-Noordhoff Groningen (3e druk).

Vandeurzen, I., Verhoeven, H., Verstraete, A., Willemsens, J. & Peters, T. (1999). *Slachtoffer- en herstelgerichte detentie. Visie- en activiteitenverslag.* Leuven: KULeuven, Onderzoeksgroep Penologie en Victimologie.

Restorative justice and its adjacent fields: complementary or competing?

Lode Walgrave

Dear Ivo,

As an experienced emeritus I must begin with a warning and a reassuring message. At the beginning of your new status, you will barely feel the difference. It comes gradually. After a few years, you will be involved less than before, and it is not always clear whether this is because you have chosen to 'emeritate' elsewhere or because they have forgotten to invite you. Gradually, you will enjoy being released from the continuous responsibility for projects, the functioning of your team or the follow-up of students. Lurking deadlines will fade away, allowing you to be selective and to concentrate on what you think is worth the effort. You will find your 'emeritarian cruise control'. Life will become more relaxed, leaving time for your beloved ones, the concerts to attend, the novels to read, the footpaths to walk. But the criminologist in you, the continuous search for better ways of doing justice after the occurrence of offending, will never settle down. You will have to live with a 'restorative justice drive'.

Restorative justice seeped into KU Leuven-criminology via two tracks. In the period 1980-1990, Tony Peters was promoter of the Research Group on Penology and Victimology. His exploration gradually brought him to understand how much mediation could serve the interests and needs of victims. In the meantime, I directed the Research Group on Youth Criminology. I discovered restorative justice as a possible 'third way', to escape the unfruitful dilemma between a punitive and a rehabilitative response to youth offending.

While both Tony and I had our offices in the same building, only a few doors away from each other, it took several years before we realised that our explorations were in fact going in the same stream of thoughts.

When Tony retired in 2001 and I in 2003, the criminology activities were reshuffled, and you succeeded us as the 'caretaker' of the upcoming restorative justice tradition in criminology at the KU Leuven. You took the lead of the Research Line Restorative Justice and Victimology. Unfortunately, Tony could not enjoy his retirement many years. I could, and I enjoyed very much the perseverance and the talent with which you brought the restorative justice heritage to further prosperity. Restorative justice became an international lighthouse of criminology at the KU Leuven. It was a pleasure to me to serve as an accomplice, a supporting sideliner in your endeavour.

Restorative justice as a field of scientific activities is subjected to theoretical and empirical critics. As a movement for change, restorative justice is confronted with institutional obstacles. Some comments and objections witness lack of understanding, misinterpretations or even irrational resistance. Well-aimed scientific critics, however, are very welcome, as they provoke further research, reflection and debate. And institutional obstacles help us learn that dreams are to be actualised in reality and they help us to temper our expectations.

Content-wise, three sources of criticism address restorative justice. The first source is the belief that punishment should remain being the mainstream response to offending. The second one is the defence of the rehabilitative approach to (juvenile) offending. The third source of criticism has its origins in the fear that restorative justice responses may endanger the genuine attention for victims' needs and interests.

This short contribution is typical for an emeritus on cruise control: relaxed, without any scientific pretentions and without bibliographic references. I will not comment on the relation/tension between the punitive premise and restorative justice. It has been argued in many publications, also by myself, that restorative justice and punishment are two different responses based on rather opposed visions on man and society. But that is less clear regarding the two other approaches, which I shall address here shortly. When I tried to prioritise restorative justice in youth justice, I experienced doubts and hesitation from those who saw the need and the interests of the young offender as the main drive. In your original field, you had to cope with scepticism from victimologists who had difficulties in understanding that victims and offenders might have common interests in a peaceful settlement of the offence.

Ivo, rehabilitation is not restorative justice, but it may (and should) complement it.

As in many countries, Belgian youth justice is predominantly oriented to the 'protection' of the children and young offenders who have committed an 'act defined as an offence'. Originally, all measures were penetrated by re-educative and assistant ambitions to the benefits of the young offender and his or her family. When mediation and community service appeared as isolated experimental practices, youth court judges and their staff saw these models as alternative ways of re-education, to confront the young offenders with the suffering and losses they had caused, not as a way to address the victims' needs. But the more the underlying restorative justice philosophy surfaced, the more hesitation emerged. Scepticism was expressed by rehabilitation agencies against the shift from focusing on the offender's needs towards addressing primarily the suffering and losses in the victims. From an object of care, the offender became a subject with responsibilities.

An important objection of the 'rehabilitationists' is that many young offenders have themselves suffered systematic social injustices and discrimination in their life course, so that it would be 'unjust' to demand from them reparative gestures while nothing is done to their own victimhood.

It is a crooked reasoning, a kind of what Sykes and Matza called a 'neutralisation technique'. Being socially excluded does not deliver a 'wildcard' to assault, steal or use private violence for example. Injustice to the young is not undone by more injustice to another victim. And the victim suffers losses, regardless of the social status of his or her victimiser. The victimising act must be clearly rejected. But the expression of the rejection must be as constructive as possible for all stakeholders. As argued in many publications, the punitive premise is more destructive than constructive. Rehabilitative responses prioritise the constructiveness for the offender, but do not, or secondarily only, consider the needs and interests of the victim.

Others try to co-opt the restorative idea, by including the 'reparation' of the offenders' societal vulnerability into the restorative objective. This option must be watched carefully. Restorative justice is reactive as a response to an offence that has already occurred. It focuses on the losses that have been caused by the offence. Rehabilitation, on the contrary, may be triggered by an offence, but it aims at preventing further misbehaviour (and ill-being) by addressing the offenders' needs that existed before the offence. The latter is, of course, very humanitarian and ethical, but it may not supplant the restorative dimension, and it is equally humanitarian and ethical to address the victims' needs. Trying to relieve the needs of the offender is a task for specific rehabilitative efforts, undertaken as complements to the restorative intervention. This distinction is crucial. If it is blurred, the intervention may shift towards focusing (again) on the needs of the offender and neglect the offence as the reason for the intervention, drifting away from the genuine victims' needs and loosening the ground for legal safeguards. This risk is certainly prominent in the institutional context which traditionally focuses on offenders' needs.

Moreover, empirical research confirms that restorative processes do certainly not worse on the rehabilitation path than the pure treatment or re-educational programmes. The face-to-face confrontation about the harm and suffering caused, the respect and support by significant others experienced during the encounter, the chance offered to make amends and to be reaccepted as a law-abiding citizen, the satisfaction felt when the reparative gestures have been carried out successfully and are valorised by significant others, all are elements which may favour the offenders' awareness and his or her motivation to conform and/or to accept rehabilitative support. Restorative encounters may function as ideal step-ups towards rehabilitative initiatives carried out by specialised agencies.

Ivo, victimology and restorative justice badly need each other.

Victimology existed long before restorative justice came up as an identifiable field of practice and research. It might be expected that victimologists would embrace restorative justice as a partner in the struggle for the rights of victims in the judicial response to crime. But Tony and you had to face scepticism from (a part of) the victimologists who held a predominantly oppositional view of the victims' and offenders' interests.

'Victims need the offender to be punished' is one of the arguments. Many victims indeed wish to see their offender punished. Punishment channelises their emotions of anger and indignation which follow after the victimisation. The institutional context of the punishment satisfies the vindication searched by victims. Victims may also opt for punishment because it is the only way they know of censuring their victimisation.

However, empirical surveys show a more nuanced and diversified image, certainly if victims are acquainted with the restorative potentials. Most victims appear to want a clear and official rejection of their victimisation, and they want respect, support and reparation or compensation (less material than social and symbolic). But some victims indeed stick to the punitive pain infliction, depending on their ideological beliefs, the kind of victimisation and the type of offender. A principled question that emerges then is whether a society pursuing constructive and peaceful relations in its midst must follow per definition the punitive wishes of the victims. After all, the traditional criminal justice responses do – rightly – not follow the victims' wishes straightforwardly, nor do the authorities follow the tax payers' wish to pay less taxes.

Victimologists also fear secondary victimisation by the restorative process itself. According to them, victims are at risk of being used in an offender-focused agenda, as 'pedagogical tools' to demonstrate to the offender the negative impact of his or her behaviour, while the genuine needs and interests of the victims are subordinated only. Victims may feel pressurised to participate in a restorative dialogue. They may feel pressurised to accept an agreement which does not respond sufficiently to their needs and interests. Finally, while traditional penal procedures shield the victims from direct confrontation with their offender, restorative processes favour face-to-face encounters, which may be too heavy a burden for many victims.

Fortunately, one of the most stable empirical findings is that victims' satisfaction is significantly higher among victims who participated in a restorative process than among those who went through a traditional procedure. Methodological issues may weaken this conclusion, but do not wipe it out. But not all victims are more satisfied. Some are even more distressed. It indicates that the risk of secondary victimisation is an issue, especially if restorative justice is implemented too unthoughtfully, as a routine. That is why it is crucially important to include the victimological point of view in restorative justice.

In my view, both restorative justice and victimology as movements have great interest in joining together in close relationship. As just said, restorative justice needs the victimological input to stay on track and avoid deviation towards sideways of rehabilitation or other extensions. Conversely, victimology needs the broader approach and ambitions of restorative justice to extend and deepen its impact. On their own, victimology and victims' movements may lead to some ornaments in the margins of the criminal justice system which will remain predominantly oriented towards inflicting the right and proportionate punishment on the offender. That is why victimology has every reason to join the ambition of maximalist restorative justice which is to reorient the criminal justice system from being guided by a punitive premise towards being primarily focused on the reparation of the individual, relational and social suffering and harm caused by the offence.

Ivo, it's all about a clear outcome-based definition.
First, we may not be naïve. The 'border-frictions' of restorative justice with rehabilitation and victimology have also a sociological dimension. Resistance is not only due to theoretical considerations. It is also provoked by institutional and personal interests, prestige and even power (let us be clear, also from the restorativists' side). But this short contribution has not any therapeutic ambition, so I will concentrate on the content.

As you have understood meanwhile, Ivo, I grasped the opportunity to repeat once again the position I held during my entire journey through restorative justice. Restorative justice badly needs clarity in its conceptualisation. Restorative justice is justice that restores. Mediation processes, conferencing and other encounters are (crucial) tools to achieve maximum possible restoration, but they are not the key to understand restorative justice. The key is the outcome pursued. If a victim suffers by a process which is meant to be restorative, the process simply has failed to be restorative justice. Restorative justice is characterised by its attempt to repair as much as possible the suffering, the harm and the social turmoil caused by the occurrence of an offence.

Advancing the process as the key element opens the gate to confusion and extension. It blurs the distinction between rehabilitation and restoration, and it rightly alarms victimologists that victims may be dragged into an offender-oriented agenda. Dialogues are not good per se. They are valued because of the outcomes they help to achieve.

I am looking forward to many more chats with you, Ivo, gradually less in audiences and meetings, but more and more at a lunch or in cafés over a beer. We both will look back as wise men enjoying our new role as outcastes – completely free of thinking and of speech, because what we think and what we say do not matter anymore.

See you soon,
Lode

Ivo Aertsen: a multifaceted academic

Kristel Beyens

1 Prelude

I met Ivo for the first time almost 30 years ago. We were both working on our PhDs and regularly exchanged experiences, doubts and uncertainties, which are so typical for this phase in academic life. This common ground immediately created a kind of 'partner in crime' feeling and a mutual understanding of the struggle with the PhD, which was so difficult to finish on top of all the other tasks we were juggling with. Ivo has always been a very active academic who was involved in different networks and who combined many interests and skills. Particular for his professional trajectory was how he combined his academic activities with a strong link with practitioners in the penal, forensic and restorative field, thus bridging the academia and the professional world. Being a student and assistant of Tony Peters, for whom I always have had a deep admiration, it was no wonder that Ivo also specialised in restorative justice, in which he became a national and international authority. The Belgian restorative justice school has become renowned worldwide, and Ivo has a great merit here. I am convinced that many contributors in this book will elaborate on this important part of his professional trajectory, so I will highlight other aspects.

As I already mentioned, Ivo is a scholar with many interests and fields of expertise. In this short contribution, I will highlight two particular 'projects' where we have intensively cooperated, namely, the Commission Holsters and our long membership of the editorial board of *Panopticon*, where Ivo was for years the leading member of the editorial subboard on 'Sentence execution and judicial aid'.

2 Commission Holsters

In 2000, a so-called Commission Holsters was installed by the then Minister of Justice, Marc Verwilghen. The goal of this commission, which was named after its President Denis Holsters, was to prepare a fundamental reform of the Belgian sentencing and sentence execution law, aiming to replace a retributive penal law by a restorative law. To do so, three subcommissions were established, namely, a subcommission for Sentence Implementation Courts, a subcommission for External Legal Position and a subcommission for Sentencing. As the Commission Holsters had to advise the federal government, the composition of the subcommisions was a balancing act of appointing members with a

French or Flemish background, where the different Belgian universities had to be represented in an egalitarian way. Taking the mission of the commission into account, namely, preparing the transition from a retributive to a restorative law in Belgium, the input of the Leuven School of Restorative Justice was very clear. And while Tony Peters was the initial representative of the Catholic University of Leuven as the proponent of restorative justice, I was the member of the Vrije Universiteit Brussel (Free University of Brussels) of the subcommission for Sentencing, due to my sentencing research background.[1] After a while, Tony Peters had to be succeeded in the commission and Ivo was his 'natural' successor. We met very regularly in Brussels to work together on preparatory texts, which gave us a lot of opportunity to reflect together and exchange ideas on the aims of punishment, on how to ensure that the judiciary would prioritise restorative and rehabilitative goals over retributive and securitative ones and on the expansion of the sentencing repertoire with community sentences.

In 2003, the report of the Commission Holsters was published. Five leading principles or proposals were put forward (see Rozie, 2004, for a short overview). *First*, and in line with the restorative mission, the leading principle of a communicative and participative justice process was put forward, pleading for informing all the stakeholders involved in the process and make room for serious debate in the court room. *Second,* some general principles for sentencing were defined, such as damage control for the offender, the victim and the society, imprisonment as the last resort, the principle of proportionality and taking the interests of all actors involved in the process into account. *Third*, the introduction of a two-phase judicial process, with the determination of the culpability in the first phase and the determination of the sentence in the second phase. *Fourth*, the inclusion of the aims of punishment in the law was proposed, to force judges to link their sentence to the aims of punishment pursued in their sentence decision. The proposed ranking of the aims was as follows: (1) communicating censure, (2) promote problem-solving and restoration of the damage due to the offence, (3) foster the rehabilitation of the offender and (4) protection of society. The last aim was considered to be the logical consequence of the pursuit of the previous aims. The *fifth* proposal of the commission was the amendment of the existing sentences that were at the disposal of the judges and the introduction of new forms of non-custodial sentences. The sentences were categorised as follows: (1) the declaration of guilt; (2) financial sentences, such as fines and specific confiscation; (3) the liberty-restricting punishments, such as deprivation of rights, work penalty and probation; and (4) liberty-depriving sentences, such as imprisonment and forced treatment. The commission also proposed that, as with the work penalty, probation should also become an autonomous sentencing option, instead of being shackled to a suspended prison sentence as a condition. This proposition met the critique of Tony Peters (1980) that 'the prisons are overcrowded because the alternatives do not work.' One of his ex-

1 I had just finished my PhD entitled 'Sentencing as a social practice' (Beyens, 2000).

planations of the failure of probation was that it was not possible to impose it as an autonomous sentence and that noncompliance with the probation conditions could lead to imprisonment. The commission's proposal to create autonomous community sentences has been taken up by subsequent Ministers of Justice and became part of the government statement of Michel I government. More than ten years later, in 2014, the Belgian Parliament voted a law to introduce autonomous electronic monitoring and autonomous probation, which was only implemented two years later, namely in 2016, under the Ministry of Justice headed by Minister Koen Geens.

There was a lot to be criticised on these proposals, which were still in their infancy, but the general impact of the work of the Commission Holsters cannot be underestimated. To prevent that this work would disappear we took the initiative with the board of *Panopticon* to organise a conference where the proposals of the three subcommissions were presented to a broader public and commented by practitioners and experts. Ivo, who was chairing the editorial board by then, was the driving force behind this conference and also behind the book that was published after the conference (Aertsen, Beyens, De Valck & Pieters, 2004). And although at the conference, the critique on the propositions of the subcommission for Sentencing was rather fierce, due to the book and the conference this report did not disappear in the cellars of the ministry after three years of hard work. The publication of the book was a difficult process – as is the case with most books – but today it is the only tangible legacy of the report of the Commission Holsters, as the original text of the report is never made available for a broader public.

3 Ivo as a leading person in the Flemish journal *Panopticon*

This leads me to the other aspect of my collaboration with Ivo, namely, as a member of the editorial board of *Panopticon*, where we were 'partners in crime' in the sub-board that was dealing with all issues on sentence implementation and judicial aid. Ivo was its first member, and for a long time he remained the main editor of this sub-board, and there I got to know him as an inspiring and precious colleague. He was the most appropriate person to lead a board with academic members and people from the field. This bridging function was an important aim of this journal and makes it quite unique in current academia. As Ivo was always very much embedded in the penal field and later on in the field of restorative justice, he knew all the important topics and sensitivities that should be dealt with in the journal. He was also a very good editor and checked and corrected all the contributions up to the last commas and spelling mistakes. But he was more than that, as he was always a constructive, critical commentator of the contributions, he always succeeded to deliver high-quality articles.

During his chairmanship of the sub-editorial board of *Panopticon* we organised two big conferences. The Holsters Conference in November 2003, with the publication of the book in 2004, and two years later, on 17 November 2015, we organised a conference on the autonomous work penalty. This sentence was introduced in Belgium in 2002 and was very successful from the beginning. This was quite exceptional and unexpected, taking the slow and difficult acceptance of the community service as a condition of probation in 1994 into account. The conference combined contributions from academics and experts from the field who were involved in the imposition and execution of the work penalty. In 2006, Ivo and I edited a special issue of *Panopticon*, which was the first academic publication on the work penalty. In our introduction (Beyens & Aertsen, 2006), we made a critical analysis of the lack of information and systematic data of the use of the work penalty, the selective interest of the judiciary in this sentence option and the vague identity and unclear policy with regard to the work penalty. For some years, Ivo and I made plans to write a book together on community punishment, but these plans have, unfortunately, never been realised.

4 The hidden side of Ivo

In this contribution, I wanted to highlight a side of Ivo that is probably less known today, as he has become this big European 'restorative justice star', a status that he absolutely deserves.

This, for many readers probably the less visible side of Ivo, is his expertise in sentencing issues and community sentences which merits to be highlighted too. He has contributed a lot to the discussions and into putting the importance of community punishments on the political agenda, as he did with restorative justice and victim-offender resettlements in Belgium and elsewhere. The perfect example of how he combined and 'sold' these interests is how he advocated to change the name of the sub-board of 'Sentence Execution and Judicial Aid' of *Panopticon* into the sub-board 'Penology and Victimology'.

References

Aertsen, I., Beyens, K., De Valck, S. & Pieters, F. (eds.) (2004). *De Commissie Holsters buitenspel? De voorstellen van de Commissie strafuitvoeringsrechtbanken, externe rechtspositie van gedetineerden en straftoemeting.* Brussel: Politeia.

Beyens, K. (2000). *Straffen als sociale praktijk. Een penologisch onderzoek naar straftoemeting.* Brussel: VUB Press.

Beyens, K. & Aertsen, I. (2006). De autonome werkstraf in België: hoe sterk het karakter? *Panopticon*, 27(4), 1-6.

Commissie Holsters. (2003). *Eindverslag van de Commissie strafuitvoeringsrechtbanken, externe rechtspositie van gedetineerden en straftoemeting. Deel II Straftoemeting.* Brussel: Ministry of Justice.

Peters, T. (1980). De gevangenissen zitten overvol want de alternatieve sancties doen het niet. *Panopticon*, 1(4), 265-270.

Rozie, M. (2004). De voorstellen van de Subcommissie straftoemeting. In I. Aertsen, K. Beyens, S. De Valck & F. Pieters (eds.), *De Commissie Holsters buitenspel? De voorstellen van de Commissie strafuitvoeringsrechtbanken, externe rechtspositie van gedetineerde en straftoemeting* (pp. 21-25). Brussel: Politeia.

The praxis of mediation or how 'stories' need theory to be credible

Kristel Buntinx[*]

My path crossed that of Prof. Ivo Aertsen over a quarter of a century ago. When I was looking for a job, after graduating as lawyer-criminologist, I ended up at *Justitieel Welzijnswerk Leuven*, working on the *Vroeghulp* project, which offered support to remand prisoners and their friends and families in the Hulpgevangenis van Leuven (Auxiliary Prison of Leuven). As a former employee, Prof. Aertsen was still in close contact with this organisation. Our first encounters at consultations or board meetings regularly ended with fascinating conversations at the counter of some bar or other on the *Oude Markt*, a central square in Leuven.

Justitieel Welzijnswerk Leuven combined support for offenders and victims in a single house – a rare combination at the time, which raised some eyebrows: 'What if a victim meets his or her offender on the stairs?' I worked there for almost eight years, and that never happened. I've never seen any drawbacks. Quite the contrary. Being under one roof with the people who worked with the victims of my offenders ensured that already at the start of my professional career I learned to take the perspective of multipartiality. That is when I first experienced the artificiality of separating the two sides to a crime. Offenders and victims are connected through the crime and that connection cannot just be severed.

It is no surprise that victim-offender mediation originated in this house. We were, in fact, doing mediation before mediation existed. I was in close contact with the victim support team[1] and would on occasion learn of a victim's questions. If I was working with the offender, I would transmit that question and let my colleague of victim support know the answer. In that way, conditional releases were proposed to the council chamber (Raadkamer) which took the desires of the victim into account. Of course, this only happened on the basis of mutual consultation and the agreement of all parties.

In the 1990s, an action research project was started in Leuven on victim-offender mediation, and I was part of the steering committee 'Victim-offender Mediation' ('Herstelbemiddeling'), where I monitored the project from the perspective of offenders. Prof. Aertsen was the lead researcher. Those were exciting times. We were on the frontline for witnessing the gradual development of 'Victim-offender mediation'. There, I first experi-

* I would like to express my gratitude to Geertjan Zuijdwegt, researcher at the Leuven Institute of Criminology, and also an author in this book, for translating my contribution into English.

1 The GDPR did not exist then. Still, we treated information about the other party with great respect for privacy.

enced the fruitful cooperation between the theoretic, academic world and the practice of mediation. In fact, it inspired me to enter the world of mediation in the year 2000. I co-implemented the project 'Victim-offender Mediation for Juvenile Offenders') for the NGO Oikoten.[2] A year later, I co-started the project 'Mediation during the Enforcement of Custodial Sentences' for the NGO Suggnomè[3] and helped to expand it to all judicial districts in Flanders.

Starting 'Mediation during the Enforcement of Custodial Sentences' was pioneering work, even though we optimally used the experiences of victim-offender mediation prior to sentencing. We immediately took on the most serious offences. Our laboratory was *Leuven Centraal*, a prison for offenders with long sentences, primarily convicted of homicide, sexual offences and armed robbery. And thus, I have changed roles along the way, but I have always been part of the steering committee 'Forum for Restorative Justice and Mediation' in Leuven until now. In fact, I still work as victim-offender mediator today.

Pioneers follow their intuition, or as some people would derisively put it, 'their gut feeling'. After all, if you start a project, you cannot fall back on established frameworks, scripts or guidelines. You can experiment, try things and work in all kinds of laboratories. It is a process of falling down and getting back up, but you learn from your mistakes and develop a practice, a method and, eventually, a framework with handbooks and guidelines. Because initially all of this is lacking, you need backing from a steering committee, a support team, experiences from all over the world and scientific research. You don't have to reinvent the wheel. And if you can learn from the mistakes of others, you, at least, won't have to make them again.

Because we had such backing, we dared to take victims of the most serious crimes to prison to meet their offenders and talk about the crimes and their consequences. We did all of this without script and without legal framework. We did it because we felt it was the right thing to do: to return the conflict to the parties involved, as Nils Christie (1977),[4] founding father of victim-offender mediation, had taught us. Eighteen years on, Moderator[5] has facilitated hundreds of encounters in cases of the most serious crimes. These experiences are invaluable. We have learned so much from them. I just want to pass on one of the most important insights.

Offenders and victims represent two sides of a single crime. They need one another; to get on with their coping process on the one hand, and on the other, to get a voice in the judicial procedure. Victim-offender mediation contributes to the coping process of both victims and offenders. Victims told me that after mediation they slept better, needed less medication, could get back to work and perform better at school. Offenders told me that, for the first time, they could look in the mirror again, or in their mother's eyes, that they

2 Now, vzw Alba.

3 Now, vzw Moderator.

4 Christie, N. (1977). *Conflicts as property*, 17, 1-15. doi:10.1093/oxfordjournals.bjc.a046783.

5 Moderator Forum for restorative justice and mediation.

felt so much lighter, that they regained perspective. For them, victim-offender mediation was a step in processing their guilt. Victim-offender mediation also gives voice to parties. In the mediation agreements, victims regularly spoke about whether punishment was still required, what a fitting sentence would be, what chances an offender should get or which conditions ought to be met for a suspended sentence or a conditional release. Offenders often appreciated this or would even propose something themselves; they would agree or disagree with the conditions and would even speak about restoration to society.

But how do we communicate all these stories and findings? How do we translate this to policy? You need an interpreter. Someone who can present your findings in such a way that they cannot be dismissed as unrealistic fairy tales. And that is why Prof. Aertsen was so important for us. He became our scientific counterpart. I don't have a ready pen, so you will find few texts, reports or articles in my name. I can tell stories, though. Stories that inspired Prof. Aertsen. And so, soon he gave me a platform. He loved to let practitioners speak.

The first time he invited me to replace him – at a conference in Norway – is indelibly stamped on my memory. The theme was mediation in the most serious crime cases. Because the audience was mostly made up of practitioners, Prof. Aertsen thought it was best that they heard my stories. So, I took the plunge, used my best English and told my story to an audience of 150 people. This was the start of many conferences, seminars and workshops in countries including Ireland, Germany, the Netherlands, Norway and Finland. In recent years, I have also taken on trainings at the Summer School and the conference of the European Forum for Restorative Justice. I once received a beautiful compliment from an interpreter who was translating my talk. He told me that he usually didn't really listen to what people say, but that he did listen to me. The story of victims who meet their offenders does something to people. People always tell me that my stories inspire them. Sometimes, this even led to the submission of a local project or to people just starting to do victim-offender mediation in cases of serious crimes. It triggered people's pioneering spirit.

In addition, Prof. Aertsen always sent visiting scholars to our mediation service to get to know our 'stories'.

This year, he invited me to teach the practical course 'Restorative Justice and Mediation' ('Herstelrecht en Bemiddeling') to criminology and law students,[6] where I had a chance to tell them about the practice of mediation.

I also experienced his support when I had to make a case within my organisation for 'Mediation in Extra-judicial Cases'. In 2013, there was serious discussion about whether Moderator should also offer mediation in extra-judicial cases. The definition we used at the time was as follows: 'Extra-judicial cases are requests for communication in situations in which, in the perception of the applicant(s), there is an offender and/or a victim, with-

---

6 I made a case to open up the course to law students, because lawyers, judges and prosecutors are our most important partners.

out them having this legal status.'[7] In other words, these cases were not known to the justice system.

The proponents argued that this was just part of our job: we were giving the conflict back to the parties involved and didn't need a legal framework for that. Parties can make up their own minds. The opponents argued that we cannot just lump everything together under the common denominator of communicative and participative justice. The term *Justice* then no longer refers to the governmental agencies in charge of law enforcement, but simply means 'justice à la tête du client'.[8]

I was on the side of the proponents, but we did not succeed in convincing the organisation; we could not find the right arguments. I even began to doubt my own opinion. But thankfully, Prof. Aertsen convinced me on a long drive to a seminar in Tübingen to stick to my point of view. In 2017, Moderator started a project entitled 'Mediation Out of the Sights of the Justice System' ('Bemiddeling buiten het vizier van Justitie').

Such fruitful cooperation is also shown in the latest project that brought Prof. Aertsen and me to the same table: Leuven Restorative City. What can the ideas of restorative justice offer a society or a city? How do you teach a city, a school or a workplace to deal with conflict? How do you prevent conflict? How do you prevent crime?

If we succeed in getting offenders and victims of the most serious crimes together to calmly engage in conversation, then I have the right to dream about the possibilities of implementing these practices and ideas on a wider scale in a society that is ever more polarised. Countless initiatives already prove that I'm right: the journalist Lidewij, who visited all her neighbours for the TV programme 'Iedereen Beroemd' ('Everyone Famous') and brought the entire neighbourhood together, the Amnesty International video in which someone gazes into the eyes of a refugee for four minutes, Radio Gaga – all initiatives that connect rather than polarise. As I heard Patrick Loobuyck say the other day, 'The counterweight for polarisation is encounter.'[9] It is as simple as that. But this story too, is one we have to get told.

And I dare to go further. After eighteen years of experience of mediation in cases of the most serious crimes it is crystal clear to me that we can use this methodology in terrorism cases. How to do so is again a pioneering work. But thanks to foreign experiences with the IRA and the Red Brigades – initiatives I learned more about through Prof. Aertsen – we also can and, more importantly, dare to take this challenge on. So, I secretly hope that when this really gets off the ground, we can still appeal to Prof. Aertsen.

7 Internal report Suggnomè (25 October 2012).
8 Newsletter Suggnomè, May 2013.
9 Theme-lunch 'Leuven without Racism' with Patrick Loobuyck on the theme: Speaking about racism in a polarised societal context.

Time and again, Prof. Aertsen has had an immensely supporting, and even sometimes a pushing and pulling role in my life. Without him, I wouldn't be where I am, but also, and more importantly, victim-offender mediation wouldn't be where it is. Thank you, Ivo.

The *praxis* of justice: one practitioner's perspective

David Gustafson

1 Introduction

This contribution to Ivo Aertsen's Liber Amicorum is likely to differ from most of the other offerings. It is likely to be less academic given that I tend to list a bit (as in the heel on a sailboat) towards the practitioner side, tacking (another of those sailing metaphors) towards the academic side from time to time, but briefly. As I reflect on that notion (the notion of 'brevity'), I recognise that it might cause some readers to smile, especially Ivo Aertsen, since he laboured with me to get my doctoral dissertation finished over a very long span of time and had to read and reread the entire thing (all 700 pages, affectionately dubbed '*Dave's kleine boekske*') in its various versions over a duration that was anything but brief. In fact, this matter proved to be the inspiration for a little light stand-up comedy at the public defence of my dissertation but, as I did then, I'll save that bit for last.

If my understanding is correct, a Liber Amicorum, such as the *festschriften* bound for Joannes Carolus Erlenwein in the 17th century or Anne Wagner's friendship book in the late 18th century are examples of the sorts of collections that had their genesis in German universities in the 16th century and quickly spread from there. In university culture, the pages often honoured the achievements of faculty or major contributors to a body of knowledge. These collections can, apparently, contain all sorts of materials and combine such disparate elements as travel journals, scrapbooks, sketchbooks, autograph books, collections of quotable quotes, proverbs, poems, essays and personal notes to friends and loved ones. Because these *festschriften* or friendship books were motivated by love and a genuine desire to honour another, once assembled they were often kept over the course of decades: a living, breathing testament to friendship, growth, accomplishment and adventure; the recognition of a life well-lived by members of the recipient's extended 'family'.

While my contribution doesn't begin to compass all those sorts of sources (that is for the whole collection to do), I will attempt to 'wedge in' a few of them: (1) a bit of history from the time of the beginnings of my relationship with Ivo Aertsen; (2) a set of learnings taken from an intensive gathering of justice stakeholder groups regarding the criteria for good *praxis* in the delivery of restorative justice programmes; (3) a poetic reflection of my own about the nature of working with survivors of devastating criminal trauma as the power of the process began to dawn on me; (4) an abstract in which I attempt to coalesce the findings reported in my own dissertation after almost 30 years of practice as a dialogue facilitator/mediator working with crimes of severe violence; (5) a quotable quote by Archbishop Desmond Tutu which could profitably be writ large over each of our programme missions and mandates; and (6) finally, the promised bit of 'stand-up' comedy. All of this, shared here while trying to stay relatively close to the main line: an amicorum motivated by deep respect, genuine philia and gratitude for all that Ivo has come to mean to me and our entire 'extended family'.

2 THE HISTORY

I have known Ivo for what proves to be a very long time: since the late Prof. Tony Peters led an expedition to the wilds of British Columbia, Canada, in 1995. That expedition, an entourage of six or eight Belgian criminologists, including many who are well-known today in restorative justice circles, included the then-young, then-blonde-haired visionary, Ivo Aertsen.

Tony Peter's dear friend and colleague, Vancouver-based victimologist Ezzat Fattah, a professor at Simon Fraser University, whom I had also come to know in my teaching role there, had suggested Tony take his Belgian colleagues to pay a visit to Community Justice Initiatives (CJI) in Langley, British Columbia, if they had interest in investigating the model programmes operated by staff there, programmes Ezzat had described as good examples of pioneering Canadian restorative justice praxis. As the story goes, following their visit to CJI, two of them, Ivo Aertsen and Leo Van Garsse, travelled home together writing, as they journeyed, the draft legislation which quickly found its way into law in Belgium; law which has governed the practice of restorative justice and victim-offender mediation since. Amazing. Not long afterwards, informed, I am told, once again, by the Canadian Victim-Offender Mediation Programme (VOMP) model, similar projects were developed and implemented for use in each of the prisons of Belgium, enabling dialogues between victims and offenders to be facilitated by trained and highly competent mediators in even the most serious of criminal offences. At risk of sounding entirely clichéd, 'What mighty oaks from tiny acorns grow!'

3 A PALAVER ON *PRAXIS*

From the beginning of the experiments in victim-offender mediation on both sides of the Atlantic, but certainly in Canada and in Belgium, there has been particular emphasis paid to good *praxis* (from Greek Praxis < *prassein,* to do) defined as: practical application or exercise of a branch of learning, and habitual or established practice or custom. Dorr (1984) has further elucidated praxis as a combination of thought and action that is required to accomplish a particular challenging endeavor. What is called for in praxis according to Dorr is 'reflective action', which is a type of activity that is constantly being evaluated and adapted in the light of its results.

In 2003, I invited Howard Zehr to come to Vancouver to help host with me a gathering of justice stakeholders, a 'Palaver on Praxis'. While the term *palaver* can connote idle, tedious, lengthy conversation which goes nowhere, *this* palaver was nothing of the sort. The invitation, titled 'Palaver on praxis: The marriage of restorative justice theory and practice' drew representatives from the judiciary, victim services, crime prevention, prosecution, human resources, aboriginal justice and policing. There were students, educators, trauma counsellors, trauma survivors, prisoners, prison volunteers and a variety of restorative justice programme managers and facilitators. This group had convened to ask – and to face – questions they saw to be of critical concern in the practice of restorative justice. Of thirteen 'critical issues' identified by these stakeholders, 'ensuring good practice' was listed more than twice as often as the next nearest items.[1] The key elements which defined 'good practice' for this diverse, educated, enlightened and potentially highly polarised group included these:

1. Safety: borrowing from the physician's Hippocratic Oath, to 'First, do no further harm';
2. Completely voluntary involvement of all participants;
3. Commitment to preparation of and meaningful follow-up with all participants;
4. Recognition:
5. that healing requires time;
6. that individuals' needs vary vastly, requiring flexibility;
7. that understanding and awareness of cultural differences can be crucial; '"Make no assumptions" needs to be a watchword';
8. The need for close adherence to principles such as Zehr and Mika 'Principles of Restorative Justice', Susan Sharpe's 'Touchstones' and practitioner values/ethics sets such as the British Columbia Charter for Restorative Justice Practitioners;[2]
9. Demonstrated, caring commitment to each individual participant is an indicator of the degree to which stated, notional values become realised values;
10. 'competence of mediators and facilitators ... [is] absolutely essential.'

The message we as restorative justice practitioners took away was clear: even those who had been strongly opposed to the use of restorative justice in anything beyond the most minor criminal offence types – and certainly opposed to the referral of anything remotely related to violent crimes, especially power-based crimes such as intimate partner violence

1 Items tied for second in terms of frequency were: 'Doing Restorative Justice in a punishment-based and bureaucratic culture'; and 'The Role of Spirituality'.

2 A Draft 'Charter' for Practitioners: See the Simon Fraser University Centre for Restorative Justice web site: http://www.sfu.ca/cfrj/fulltext/charter.pdf.

and any form of sexual assault – would support our programmes and even refer their constituents IF (and only if), these sorts of tenets governed and were the basis of standards for programme practitioners and steadfastly adhered to. Recent work in British Columbia, headed by staff at CJI, has produced such a set of standards for any programmes willing to become signatories.

I love words. And I often search out their etymologies to ensure that I understand their deepest meanings, how they have been used historically and how they apply to things I am attempting to describe in the present. Sometimes that requires borrowing from another language, where a term might be more adequate and nuanced than any in the vocabulary of my own first language. There are a few such terms which I have borrowed from Greek to help in defining and describing the commitment required of practitioners working with programme participants impacted by serious and often highly traumatic criminal incidents. The first of these is *paraclete*, from *para* (*beside*, or *alongside*) and *kalei^n* (*to call, encourage, exhort*).[3] It denotes an advocate, one called to aid or support; hence, the *Consoler*, *Comforter*, or *Intercessor*, a term applied to the Holy Spirit in Christian tradition, but in the earliest uses of the term in Roman times denoting, more widely, 'an advocate (a legal representative)'. For me, given what I have experienced over 30 years now and witnessed as highly competent victim-offender mediators/facilitators accompany desperately wounded people in search of some respite, the word has come to connote all of those things: Consoler, Comforter, Intercessor; a trusted (and trustworthy) counsellor, a compassionate companion, someone deeply devoted to another's physical, psychological and spiritual well-being.

4 A poetic reflection on vocation

Since, as I noted earlier, an Amicorum can include many different kinds of materials, it seems to me fitting to insert at this point a sort of poetic reflection I wrote many years ago following an intense trip to the interior of British Columbia to meet with survivors of serious criminal trauma in their homes. In it, I tried to describe the nature of our work; work that I have come to see as far more than an occupation as a victim-offender mediator but, rather, as a vocation, as a *paraclete* to the most wounded of the wounded, on both sides of the razor's wire:

> BEAUTY FOR ASHES
> We were exhausted. We drove on, mile after mile, along the west bank, high above British Columbia's Okanagan Lake, saying little; each of us quieted, reflecting on the experience of the past few days. Each of those days had been spent with survivors of serious crimes committed against them and their loved

3 Collaborative International Dictionary of English.

ones: the senseless murder of a son, a brother; a decade of torturous child and adolescent emotional and sexual abuse in a totalitarian 'family' cult. We had just left the survivor of the latter, a woman of indomitable spirit, yet grieving the loss of so much and facing into tomorrows which, to her, held out a prospect almost as bleak as the forty years of yesterdays.

Listening, listening. To the stories of pain and unmet need, respecting the tellers' sense of what is still required for them to find a greater degree of healing and that too often used and highly elusive word 'closure'. They are the experts in their history, their day to day lived experience, and we, at best, are positioned and equipped to be the cautious process guides, to bear witness and to provide devoted accompaniment to them for this stage of their journeys.

In each case, over these past few days, we have been given a sacred trust: each of these people have made decisions to begin to participate in a program run by our agency which works with victims of the most serious crimes in the Canadian Criminal Code, and with the perpetrators incarcerated (and who take responsibility) for those crimes.

As I drive, I reflect on how little we have to offer in the face of such immense human need, such lingering grief and darkness. Yet, I know too, the truth of what they tell us: that our caring, a combination of professionalism and devoted personal attention, increases hope and offers them greater prospect of healing than anything else they have received so far in the search for justice. Small comfort.

The scene as the road stretches out before us seems fitting commentary for our thoughts. Counterpane and counterpoint, the interplay of light, and deepening shadow. Dusk comes on, hastened by the approach of ominous charcoal storm clouds, boiling up the valley, vapour in a venturi, jealously, petulantly pulling the shade on the magnificent vista to the horizon, obscuring our view of the Cascades to the South. Sheets of rain, like slates on a medieval roof appearing softened at the edges by the distance, began to layer the hillsides along the entire eastern shore along the lake. Ancient builders atop a mountain cathedral, laying slate.

The road ahead is dry. Only whitecaps on the lake and sharp gusts at our elevation augur danger, anything amiss. We are miles west of the storm, watching as the remaining wash of pale background sky is painted over with what seems a slashing broad brush, by thickly applied raw umber – no apparent room for subtlety – the storm is winning. 'Where, when we need them,' I try to lighten up, 'are the Group of Seven.'[4] Grey, black and umber hues scroll up,

4 Most Canadians would instantly recognize this reference. The Group of Seven, also sometimes referred to as the Algonquin School, was a group comprised of some of Canada's best-known and revered landscape painters, many of their works iconic in Canadian art history.

from the middle of immense Lake Okanagan to highest heaven. We drive on, no alternative course, toward deepening darkness and collision with the storm. Then Light. One tiny shard. Piercing through the darkness at what appears its thickest point. And as it comes, the scene becomes transfigured. Words don't describe the transformation. We don't try. I try to get my head around the science: isobars and millibars, a wedge of pressure splitting cloud, systems colliding and recoiling. I give it up in favour of mute witness. The light breaks through, opening the rent created, transforming everything it touches. Umbers are eclipsed, turning to magenta, then deep rose. Soft purples, emerge, then blues again, scarlet, and myriad greens. The shaft of light itself is all of these, combining, at its heart, in a vein of purest gold.

I dare to break the silence, to quietly voice a thought, a scripture taught me by my mother: 'A light shines in the darkness, and the darkness has never overcome it.'

And suddenly I see our work, our vocation, in a new, more humble yet more adequate way. A shard of light in the darkness; a glimmer of hope for at least the possibility of an exchange of beauty for ashes. It seems fitting to risk a few more words, though I am humbled, a man of unclean lips and on holy ground; words written by a friend and fellow-sojourner that seem to describe what we do, inviting still others to join us:

War Weary World
Come and see.
Maybe our lives can be a sacrament,
Love's presence, in a world that's bent.
Another's first foothold
On the way
To hope.

Martha Keys Barker

The metaphor of light appearing in darkness and a growing sense of personal vocation have continued to play out now for almost 30 years, as the programme we began against all odds in 1990 slowly began to impact correctional policy in Canada. In 2004, beyond any dreams we had ever had for it, the model we began in British Columbia was established as the model for the nation and 'rolled out' as a programme available to all of the victims of serious crime and to the offenders responsible for their harms from coast to coast in Canada. The following abstract is from my doctoral dissertation completed at KU Leuven under Ivo Aertsen's supervision which investigated the outcomes for participants in the first decade of the programme's operation. In fact, if not for the support of the members of my doctoral committee, Stephan Parmentier, the gracious Johan Goethals and Ivo's challenge to stay the task and complete it – in addition to his personal support and supervision – this piece of research would never have seen the light of day.

5 Encountering 'the other': victim-offender dialogue in serious crime (abstract)

This study examines the Canadian VOMP to determine the answers to the primary research question: *What are the major impacts and outcomes of facilitating dialogue encounters between victims and offenders in crimes involving severe violence?*

Utilising a qualitative, multiple-case-study methodology involving a sample of 25 cases in which victims and offenders met one another face to face demonstrated positive outcomes for both victims and offenders. (Twenty of the cases were chosen at random and five more were selected 'purposively' to address sampling anomalies in the random sample. The 25 resulting cases were chosen from a data pool of 166 cases in which participants had met one another in dialogues facilitated by the author and one other trained facilitator.)

Of the victims ($N = 34$) 33 out of 34 (97 per cent) felt disempowered by their engagement with the criminal justice system prior to their VOMP participation. Following participation, victims reported that the programme had 'empowered', 'enabled' and provided them opportunity to accomplish objectives, obtain information and/or to 'say their piece' and 'impact offenders' thinking'. Prior to VOMP 32 out of 34 victims had either been diagnosed with PTSD (21 out of 32 or 65.6 per cent) or were highly symptomatic (11 out of 32 or 34.3 per cent). Following their VOMP process, all 32 victims, including those most highly traumatised and suicidal, reported considerable 'healing' and recovery, confirmed by marked reduction in their PTSD symptoms. Further, 11 out of 24 adult victims credited VOMP with enabling them to transform their experience of victimisation, finding new vocation, which enabled them to serve others in profound and remarkable ways.

Findings for the offenders ($N = 28$) were similarly positive. Where known, the trauma history of 13 out of 28 offenders indicated they had been sexually or physically abused as children. Following VOMP, 24 out of 28 reported their experience as having been profoundly powerful, enabling them to come to peace with much in their own traumatic histories and precipitating significant healing for them. Prior to VOMP, offenders demonstrated varying degrees of victim empathy but, following their face-to-face meetings, 26 out of 28 offenders reported and demonstrated an increase in empathy. Two of the 28 offenders serving 'life' sentences are currently still incarcerated. Three of the 26 who have been released reoffended and were returned to prison. A total of 23 out of 26 are desisting (88.46 per cent). Apology and forgiveness played a role in the majority of cases with 23 out of 25 offenders offering an apology to their victim(s). In 22 out of 25 cases offenders also offered amends that had value and importance for victims and in 22 out of 25 cases forgiveness was offered by victims and received by offenders. A number of unanticipated outcomes were revealed: seven offenders took responsibility for crimes for which they had never been charged or were acquitted at trial. One such case involved an offender serving a life sentence for one murder who confessed to a formerly unsolved cold case murder. Another unanticipated outcome was the 'ripple effect' that saw approximately 1,650 individuals positively impacted 'downstream' by the outcomes for the programme participants.

The significance of this study is that it advances research about the use of restorative justice in serious crime, addressing some of the most controversial issues regarding the use of restorative justice in crimes of severe violence, domestic violence, sexual assault and situations of disproportionate power involving adult offenders and child victims. Finally, recommendations are made regarding how the findings of this study might impact policy and practice, and suggestions are provided regarding possible future research projects.

6 Archegos and the law of love

Another of the terms I have borrowed from the Greeks is 'archegos', a noun which seems to capture the almost sacramental sense of vocation Martha Barker's poem, cited previously, invites us to take up and shoulder. That seems to be what it takes to enable and facilitate the healing outcomes that these powerful processes can potentially produce in the lives of victim and offender participants impacted by the most serious criminal offences imaginable. The term *Archegos* means a 'way-maker, or a pioneer'. It might be used to describe someone who courageously swims ashore from a ship breaking up on the reefs to secure a line along which other survivors make their way to safety. Perhaps less dramatically, in the search for truly healing justice, the term could also connote the leaders who by virtue of consistent commitment to good praxis – '"reflective action," activity that is constantly being evaluated and corrected in the light of its results' – teach and model for others this sort of *praxis*, challenging everyone under their tutelage or purview to do the same, with constant commitment to improving the practice, evaluating, reflecting upon, honing and improving every aspect of service delivery as an ongoing part of the work. That commitment is one we, in Canada, have also seen modelled in Europe, and perhaps particularly in the leadership of people like Ivo, who has demonstrated this type of sacrificial commitment to the wisdom of what he has discerned, researched, studied and through the decades has come to know in the marrow of his bones. Ivo has been and will yet be *archegos* for many.

Some of us discover our vocations in becoming *paracletes* to nations, as Archbishop Desmond Tutu has done. Others among us, however, are 'called alongside' wounded others in their ones and twos. Those who shoulder the mantle as *paracletes* or (even unwittingly) fulfil the challenge of being an *archegos* almost inevitably are people who have transcended any reliance on punishment models or the belief that violence can be redemptive and can accomplish healing ends. They seem to be people who 'get' that; they not only understand but apprehend and live out the higher law of love, recognising, as Tutu (1999) did, that:

> Love is much more demanding than law.
> Love is stronger than hate,
> Life stronger than death,
> Light stronger than darkness;
> Laughter and joy,
> and compassion
> and gentleness
> and truth,
> all these are so much stronger
> than their ghastly counterparts.

7 Coming 'full circle'

So, to complete the circle, I return to the reference I made at the beginning to the piece of 'stand-up comedy' at the public defence of my dissertation in Leuven. As the question-and-answer section of the agenda concluded I reported that, as a good researcher must, I had examined the claim that KU Leuven was actually founded way back in 1425 and had determined that all the evidence pointed to the truth of that assertion. 'But', I added, 'there is one rumour circulating here that I must attempt to dispel before I return to Canada: that being the rumour that "Gustafson began to write his dissertation in the following year."' 'Although it may seem that way to my jury and the members of my supervision committee, *that rumour*', I said, with a dead-pan expression, but emphatically, 'is entirely untrue'. After a moment's silence, as the audience tried to discern whether I was being absolutely serious, laughter rang out in the auditorium. It was a fun moment at the end of a long journey. And the point of adding this little anecdote here is to offer one more accolade to Ivo, who has been mentor, teacher, guide, supervisor and friend through the duration: I am convinced that were that rumour *true* (i.e. that I *had* been labouring at my dissertation since 1426), dear Prof. Dr Ivo Aertsen – given his demonstration over decades of commitment to his students, of patience and diligence, of encouragement and advocacy – would have walked alongside me for the entire time, *archegos* and *paraclete*, providing each of those elements of his own character, until the final word was written. Thanks, Ivo, profound thanks!

References

Dorr, D. (1984). *Spirituality and Justice.* New York: Orbis.
Tutu, D.M., (1999). *No Future without Forgiveness.* New York: Doubleday.

The mystic life of a mediator: mediators as reflexive practitioners

Kris Vanspauwen

1 Introduction

The academic legacy of Ivo Aertsen is – among other things – also one of action research. With this short account, I would like to pay tribute to that legacy. After more than a decade of being a mediator in cases between victims and perpetrators in the most diverse forms of crimes, I can quote the three holy principles of a restorative justice process by heart: mediation is a voluntary process, a confidential process and a process led by a neutral third party.

I am going to challenge each one of them briefly, in an attempt to say that the role and position of a mediator in a restorative justice process is not always value free. Even more, I am convinced that the intervention of the mediator in a process is often decisive. By taking up this challenge, I am not arguing at all for a reconsideration of the restorative justice principles. I am raising attention to the fact that we are in need of more action research and evaluation on the role of the mediator if we want to draw a clearer and more realistic picture of the practice. My reflections are based on my own experience as a practitioner rather than on empirical grounds of a researcher. Forty years after Nils Christie's *Conflicts as Property*, we could perhaps write a story about mediators as the professionals?

During my years as a mediator there were quite a lot of successful cases, there were many more failed cases and there were all types of cases where success and failure were hard to judge. I hardly ever talked about my 'failed' or 'hard-to-judge' cases. In the past years, I have scrutinised my own behaviour as a mediator, and to some extent, I have also compared my cases in a quantitative way with those of my fellow mediators. The method of researching one's own behaviour is also known as the 'reflexive practice', better known in the fields of social work and psychotherapy. Rather than convincing the reader of my statement about the decisive and underestimated role of the mediator in a process, my aim here is to call for the introduction of *reflexive practice* as a research method in the field of restorative justice. Therefore, I was very happy to read recently when Christa Pelikan praised Gerd Delattre for his big contribution to the restorative justice field as a reflexive practitioner. And indeed, I agree, restorative justice practitioners could contribute significantly to the restorative justice community by talking and reporting more in-depth about their reflections in both 'successful' and 'failed cases'.

The field of restorative justice has been a subject of much repetitive research in the past decades. Important topics were neglected. The role and the effect of the figure of the mediator in the process is one of these neglected subjects. There are probably practical and methodological obstacles. Placing the mediator in the position of the researcher evaluating his or her own behaviour is an innovative approach to overcome this obstacle. Maybe there are also strategic reasons for not delving into the diaries or the heads of mediators. After all, there is something 'mystic' about the figure of the mediator. Let us unveil at least one of those narratives. I organise my account around the three principles: neutrality, voluntariness and confidentiality.

2 The unmistakable interest of a mediator

The first and foremost excuse of a mediator about his or her possible (and disputable) role in the process is the principle of neutrality, sometimes also described as 'impartiality'. It is generally accepted that a mediator is the process facilitator who leads a fair and equal process for both parties. There is little doubt that a mediator's role becomes questioned. Even when a case fails, it is quite uncommon I would say to question the role of the mediator. In that sense, I feel the field of mediators is not very self-critical. I started to have more interest into my role as a mediator when I noticed quite a few differences in the annual figures of the mediation cases based on the individual level of the mediator. Among the differences, I saw a consistently higher number of the face-to-face encounters for some mediators and very low figures for others. This means that some mediators succeeded more easily in bringing the conflicting parties around the table than their colleagues did. It is clear that some mediators therefore do not hesitate to be more decisive and guiding in the process. It would be interesting to know more about the techniques and tactics and to compare the approaches of both types of mediators. These figures elicit something about the style, the role and the freedom of the intervention of the mediator.

I observe also a hesitation among mediators to engage more fully in 'nasty' cases, protracted conflicts and conflicts that seem 'unsolvable'. Neighbourhood disputes and, to a certain extent, also domestic violence cases are good examples. At the same time, these are often cases that have a great impact on a broader context and on our society. Murder cases are serious crimes, but their impact on the society is often less pervasive than let's say neighbourhood conflicts. Moreover, murder cases are often success cases compared to the nasty cases. I see an interest or preference of the mediator to work with the very serious crimes. It would be interesting to study the attitude of mediators towards these different types of conflicts and what makes them enthusiastic or recalcitrant to work with either of them.

3 Engage personally with parties

In the Flemish practice of victim-offender mediation, the majority of the cases are initiated after a referral by the judiciary. In the remaining part of the cases, most of the applications or requests come from the offender's side. In the first case, this means that both the victim and the offender are informed about mediation by means of standard letter. It is important that parties are informed in a correct, complete and neutral way. This way a victim or an offender can make an informed and voluntary choice. Voluntariness is an important principle. Parties should have the free choice to engage in a victim-offender mediation process. Research has shown, however, that the standard letter is often viewed as too formal, too distant and often too complicated. Moreover, the letter often arrives in the mailbox at a time that parties receive many more correspondences related to the judicial procedure. It is often overwhelming, and the letter often ends up in the trash.

After having been informed about the criminal file, and too often followed by a non-response on the mediation offer, I found myself in situations where I could clearly imagine the value and the usefulness of a victim-offender encounter. Sometimes, my assumptions were based on past experiences in similar cases. Sometimes, I got convinced by the story of the responding party, either the victim or the offender. And then I had a choice: close the application or try and actively contact the other party again. This choice of sending a reminder can become a standard procedure to inform that the other party has shown interest in the mediation offer. Sometimes, this second letter triggers the interest of the other party. My experience was that parties responded more often when the reminder was more personalised. I realised that many colleague-mediators had also replaced the folder named 'standard reminders' with a folder named 'personalised letters'. Mediators often developed their own slightly adapted versions of letters for the victim or the offender. A step further is a telephone call. When parties are contacted personally by telephone, a positive response for an informative meeting about the possibilities of mediation followed even more often. This 'personal' way of working with parties is often referred to as the 'intrude technique' in the circles of mediators. For the 'uniformists' among us, a telephone call or a personalised letter means a breaching of the principle of voluntariness. Some mediators would call this an active engagement towards parties. Apart from the question on the moral boundaries of the mediator, it is clear that there are differences in the style and approach of a mediator in the first communication with the victim and the offender. And these differences clearly have an impact on the further processes of a case. Moreover, they often determine whether or not a mediation case will be initiated. It would be interesting to study more in-depth the motives and actions of mediators.

4 A public process to create broader support

The Belgian Mediation Act provides a responsibility for the judiciary to inform all victims and offenders involved in a judicial procedure about the existence of mediation. And yet, more than a decade later, there is still a lot of resistance among prosecutors and judges to refer cases to the mediation service operating in their district. During the many conversations with various prosecutors and judges, I often got the response in the sense of 'We know the processes are confidential. So after referring a case, we never hear back about the outcome. And that is correct. But that is also frustrating.' Confidentiality of a mediation process is a key principle. Certainly if it relates to the confidentiality towards the referrer and, most notably, towards the judicial authorities. My experience is that when it is very well discussed with both parties, it often seems a good choice to inform the legal authorities to a certain extent about the mediation process. As long as the legal guarantees of both parties remain safeguarded. Making a mediation process more public as it is now creates also opportunities to make stakeholders and society more responsible and more supportive in the aftermath and follow-up of a case. The peacemaking circles in Canada are a good example.

Confidentiality can also become a critical issue when the referrer is the victim assistance programme of the victim or the therapist and/or psychiatric unit of the offender. In either case, it is often in the interest of both the victim and the offender that a mediation process can be integrated in the assistance or therapy process. As for the other principles, there is little or no research conducted on the way in which mediators use the concept of confidentiality in their practice. It is certain that they take a considerable degree of freedom to implement the concept of confidentiality at their discretion. That is at least the case for the Flemish and probably also the Belgian practice of mediation, where the mediator is often far too dependent on the referrer, and, more particularly, the prosecutor or the judge. It is therefore also crucial to compare the differences between mediators in their approaches on the use of confidentiality.

5 Conclusion

In this brief account, I have tried to make the case for using a rather new research method to study the role and impact of the mediator in restorative justice process. If we want to deepen our knowledge about these processes, but, more importantly, if we want to contribute to the development of quality standards of restorative justice in general, I think it is necessary to start listening more carefully to the mediator as the *reflexive practitioner*. It requires, however, some engagement and commitment of the mediator.

To Ivo

Estelle Zinsstag

DEAR IVO,

Hesitating whether to write something academic or something more personal for this endeavour in your honour and after some discussions with the editors of the *Liber Amicorum*, I have decided to go towards the more personal and in the style of a letter, speaking directly to you. You are a modest, rather private, cosmopolitan *Vlaams* – in my 'southerner' (or proud person from 'nowhere'[1]) opinion anyway – that is, you are a little stern sometimes, rather reserved and not overly talkative in some situations – and therefore am not sure this will really be to your taste ... but this is not only for your benefit and I do think that a big heart like yours should be treated to some flattery, even if only to inspire others!

After a rather complicated and eventful start, due to a challenging (in many respects) two-year European project (on conferencing), our collaboration almost ended there and then, during a meeting in your office in July 2011, with the (not very restorative) words, 'I don't think I can ever work with you again' – your words then but the feeling was quite mutual ... After having said these damning but quite memorable words, and others, during that almost fateful meeting, as I was just about to leave your office, we changed the topic and you asked me point blank what I thought about an idea you had for an international journal dedicated to restorative justice. You had been discussing it for a while already with Lode Walgrave, Stephan Parmentier and others, but it was not advancing, as you could not find the right pitch, and the project had been stalling. I replied that it sounded like quite an exciting idea (and it was), we discussed it in some more details, about what next steps should be taken, what the concept could be, what publishers could be approached and so on, but we left it at that, since for now we could not imagine ever working together again ...

A few months passed, but the idea never left either of us, and we decided to meet again and started working on it more seriously, with a newly created quintet at its helm – the editorial team – consisting of our colleagues Lode Walgrave, Inge Vanfraechem, Stephan Parmentier and the two of us. It was fairly straight sailing from there and *Restorative Justice: An International Journal* (RJIJ) was born fairly soon thereafter, with an enthusiastic Richard Hart to publish it and an editorial and international advisory board con-

1 This is what Prime Minister Theresa May called persons like me in 2016 in a 'great' speech against cosmopolitanism, citizens of the world and so on.

sisting of the *crème de la crème* in international restorative justice research, just as passionate and eager as we were. Quite the dream setup.

This was the (true) start of a strong, trusting and forward-looking collaboration, which has only grown over the last ten odd years! RJIJ was one of the projects we have been involved in together, but Ivo, you have consistently had your door open and an attentive ear to all my (sometimes wild) ideas for projects and other initiatives which resulted in some epic adventures, some of which I will talk about here.

At the Leuven Institute of Criminology and in particular in y(our) research line on 'Restorative Justice and Victimology' you have managed to bring together a very cosmopolitan crowd, mixing quite successfully local, indigenous assistants and researchers with an international cohort of academics, practitioners and other fans. You have imposed on us at times your 'workaholism' (i.e. the never-ending hours of work, day and night); you have not only 'forced' on us 'thinking days' (and I tend to really dislike these types of gatherings and exercises) but also enabled through your generosity (using moneys you had earned from your consultancy work among other sources – it has to be said that this is rather unheard of in academic or other circles – for many of us to attend conferences or undertake work-related travels. This in turn though created a strong, faithful and dedicated group, which could, for example, pull together to write up a complicated funding application in no time and with some success. You have 'inflicted' on us an incredible work ethos. You are, for example, not only capable of taking harsh criticism but also praise with calm and stoicism and have always been open to discuss problems, take advice and for me to correct your English on quite some occasions – few bosses can claim such humility! I do not think you are the best of mediators, which is a bit of an oxymoron for a restorative justice expert like you (you did try it on occasion on me and others), but that is I think because you are too keen to accommodate and be fair to explosive and demanding personas, which you seem quite drawn to, and of which you have had a fair collection of in your team, me included, of course.

To come back to the journal for a minute, it has not been straight sailing after all. After a successful launch, you and I took the helm, and worked with much enthusiasm and commitment with the editorial team, boards, publishers, copyeditors, other marketing staff and so on and although both quite democratic in our ethea, it has happened on occasion that we took undemocratic decisions, like the choice of RJIJ's cover – but I am so proud we did on that particular occasion, as I am still convinced it was by far the best choice and still regret having lost it to the 'corporate sharks' of Taylor & Francis who took away RJIJ from us. We still have so much work awaiting us on the 'relaunched' journal *The International Journal of Restorative Justice* with Eleven, which should keep us out of trouble for a while still.

A project which you enabled by your curiosity, open-mindedness and vision was born from your trust and instinct in my abilities – which I am so grateful for. I am talking here about a project that is so very close to my heart and which is the European Commission-funded Daphne project on sexual violence and restorative justice. As said, as I did sometimes, I came to your office one day, throwing at you an idea which had been going around my head for a while for a project which could maybe fit in one of the calls of the European Commission. You listened distractively, worried about other urgent work, but for a while only, as your senses were suddenly pricked by interest. As I continued explaining and expanding, you told in your usual calm, professional – slightly impersonal – tone, yes, this could have potential, and sent me out to write a page with the concept and that we would pick it up from there. What ensued was a marathon to write it up, find the right partners, the right setup, the right outcomes and so on, but it resulted in an amazing collaboration between eight partners from seven European countries, from practice to policy and to academia; we amassed so much data that we are still working on the results some years after it 'officially' ended. The work we achieved with this project is so wide-reaching that there is still a regular stream of invitations to discuss the results of this project coming our way. These results have indeed shaped practice in a number of ways and countries, have changed very sceptical minds and have had far-reaching impact – an important but not always straightforward role for academia these days.

You invited me to come along in 2014 to Oñati in Spain for an ILLS seminar on sexual abuse in the church and other institutional settings. This was such an intense but thought-provoking gathering and, thus, experience, through not only the people who participated and the themes addressed but also through a remarkable evening. After a long day of academic endeavours, as we were wondering around this little jewel of a town, five of us lost the rest of the group (Marie Keenan, Anke Bisschops, a Polish Priest whose name now escapes me and the two of us) and ended up in a mediocre restaurant having one of the most interesting and personal discussions. The discussion was light and serious at the same time; it was about religion, spirituality, philosophy and other topics along that line and the vast differences between the five of us on these topics could have been staggering, but the fact that we could talk about it, explain our points of views with such freedom, debate and agree to disagree was quite extraordinary and memorable (for me anyway) and filled me with hope and a renewed positive outlook on the world.

We were both invited in 2016 to Teheran (Iran) to speak at the first national conference on restorative justice organised by the School of Law at Tarbiat Modares University. You could not make it, but I went and it was an incredible journey in the company of the illustrious John Braithwaite, Heather Strang, Jacques Faget, Evelyn Zellerer and many other colleagues from around the world. I also met some incredibly passionate and keen local colleagues from Tarbiat Modares University, among whom Mohammad Farajiha and Hajar Azari who must be mentioned particularly but also their students and colleagues. While there, I discussed with them about possible collaborations and the setup of links between our universities and countries. So I then came back to Leuven with lots of ideas, hopes and wild plans, and that is how we came to organise an incredible seminar in Leuven, with little funds and quite a complicated setup. Indeed, we organised a (properly) cross-disciplinary, interdisciplinary and multidisciplinary seminar involving the faculties of theology, gender studies and law at KU Leuven and of law, women's studies and literature at Tarbiat Modares University and other universities in Teheran. The seminar was called 'Gender, religion, law and society: exchanges between Iran and Belgium'. Quite the programme, a bit ambitious but what an extraordinary gathering. It was a day-and-a-half where we levitated out of the realm of daily depressing world politics and where we were just a group of humans exchanging on our research interests, results, finding many common points, disagreeing on others. I do really hope that we will manage to finally do the second round in Teheran as planned as it is now overdue.

There are many other topics that I could have addressed in this *Liber* in your honour, from the writing-up of a project for an EU funding proposal on the right of women in Muslim communities and their access to the European victims' directive to accepting to come to Scotland to comment on the new developments of restorative justice (you had already come several times before for the same reason over the past two decades and were a little sceptical but still came) to your support for my book series project which I have started with Tinneke Van Camp entitled *Studies in Restorative Justice* or for the creation of the new working group on restorative justice at the European Society of Criminology with Kerry Clamp, you have always been supportive even if the ideas did not always make sense to you, or not straight away at any rate. You have been a mentor, supporter and incredible collaborator, and I really thank you for that!

Through the journal and other projects, we have travelled literally to all four corners of the world together, from Budapest, to Hong Kong, Recife and Porto Alegre in Brazil, to Milan, Bilbao, San Francisco and Sarajevo to name but a few. Through all this travelling we have met and collaborated with some incredible people and continue to do so. We have shared glasses of wine in exotic places, only after having worked hours on end instead of going and discovering these incredible places, which we would do then briefly and *au pas de charge* in usual Ivo style! Still, from eating a steak (which possibly was dog or some other poor creature's meat) in a tiny joint in Hong Kong to one of the best steaks in one of the famous barbecue parties on the beautiful terrace of Daniel and Raffaella's in Porto Alegre, what adventures we have had. And I know these are not the last ones, so I look forward to Teheran, Perth and whatever else is expecting us in the near future. Do enjoy some time to yourself, with Charlotte and all your family and friends, you have certainly deserved it!

Estelle

Part III
European journeys

The praxis of Ivo Aertsen

Christa Pelikan

Thinking about Ivo Aertsen and praxis he appears before my inner eye in two contexts: first, the European context, more precisely in his work for the promotion and development of restorative justice in the whole of Europe, and second, in relation to theoretical thinking, to connect theory and practice. I will therefore dedicate this contribution to those two fields: to European praxis and to theory-informed praxis.

1 European praxis

Ivo Aertsen is one of the most 'European' persons I know. And his praxis is indeed a European one. I got to know Ivo in Strasbourg, and during one of our first meeting days he proposed to me to pay a visit to the parliamentary assembly congregating in the Palais de L'Europe – nothing special, an ordinary session with non-spectacular topics being discussed.

While working together in the Committee of Experts on Mediation in Penal Matters we became friends. We have recently remembered this event and the work invested in drafting the first recommendation on mediation in penal matters.

In the course of the *Erinnerungsarbeit*, on digging up and activating one's memory, I became aware of the extent in which the style and the overall spirit of working for restorative justice has been shaped in the course of working within this committee. It was serious, albeit pleasant work carried out with mutual support and understanding of the participants. Ivo's seriousness and his sense of dedication to the cause of laying the foundations for an alternative handling of 'matters following from crime' were conveyed to the whole assembly that consisted of very able and highly competent professionals. The 'guests' from Canada are a very striking example of this orientation: both Ezzat Fattah and David Daubney participated – and contributed profusely – without having any voting rights in this committee. Most importantly, this spirit materialised in the way that public prosecutors from Cyprus and from Slovenia made the promotion of restorative justice in their respective countries their task and their mission. Not for all the participants, but certainly for some of them, working in the committee was the beginning of their involvement with restorative justice.

The conviction that the restorative justice idea had a chance only when professionals, practitioners, researchers, administrators of different countries worked together in an effort to implement what had been set out in the recommendation became the driving force that resulted in founding the European Forum for Victim-Offender Mediation and Restorative Justice (which later became the European Forum for Restorative Justice – EFRJ). The establishment of the EFRJ was the expression of this European spirit and perspective. A sufficient number of participants of the Council of Europe committee had been contaminated by Ivo's energy and his unflinching effort to promote restorative justice and were ready to join these efforts.[1] In the years following the founding of the EFRJ, you could see Ivo proselyting on the occasion of various conferences, in the course of specific visits to European countries – talking, talking, talking; giving advice, dispensing information, providing encouragement.

Poland was one of the first targets where Ivo and a number of other members of the EFRJ participated in a conference where Polish judges and public prosecutors became acquainted with restorative justice. This event is a good example of both the promise and the difficulties encountered when following this task. In Popowo, where we travelled together by bus from Warsaw we were met with both curiosity and interest and a lot of scepticism on the side of the representatives of the Polish judiciary. I remember quite vividly the role-play we staged to illustrate what victim-offender mediation would mean – what kind of solution and what paths of solution could be realised, and how it worked. The choice of a case had been left to the Polish audience and – not coming as a surprise to the experienced organiser of this kind of role-play – they had chosen an 'unsolvable' case. They triumphed with a mixture of uneasiness and malicious glee since they thought that they had proven to us that we were caught in an unrealistic perception of the realities of crime and criminal justice. We were a bunch of well-meaning, starry-eyed idealists. I am here dwelling on this negative experience at some length in order to show the obstacles and difficulties met.

I mentioned this also to point to a special quality that Ivo displayed on these occasions. His ability to resist getting angry and to despair, his readiness to persist. And he was right, something was set in motion in Poland. A praxis of victim-offender mediation evolved, albeit on a small and restricted scale – but with a number of dedicated people who continued to apply their energy and their considerable creativity in further developing this praxis. I am talking about Ivo's diplomatic skills – that were not skills *l'art pour l'art* but an expression of his will to achieve progress, European progress for restorative justice; this diplomacy was – and is – an expression of a praxis. Maybe the term *diplomatic skill* is not adequate at all. Rather, it is the effort to understand the position of the other and to resort to those arguments and to a line of reasoning that takes into account the other's stance, his or her ecological framework or embeddedness. It is, in fact, a truly

1 At the same time, Erich Marks from the German TOA bureau had asked me to prepare a statement of intent and a kind of explanatory memorandum to apply for financial support at a German organisation to obtain the means for setting up an umbrella organisation that would carry on and further promote restorative justice in Europe. It was easy to establish contact with the Belgian endeavour and to join forces. Belgium and Leuven with its university provided the more favourable ground to construct such an umbrella organisation.

'restorative' attitude one could say (although I prefer to avoid the overusage of the term), an attitude that attempts to recognise the other. I have been writing about recognition as a kind of reciprocal interaction that is apt to overcome opposing forces. Mutual recognition affords standing up to the tension of recognising the other as different and simultaneously holding onto one's own difference. Thus, it is more – and more far-reaching – than diplomatic compromising.

Another striking example of this quality – one I was able to observe while participating in it – was the effort of the EFRJ to support the introduction of a restorative justice praxis in Turkey. Aside from the conference taking place there in 2012, assembling an impressive number of experts from all over the world, the authorities of the criminal justice system had organised a round table with a smaller number of experts (Mark Umbreit, Ivo and myself and a number of public prosecutors interested in the matter) in order to discuss concrete ways of implementing restorative justice in Turkey. One of the contentious points was the conviction on the Turkish side that only persons with legal training were suited to act as mediators in penal matters. It was stated that it was impossible for persons without such training to acquire the necessary understanding to conduct mediation in the field of criminal law (whereas they regarded the acquisition of the necessary competence and skill to act as a mediator being well within the capacities of a law person). The Turkish colleagues insisted that conditions within the criminal justice system in Turkey as well as the expectations of the general public would not accept non-lawyers, because of their lack of authority. Again I remember Ivo's soft insistence while emphasising the importance of the role of public prosecutors in the whole process and their discretion as to the referral of cases as well as to the ultimate dropping or continuing of the indictment (or the penal procedure) after mediation had taken place. His clever way of handling the discussion and his serious efforts to understand the position of the prosecutors have not least remained in my memory because I myself went ahead with advancing my idea of the prosecutors 'going to sleep' while the mediators went about their task, which is to follow a different rationale from that of the law people. Of course, the prosecutors were not at all pleased with the image of themselves being asleep: it insinuated the idea of being passive and lazy. This was not what I had intended to convey, but obviously I was too insensitive and too much concerned with my own nice ideas. Ivo had taught me a lesson!

Ivo worked towards a European restorative justice praxis in the course of so many projects the EFRJ had taken on board and executed. He was able to master and activate the energies and the knowledge and the competence of members of the EFRJ or of other members of the 'Leuven group'. Again, I remember most lively the conference in Chisinau as part of the project 'AGIS 2: Meeting the challenges of introducing victim-offender mediation in Central Eastern Europe'. A general spirit of 'change is at the doorsteps and we will contribute to it' was palpable throughout the event, and it was especially the colleagues from Moldova who were surprising and delighting the others with their enterprising attitude and their creativity. Ivo's tireless efforts kind of sprang over and 'contaminated' the members of the steering group. On the other hand, these events and these experiences also worked as an inspiration for Ivo and his 'crew'. These were the heydays of the EFRJ when we went to the different Eastern – then Southern European cities, visited local programmes, got inspired and conferred inspiration.

There was another quality of Ivo's work and of his personality that came to bear upon the praxis he helped to spread in Europe. This was the quiet steadiness of his work and his lectures and the way he conducted sessions and led discussions. I do not talk about his quality as a workaholic; in fact, this is ambiguous. Of course, it is a great asset, but it became also a burden on his team. It was not easy to admit that you could not stand up to his working capacity – some could, but for others it was just too much. I think this was a hard lesson for him to learn. I remember when, at a dinner at the closing of project ALTERNATIVE, he was talking about his parents and his family of origin, the hard-working life they had led and that had always stood before his eyes and, I guess, had shaped his mind. 'They were working from morning until late in the evening, they knew nothing else – and that's what I got to know'; it came as an explanation and as a kind of excuse for his working so relentlessly.

Back to the European praxis once more: the support Ivo provided for restorative justice developments in Georgia. Due to the initiative of Renate Winter whom I knew since I did research at the Viennese juvenile court, I had paid a visit to Tbilisi as early as 2011. Ivo and I have never been together in Georgia – but both of us have done work there and enjoyed it especially. It is the youngest example of expanding the influence of the EFRJ, of going east once more, even beyond Europe. As such, it is a repetition and it is the ideal type of the kind of support the EFRJ is able to provide – and very competently so. Realising restorative justice praxis meant establishing strong links to the group of practitioners working in Tbilisi, links of support and links of ongoing exchange with people and groups of people, legal professionals and social work practitioners active in the new areas. In the case of Georgia, Ivo promoted these predominantly young and enthusiastic people – apart from giving lectures by attempting to establish closer ties to the EFRJ and further support activities, seminars and conferences.

2 Theory-informed praxis

Several times in the course of a lecture, or a discussion when Ivo mentioned Belgium, he spoke of 'my small but complicated country' – ironically, albeit with a certain warmth – but without sentimentality. I think this is important: this realistic, sceptical but ultimately accepting relationship with one's place of origin – as the place from where to go out into the 'wider world'. We have therefore to start from Belgium or, more specifically, from the situation at the University of Leuven. In Leuven, we found from the outset a model of close cooperation between theory and praxis – as exemplified in the work of Ivo's predecessor Tony Peters and also in that of his colleague Lode Walgrave. I got the impression that the work of the organisation Suggnomé (currently Moderator) had inspired research in the field of victim-offender mediation and restorative justice and that *vice versa* Suggnomé profited immediately from the research done at the university. There was mutual appreciation, and there was continuous exchange. It rested to a large degree on personal relationships: Ivo and Leo van Garsse (Belgium's first mediator) did get along with each other very well. Leo was one of those highly reflexive practitioners who are the 'backbone' of every new theory-induced sociopolitical development. Ivo was the friend and colleague who stood next to him, assisting, providing constructive critique and, thereby, valuable support. Ivo himself has numbered the close relationship between theory and praxis as one of the preconditions that made for the success of victim-offender mediation in Belgium.

Once again this theory-praxis relationship materialised in various projects, especially the big 'COST project: Restorative justice developments in Europe'. It comprised four working groups. The third one was specifically dedicated to theoretical work. It proved a most fruitful endeavour, as the book that was published was an outcome of this working group: 'Images of Restorative Justice Theory' made some valuable contributions. In fact, there were several books that can be called the 'fruits' of this big project. I want to mention one that bore witness to a new development, a new strand of interest within the EFRJ that was strongly supported by Ivo. It was derived from Working Group 4: 'Violent state conflict and mass victimisation' that was established later and added to the already existing three working groups. This group had published the important volume 'Restoring justice after large-scale violent conflict. Kosovo. DR Congo and the Israel-Palestinian case' where Ivo Aertsen, Jana Arsovska, Holger-C. Rohne, Marta Valinas and Kris Vanspauwen acted as editors.

Ivo was not a member of the 'theory-group' but participated in the general discussions on the project that brought together the different workshops. This brings me to reflect on the understanding of 'theory' that became a topic of controversy within the special group as well as within the larger project. It appeared that 'theory' meant different things for different people. Especially those from the continental or, more specifically, the German and Roman (French, Italian and Spanish) tradition, followed an understanding of theory as the construction of large (or at least middle range) edifices of theory, for example, system theory, functionalism, structuralism or symbolic interactionist theory. The notion of 'crime' has to find its place and its importance within such theories or pieces of theory derived from the grand theory. The colleagues with Anglo-American training used to denote as theory (or theoretical) anything that was not part of the sphere of practice. I came to understand that theory was almost identical with research, with empirical research and the procurement of empirical evidence about the working of restorative justice at its core. Ivo tended to share the Anglophone understanding; anyway, he strongly supported and admired solid empirical research and its contribution as underpinning the promotion of restorative justice. This was the Leuven tradition, and he kept proposing it to any newcomers in the field. Since it was also the tradition of the Institute for the Sociology of Law and Criminology (IRKS) and since I had done empirical research in the way of accompanying research that had supported the introduction of victim-offender mediation in Austria, we could reach an understanding easily.

As concerns the theory-praxis relationship I would contend – and once more I rely on my memory – that Ivo found his congenial partner in Siri Kemeny, an administrator-practitioner with lots of concrete experience and – most important – with a keen interest in theory. Siri really 'believed' in the importance of theory for furthering a sociopolitical understanding of restorative justice as a precondition of its firm establishment within society. Siri and Ivo shared this conviction, and this shared conviction was – apart from their enjoyment of merry-making – the basis of their excellent cooperation. It was a lucky chance, a *Glücksfall* indeed.

Starting around 2009 and most pronounced with the project ALTERNATIVE a new chord was struck. In the prolegomena of the project, a type of merging of theory and praxis was put forward that went beyond a mere mutual influence. ALTERNATIVE was to have at its core four intensive case studies (which mainly took the form of action research activities) built around, supported by and mutually feeding into three more theoretically oriented work packages and, thus, into the project as a whole. These different parts together were to produce a spectrum of theoretically grounded and empirically tested models of dealing with conflicts in intercultural settings by restorative justice-oriented processes. The four case studies were located at four different sites. The action research in each of these sites was dedicated to different levels of intercultural conflicts in a few selected security sensitive areas: (1) *at the micro level* – everyday conflicts between local residents and residents with migrant background in public/social housing (Vienna); (2) *at the meso level* – conflicts in a small town with Roma and non-Roma inhabitants (Hungary); (3) *at the meso/macro level* – interethnic conflicts within three multi-ethnic and multicultural regions: conflicts between Serbs, Albanians, Muslims and Croats (Serbia); and (4) *at the meso/macro level* – civil conflicts at three sites: conflicts between a local community and gangs of youths; between long-term residents and recent immigrants; and intercommunity sectarian conflict (Northern Ireland). The theoretically oriented work packages dealt mainly with alternative epistemologies of justice and security, with conflict and conflict resolution approaches and with restorative justice models' application and their relevance for European policies.

With the concept of alternative epistemologies, Brunilda Pali had put forward pieces of a grand theory as the guiding star of the theoretical work within the project. It was declared as the aim of the research effort 'to develop a coherent theoretical framework for an alternative understanding of security and justice'. It started from a critical analysis of 'the existing epistemologies of thinking, talking about, and doing justice in current democratic societies, especially in relation to the discourse on human security' and to 'offer a new theoretical understanding based on alternative epistemologies of doing justice and enhancing security in democratic societies on how to tackle conflict, especially in intercultural settings in a constructive and transformative way.' The inclusion of these concepts in the theoretical work packages but according to the overall linking of theory, research and praxis in ALTERNATIVE also as orientation or rather as grounding for the analysis and the action research in the four research sites provided what we meanwhile call a challenge. In fact, almost any kind of task or difficulty is called 'a challenge', but this really was 'a call to stand up to a new task'. And in almost all the work packages, the members of the groups struggled to make their research and their praxis meet the expectations that came with this theoretical orientation. Ivo had to make this effort as well, and he did it in an admirable way. He really made himself acquainted with the intellectual framework of epistemology to a degree that enabled him to present this part of the project to the outside whenever it was required – in a very clear and convincing way.

This was once more proof of Ivo's high communicative qualities and, moreover, of his readiness to engage seriously with his colleagues' ways of thinking and of supporting new paths of making theory relevant for praxis. ALTERNATIVE was also about praxis. We had intense discussions on action research, what kind of research strategies it comprised, where we had to draw the lines between the researcher and the researched and where to tread new paths of cooperation. There Ivo was one of those insisting on 'maximum feasible' involvement of the men and women at our research sites.

3 Conclusions

In general, I have seen Ivo always accepting a wide range of theoretical approaches, and I remember him only once wrinkling his nose when he read one or two paragraphs I had included in the theory paper that is part of the report on the project 'Building Social Support for Restorative Justice'. I had written about psychoanalytical theories put forward as contributing to certain developments that might underpin an increased reliance on self-activity of victims and offenders and an increasing affinity towards compensation and restoration instead of punishment. 'Do we really have to refer to psychoanalytic concepts?' he asked. But when I tried to defend their potential explanatory power he consented to leave the paragraphs there. Maybe he made allowances for the Viennese lady and wanted her to follow her whims? I remember the incidence as a pleasant one – not at all rigidly contentious but carried by an effort to understand each other and to learn from each other. And I have learned so much from Ivo! Until this day I look forward to each occasion when I meet him, to enquire how he is and to give him a big embrace as an expression of our friendship.

My long restorative journey with Ivo Aertsen

Dobrinka Chankova

My personal acquaintance with Ivo Aertsen was in the distant 1996, in the context of the Council of Europe Committee on mediation in penal matters. We were both nominated by our governments to work at a scientific level for the promotion of victim-offender mediation in Europe. While Ivo Aertsen was one of the key persons in the Committee, at that time I had some expert knowledge (but quite limited as the idea was an absolute novelty for Bulgaria) and was also the least experienced. However, the Committee accommodated me, and I was (and still I am) proud with the result – Recommendation No. R (99) 19 of theCommittee of Ministers to the Member States concerning mediation in penal matters. I was fortunate always to sit by Ivo, to communicate formally and informally with him and to receive big portions from his deep knowledgeon the subject. This interaction, I dare say, has influenced my whole professional career.

The Council of Europe Committee was constituted not only by experts but also by great visionaries, and it was committed to pioneering work. A logical consequence after the successful end of the Committee's mandate was the decision of some researchers (Ivo among them) to establish a sustainable structure for the further development of mediation in penal matters and restorative justice as a doctrine. After careful preparation, in December 2000,the European Forum for Victim-Offender Mediation and Restorative Justice (now European Forum for Restorative Justice, herein after referred to as EFRJ) was officially established in Leuven, Belgium, and Ivo Aertsen was elected as its first chair. I remember very well that moment, as in order to be able to attend and to sign the Constitution of the EFRJ I had to do the impossible and move a meeting in the frames of an international project from Paris to Brussels. During the following years, every time I visited Brussels, I stopped in Leuven (with or without good reason) taking the risk to 'steal' the precious time of EFRJ's staff. But I could not refrain from this. And Ivo (and the others) always had or made time for me, with new books, journals and ideas to share.

One of the first EFRJ's great initiatives was the COST Action A21 Restorative Justice Developments in Europe (2002-2006), and I had the chance to participate in it. Lasting four years, this project not only created strong researchers' networks and produced important publications but also led to lifelong friendships. Needless to say that Ivo Aertsen as a chair of the COST Action has had a crucial role in all of these contributions.

One of the first meetings of the COST Action was in September 2003 in Lisbon. I had already committed to developing a questionnaire for creating new restorative justice models in Europe.However,the meeting was scheduled quite soon after my return from a long stay in the United States, and I was a little unprepared. Yes, I had a draft, but within the working group it was much criticised and that led to the phrase: 'Please, criticise me but not crucify me!,' which was used long after Lisbon meeting as an idiom for the work in the COST Action.

It was hard work, no doubt. More than 20 countries participated; some of them with several experts, everybody with his or her own understanding, vision, vocabulary and different levels of proficiency in English. But Ivo has managed it! He has had time for everybody and everything; he was wisely finding a solution to many difficult situations, acting always after deep reflection, decisively but at the same time gently. And some of the problems were heavy, indeed; for example, disputes with the European Commission's bodies, most of them on financial ground, delayed payments for eight months or refusal of payments. But even then, Ivo's mediator skills helped. He always defended project participants, their rights and interests successfully. I have never met a better chair ofa project. At the end of the action, it was not only me who was asking: 'How will life go further without our COST project?' It was a kind of university for many of us; it became a lifestyle.

There were many other projects, and the contribution of the EFRJ and Ivo personally for restorative justice developments on European and global scale is well-known and widely recognised. But I will particularly mention one more – AGIS project – Meeting the challenges of introducing victim-offender mediation in Central and Eastern Europe (2004-2005). This project was a bright expression of the care of the EFRJ for the countries in the region, Bulgaria included – new democracies, with very punitive criminal justice systems, lacking information about new penal policies, not to mention experience, traditions and so on. I estimate this project as a tremendous achievement as it contributed towards introducing victim-offender mediation and reforming the criminal justice system in many countries from the region in a restorative way. To my deepest regret, my own country did not profit enough from the project results as the policy-makers were not ready for such a big transformation. Although at the final AGIS Project meeting in Sofia in October 2005 the responsible Deputy Minister of Justice, Members of the Parliament and other key persons attended, and during the next decades numerous other initiatives for promotion of restorative ideal and practices were undertaken, mainly by academics and NGOs, but Bulgaria is still behind other countries in the application of restorative instruments.

But Ivo Aertsen never stopped paying attention and observing the developments in the region. In one of the issues of *Restorative Justice: An International Journal* in 2015, there was a special section 'Notes from the field: developing restorative justice in states in transition'. Five articles following the latest achievements in Croatia, Hungary, Poland, Romania and Bulgaria were published. I had the difficult task of analysing Bulgarian results and the pleasure to co-author with Ivo the summarising article. In fact, it was not a pleasure the whole time. After rewriting and editing several times, I was frustrated and at the final stage simply said: 'I have no time for further improvements.' But even then Ivo persuaded me to reconsider the article. Reasonably, and because he does not like anything less than perfect (of course, to the largest extent possible in our case).

I am personally thankful to Ivo for many other reasons. He was my top consultant numerous times, during the past 23 years, while developing research papers, initiating projects undertaking policy-oriented actions. His advanced knowledge in many other fields – victimology, prisons, penal reform and education – I recognise and deeply respect even now, being myself a full professor. And I am very happy that Bulgaria will host the EFRJ Summer School in 2021, partly because it was my idea to start organising such schools.

But Ivo Aertsen was an important factor not only for my professional developments. He was and still is a great catalyst for the advancement of Bulgarian restorative justice theory and practice. Now I can proudly say that we have a restorative justice community among academia and the NGO sector, mainly due to the personal contacts with him and the EFRJ.We are still a rather small community, but a growing one. We are organising national restorative justice conferences every year; we have been celebrating the restorative justice week for decades; and we are teaching restorative justice in many universities, schools and beyond.

Maybe it is a good occasion to admit that I refused to participate in some of EFRJ's events because I was afraid that I would meet Ivo and I had not enough good news. That was and still is a motivation for action.

Finally, I could announce that the long-prepared Bill for diverting juvenile offenders from the criminal justice system and application of restorative practices is almost ready. Many restorative initiatives were undertaken in prisons and probation. Restorative justice is an important part of school ethos. And a big part of academia is now a restorative justice proponent.

So, I am deeply grateful to Ivo Aertsen – the friend, the 'engine' for action and the real 'institution' in the restorative justice field.

THANK YOU, IVO!

Enhancing the role of the judiciary in restorative justice: challenges for Poland

Beata Czarnecka-Dzialuk

1 Introduction

The beginnings of making Polish judges and public prosecutors aware and interested in restorative justice have been promising. The input of Professor Ivo Aertsen[1] to this has been remarkable. Several times in the late 1990s, he visited Poland to speak to them on the Belgian experience with victim-offender mediation. I will write more about this in the chapter, but first I will go back a few years earlier to share my personal experience of the support received from Ivo to learn about restorative justice and to get involved in implementing it in practice. In the beginning of 1990s, while elaborating my doctor thesis on proceedings in juveniles cases, and being also concerned with victimology, I turned my attention to those measures and methods that have an educational impact on juveniles and teach them to take responsibility for the consequences of their actions and consider the interests of those they have wronged. I have included in the conclusions of my book (Czarnecka-Dzialuk, 1993: 187) that programmes like victim-offender mediation might be needed to improve the reaction towards juvenile criminality.

In 1994, I went on a short study visit to Belgium. I succeeded in getting an ad hoc appointment with Ivo, who agreed to meet with me despite being very busy that day, in between his university work and picking up his children from school and pre-school. He gave me lots of theoretical and practical information, suggested institutions to visit and other people to meet. After few years, he delivered useful remarks on the draft of the first Polish experimental programme of victim-offender mediation in juveniles cases and then on the idea of the action-oriented research project. Even during the conference 'Restorative Justice for Juveniles' in Leuven in 1997, despite being busy with organisational matters, in a longer break, Ivo explained to me the research tools that he used in his research, translating them from Flemish into English. Then, several times he has answered my e-mails with urgent questions on how to deal with certain problem or challenge with our experimental programme. I had a feeling that I kept asking too much. But then I have already experienced the hospitality of Ivo and Charlotte (his wife), as have other Polish colleagues invited to stay at their place during conferences. This will never be forgotten.

1 I hope it is not improper for me to call him Ivo after more than 25 years of doing so.

2 On the role of the judiciary in restorative justice in Poland

Ivo has informed many Polish judges about the Belgian experience with restorative justice. These judges took part in the conferences co-organised by the Council of Europe and the Institute of Justice by the Polish Ministry of Justice in 1997 and 1998 in Popowo and in another seminar in 1998 in Warsaw. The subject of the first one was the use of victim-offender mediation in juveniles cases and the other was criminal cases for adults. The interest was so great that, thanks to this, Ivo Aertsen and Martin Wright planned to spend about a week in Poland to take part in the international conference on psychology and law in Cracow; another seminar was also organised to take place just a few days later in the Ministry of Justice to enable more judges and public prosecutors (about a hundred) to listen to their lectures. Others could learn from the publication (Czarnecka-Dzialuk & Wójcik, 1999) that resulted from the first conference. Ivo has explained in detail how different mediation programmes work, pointing out benefits and certain problems that each kind of programme might face. During the discussion he has answered many specific questions, like how to organise the cooperation of judges and mediators (Aertsen, 1999: 60-75, 134-138).

After introducing in Poland the victim-offender mediation into the codes of criminal law and criminal proceedings (in 1997) and then into the law on proceedings in juveniles cases (in 2000), it became evident that its use was much lower than was expected after seeing judges' interest during the first conference. Some research on magistrates' opinion has been carried out in order to search for explanations. I would like here to elaborate more on those surveys conducted to gauge the opinion of magistrates and probation officers. I was personally involved in these surveys.

In 2010, a survey on measures applied towards juveniles on mediation issues, with a number of questions concerning mediation, carried out at the Institute of Justice (Czarnecka-Dzialuk & Wójcik, 2011) has shown that less than half of the 311 Family Court judges who responded to the survey had ever referred a case to mediation and only a third of the 1,063 probation officers had ever suggested it. The reason might be that just under 29 per cent of the judges and 43 per cent of the probation officers had participated in special mediation training. Half of the respondents pointed out the educational aspects of mediation, and almost 40 per cent observed that mediation made amends and offered satisfaction to the injured party. The effect of mediation on the speed of the proceedings was viewed positively (curiously, by a fifth of probation officers as opposed to a tenth of judges). Ninety-four per cent of probation officers and only a little more than 50 per cent of Family Court judges were in favour of mediation being used more frequently. There was a clear connection between undergoing training and later referring cases to mediation and promoting its greater use. Another important finding was that personal experience in referring cases to mediation has a major impact on the perceived need to do so. Almost 70 per cent of Family Court judges who had mediation experience wanted to see it more widely used. Conversely, almost 70 per cent of judges who had never referred a case to mediation saw no such need.

In order to broaden the use of mediation in juvenile cases, the surveyed judges indicated activities such as informing the parties about mediation by the police, promoting mediation in the media as well as improving access to mediation services. It is interesting that only 5 per cent of judges (and 6 per cent of probation officers) mentioned a need to change the provisions regarding mediation.

Further qualitative studies at the Institute of Justice aimed at showing what prosecutors and judges who impose sentences in criminal cases think of mediation were conducted. In designing them, the intention was to get more in-depth information than it is possible from surveys and also to enable discussion among participants. This method has also weaknesses, as it has not been representative and impartial. Most of the participants selected (they volunteered or were appointed by superiors) had already a positive attitude towards mediation. Opponents rather did not appear (there were not more than two), and at the end of the meeting they apparently have changed their opinion on mediation, although some had no personal experience with mediation[2] (Czarnecka-Dzialuk, 2013a: 113-120, 2013b: 980). The judges participated in focus group discussions in four groups at the end of 2011, and the prosecutors, likewise in four groups, a couple of months later. Almost 50 people took part in the group interviews.

This research confirmed that mediation is efficient. All the magistrates taking part in the discussions thought that mediation had a large potential and was an effective way to resolve disputes, given that the parties seldom returned to the prosecutors or the courts but came to a permanent reconciliation through mediation that most often ended in an agreement and did so relatively quickly. Cases referred to mediation most often end with agreement and thus in relatively short time; cases that lasted for months or years are sometimes being solved after two mediation sessions. Mediation is a real chance for the parties. Regardless of whether it ended in agreement, mediation was the first opportunity for the parties to sit down for a quiet discussion. The magistrates stressed their personal satisfaction with making it possible to rectify situations and expressed their feeling that mediation had been a good lesson for society. They noticed its educational influence on the offender. With successful mediation some concrete situations have been evoked, for example, peaceful holidays for the parties and their families.

The magistrates have pointed out that mediators played a key role for mediation to be effective as they have specific knowledge (not necessarily legal knowledge, although some understanding of the law is essential), the skills and personal capacities essential for approaching the parties, intuition and emotional intelligence. All this, however, laid bare the problem of not being able to verify the competence of mediators. This does nothing to

---

2 I presented the results of this research in the report 'Mediation prospects and barriers: the voice of Polish magistrates', which I delivered at an international conference of the European Forum for Restorative Justice in Helsinki.

build confidence in them, in particular if mediators handling criminal cases are not required to complete specialist training that complied with specified standards, as is the case with mediators authorised to mediate in juvenile cases.

The magistrates indicated several obstacles in referring cases to mediation. The concern that the injured party would feel that having the case referred to mediation meant that the justice system simply wanted to offload it and the concern that the attitude of the injured party would have too great a bearing on the outcome of the case were shown to be barriers to the practical use of mediation. At the same time, lacking the means to purchase a ticket to come to a meeting can sometimes result in a failure to agree to mediation. Inadequate mechanisms to enforce the obligations laid down in mediation agreements were also brought up in discussions. The participation of lawyers in mediation can create problems, as they place undue weight on interests and claims. There were various opinions on mediation in domestic violence cases where, on the one hand, great care had to be taken to ensure that there is certain balance among parties; on the other hand, it was noticed that the injured party was in a strong negotiating position. There was a divided opinion over whether cases should be referred to mediation more often by the police, who have not previously had any experience with this issue. Finding the best moment to suggest mediation to the parties was also mentioned as problematic. It is not always a case of 'the sooner the better' as the parties may not be ready for mediation the moment the case becomes a police matter. This is why it is sometimes worth suggesting mediation again after a certain time.

Mediation is valued, but judges and prosecutors would like to see this remedy give them more benefits in conducting proceedings. Above all, those in the discussion groups pointed out the need for provisions enabling cases to be discontinued due to a successfully concluded mediation where the accepted obligations have been performed. They expressed that they are in favour of expanding the catalogue of offences prosecuted on complaint where mediation should be used more often. This also applies to cases brought to court with a voluntary submission to a penalty where the interests of the injured party are not sufficiently protected. Such cases constitute more than 55 per cent of the proceedings that prosecutors bring to court. The procedure for case referrals (enabling it in earlier moment) and reception of agreements for mediation should be simplified.

Prosecutors and judges claimed that the main obstacle to mediation is the fact that the public prosecutor's office is 'governed by statistics' and that their performance was assessed on completed cases. Those who work in large cities especially complained about this pressure. In spite of the provision, the time of mediation is not included in the time of preparatory proceedings, the computer information system shows also cases referred to mediation were kept pending for long periods; they remain in prosecutor's docket. Mediation, even when viewed as successful in terms of reaching the agreement, in practice does not have the meaning of success for public prosecutor, bearing in mind what has been said earlier about the evaluation of their performance. Although they initially claimed that mediations drag out proceedings, they later admitted in discussions that cases take months to come to trial, a time during which mediation could achieve a great deal. Some judges and prosecutors declared that even if they would get remarks on the duration of proceedings, they would keep referring cases to mediation, simply because it is a good reaction. However, many respondents conveyed that in general there was no knowledge of mediation and little awareness of its existence.

Other research concerning the discussed topic conducted in Poland showed similar findings. Survey on the opinion of two groups of judges – those who refer cases to mediation and those who never did it – carried out in the Institute of Justice in 2004 has shown that those with more experience accept mediation much more than others (Wójcik, 2007: 555). A pilot study in Lublin area (survey of 60 respondents: judges, public prosecutors and barristers, 20 respondents in each group) showed moderate level of knowledge about mediation and their ambivalent or negative attitude towards mediation proceedings, even if they indicated the advantages of solving conflicts through mediation. It is worth mentioning here that respondents pointed out only benefits of legal character while psychological benefits were omitted. Lack of knowledge results in the fear and reluctance to undertake unknown dealings (Lewicka-Zelent & Niedźwiadek, 2014: 78). Sceptical attitude of magistrates to mediation has been reported also by mediators surveyed in 2001 and 2002. As Zalewski (2003, 2009, 2015) has written, 77 per cent of them encountered lack of understanding of mediation's significance on the part of judges and prosecutors. Mediators also felt lack of cooperation from the judiciary system, in particular the lack of training and lack of room. Thus, it is concluded that the attitude of magistrates and lawyers might be the reason for the low number of referred cases and one of the barriers to developing mediation.

Another survey in the Silesian district (Katowice, Gliwice; among 174 respondents there were 64 judges and 110 public prosecutors) shows participants' lack of knowledge or misconception about mediation goals and possibilities for the criminal proceedings. Among the reasons given for justifying not referring cases to mediation were lack of cases suitable for mediation and making the time of the proceedings longer (see also Cielecki, 2006: 52) and lack of the possibility to discontinue the preliminary proceedings when the mediation successfully led to the parties reaching an agreement. Nearly 60 per cent of the respondents were in favour to broaden the use of mediation; however, 86 per cent of public prosecutors and 27 per cent of judges admitted that they did not refer any case to mediation in the previous three years. The respondents' suggestions to overcome the barriers were the same as in other research – introducing the possibility to close the case after successful mediation and changing the way of registering the lengths of proceedings in the statistics (Sitarz, Jaworska-Wieloch, Lorek, Sołtysiak-Blachnik, Zawiejski, 2012:148; Stańdo-Kawecka, Deszyńska 2013).

The survey carried out among 122 prosecutors in the area subordinated to the Gdańsk Court of Appeal shows similar results in answering the question on how often they refer a case to mediation. Almost 92 per cent said that they did so rarely or very rarely (out of which 72 per cent answered *very rarely*). The majority of prosecutors do not refer cases to mediation (*sometimes* – 35 per cent; *never* – 59 per cent), but they think that mediation is necessary in creating civil society (*yes* – 59 per cent; *not or definitely not* – 24 per cent). Qualifications of mediators were assessed as sufficient only by 18 per cent of the surveyed. Almost 68 per cent of the surveyed were not able to assess the work of mediators. Answer to the question whether it is possible to achieve the effect of resocialisation through mediation was mostly negative (*not or rather not* – 62 per cent; *yes* – 27 per cent). The majority also thinks that mediation does not fulfil the social sense of justice (*not or absolutely not* – 66.4 per cent; *yes* – 24.5 per cent).

Judges from the same area and also judges from Mińsk and Białystok rarely encounter mediation (73 per cent – *rarely* or *very rarely*), but they think that mediation is generally a good method of solving disputes (56 per cent) although it is rarely effective (*in neither case* – 48 per cent; *three and more* – 30 per cent). Judges' attitude towards mediation have been positive – mediation contributes to civic society (*yes or rather yes* – 79 per cent) and fulfils its role (*yes or rather yes* – 40.3 per cent; *not or absolutely not* – 29 per cent). They regard qualifications of mediators as sufficient or high – 40 per cent, and insufficient, low – 24 per cent. Thirty per cent of judges could not assess the work of mediators. Judges have a different opinion from prosecutors with regard to the possible effect of resocialisation. The majority thinks that it can be achieved through mediation (*yes* – 51 per cent; *not or rather not* – 37 per cent). In spite of that, the majority of judges, as well as the majority of prosecutors, think that mediation does not fulfil the social sense of justice (*yes* – 30.6 per cent; *not or rather not* – 54.8 per cent) (Zalewski, 2015).

Diagnosis of the use of mediation and of the reasons for its lower-than-expected popularity elaborated few years ago by Agrotec Polska for the Ministry of Justice[3] indicates several matters bounded with magistrates' attitude towards mediation as barriers. Among the causes of the low popularity of mediation among judges are: judges believing firmly in their own conciliation abilities, the schematic way of thinking and proceeding by judges, low training activity, low quality of conciliation agreements, the problem of qualification of cases for mediation, ineffective mediation referral process, insufficient information on mediators, lack of incentives for judges to refer cases to mediation and belief that conciliation obligations will not be fulfilled. Judges are often unable to present to the parties the potential advantages of mediation, such as avoidance of secondary victimisation caused by unpleasant and stressful contacts with official institutions, the possibility to express their emotions and the perpetrator understanding the mistakes made and the necessity to change their behaviour.[4]

Therefore, it is recommended to enhance awareness, through trainings and exchange of experience, of differences between the roles of judges and mediators and their mutually

3 Final report www.mediacja.gov.pl/files/doc/rk-mediacje-agrotec-16.09-en.pdf (last accessed 5 May 2019).
4 As above, p. 21.

complementary competences and not competition. The training programme should include practical exercises on how to inform the parties on the possibility of mediation by presenting the associated advantages and discussing clearly the course of mediation itself. The parties to the conflict must understand the nature of mediation and be able to give their informed consent to participate in mediation. It is recommended to provide an opportunity for the mediator to conduct an information meeting, concerning mediation, and the costs of this meeting should be included in the costs of legal proceedings covered by the State Treasury (both parties should be able to participate in the meeting free of charge).

3 Conclusion

After extensive research on magistrates' opinion on mediation, pointing out problems and concluding with similar proposals, it seems it would be easier to improve the situation and enhance the role of judiciary in restorative justice. In practice, however, it is not so. There are (or were) certain steps forward. For instance, coordinators for mediation have been appointed in the public prosecutor's office and in the courts. According to the Sec. 16a of the Law on the System of Common Courts, the coordinator for mediation in district and regional courts acts to promote development of mediation, provides efficient communication between judges and mediators and cooperates in organising information meetings.[5] Few years ago, some of the magistrates who took part in focus group discussions had never met the coordinators, which suggests that this function happens to be treated just as an official one ('on paper'). However, those who met an actively engaged coordinator have underlined their efforts to organise Mediation Week, certain meetings and trainings.

Mediation appears more often in the trainings for judiciary (however, probably still not sufficiently) and in the university curricula. However, it was not easy to find magistrates to take part in the 'attractive training' (those who joined evaluated it so) organised in Warsaw within the framework of the European Forum for Restorative Justice project.[6]

The long-awaited-for legal provision by magistrates, allowing for the discontinuance of criminal proceedings after successful mediation (Art. 59a of the Criminal Code, adopted in 2013) was repealed just nine months after coming into force when a new government came into power. The explanatory memorandum to the Bill of March 2016 criticised it for 'making possible to avoid responsibility for quite serious offences and

---

5 The law on the system of common courts of 27 July 2001, *Journal of Laws* (Dz.U) 2019, item. 52.

6 'Developing judicial training for restorative justice: Towards a European approach'. Retrieved from www.euforumrj.org/developing-judicial-training-for-restorative-justice-towards-a-european-app.

provoking pressure on the injured party to submit the motion' (without any empirical evidence).[7]

The problem of magistrates' lack of confidence in mediators' competence is not solved sufficiently, as there is still no requirement for them to complete standardised quality training (such requirement is provided only for those mediating in juveniles' cases). The Law on the System of Common Courts points out just 'having knowledge and skills in leading mediation' that can be confirmed by simple statement (Arts. 157a and 157b §2). A lot still needs to be done. In my opinion, the main barrier to enhance the role of judiciary in restorative justice rests in the knowledge, the awareness and their will (but also the will of those shaping criminal policy). After 20 years, I would like Ivo to come again to Poland in order to share his experience in mediation matters and to inspire again new public prosecutors and judges as he did that time.

References

Aertsen, I. (1999). Victim-offender mediation in Belgium: legal background and practice. In B. Czarnecka-Dzialuk & D. Wójcik (eds.), *Mediation in juveniles cases* (pp. 60-75). Warsaw: PWN.

Cielecki, T. (2006). Zarządzanie zmianą – refleksje o polityce kryminalnej w Polsce na tle wprowadzenia mediacji w prawie karnym. *Mediator*, 1, 52-64.

Czarnecka-Dzialuk, B. (1993). *Nieletni sprawcy czynów karalnych przed sądem rodzinnym*. Warsaw: Agencja Scholar.

Czarnecka-Dzialuk, B. (2013a). Perspektywy i bariery mediacji w opinii prokuratorów i sędziów. In L. Mazowiecka (ed.). *Mediacja karna jako instytucja ważna dla pokrzywdzonego* (pp. 89-116). Warsaw: PWN.

Czarnecka-Dzialuk, B. (2013b). Mediacja w sprawach karnych w opinii sędziów i prokuratorów. In A. Błachnio-Parzych, J. Jakubowska-Hara, J. Kosonoga & H. Kuczyńska (eds.), *Problemy wymiaru sprawiedliwości karnej. Księga Jubileuszowa Profesora Jana Skupińskiego* (pp. 978-988). Warsaw: LEX a Wolters Kluwer business.

Czarnecka-Dzialuk, B. & Wójcik, D. (eds). (1999) *Juvenile Offender-Victim Mediation/ Mediacja. Nieletni przestępcy i ich ofiary* (English and Polish version in the same volume), Warsaw: PWN.

Czarnecka-Dzialuk, B. & Wójcik, D. (2011). Reagowanie na czyny karalne i demoralizację nieletnich – koncepcje teoretyczne, statystyki i opinie sędziów rodzinnych. In A. Siemaszko (ed.), *Stosowanie prawa. Księga jubileuszowa z okazji XX-lecia Instytutu Wymiaru Sprawiedliwości* (pp. 868-922).Warsaw: LEX a Wolters Kluwer business.

7 Available (in Polish) at: http://orka.sejm.gov.pl/Druki8ka.nsf/0/0DCDFBC92E81FB4CC1257F47004B0C7D/%24File/207.pdf (last accessed 6 June 2019), p. 18.

Lewicka-Zelent, A. & Niedźwiadek, K. (2014). Mediacja sądowa w opinii sędziów, prokuratorów i adwokatów. *Probacja*, 3, 63-80.

Sitarz, O, Jaworska-Wieloch, A., Lorek, D., Sołtysiak-Blachnik, A. & Zawiejski, P. (2012). Mediacje karne w opiniach stron postępowania oraz sędziów i prokuratorów - wyniki badań ankietowych. Część II: Opinie skazanych oraz sędziów i prokuratorów. *Czasopismo Prawa Karnego i Nauk Penalnych*, rok XVi, 4, 123-148.

Stańdo-Kawecka, B. & Deszyńska, J (2013). Final national report of Poland - *The 3E Model for a restorative justice strategy in Europe*. Retrieved from http://3e-rj-model.web.auth.gr/files/national_reports/Poland.pdf (last accessed 5 June 2019).

Wójcik, D. (2007). Poglądy sędziów na temat mediacji w sprawach karnych. In K. Krajewski (ed.). *Nauki penalne wobec problemów współczesnej przestępczości. Księga jubileuszowa z okazji 70. rocznicy urodzin Profesora Andrzeja Gaberle* (pp. 555-568). Warsaw: Wolters Kluwer Polska.

Zalewski, W. (2003). Mediacja w polskim prawie karnym - teoria i praktyka, *Przegląd Sądowy*, 6, 92-115.

Zalewski, W. (2009). Sprawiedliwość naprawcza w Polsce. *Iuris Effectus. Kwartalnik Krajowej Szkoły Sądownictwa i Prokuratury*, Numer specjalny.

Zalewski, W. (2015): Poland. In F. Dünkel, J. Grzywa-Holten & P. Horsfield (eds.), *Restorative Justice and Mediation in Penal Matters - A stocktaking of legal issues, implementation strategies and outcomes in 36 European countries* (pp. 637-672). Mönchengladbach: Forum Verlag Godesberg.

Justice, security and victims: linking theory and practice

Vesna Nikolić-Ristanović and Sanja Ćopić

1 Introduction

Justice, security and victims are the topics which both authors of this chapter have been interested in for quite a long time. This is not surprising that, while doing our own research, both of us came across the work of Ivo Aertsen very early, and we found it inspirational and valuable for our own research and activism in Serbia. The fact that in his work Ivo tended to deal with the issues of justice, security and victims from both theoretical and practical point of views, as part of interdisciplinary policy and practice-oriented criminological research in the field of victimology, penology and restorative justice, is of particular importance. Moreover, application of research results for the creation of mechanisms for reduction of crime and the advancement of human rights (e.g. victim support, prison programmes, victim-offender mediation, restorative justice in intercultural context, transitional justice, initiation and development of the European Forum for Restorative Justice etc.) was the exciting common denominator for our efforts to make the world we live in a better place.

We recognised our common interests in both topics and the approach Ivo has used. We read his publications and attended the conferences, seminars and similar events he organised and/or took part in them. On different occasions we met him in person and started different ways of professional cooperation with him as well as with his colleagues from the Leuven Institute of Criminology (LINC). This resulted in joint projects, but inevitably this led to friendship as well.

This chapter aims to acknowledge the importance Ivo and his work had for our policy- and practice-oriented research in the use of restorative justice in different settings: to empower victims and foster dialogue in Serbian post-conflict social context and to raise the awareness of prisoners about victims and restorative justice in order to prevent future victimisations. This is a unique opportunity for us to share our personal and professional experiences, inspirations, challenges, ideas and other ways we got food for thought and spirit during our more-than-a-decade-long cooperation with Ivo.

The chapter is divided into two parts. In the first part, we share some memories which have a rather personal meaning for us because they are connected to building personal relationship with Ivo as a colleague and a friend. In the second part, we present theoretical concepts and practical mechanisms developed by the Victimology Society of Serbia

(VDS) in relation to applying restorative justice in different settings: applying restorative approaches in multi-ethnic communities in Serbia within the project ALTERNATIVE on developing alternative understandings of security and justice through restorative justice approaches in intercultural settings, which was promoted and coordinated by Ivo,[1] and developing and piloting victim awareness-raising programme in the female prison in Serbia.

2 Ivo as a colleague and a friend: how we got to know each other

Both authors of this chapter became familiar with research of Ivo Aertsen first through his books, papers and conference proceedings and then through different projects and discussions with Ivo's colleagues from the LINC. For Vesna, the first encounter with the Leuven team was in 2002, when she was invited by Professor Stephan Parmentier to take part in the *Expert seminar on reparation for victims of gross and systematic human rights violations in the context of political transitions.* On this occasion, she also met other colleagues involved in research on restorative justice in general and in its application in post-conflict societies in particular. This was the beginning of a long and fruitful cooperation, which led to Vesna's involvement in the COST project, *Restorative justice developments in Europe*, coordinated by Ivo. Her participation in this project was linked primarily to the international workshop, *Restorative justice and contact hypothesis in dealing with ethno-national conflicts* that was *held at the* Bar-Ilan University in Tel Aviv (Israel) in 2006.

The workshop was organised on the occasion of the meeting of the COST project working group whose aim was to explore the potential of restorative justice in dealing with the aftermath of violent conflicts in various (post-)conflict areas (Aertsen et al., 2008). Vesna was invited to speak about the situation in Serbia, which was followed by the invitation to write the chapter for the book Restoring justice after large-scale violent conflicts: Kosovo, DR Congo and the Israeli-Palestinian case *(2008)* edited by Ivo and several other colleagues. The book is a fascinating collection of papers with examples which give hope that restorative justice can bring real change even in the societies with very complex and lasting conflicts, divisions and prejudices. It showed that in every post-conflict society there is some seed of restorative practices that can be cultivated again and used as a tool for achieving peace through constructive communication and mutual understanding.

---

1 The research project *Developing alternative understandings of security and justice through restorative justice approaches in intercultural settings within democratic societies – ALTERNATIVE* received funding from the European Union's Seventh Framework Programme (FP7-SEC-2011-1) under grant agreement no. 285368. The project aimed to provide an alternative and deepened understanding of justice and security based on empirical evidence of how to handle conflicts within intercultural contexts in democratic societies in order to set up security solutions for citizens and communities.

Vesna was given a very challenging task – to elaborate on the potential in Serbia for dealing with the killings in Racak (Kosovo) through an overview of informal mechanisms as positive examples of restorative efforts in dealing with conflicts between Albanians and Serbs in post-war Kosovo (Nikolić-Ristanović, 2008). This happened to be a very important learning experience in her research and activist effort in looking for the model of reconciliation that best suits the needs of Serbia and other countries of the former Yugoslavia. But this was not the only time when Ivo's suggestions were precious for helping Vesna to put her ideas into a broader and clearer perspective. She was and still is particularly grateful for Ivo's help in revising her article *Communication about the past and reconciliation: Lessons from the Western Balkan*, which was at the time submitted for publication in the *Restorative Justice: An International Journal* (Nikolić-Ristanović, 2015). She particularly remembered how Ivo found time to discuss the article when they met in Leuven at the end of the ALTERNATIVE project. She was hosted by Ivo and his wife Charlotte in their nice house at the outskirts of Leuven. Vesna enjoyed their hospitality very much and was particularly grateful that, in spite of many obligations, Ivo found time to go through the article with her and make some final comments.

During her research stay in LINC in 2009, Vesna had various opportunities to communicate with Ivo and to get to know him on a more personal level as well. Moreover, she was honoured by being invited by Ivo to give a lecture to his master students of the restorative justice course, focusing on the potential of restorative justice in Serbia to deal with the killings in Racak (Kosovo). The lecture was based on her chapter in the previously mentioned book (Nikolić-Ristanović, 2008). The image that she got at that time about Ivo has not changed much over time. Hard working and passionately devoted to his professional tasks, which are firmly embedded in his overall life, on one side, and on the other side, his being a nice, warm and supportive person who always managed to find time to spend with colleagues in more informal ways. Vesna remembers the day when she was about to leave Leuven after her research work. Stephan Parmentier invited her and her husband for a lunch in the Sicilian restaurant, not far from the university. Ivo was invited, too, but he had some strict deadline to meet, and, when Stephan, Vesna and her husband were convinced that he would not be able to come, he showed up. Of course, he did not have time to join the others in mouth-watering lunch accompanied with great Italian wine degustation. But Vesna and the others did have a nice chat with Ivo and appreciated very much that, in spite of time pressure, he decided to come and say goodbye.

Sanja met Ivo for the first time in Leuven in 2002. She attended the *International summer course in human rights*, which was a two-week course hosted by the University of Tilburg in the Netherlands and the University of Leuven in Belgium. As she had already started to think about developing her PhD project proposal on restorative justice, she came across various pieces of Ivo's work. Being in Leuven and meeting Ivo was not to be missed. During her one-week stay in Leuven, she asked some of the professors how to find Ivo at the university, and she got directions. The university building had been repaired, and she needed time to move through the corridors to get to Ivo's office. Sanja found him working, surrounded with books and piles of papers all over his small office. Although the meeting was not arranged in advance and Sanja just barged in, Ivo's generosity and hospitality was amazing. In spite of being busy, he found time to talk to her. They had a short, but very fruitful and pleasant conversation, and Sanja left Ivo's office with plenty of ideas and a big bundle of photocopies of articles and book chapters published on various aspects of restorative justice. That was the best present Ivo could give her. These materials were a real treasure since at the time it was not easy to get relevant publications in Serbia, and buying them was a rather expensive thing to do. She used these reference materials when she wrote her PhD dissertation on restorative justice and the criminal justice system in which she quoted the works of Ivo and his Leuven colleagues, and she still keeps all these papers on her book shelves. Next time, she met Ivo in Sofia (Bulgaria) in 2005 at the Third Regional Seminar of AGIS project, *Meeting the challenges of introducing victim-offender mediation in Central and Eastern Europe*, which was organised by the European Forum for Restorative Justice. As always, Ivo's presentations and discussions were a valuable source of information and ideas for working in the field of restorative justice. These were important moments that paved Sanja's research interests in restorative justice, and she remains active in this field till today.

In 2008, the Victimology Society of Serbia hosted the annual general meeting and conference of the Victim Support Europe (VSE) entitled, *Taking the victims agenda forward*, which was held in Belgrade. For the first time, the concept of the VSE's annual conferences was changed a bit and several thematic workshops were organised. One of them was dedicated to supporting victims of terrorism. It was designed and facilitated by Ivo. He developed discussion around the findings of the EU-funded research project on developing standards for assistance to victims of terrorism and restorative justice. The workshop focused on three important issues: explaining and understanding key characteristics of terrorism; analysing the consequences of terrorism on primary, secondary and tertiary victims; and exploring possible ways of addressing victims' needs in the aftermath of terrorist attacks. In this context, the possible role of restorative justice principles and practices in dealing with victims of terrorism was assessed as well.

Our cooperation developed over time was particularly intensive during the preparation and implementation of the ALTERNATIVE project. We had the opportunity to meet regularly and discuss various issues – from theoretical concepts and action research design, to the research findings and their further use to feed the initial theoretical framework and, thus, linking theory and practice all the time. VDS hosted one of the project's Steering Committee meetings in Belgrade in winter 2014. This was Ivo's second visit to Belgrade and the VDS. Researchers from all partner organisations, including the authors of this chapter, had fruitful discussions about action research in different countries, including Serbia, and we all got useful feedback about our own work from the colleagues, including Ivo. These were the moments of inspiration and intellectual exchange, which fed our thoughts and shaped our further work. From that meeting, as well as from other project meetings, we have nice memories not only about discussions related to the research and organisation of the work but also about the ways how Ivo wisely supported us in coping with many personal challenges we faced during the project time. Moreover, we keep some great memories about numerous moments of relaxed socialising after working hard.

We hope to have Ivo's support in future work as well and to continue our fruitful cooperation. And, in this regard, we have to express our deep honour and happiness that just a few months before this manuscript was prepared for publishing, Ivo had kindly accepted the invitation from the Victimology Society of Serbia to be the keynote speaker at the Tenth Anniversary Conference of the Victimology Society of Serbia entitled, *Victimisation and diversity: towards holistic approach to victimology and victims' rights*, which is going to be held in Belgrade in November 2019.

3 Justice, security and victims as our common points of research interest

Justice, security and victims are some of the common points of research interest for both Ivo and the authors of this chapter. In this part, we provide some lessons learnt as well as some challenges and experiences from the projects that included developing, testing and upgrading of some restorative approaches in different settings in Serbia. The first one relates to applying restorative justice to empower victims and foster dialogue in three multi-ethnic and intercultural communities in Serbia within the project ALTERNATIVE. The other one refers to developing and piloting a programme in the women's prison in Serbia that raises awareness about restorative justice and the impact of a crime on a victim.

3.1 *Applying restorative approaches in multi-ethnic communities in Serbia*

Dealing with past and present-day conflicts that have their roots in the war-period is of pivotal importance for enabling people in the post-conflict societies to rebuild mutual trust and social relationships, prevent further divisions or eruption of new conflicts, to reconcile and to re-establish democracy and social justice. As suggested by some research, the transitional justice discourse in Serbia has been strongly influenced by legal approaches (Fischer, 2016a, 2016b; Nikolić-Ristanović & Ćopić, 2016). Although relevant, legal approaches suffer from various shortcomings (Minow, 1998: 30-31); thus, they need to be complemented with non-judicial mechanisms, including restorative approaches that foster encounters and dialogue (Foss et al., 2012).

In 2002, the VDS initiated efforts to find a model which might alleviate existing conflicts and also prevent future conflicts in Serbia. These resulted in the establishment of the *Association 'Joint Action for Truth and Reconciliation'*, which presented a framework for developing the so-called Third Way model of communication about conflicts (Nikolić-Ristanović, 2015). The Third Way model is defined as a non-conflicting, inclusive, two-way communication of people with different experiences of war and other conflicts about the past and implicates dealing with all crimes, victims and perpetrators, regardless of their ethnic identities, political affiliations or other personal features. This approach is based on mutual respect, two-way communication, care about human rights, empowerment and reintegration of all persons affected by conflict by using a wide range of restorative approaches for establishing truth and reconciliation and a proactive approach in dealing with the past (Nikolić-Ristanović & Srna, 2010). Its aim is to restore trust as well as reconciliation between various social groups in Serbia and the region. Thus, it is not surprising that Ivo Aertsen as well as some other authors have recognised the Third Way model of communication as a possible way of applying restorative justice in post-conflict societies (Liebmann, 2007; Aertsen et al., 2008).

The Third Way model of communication has been developed over time. In 2014, it was tested, re-examined and upgraded in the context of action research conducted by VDS within the project ALTERNATVE. It was done in the form of participatory seminars entitled, *From the conflict towards peaceful life in the community*, which were conducted in three multi-ethnic and intercultural communities in Serbia who were more directly affected by the wars in the former Yugoslavia (Nikolić-Ristanović et al., 2018a). Seminars presented a process of bringing together citizens, representatives of civil society organisations and state institutions on the local level into dialogue. The core part of this intervening process was on raising awareness and working towards capacity-building of the participants for dealing with conflicts with the use of restorative approaches and their dissemination in their social networks.

The seminars consisted of three mutually linked thematic workshops focused on communication about conflicts, victimisation and security; recognising similarities in different experiences; and learning and upgrading knowledge about restorative justice and testing the restorative circle model (Nikolić-Ristanović et al., 2018a). The main methodological approach of the action research was setting the laboratory/experiment conditions for optimal contact and communication between members of different groups as the seminar participants, which allowed for exploring the applicability of the Third Way model of communication and coming to ideas about its possible further development. This included three main components. First, we took care that most of the conditions for optimal contact are met (Allport, 1954; Amir, 1998; Nikolić-Ristanović, 2015; Pettigrew,

1998). Second, the communication framework was set as a part of ground rules, with elements of mindfulness[2] included. Third, different relaxation and empowering techniques, including yoga, breathing techniques and meditation, were used throughout seminars as the generator of inner peace and positive personal and intergroup change. In addition, a restorative circle model was tested. Therefore, we intended to explore how seminar participants communicate/change their communication patterns about difficult topics, including their own conflicts/victimisations and related needs, when conditions are controlled and space is created for them to feel safe and relaxed. In addition, we tried to demonstrate and give people in the local communities a kind of a tool which could be used for dealing with/solving problems, tensions and conflicts that may prevent future conflicts and enhance both inter- and intra-ethnic relationships. In this way, the seminars provided a space for experiential learning, networking and building relationships and cooperation. At the same time, the Third Way model was re-examined and upgraded in relation to both theory and practice.

What we learnt from this action research can be summarised as follows: the Third Way model of communication, and the restorative circle model, are applicable and appropriate approaches for multi-ethnic communities in Serbia for conflict prevention and transformation. Communication patterns can change when conditions for optimal contact are met, which enables constructive communication (dialogue). Communication framework (a framework for restorative dialogue) is important: it provides a space for mutual respect and trust, fosters openness and enables mutual understanding and support. This enables people to communicate about difficult issues in an easier way. Recognising similarities in different experiences may contribute to a better understanding of one's own self, for understanding others and for making people feel closer to each other, which in turn prevents estranging. The importance of using different aspects of yoga that contributes to concentration on the present (mindfulness) as well as to inner peace and balance (e.g. breathing techniques, relaxation and meditation) was also recognised within the action research. Therefore, the upgraded Third Way model is envisaged as an approach that would rest upon the following elements/components: conditions for optimal contact; communication framework in the spirit of restorative justice, yoga and mindfulness; peacemaking/restorative circle model (a circle format); and a solution-focused approach (Nikolić-Ristanović et al., 2018a). This may make this approach a unique and original model of conflict transformation in intercultural settings, not only in the region of the former Yugoslavia but also in a broader intercultural context (Vanfraechem & Aertsen, 2016).

---

2 A mental state achieved by focusing one's awareness on the present moment, while calmly acknowledging and accepting one's feelings, thoughts and bodily sensations. It is used as the part of meditation and as a therapeutic technique.

3.2 *Introducing restorative justice in prison settings*

Introducing restorative approaches in prison settings is another possible way of implementing restorative justice in practice. It is argued that restorative justice can bring more humanity into prison systems; it may help in the treatment of prisoners and contribute to their preparation for release and reintegration. On the other hand, introducing victims' perspectives, either through their direct involvement in restorative justice programmes implemented in prisons or through initiatives that raise prisoners' awareness of victims, contributes to victims' visibility, empowerment and healing. Taking that as a starting point, in 2015, the Victimology Society of Serbia developed the *Program on raising awareness about the impact of a crime on a victim and on restorative justice*[3] as a part of its long-term advocacy and support to female prisoners (Nikolić-Ristanović & Ćopić, 2015; Ćopić & Nikolić-Ristanović, 2018; Ćopić & Nikolić-Ristanović, forthcoming). The programme, which was piloted in the women's prison, presents an example of victim awareness programme oriented towards teaching prisoners to accept ideas and values of restorative justice; to be aware of victims' feelings, needs and rights; and to address their own criminal behaviour. To our knowledge, this was the first programme based on restorative justice principles that was implemented in a prison setting in Serbia. It was primarily inspired by different victim awareness programmes implemented in prisons worldwide, but it was also informed by other experiences of implementing restorative approaches within the prison settings, including the one in Belgium, in which Ivo was invloved (Aertsen, 2006, 2012).

There were four main aims of the programme: first, acquiring better understanding and developing a positive approach towards one's own self and others and overall personal growth; second, becoming familiar with restorative justice principles and communication skills in the spirit of restorative justice; third, raising awareness of participants about the impact of crime on a victim and victims' needs in the aftermath of harmful events and on restorative justice in order to prevent future victimisation (both during their stay in prison and after release) and divert them from committing new crimes; and fourth, becoming familiar with yoga and mindfulness and their transformative/restorative potential. The programme was implemented in a form of a series of six workshops followed by the evaluation interviews with female prisoners who took part in the entire programme (with six out of twelve who started the programme). The main methodological framework for implementing workshops was interactive group work with the use of different techniques: presentations; discussions; video materials; different exercises;

3 The programme was developed and piloted within the project *Promoting alternative sanctions and restorative justice measures*, which was implemented in partnership by the Center for Democracy Foundation and the Victimology Society of Serbia during 2014 and 2015. The project was supported by the Delegation of the European Union to the Republic of Serbia within the framework of the programme entitled *The European instrument for democracy and human rights*.

drawings; questionnaires; case studies; relaxation exercises, including yoga and meditation; and listening to music and singing. The entire programme had the form of a feminist action research, which reflected in its permanent development and adjustment to the needs of prisoners.

In order to secure a safe, supportive and trusting environment for programme delivery, the following principles were established: 'far-close', that is, gradual and controlled narration about participants' experience of victimisation and their victimising behaviour towards others; focusing on and emphasising values each woman possessed (verbally, through contact etc.); strengthening mutual respect and empowering women (through congratulations, saluting each other etc.); including relaxation exercises, such as yoga; and focusing on positive thoughts and feelings. This also encompassed a communication framework, in the spirit of restorative justice, which the participants were introduced to at the beginning of the programme and reminded about throughout the programme delivery. During the programme delivery, by using different methods, trainers endeavoured to strengthen women's ability to recognise different forms of victimisation, victims' needs and feelings; to strengthen their own capacities and resources and to make them think about alternative ways of dealing with problems in a more constructive way with the use of restorative dialogue. The programme also encompassed writing an (apology) letter to person(s) the participants had hurt.

At the end of the programme, based on evaluations, it was concluded that the participants' understanding of the impact of crime on victims and their families as well as on themselves and their own families increased. Female prisoners became familiar with and accepted restorative justice principles in general, and in particular, the restorative way of communicating with others. They also became familiar with and accepted yoga/mindfulness exercises as a form of self-help and help in solving problems with others.

4 Conclusion

Experiences of introducing restorative approaches in Serbia presented in this chapter suggest the relevance of restorative justice for conflict transformation and establishing security based on trust and relationships in various intercultural contexts (post-conflict communities, prison setting etc.). Restorative justice is an important social force that contributes to the revival of participatory democracy, which needs to be more inclusive, responsive and just (Walgrave, 2008: 194-195) and contributing to social justice. This seems particularly relevant for societies such as Serbia that are predominantly authoritarian and punitive, where justice is still very much attributed to retributive (legal) justice. Although relevant, legal justice is quite often not sufficient for the restoration of trust and relationships, and it usually leaves those who suffer (victims) on the margins of social response to crime, conflicts and other injustices. Restorative approaches, on the other hand, enable active participation and support for all those who feel victimised, with the final aim of reintegrating them into the society and closing the cycles of violence (Nikolić-Ristanović, et al., 2018b). In this regard, it is important to stress that the experiences presented in this chapter proved the relevance of accepting a broader notion of the victims, including both those directly and indirectly injured, as well as primary, secondary and tertiary victims (Spalek, 2006; Vanfraechem, 2012; Nikolić-Ristanović et al., 2018b). This is relevant not only for the post-conflict settings but also for working with prisoners. Restorative approaches may help in overcoming negative consequences of selective recognition of victims and hierarchies of victimhood. They may also help avoid binarism and allow overlaps between victims and perpetrators/responsible parties (Fattah, 1993 according to Vanfraechem, 2012); restorative approaches should work towards empowering all those who suffer, while recognising or taking into account the parties' or participants' individual traits and personality.

The essence of restorative approaches is interactive communication and dialogue (Foss et al., 2012). Both examples of introducing restorative approaches in Serbia proved the relevance of communication in the spirit of restorative dialogue as a tool for solving, transforming and preventing conflicts, problems and tensions in intercultural fields characterised by diversities, or even controlling environments such as prisons. Restorative justice may play a role in building trust and developing confidentiality and relationships, which are key preconditions for active participation and establishing dialogue that may help with making people come closer to each other and preventing their estrangement and increasing their security. In such a context, security should be understood as a 'sense of safety people experience' in different fields of social life (Vanfraechem, 2012: 6). Therefore, security is primarily understood in terms of human security, which focuses on the protection and empowerment of individuals, including victims. However, for the dialogue process to be successful, it is important that it meets some preconditions, such as power balance, refraining from mutual blaming, respectful active listening and mutual understanding and respect for diversity (Nikolić-Ristanović & Srna, 2010: 51). In so doing, meeting conditions for optimal contact and setting communication rules, as also suggested by Serbian experience, is important.

Introducing restorative approaches into different settings and contexts also proves to be a valuable learning experience: it helped in broadening the understanding of the concepts of security, victims and justice, including restorative justice. A broader understanding of the concepts justice, security and victims proved to be useful for dealing with victimisation and empowerment of victims in both projects presented in this chapter. Reimagining these concepts through restorative justice lenses, in both theoretical analysis and testing them in practice, was very useful for developing restorative mechanisms in Serbia. Presented experiences also helped in recognising the potential that restorative approaches may have in a much wider context of people's everyday life and in various situations, settings and relationships. Thus, restorative justice is to be considered not only as a form of justice but also as an approach, intervention, practice or as a way of life. It offers a ground for exploring and studying the interplay between the lives of citizens and their justice needs and the legal and institutional mechanisms for meeting these needs. In this regard, action research has proved to be an important scientific tool which offers a methodological framework for constant exchange between theory and practice.

References

Aertsen, I. (2006). The intermediate position of restorative justice: the case of Belgium. In I. Aersten, T. Daems & L. Robert (eds.), *Institutionalizing restorative justice* (pp. 68-92). Devon: Willan Publishing.

Aertsen, I. (2012). Restorative prisons: Where are we heading? In T. Barabas, B. Fellegi & S. Windt (eds.), *Responsibility-taking, Relationship-building and Restoration in Prisons* (pp. 263-276), Budapest: OKRI.

Aertsen, I., Arsovska, J., Rohne, H.-C., Valiñas, M. & Vanspauwen, K. (eds.), (2008). Restoring justice after large-scale violent conflicts: Kosovo, DR Congo and the Israeli-Palestinian case. Cullompton: Willan Publishing.

Allport, G. (1954). *The nature of prejudice*. Reading: Addison-Wesley.

Amir, Y. (1998). Contact hypothesis in ethnic relations. In E. Weiner (ed.), The handbook of interethnic coexistence (pp. 162-181). New York: Continuum Publishing.

Ćopić, S. & Nikolić-Ristanović, V. (2018). Podizanje svesti osuđenih lica o restorativnoj pravdi i pravima žrtava: Primer programa sprovedenog u zatvoru za žene u Srbiji. *Temida*, 3, 385-410.

Ćopić, S. & Nikolić-Ristanović, V. (forthcoming). Introducing restorative approaches in prison settings: an example of a victim awareness program in Serbia. In J. Joseph (ed.), *Contemporary developments in victimology: an international perspective.*

Fischer, M. (2016a). Dealing with the past from the top down and bottom up – challenges for state and non-state actors. In M. Fischer & O. Simić (eds.), *Transitional justice and reconciliation – lessons from the Balkans* (pp. 25-60). Oxon: Routledge.

Fischer, M. (2016b). Dealing with past violence as a long-term challenge – lessons from the Balkans. In M. Fischer & O. Simić (eds.), *Transitional justice and reconciliation – lessons from the Balkans* (pp. 245-262). Oxon: Routledge.

Foss, E. M., Hassan, S. C., Hydle, I., Seeberg, M. L. & Uhrig, B. (2012). Report on conflicts in intercultural settings. Oslo, Norway: NOVA. Public deliverable 2.1. of the ALTERNATIVE project. Retrieved from www.alternativeproject.eu/assets/upload/Deliverable_2.1_Report_on_conlicts_in_intercultural_settings.pdf (last accessed 3 September 2015).

Liebmann, M. (2007). *Restorative justice: how it works.* London: Jessica Kingsley Publishers.

Minow, M. (1998). *Between vengeance and forgiveness – facing history after genocide and mass violence*. Boston: Beacon Press.

Nikolić-Ristanović, V. (2008). Potential for the use of informal mechanisms and responses to the Kosovo conflict – Serbian perspective. In I. Aertsen, J. Arsovska, H. C. Rohne, M. Valiñas & K. Vanspauwen (eds.), *Restoring justice after large-scale violent conflicts: Kosovo, DR Congo and the Israeli-Palestinian case* (pp. 157-183). Cullompton: Willan Publishing.

Nikolić-Ristanović, V. (2015). Communication about the past and reconciliation: lessons from the Western Balkan. *Restorative Justice: An International Journal*, 3(2), 188-211. doi:10.1080/20504721.2015.1069090.

Nikolić-Ristanović, V. & Ćopić, S. (2015). Programs for female prisoners and positive criminology and victimology: the case of Serbia. In N. Ronel & D. Segev (eds.), *Positive criminology* (pp. 319-338). Oxon: Routledge.

Nikolić-Ristanović, V. & Ćopić, S. (2016). Dealing with the past in Serbia: achievements in the past 20 years. In M. Fischer & O. Simić (eds.) *Transitional justice and reconciliation – lessons from the Balkans* (pp. 141-168). Oxon: Routledge.

Nikolić-Ristanović, V. & Srna, J. (2010). Pomirenje sa sobom i drugima: od pristupa ka modelu. *Temida*, 1, 43-58.

Nikolić-Ristanović, V., Ćopić, S., Petrović, N. & Šaćiri, B. (2018a). Reimagining security and justice in post-conflict societies through restorative lenses. In B. Pali & I. Aertsen (eds.), *Restoring justice and security in intercultural Europe* (pp. 110-125). Oxon: Routledge.

Nikolić-Ristanović, V., Ćopić, S., Petrović, N. & Šaćiri, B. (2018b). Conflicts, victimization and restorative justice in intercultural settings: an example of action research in Serbia. In I. Vanfraechem & I. Aertsen (eds.), *Action research in criminal justice – Restorative justice approaches in intercultural settings* (pp. 99-116). Oxon: Routledge.

Pettigrew, T. (1998). Intergroup contact theory. *Annual Review of Psychology*, 49, 65-88. doi:10.1146/annurev.psych.49.1.65.

Spalek, B. (2006). *Crime victims: theory, policy and practice.* New York: Palgrave MacMillan.

Vanfraechem, I. (2012). Deliverable 8.1: work document on operationalisation of theoretical concepts. Leuven: KU Leuven (Deliverable 8.1. of FP7 project ALTERNATIVE – Developing alternative understandings of security and justice through restorative justice approaches in intercultural settings within democratic societies).

Vanfraechem, I., & Aertsen, I. (2016). *Justice and security through restorative justice approaches to conflicts in intercultural settings – final report.* Retrieved from https://cordis.europa.eu/docs/results/285/285368/final1-alternative-final-report-june-2016.pdf (last accessed 30 May 2019).

Walgrave, L. (2008). *Restorative justice, self-interest and responsible citizenship.* Cullompton: Willan Publishing.

A conversation about Ivo Aertsen

Renate Winter and Maia Chochua

Dear Maia,

Just recently I heard that Professor Aertsen, our Ivo, will retire in October this year. Difficult to imagine, really!

It seems to me that it was not long ago that I met Ivo and started to work with him in order to change the punitive juvenile justice system. I do not even recollect exactly where we met for the first time and where I heard for the first time a discussion about restorative justice, a topic I knew only from books. Was it between 1996 and 1999 at the Council of Europe, where he was a member, dealing with mediation in penal matters and me with international mediation in family matters?

Was it in Vancouver where he did research work in 1996? I don't know anymore, I just know that I was mandated by the UNDP to go to Bhutan to discuss mediation and that I immediately asked Ivo to come with me, hoping that his voice would be strong and his arguments convincing as he was the practitioner and me only the judge (judges are not always really welcome, as you know). It turned out that both of us had to learn a lesson, as penal mediation as well as family mediation already had a well-established place in Bhutanese society. The extra lesson I learned from him there was not to be afraid when bringing new developments to a justice system, as conservative or punitive it might be. Austria was at a crossroads at this time, wishing to change its juvenile justice system, and I had familiarised myself with the Belgian and Dutch methods to avoid to get children in the justice system altogether. It was Ivo through my continuous contacts with him, be it in Sion, Switzerland where both of us are members of the Scientific Committee – he for the European master in mediation, me for juvenile justice – be it during his time as Chair of the European Forum for Victim-Offender mediation and Restorative Justice, who taught me (with a lot of others) how to assist introducing restorative justice in my own country. I met him again in Vienna in 2006, during a seminar 'Restorative Justice in the European Judicial Area' co-organised by him, and in Helsinki for another seminar, again co-organised by him on 'Restorative Justice and Victim-offender mediation in Europe'. All the time I was impressed by his great knowledge about challenges and progress in countries around the world and how he continued to use and develop Braithwaite's and Zehr's ideas further. He continued to assist in Warsaw, in Almaty, in Montreal, in Belgrade, in Porto, in Turkey and everywhere my judge and prosecutor colleagues started to ask themselves if they should change direction.

Finally we got him (you remember how the two of us worked for that) to Georgia, thinking about future meetings, seminars, round tables, etc.

And now? What now? I have difficulties to imagine that he would not continue at all anymore! What do you think? How to continue?

Looking forward to hearing from you!

Warmest

Renate

What a news dearest Renate!

First time I met Ivo, about 7 years ago, I wished I was still a student and Ivo was my professor. Having soon realised that this was already a missed opportunity, I immediately started to think of the ways to make sure that he comes back to Georgia to share his incredible knowledge, experience, dedication and vision to more professionals to broaden their vision and expand their restorative imaginations. I still remember how fascinated I was when I first listened to Ivo's inspiring speech at our Restorative Justice Conference at the very early stage of our reforms. I remember faces and reflections of the impressed participants, long queue of questions on practices, policies, legislations, theories and research. Answers – always appealing and convincing. It was amazing to observe the process of transformation in people's minds. Transformation that has led to fundamental changes in juvenile justice system of Georgia and has also supported us to become part of the larger movement of restorative justice.

While promoting restorative justice in Georgia, we have witnessed first-hand this remarkable transformation. We have seen how individuals can be reintegrated back into the society; how victims of crimes can become the best defence against repeat offenders if their voices are heard; we have seen Georgians find a measure of peace through restorative justice processes; Ivo's persuasive evidence-based arguments led even our law enforcements to see the difference between isolation and rehabilitation. This transformation instils deep confidence that restorative justice is our surest path to prevent recidivism and to ensure a safer society.

May I be a bit selfish and imagine that if Ivo retires he will have more time to travel and support countries like Georgia that want to further develop and promote restorative justice. There is so much more to be done. Do you think we can convince him to continue?

Until very soon,

Maia

My dear Maia,

I do know the feeling you describe, I had it myself many times, especially when I had some discussions with Ivo, pointing out that something (like no punishment at all) wouldn't work or wouldn't be accepted. The first question of Ivo on such occasions was always: 'Why not?' In arguing then your point of view, you found out for sure about your own bias, your own hesitation to really change, your own lack of courage to go for the most effective instead of the usual. It was because of Ivo's notion of not only 'rechtvaarding', 'according to the law' but as well 'doing the right thing', that I started to see that punishment only never has been effective, never since Hammurabi's time, and to ask myself why it should do so now?

I am certainly not the only one having been influenced by Ivo, taking into consideration that he assisted countries in Latin and Central America, European countries like Finland, his own country Belgium, Slovakia, Russia, my own country, Austria, Poland, Serbia, Portugal and others with other systems like Uzbekistan and Canada. Always, when I visited a country after he has been there, I noticed his influence at work already!

On top of it, you never know if he will discuss from a social welfare point of view, from a psychologist one, a criminological one, an educational one or a purely legal one. Lately, in Georgia, we even heard medical reasoning!

Oh, apropos Georgia: yes we should indeed turn this unfortunate issue of retirement into a very positive one of regular visits for seminars, round tables, academic discussions, training sessions for practitioners in restorative justice and mediation specifically, not only for Georgia, but for the whole region! Quite a lot of countries in our region have some notions about restorative justice (or would like to believe that they have), mostly partially at best, often not knowing even about basics and certainly not in an orderly and structured approach. Shouldn't we use the momentum of their interest in 'getting the right thing' from the right person?

Could you imagine a programme, considering the many needs for mediation in many different fields, of community service that is not regulated in most of the countries, in further increasing the number of the restorative measures available like family/community/peer conferencing for the region? Ivo (involving as well his friends and colleagues) could most importantly be of assistance in this regard, both educating and convincing.

Any ideas?

Warmest,

Renate

Dearest Renate,

Absolutely! Ivo is always an inexhaustible source of information, knowledge and inspiration. He has 'poisoned' us with restorative justice, exactly the same way you 'poisoned' us with juvenile justice. This is not for nothing that in Georgia we call him the Father of Restorative Justice and you the Mother of Juvenile Justice. I truly believe that there is only one way to go and this is the way forward. We will stay committed to the values and open possibilities that restorative justice provides.

It was Ivo again who supported us to design and institutionalise certified training course for mediators. He trained our mediators, social workers, judges, prosecutors, investigators, lawyers. He led a number of policy discussions with decision makers. With him we developed a vision on further expending borders of restorative justice that we currently follow. We have ambitious plans that we certainly want to implement together with him.

And you are absolutely right – it is his holistic approach and knowledge from criminology to psychology and beyond that makes his proposals so convincing for professionals. There is so much of his input that, today, Georgian experience is used as a model in the region.

In one of his interviews with a local Georgian magazine, "Liberali", he said, "The existence of restorative justice in the country, first of all, enhances justices system. It helps to effectively fight against crime. Effective means that measures that had been carried out are presumed just. In many countries, the bridge between justice system and society is broken. The level of trust is also low. This is exactly where restorative justice can play its role. Systems like this better responds to the needs of society."

We in Georgia will always appreciate Ivo's input in building bridges between the justice system and the society. But again, we still need his support.

Warmest,

Maia

Dear Maia,

Ok, let's look forward and continue striving for a better system in Georgia and the region together with Ivo and his organisation! Maybe at the end of the day we would not need to travel to New Zealand any longer to find new ideas and outstanding examples, the region might be able to become one!

As Ivo is still a member of the Executive Committee of the World Society of Victimology (he didn't say that he wanted to stop) so we could continue planning in this regard as well, as getting the status of victim, bearing rights, is a major undertaking here in Georgia with a quite problematic procedure.

And one more thing: Ivo is editor-in-chief of *Restorative Justice: An International Journal* – another chance to continuously learn from him and to participate in further developing Ivo's notorious and most enchanting concept of 'doing justice', of accepting that justice is not only a principle, a theory, a contract between citizens of a country, a humanistic idea, a possibility to survive in the jungle, but a skill, something that could be 'done' and 'should be done'.

'RECHTVAARDIG', IVO, ISN'T IT? We thank you for that!

Renate

Dearest Renate,

For me, working with Ivo is an extremely creative, inspiring and fun process. His wit, sophistication and personal skills make the age difference almost disappear. While saying this, I express the view of our whole team and all the professionals he has worked with in Georgia.

In fact we have to thank you for introducing us to Ivo. Thanks to the endless efforts of you, Ivo, Christa Pelikan and Michael Koenigshofer, we have strong fundamentals now.

We have bridged the distance between conventional justice and restorative justice, and most importantly this has effected the lives of thousands of children.

There is so much more we could say about Ivo. Last but certainly not least, I would like to thank Ivo for introducing us to the European Forum for Restorative Justice – the big family of competent, interesting, dedicated, inspiring, progressive people – change-makers within their countries and beyond. Thank you Professor Ivo!

Until very soon, I hope,

Maia

Ivo Aertsen and the growth and development of restorative justice

Tim Chapman

1 Introduction

In September 1999, Recommendation No. R (99)19 of the Committee of Ministers to member states concerning mediation in penal matters was adopted by the Council of Europe. In October 2018, Recommendation CM/Rec(2018)8 concerning restorative justice in criminal matters was adopted by the Committee of Ministers. Ivo Aertsen had a significant influence on both documents.

In 1998, a group of committed people from eight European countries who were active in the field of penal mediation began cooperative work funded by the European Commission's Grotius programme. Ivo Aertsen was a key player in this initiative, and the Catholic University of Leuven where Ivo worked was the administrative centre for the project. In 1999 there was a conference in Leuven on 'Victim-offender mediation in Europe: Making restorative justice work'. This led to the formation of the European Forum for Victim-Offender Mediation and Restorative Justice (currently European Forum for Restorative Justice, herein referred to as the EFRJ). Ivo Aertsen was elected as the first Chair of the EFRJ.

In 2018 the EFRJ held its highly successful tenth international conference in Tirana, Albania. In 2020 the EFRJ will celebrate its twentieth anniversary. It now has more than 460 members, including nearly 100 organisations from Europe and beyond. I am the current Chair of the EFRJ and I cannot over-estimate the impact that Ivo Aertsen has had and continues to have on restorative justice in Europe and throughout the world, on the EFRJ and on me.

2 Stages in the development of restorative justice

The EFRJ was 18 years old at its conference in Tirana in 2018. It struck me that it had 'come of age'. By this I mean that the EFRJ and, by implication, restorative justice had achieved a level of acceptance and respect that a mature movement would expect. This stimulated me to explore the theory of stages of human psychosocial development as a metaphor for the development of restorative justice (see Erikson, 1950, 1959, 1968; Erikson & Joan, 1997).

While there has been a long history of mediation in Europe, victim-offender mediation was a fledgling service within most criminal justice systems in 2000. The Council of Europe Recommendation No. R (99)19 and the EFRJ led by Ivo Aertsen were critical to nurturing this new approach to justice and encouraging governments to trust its efficacy. At this stage the pioneers in research and practice helped to define the field of restorative justice, to develop frameworks of practice and the competence of the practitioners. Restorative justice thrived and gained a firm footing in several countries such as Finland, Norway, Germany, Austria, Belgium and Northern Ireland between 2000 and 2010. However, there were many countries which struggled to implement anything approaching a comprehensive provision of restorative services.

Around this time much of the restorative movement entered what I characterise as its 'adolescence' phase. This was as Erikson understands it as a struggle between finding and asserting a distinctive identity and role confusion. Restorative justice asked itself 'who am I and what can I do?' This was particularly apparent in English-speaking countries such as the United States and the United Kingdom and was amplified by an increasing use of social media.

It involved distinguishing itself from formal criminal justice systems (restorative justice as good and the criminal justice system as bad) and asserting that restorative justice or practices were 'awesome' and could be applied almost everywhere. Just as some were attempting to define restorative justice, others were adding the word to any practice which seemed positive even if such practices had existed long before the emergence of modern forms of restorative justice. Respectful, relational and proactive approaches to education, policing and corrections were termed restorative practices.

This was a necessary stage of development which was largely tolerated affectionately by the grown-ups in various systems. It resulted in greater public awareness of restorative justice even if it was accompanied by confusion as different restorative organisations competed for attention and the increasing resources for training and delivery. During this time, in order to stand out and achieve credibility restorative practices appropriated indigenous practices and therapeutic concepts such as 'healing' and claimed ownership of a range of psychological theories and qualities such as trauma and empathy.

This move from restorative justice to restorative practices involved a retreat from the core value of restoring justice when an injustice has occurred. The grown-ups were generally not willing to let restorative justice encroach such a critical area of practice. It has to be acknowledged that serious research into the effectiveness of restorative justice was also being conducted in order to persuade the adults to support restorative justice as a means to achieving the aims of the criminal justice system.

This compulsion to promote, 'look at me, look at what I can do', was not as prominent in Europe. This was in part due to a different criminal justice culture which was not so focused on reoffending as the measure of its effectiveness. It was also due to Ivo Aertsen and other leaders in the field who resisted the hyperbole and continued to work on clear, practical and research-informed definitions of restorative justice. Critically Ivo Aertsen never conceded to the pressure to dilute the central importance of justice to restorative justice.

The adolescent phase of development is all about 'ego'. Like many teenagers we felt that we knew it all and the older generation were too conservative. The problem with this self-promotion is that you end up just talking to people who have the same values and beliefs as you do. This leads to isolation from ordinary people in society and marginalisation in the systems that serve those ordinary people.

In 2012 Ivo Aertsen invited me to engage the University of Ulster in the ALTERNATIVE action research project over four years along with research organisations from five other European countries. This was a well-funded (EU Framework Programme 7) project which inquired into the contribution of restorative justice in relation to conflicts in intercultural settings. This research opened my mind to the possibilities of restorative justice beyond the criminal justice system without compromising on the value of justice. This unique project was both founded on the direct lived experience of people living in communities experiencing conflict and informed by critical social theory.

Through this programme I realised that we should not start from the position that restorative justice is some new wonderful approach that we need to 'sell' to the world. We should start from an understanding of the reality in which people live, their 'lifeworld', and with them generate inclusive, participative and transformative solutions (which may or may not be called restorative).

Speakers, such as Fania Davis, Vincenzo Ruggiero, Claudia Mazzucato and Tali Gal, at the 2018 EFRJ conference in Tirana urged the restorative movement to engage with the real injustices that people are experiencing and with the systems of government which need help to change so that they can address these injustices. I felt this was a call to stop being so obsessed with ourselves and to seek relationships with people and systems with whose values we may feel uncomfortable.

This was a signal that restorative justice has come of age and needs to act like a grown-up. It represented the beginning of a transition from an ego-system to engagement with the eco-system. Without the influence of Ivo Aertsen, I would not have come to such a realisation. For that I will always be grateful.

References

Erikson, E. H. (1950). *Childhood and society* (1st ed.). New York: Norton.

Erikson, E. H. (1959). *Identity and the life cycle*. New York: International Universities Press.

Erikson, E. H. (1968). *Identity, youth and crisis*. New York: Norton.

Erikson, E. H. & Joan, M. (1997). *The life cycle completed: extended version*. New York: Norton.

Restorative justice: university education, theoretical and practical training for operators, raising community awareness

Grazia Mannozzi

Recede in te ipse quantum potes; cum his versare qui te meliorem facturi sunt, illos admitte quos tu potes facere meliores. Mutuo ista fiunt, et homines dum docent discunt.
(Lucio Anneo Seneca, Lettere a Lucilio, 1, 7)[1]

1 Training for restorative justice

Training is one of the crucial points of restorative justice. The term should be widely understood to include not only university education and specific mediator/facilitator training, but also raising awareness among *stakeholders* and encouraging a restorative culture in the community.

This general definition of the word *training* refers to an opportunity of mutual work and commitment, to which supranational, international and European sources devote important comments and provide some guidelines.

The Council of Europe's Recommendation CM/Rec (2018)8 expressly indicates how restorative justice should be considered not (merely) as an *alternative*, but rather as a complement to criminal proceedings (Cunneen & Hoyle, 2010).

In the first case, restorative justice may be used merely as a diversionary measure; in the second, restorative justice needs to open a dialogue with the criminal justice system, by operating in parallel or in synergy with it.

This is a relevant statement, as the role played by restorative justice compared to the penal system shapes institutions, recipients and training methods.

First, the complementary nature of restorative justice to the criminal justice system implies that a general approach to restorative justice can be used, that is, regardless of the seriousness of the offence and at whatever stage and level of criminal proceedings. This suggests that the training range should be just as far-ranging to include not only mediators and facilitators but also jurists and justice service staff.

---

1 'Withdraw into yourself, as far as you can. Associate with those who will make a better man of you. Welcome those whom you yourself can improve. The process is mutual; for men learn while they teach.' (Seneca, *Letters from a Stoic*, 1, 7)

It is, therefore, appropriate that jurists, especially magistrates and lawyers, already receive training in *restorative justice* during their university studies by including restorative justice, possibly as a mandatory subject in the law course content.

And, if possible, basic training in restorative justice not just as a form of non-retaliation justice, but rather in a dialogue, community, inclusive form should be experimented even earlier, that is, within the entire school cycle prior to university (Brown, 2018; Karp, 2014; Morrison, 2015; Wachtel, 2016).

The importance of training expressed in the 2018 Recommendation is also supported by Directive 2012/29/EU, in which Recital 61 asks for:

> Any officials involved in criminal proceedings who are likely to come into personal contact with victims should be able to access and receive appropriate initial and ongoing training, to a level appropriate to their contact with victims, so that they are able to identify victims and their needs and deal with them in a respectful, sensitive, professional and non-discriminatory manner.

The subject of training is expanded, more specifically, in Article 25 of the Directive, where it distinguishes between four action plans according to the recipients and the role they play in interacting with the victims of crime. More specifically:

(a) As regards *officials* likely to come into contact with victims – first and foremost police officers and court staff – the Directive requires that:

> they receive both general and specialist training to a level appropriate to their contact with victims to increase their awareness of the needs of victims and to enable them to deal with victims in an impartial, respectful and professional manner.[2]

(b) As regards the *judiciary*, although the Directive explicitly states the latter should maintain its autonomy and independence, it envisages that:

> Member States shall request that those responsible for the training of judges and prosecutors involved in criminal proceedings make available both general and specialist training to increase the awareness of judges and prosecutors of the needs of victims.[3]

2 Art. 25, para. 1, Directive 2012/29/EU of the European Parliament and of the Council of 25 October 2012 establishing minimum standards on the rights, support and protection of victims of crime, and replacing Council Framework Decision 2001/220/JHA.

3 Art. 25, para. 2, Directive 2012/29/EU.

(c) As regards the *legal bar*, without prejudice to the respect for the independence of the legal profession, the Directive requests Member States to recommend 'that those responsible for the training of lawyers make available both general and specialist training to increase the awareness of lawyers of the needs of victims'.[4]

(d) Lastly, as regards training of staff working for victim protection associations and mediators/facilitators, the Directive envisages that:

> Member States shall encourage initiatives enabling (...) to receive adequate training to a level appropriate to their contact with victims and observe professional standards to ensure such services are provided in an impartial, respectful and professional manner.[5]

Unlike the two documents mentioned above, the Basic Principles of the United Nations do not mention training for jurists and stakeholders and only stress the importance of initial and continual training for facilitators. Nevertheless, they state that:

> There should be regular consultation between criminal justice authorities and administrators of restorative justice programmes to develop a common understanding of restorative processes and outcomes, to increase the extent to which restorative programmes are used and to explore ways in which restorative approaches might be incorporated into criminal justice practices.[6]

That kind of consultation is of fundamental importance as it contributes to promoting a deepening in knowledge and the implementation of joint projects. In that, the universities' role could be of a strategic importance. The 'third mission' in universities allows to generate knowledge outside academic environments, to the benefit of the social, cultural and economic development. Third mission activities – and research and teaching restorative justice could be one of them – strengthen dialogue, interaction and mutual understanding among university, justice system and society (included in its components like volunteer and not-for-profit sector).

A less valued profile in supranational documents is the one of research in the field of restorative justice. Research is instead to be considered a fundamental element in the development and implementation of restorative justice.

4 Art. 25, para. 3, Directive 2012/29/EU.

5 Art. 25, para. 4, Directive 2012/29/EU.

6 Art. 21, Basic Principles on the Use of Restorative Justice Programmes in Criminal Matters, ECOSOC Res. 2000/14.

It not only offers a solid framework of meaning with respect to the discourse on restorative justice but above all it allows us to read the practice, to orient it and also to make teaching more coherent, effective and vital (Pali & Walgrave, 2019).

I will start, therefore, with some comments on the importance of restorative justice in a jurist's university training and then move on to other training areas, noting immediately that improving awareness in the community is of fundamental importance (Pelikan, 2019: 7).

2 The jurist's university education on restorative justice: rationale and powers

Teaching is a moral action (Lodigiani, 2019: 27).

Behind the need for a jurist's university training to acknowledge restorative justice lie not merely legal, but also philosophical and cultural grounds.

The legal grounds should include mainly the importance of restorative justice in supranational sources – where it is referred to as a fast track to solve criminal conflict and is also given its first 'official' definitions – and the acceptance of said sources by individual European and non-European States.

In the individual States, restorative justice and victim-offender mediation – one of the main, most structured methods, which already appears in the EU Recommendation 99 (19) concerning Mediation in penal matters – were given legislative recognition on various levels: as part of juvenile and adult justice, as a diversion technique, as a form of extinguishment of offence, in the probation area and as a component of the enforcement of sanctions (Dünkel, Grzywa-Holten & Horsfield, 2011).

Restorative justice is being taken into consideration more widely and is increasingly acknowledged in legislation. It implies the need to guarantee that restorative justice can constitute a co-essential, qualifying subject in university courses devoted to cooperation and development, peace building, political science and law.

A university training for jurists in the fundamentals, contents and methods of restorative justice can contribute to improving sensitivity, which enables them to overcome formalistic visions of the offence, value the victim's role, limit excessively severe sanctions (Chartrand & Piché, 2019) and nurture the person's dignity.

In addition to the legal grounds, the philosophical grounds are also in favour of restorative justice training for the jurist.

In fact, in order to escape the risk of becoming a self-referential system, the law has to be philosophically justified, commencing with options in terms of values regarding the concept of justice (Lombardi Vallauri, 2012: 213). To discuss the claim above, it would be opportune to recall the assumption of a historic difference between *justice* and *law*. 'The law – Jacques Derrida observed – is not justice. Law is the element of calculation, and it is just that there be law, but justice is incalculable, it requires us to calculate with the incalculable'[7] (Derrida, 1994: 66).

This *difference* has its roots deep in a primordial religiousness – which, in the myth, places justice as truth (*dike*) in the presence of Zeus (Curi, 2003: 61-71) and the law (*nomos*) for men. Even more clearly, in Christian, theological thought, the distinction between law and justice runs through the entire Old Testament (Bovati, 1986), where justice as supernatural order goes beyond the human dimension.[8]

Umberto Curi states to this regard:

> Even the incunabula of Western cultural tradition do not equate these two concepts, but rather show a radical, relentless difference. We can even state that the existence of law is proof of the non-existence of justice, of its absence from the horizon of human relationships. We would have no need for law – nor was there a need for law in certain social structures, as studies of cultural anthropology have shown – if there were justice. Conceptually and historically law appears to begin from this deviation[9] (...). (Curi, 2003: 70)

Thus, *law*, which is an uncertain, changeable instrument, used in the perpetual search for *justice*, opposes the ideal of justice as truth or as a virtue and, therefore, as the absolute ideal.

If criminal law is only taught by focusing on its legal provisions, the discourse on 'justice' will inevitably be relegated to the background without ever rising to the status of a central value. This issue is, on the contrary, spurred on to return to its far-reaching meaning, when the system of criminal regulations and punishments is implemented in the perspective of restorative justice (Braithwaite, 2013).

Restorative justice brings the *meaningful grounds of the criminal precept* back to the centre of the conflict, considering it mainly relevant to the victim's needs and not solely to the 'need to punish' the offender, but above all by excluding the logic of the dispute and revenge from the way the conflict is handled. Vice versa, ordinary justice with its dynamics of 'win-lose game' can end by encouraging an instrumental use of law. As in the '*sporting theory of justice*' opposed by Pound (Sherman, 2007), there is a risk that the competitive spirit shaping the process transforms the dispute from a clash on a *question* (injurious event or a breach of law) to a clash between *people*. This leads to a double consequence: from an ethical viewpoint not only does it not push the litigants to become aware of their true motives, but neither does it go beyond mere tolerance to achieve a true acknowledgement of the other; on the practical side, it almost always confuses the truth with victory, leaving the defeated party alone with resentment and desire for revenge.

---

7 Own translation.

8 See Psalm 84, 11-12.

9 Own translation.

Moving on to the cultural grounds, it is clear how restorative justice tends to be used in various sectors of community life. We only have to think of how restorative justice methods are used to handle conflicts, which develop in schools, at work or in the community, in interreligious and intercultural settings, involving immigrants, refugees (Pali, 2017), street group violence (Gavrielides, 2012) or even terrorism. Restorative justice also sets out to be the driving force behind a perceptible change in local communities: we need only consider the phenomenon of restorative cities, where the community becomes a 'player' and not merely the recipient of restorative policies. As a form of justice that 'heals', restorative justice has become key for developing a 'comprehensive' approach not only to the offence but, more generally, to the ethics of human relations (Reggio, 2010: 13), interpersonal relations and relations between groups, fostering cooperative dynamics and *win-to-win* logic.

3 Teaching restorative justice to launch dialogue among disciplines for a holistic training of the jurist

Just because it moves from a perspective of *justice* and not merely of *law*, the conceptual universe of restorative justice requires first and foremost *multilevel teaching*, open to multidisciplinarity (Derrida & Rovatti, 2001: 54; Pointer & McGoey, 2019) and a reasoned crossover between the disciplines (Pointer & McGoey, 2019; Canestrari, 2008: 8).

The assumption I am making here is that the scientific autonomy of restorative justice can make a fundamental contribution to the *complete, globalised training of the jurist*, as it enables attention to be brought back to a concept of justice as seen in its legal-philosophical entirety.

Different *interdisciplinary* courses can be started up in a course on restorative justice: the connection between psychology, anthropology, criminology, victimology and law is fundamental.

3.1 Restorative justice and psychological science

The need for a connection between restorative justice and psychological science is undeniable. By comparing with the different methods of restorative justice, the psychological disciplines can offer an interesting platform of comprehension.

Listening is a benchmark of restorative justice (Umbreit, 2001). To this regard, some major research has been conducted by Gordon on communication barriers (Gordon, 1970) and by Carl Rogers on active listening (Rogers & Farson, 2015). Whether in a circle or during mediation, the whole body should be listening and the mediator/facilitator has to nurture the parties' skills to listen empathetically (Rogers, 1980; Goleman, 1995), in order to be able to detect the needs underlying the layer of conflict. Knowledge of communication barriers could help to create a style of interaction to avoid those interjections that hinder dialogue and could bring the conflict back to stagnation.

In programmes of restorative justice, it is important to identify the real needs of the conflicting parties by using empathetic listening to reopen communication channels. Knowing how to facilitate acknowledgement of a person's needs can benefit from Maslow's hierarchy of needs (Maslow, 1954), which helps explain why programmes of restorative justice go beyond the perspective of an exclusively material repair to access forms of symbolic reparation (Simmel, 1900).

As is well known, emotions play a fundamental part in programmes of restorative justice. This works in the view mapped out initially by Ekman and Plutchik, according to whom there are primary and secondary emotions and emotions that are the result of a combination of the aforementioned categories of emotions (Ekman, 1999; Plutchik, 1962).

3.2 *Restorative justice, criminal law and criminal procedure*

Restorative justice is intended to cross over with a series of typically criminal and procedural questions (Pelikan, 2019: 5).

The fundamental question is that of alternativity or complementarity between restorative justice and the criminal justice system (Pali & Pelikan, 2014).

Compared to substantive criminal law, working on restorative justice means drawing attention back to the *value* protected by the incriminating provision and to the *sense of the punishment*. As regards the first perspective, the idea of *reparation* also forces us to reflect on the nature of the behaviour, which can decrease or annul the damaging or dangerous consequences of the crime. Restorative justice also encourages to reflect on how to handle criminality in companies, where the victims are widespread, often unaware of being victimised and hard to identify (Aertsen, 2018).

As regards the finality of the sentence, restorative justice forces our attention back as much to the fragility underlying the principle of *proportion*, anchored to a mythological and pre-religious dimension, as to *prevention* and to the difficulties of an empirical verification of models of general prevention and rehabilitation.

Restorative justice invites us to take into account the practicality of answers constructed via *positive* and not merely *repressive* contents. Donini wrote:

> In fact, we are no longer capable of understanding the 'sense' of the punishment, understood as doubling the wrong, as adding wrong to a wrong already committed. For us, this a point of no return compared to the past. A Copernican revolution is underway, which now touches the essence of criminal law, the challenge of its possible focus on human interests.

Compared to procedural law, restorative justice forces us to tackle themes of the victimhood (Aertsen, 2017), admission of guilt, the guarantees of questioning and, generally speaking, the problematic aspects of the mechanisms of a stay of proceedings and of plea bargaining.

The awareness that an approach of reparation towards the victims should be encouraged could also promote a reflection on the legal bar's codes of ethics towards a lawyer/client relationship that would give qualitative feedback even within the proceedings and institutions (Foley, 2015).

Teaching restorative justice also implies a connection with the meaning of guarantees, with the spirit of negotiation running through the *adversary* proceedings and with the applicative paths of differential proceedings.

3.3 *Restorative justice and criminology*

As restorative justice moves from the central position of the victim and from the idea of repair, it requires constant dialectics with the science of criminology and victimology. The latter especially can help to understand both the type of victims and their possible role in the genesis of the crime.

Equally important is the reflection on the amount of damage in order to link it to the sense of material and symbolic repair.

The criminological investigation also appears fundamental to our understanding of the spirit of the mediation and of how to assess the techniques to intervene on the attitude of the offender, who expresses the desire to refuse or remove the knowledge of having committed a crime: teaching mediation requires, for example, a close analysis of the 'techniques to neutralise' the sense of guilt, as restorative justice can be used to work on some of these.

Empirical-criminological research is also indispensable to verify the effectiveness of the mediation via a statistical analysis dedicated to the type and seriousness of crimes mediated, to the results of the mediation and repair, to the victims' and offenders' level of satisfaction compared to resorting to restorative justice, to desistance (Sherman et al, 2015).

3.4 *Restorative justice and legal anthropology*

The contribution of legal anthropology in teaching restorative justice was, at least initially, significant. It brought an awareness of procedures to solve conflicts that are typical of 'simple societies' (Sylvester, 2003) or ethnic minorities, which included family group conferencing. Nevertheless, it encourages the awareness that the transplantation of conflict handling methods typical of the simple societies or belonging to informal justice (Grande & Mattei, 2008) must be faced with a deep knowledge of culture and history.

More generally, an understanding of the 'spirit' of mediation thrives on the anthropological contribution, which tends to explain how mediation encourages the offender and the victim to reformulate their own inner worlds in a community context.

3.5 *Restorative justice and philosophical anthropology*

Justice is an essential component for managing human relationships that has the centrality of human being and the way he/she relates to others as an axiological assumption.

Describing the concept of justice in terms of 'reparation' means advocating once again the search and pursuit of the respect for the anthropological structure: what protects, takes care of and develops the individual as a person is good; what degrades, exploits or destroys a person is bad. Justice, law, value, acknowledgement: restorative justice can be interpreted within such a concatenation.

Restorative justice gives priority to the person and not to the abstract law and leads to a reconsideration of criminal justice. It is an unavoidable need, especially as regards the recognition of human rights.

This is where the challenge for an authentic laic view of law is played out: first and foremost, because the offence to a juridical good may not have a universal character, as it may belong to a sphere of values that differ from that of the offender, which the latter cannot be a part of. Nevertheless, it is important for the victim, who is entitled to reparation. Secondly, because by abandoning the search for universal values in the precepts, restorative justice implies it acknowledges the humanity of the other as the sole, true, universal set of values. Teaching restorative justice is, therefore, also required to work on the ethical and normative aspects of a human relationship, which stem from this universal 'humanity'.

3.6 *Restorative justice and ethics*

Ethics and law both refer to the moral quality of human experience. Even before they control areas of knowledge, norms or rules, ethics and law outline the shapes and moments of human experience.

Restorative justice is linked to ethics in several ways.

According to Dignan (2005: 94-107), moral discourse is one of the intellectual foundations of restorative justice movement.

Restorative justice deals with *moral emotions* such as shame, embarrassment and regret (Lauwaert & Aertsen, 2016: 233, 360). But at a deeper level, restorative justice encounters ethics in the field of individual responsibility. Indeed, as a 'medium' for justice, law is a fundamental, relational, human experience, based on *responsibility*.

Rather than responsibility for the past, restorative justice relies on responsibility for the future: an active responsibility, which invests in change and in the future, with a view to repairing and creating relationships. This is one of the ways through which ethics comes into play: if ethics and law are to be kept separate as regards the choices of primary criminalisation, we also have to acknowledge that law is called once again to meet ethics in terms of responsibility *towards* the other person (Lèvinas, 1984). Restoring an offence, therefore, implies first and foremost to search for the other as a person, opening spaces of acknowledgement, the results of which can be a communal choice to take a step back or to open up to the person's return. This brings the logic of restorative justice closer to a secular and ethical interpretation of the dynamics of forgiveness (Arendt, 1958), without superimposing on it. Colombo wrote:

> The one who forgives is responsible for reaccepting; the one who is forgiven is responsible for judiciously using what they receive, i.e. being reaccepted. Both are responsible for mending the relationship that had been torn apart. (Colombo, 2011: 87).

3.7 *Restorative justice, language and literature*

Teaching restorative justice also includes renewed attention to language. Compared to the penal handling of the conflict, restorative justice has encouraged a cultural change, which implies a 'new' vocabulary to think of the crime and its consequences: in fact, it offers uncommon words to think of and conceptualises the conflict.

Nils Christie has, however, shown a certain perplexity towards this vocabulary, commencing from the term 'restorative justice'. It evokes victims, offenders, compensation and redress, lexical categories and, first and foremost, the typical concepts of the penal definition of conflicts. Therefore, it appears too steeped in the criminal law it hopes to overcome. Consequently, Christie proposes to use the more neutral linguistic formula of handling conflicts: a 'less heroic terminology' – he claims – 'but also less open to abuse and misleading expectations' (Christie, 2013: 19).

Aertsen underlines that restorative justice may replicate the conceptualisation of victims and offenders as they have developed within criminal law (Aertsen, 2017: 357).

In any event, the language of restorative justice continues to differ qualitatively and lexically from that of criminal law, as such legislative structures have criteria of different legitimisation and, secondarily, because they use different operational instruments. The intrinsically empathetic and functionally cooperative language, typical of restorative justice, acts as a counterpoint to the intrinsically authoritarian and functionally prescriptive language, typical of criminal law.

The common semantic feature between these two languages is the formal definition of an unlawful act, even though the offence in the restorative justice paradigm, as we have seen, is considered not as an expression of aggression towards the established order, but rather as a 'violation' of the victims' individual rights.[10]

The path to understanding the different linguistic registers of criminal justice and restorative justice can also be facilitated by the contribution of literature. Martha Nussbaum wrote:

> Citizens cannot relate well to the complex world around them by factual knowledge and logic alone. The third ability of the citizen, closely related to the first two, is what we can call the narrative imagination. This means the ability to think what it might be like to be in the shoes of person different from oneself, to be an intelligent reader of that person's story, and to understand the emotions and wishes and desires that someone so placed might have. The cultivation of sympathy has been a key part of the best modern ideas of democratic education, in both Western and non-Western nations. (Nussbaum, 2010: 111)

In order to apply the law, which regulates life, the jurist should know life through its shades of meaning and sense linked to the uniqueness/unusualness of concrete cases. In this dynamic of understanding, the contribution of literature can be just as meaningful compared to the one offered by analysing court cases, which are, nevertheless, conveyed using a technical language to rewrite the parties' experience under the lens of the substantive-procedural legal categories. Thus, literature offers the jurist the opportunity to reflect empathetically (Bergman Blix & Wettergren, 2016) on many questions of fact, which usually remain beyond the logic of the court case, but which are essential to contextualise a criminal episode in the perspective of restorative justice.

The contribution of art and image can be considered equally significant: 'art can mediate, enhance and make tangible new understanding of the notion and practice of justice' (Pali, 2014: 85).

10 DIRECTIVE 2012/29/EU (Whereas 9); Recommendation CM/Rec (2018)8 of the Committee of Ministers to member States concerning restorative justice in criminal matters, according to which 'crime involves a violation of individuals' rights and relationships'.

4 MEDIATOR/FACILITATOR TRAINING

On the basis of Article 25 of the Directive 2012/29/EU – which explicitly highlights the importance of both initial and continual *training* for those providing victim support and restorative justice services[11] – mediators and facilitators are required to have not particularly specific skills. There are actually no professional skills more appropriate than others to qualify the figure of mediator/facilitator. However, they will need linguistic-relationship skills and be people-oriented to handle not only the, at times, intense emotions and feelings, the silence and the mild language of tears, but also the emotional petrifaction typical of the vertices of incommunicability, loneliness and suffering correlated to a conflict (Borgna, 2017: 43, 117).

In mediators' and facilitators' training, the so-called experimental learning is of fundamental importance. It often takes the forms of role play but can also take advantages of games (Pointer & McGoey, 2019), the arts (Liebmann, 1989 and 2007) or storytelling (White, 2007).

Some of the major supranational documents include the Recommendation R(99) 19 of the Council of Europe, regarding the qualification of the mediator in penal matters and the Guidelines for a better implementation of the existing Recommendation concerning mediation in penal matters CEPEJ(2007)13.

The Recommendation requires mediators to:

- be recruited from all sections of society and possess a good understanding of local and community cultures (Art. 22);
- receive not only initial training before taking up mediation duties, but also in-service training (Art. 24);
- be trained to provide for a 'high level of competence, taking into account conflict resolution skills, the specific requirements of working with victims and offenders and basic knowledge of the criminal justice system' (Art. 24).

The Guidelines for a better implementation of the existing Recommendation specify a list of subjects, in which mediators should be trained (including knowledge, skills and practical experience) (Art. 20). They ask States to recognise the importance of establishing common criteria to permit the accreditation of mediators and/or institutions, which offer mediation services and/or train mediators, including, in a transnational perspective, a certificate of European mediator (Art. 21).

11 Directive 2012/29/UE.

5 The training of magistrates, lawyers and prison personnel

In the light of what we have discussed so far, restorative justice should become an integral part of the mandatory, continual training for magistrates and lawyers.

The former are called to report and promote programmes of restorative justice at every stage and level of proceedings. They can encourage collaboration with public or private restorative justice centres in the territory.

The latter can inform the people they assist of the available restorative justice programmes.

Even prison personnel (educational staff, social workers, experts, prison police officers) play a considerable role in implementing programmes of restorative justice. It is important to also realign the role of prison personnel with restorative justice and this implies an overhaul of the educational role within social reintegration.

6 Raising awareness in the community

To encourage a restorative culture to spread, we also need to work on raising awareness within the community and with social workers in the territory, who intend to adopt a restorative approach.

The level of raising awareness is fundamental and delicate and requires a careful selection of the contents to be imparted. To avoid the ever possible risk of an improper use of restorative justice methods, raising awareness would have to be proposed not on operational methods of restorative justice, but rather on its essential values, its potential and its limits. On the one hand, in fact, we need to avoid restorative justice being misunderstood as a weak, do-good dynamic. On the other, we need to ward off the risk of inadequately trained people from spontaneously adopting potentially risky, improvised approaches of restorative justice.

One of the keynotes of restorative justice is actually to avoid so-called secondary victimisation, especially where conflicts of criminal importance are concerned. Secondary victimisation is often linked to methods of approach that are insufficiently professional, respectful and aware of the values at stake compared to conflicts of criminal seriousness and of the guarantees behind restorative justice.

The level of awareness moves from a scientific-popular communication, which pays attention to the principles, outcomes, benefits and risks of restorative justice and which is conducted using accessible, appropriate language for the recipient target.

7 Training for restorative justice and being trained by restorative justice

Understanding restorative justice and the spirit of mediation means more than just knowing part of the law: it means reflecting on the relationship between the individual and the law and on how to apply the law *with a spirit of justice* (Derrida, 1994: 67).

In some respects, restorative justice reminds us of the gift of *aidos* Zeus gave mankind. Ost wrote:

> What would it matter whether or not we had law, if the essential were not guaranteed: a favourable disposition towards it, an inclination for civilisation and a certain capacity for inner life, in a concept which demands self-respect? Aidos involves something more than just "observing the rule for itself"; it appears to be linked to justice, as a principle of organising relationships between men. (Ost, 2004: 37)

Ost's words catch an essential point: restorative justice is also an 'art' for the care for the *self* and for recomposing the dynamics of *social relations*. Training for restorative justice actually also implies allowing oneself to be trained by restorative justice, by recovering a 'can be' attitude, which combines with a 'can do' attitude (Morineau, 1998).

Training in restorative justice implies having first worked and continued to work on oneself, on one's own listening skills, communication methods, without facing proven and removed shame, without experimenting trust dynamics or learning to recognise in the other the *person* whenever and wherever beyond the acts actually carried out. It is impossible to separate training for restorative justice from a deep reassessment of one's own lifestyle, by starting to be empathic towards ourselves (Rosenberg, 1998). This divergence is always possible in other professions where, on the contrary, a 'mask' is sometimes required to be worn to shield the person.

References

Aertsen, I. (2017). Recalibrating victimhood through restorative justice: perspectives from Europe. *Restorative Justice: An International Journal*, 5(3), 352-367. doi:10.1080/20504721.2017.1390997.

Aertsen, I. (2018). Restorative justice for victims of corporate violence. In G. Forti, C. Mazzucato, A. Visconti & S. Giavazzi (eds.), *Victims and corporations. Legal challenges and empirical findings*. Milano: Wolters Kluwer. Retrieved from https://asgp.unicatt.it/asgp-VictimsCorporations_Ebook_2018.pdf (last accessed May 2019).

Arendt, H. (1958). *The human condition*. Chicago: The University of Chicago Press.

Bergman Blix, S. & Wettergren, Å. (2016). A sociological perspective on emotions in the judiciary. *Emotion Review*, 8(1), 32-37. doi:10.1177/1754073915601226.

Borgna, E. (2017). *Le parole che ci salvano*. Torino: Einaudi.

Bovati, P. (1986). *Ristabilire la giustizia. Procedure, vocabolario, orientamenti* [An Bib 110], Rome.

Braithwaite, J. (2013). Ten responses to 'words on words'. 1. Western words. *Restorative Justice. An International Journal*, 1(1), 20-22.

Brown, M. (2018). *Creating restorative schools: setting schools up to succeed*. St. Paul: Living Justice Press.

Canestrari, S. (2008). Per un modello "aperto e condiviso" di scienza penalistica. *IUS17*, 7-10.

Chartrand, V. & Piché, J. (2019). Abolition and pedagogy: reflections on teaching a course on alternatives to punishment, state repression and social control. *Contemporary Justice Review*, 22(1), 23-42. doi:10.1080/10282580.2019.1576129.

Christie, N. (2013). Words on words. *Restorative Justice. An International Journal*, 1(1), 15-19.

Colombo, G. (2011). *Il perdono responsabile*. Milano: Ponte alle Grazie.

Cunneen, C. & Hoyle, C. (2010). *Debating Restorative Justice*. Oxford: Hart Publishing.

Curi, U. (2003). *Il farmaco della democrazia*. Milano: Marinotti.

Derrida, J. (1994). *Force de loi. Le «Fondement mystique de l'autorité»*. Paris: Galileé. Ital. translation *Forza di legge*. Torino: Bollati Boringhieri, 2003.

Derrida, J. & Rovatti, P. A. (2001). *L'università senza condizione*. Milano: Cortina.

Dignan, J. (2005). *Understanding victims and restorative justice*. Maidenhead: Open University Press.

Dünkel, F., Grzywa-Holten, J. E & Horsfield, P. (eds.). (2011). *Restorative justice and mediation in penal matters: a stocktaking of legal issues, implementation strategies and outcomes in 36 European countries*. Godesberg: Mönchengladblach.

Ekman, P. (1999). Basic emotions. In T. Dalgleish & M. Power (eds.). *Handbook of cognition and emotion*. Sussex: Wiley.

Foley, T. (2015). Institutional responses to child sexual abuse: how a moral conversation with its lawyers might contribute to cultural change in a faith-based institution. *Legal Ethics*, 18(2), 164-181. doi:10.1080/1460728x.2015.1125652.

Gavrielides, T. (2012). *Waves of healing: using restorative justice for street group violence*. London: Independent Academic Research Studies Publications.

Goleman, D. (1995). *Emotional intelligence*. New York: Random House.

Gordon, T. (1970). *Parents effectiveness training*. New York: Three Rivers Press.

Grande, E. & Mattei, U. (2008). Giustizia allo specchio. *Antropologia*, 8(11), 25-39.

Karp, D. (2014). *Little book of restorative justice for colleges and universities: repairing harm and rebuilding trust in response to student misconduct*. New York: Good Books.

Lauwaert, K. & Aertsen, I. (2016). With a little help from a friend: desistance through victim-offender mediation in Belgium. *Restorative Justice: An International Journal*, 4(3), 345-368. doi:10.1080/20504721.2016.1245913.

Lèvinas, E. (1984). *Èthique at Infini. Dialogues avec Philippe Nemo.* Paris: Librarie Arthème Fayard.

Liebmann, M. (eds.). (1989). *Art therapy in practice.* London: Jessica Kingsley Publisher.

Liebmann, M. (2007). *Restorative justice. How it works.* London: Jessica Kingsley Publisher.

Lodigiani, G. A. (2019). Conoscere per conoscersi ed interpretare, agire insegnando e insegnare agendo. *Cultura religiosa e scuola*, 18(1), 15-33.

Lombardi Vallauri, L. (2012). *Corso di filosofia del diritto.* Padova: Cedam.

Maslow, A. H. (1954). *Motivation and personality.* New York: Harper and Row.

Morineau, J. (1998). *L'esprit de la Médiation*, Toulouse, Erès.

Morrison, B. (2015). Restorative justice in education: changing lenses on education's three Rs. *Restorative Justice. An International Journal*, 3(3), 445-452. doi:10.1080/20504721.2015.1109367.

Nussbaum, M. C. (2010). *Not for profit. Why democracy needs the humanities.* Princeton, NJ: Princeton University Press. Ital. translation *Non per profitto. Perché le democrazie hanno bisogno della cultura umanistica.* Bologna: il Mulino, 2011.

Ost, F. (2004). *Raconter la loi. Aux source de l'imaginaire juridique.* Paris, France: Odile Jacob. Italian trans. *Mosè, Eschilo, Sofocle. All'origine dell'immaginario giuridico*, Bologna: il Mulino, 2007.

Pali, B. (2014). Art for social change: exploring restorative justice through the new media documentary inside the distance. *Restorative Justice: An International Journal*, 2(1) 85-94. doi:10.5235/20504721.2.1.85.

Pali, B. (2017). 'Cultural' problematisations in the restorative justice discourse. In I. Aertsen & B. Pali (eds.), *Critical restorative justice* (pp. 175-191). Oxford: Bloomsbury.

Pali, B. & Pelikan, C. (2014). Con-texting restorative justice and abolitionism: exploring the potential and limits of restorative justice as an alternative discourse to criminal justice. *Restorative Justice: An International Journal*, 2(2), 142-164. doi:10.5235/20504721.2.2.142.

Pali, B. & Walgrave, L. (2019). A conversation with Lode Walgrave. *Restorotopias*, 28 January 2019. Retrieved from www.restorotopias.com/author/restorotopias/ (last accessed 31 May 2019).

Pelikan, C. (2019). Imagination and experiences: some forethoughts and afterthoughts on the 10th conference of the European Forum for Restorative Justice in Tirana. *The International Journal of Restorative Justice*, 2(1), 3-12. doi:10.5553/ijrj/258908912019002001001.

Plutchik, R. (1962). *The emotions: Facts, theories and a new model.* New York: Random House.

Pointer, L., & McGoey, K. (2019). Teaching restorative practices through games: an experimental and relational restorative pedagogy. *An International Journal of Restorative Justice*, 2(1), 34-48. doi:10.5553/ijrj/258908912019002001003.

Reggio, F. (2010). *Giustizia dialogica, Luci e ombre della Restorative Justice.* Milano: Franco Angeli.

Rogers, C. R. (1980). *A way of being.* Boston: Houghton Mifflin Company.

Rogers, C. R. & Farson, R. E. (2015). *Active Listening.* Eastford: Martino Fine Books.

Rosenberg M. B. (1998). *Nonviolent communication.* Encinatas: Puddle Dancer Press.

Sherman, E. F. (2007). Dean Pound's dissatisfaction with the 'sporting theory of justice': where are we a hundred years later? *South Texas Law Review*, 48, 983-1002.

Sherman, L. W., Strang, H., Mayo Wilson, E., Woods, D. J. & Ariel, B. (2015). Are restorative justice conferences effective in reducing repeat offending? Findings from a Campbell systematic review. *Journal of Quantitative Criminology*, 31(1), 1-24. doi:10.1007/s10940-014-9222-9.

Simmel, G. (1900). *Philosophie des Geld.* Berlin: Duncker & Humblot.

Sylvester, D. J. (2003). Myth in restorative justice history. *Utah Law Review*, 1145-1496.

Umbreit, M. S. (2001). *The handbook of victim offender mediation. An essential guide to practice and research.* San Francisco: Jossey Bass.

Wachtel, T. (2016). A restorative practices perspective: Governance and authority. *MinoriGiustizia* (1), 49-56. doi:10.3280/mg2016-001006.

White, M. (2007). *Maps of narrative practice.* New York: W.W. Norton.

Part IV
Global challenges

Restorative justice and access to justice: in search of new perspectives for criminal justice in Brazil[1]

Raffaella da Porciuncula Pallamolla and Daniel Achutti

1 Introduction

Restorative justice stands out in the contemporary international scenario as a way of resolving conflicts that are distinct from that imposed by the traditional penal model. Inspired by various theories and movements – such as penal abolitionism, the victims movement, victimology and the critiques against the traditional criminal justice system presented by labelling approach theory and critical criminology[2] – restorative justice emerges as a response to the little attention given to victims in the criminal procedure and due to the failure of the prison penalty to promote rehabilitation of those convicted.

The principles of the restorative justice model[3] are different from those that support the traditional criminal justice model and mainly involve the participation of the victim in the resolution of conflicts, reparation of the damage and the offender taking responsibility in a manner that is not stigmatising and exclusionary. It uses conflict resolution practices based on a dialogue between those involved in the crime in order to allow the parties to define what should be done in relation to the offence and the harm caused to the victim. It can also be said that this model aims at constricting the criminal justice system above all in terms of reducing the imposition of punishment.[4]

---

1 This chapter is a tribute to Prof. Ivo Aertsen, to whom we are very grateful for the opportunity of conducting part of our research projects at the Leuven Institute of Criminology (LINC) of the University of Leuven (Belgium) and to experience its unique *restorative environment* within the members of the research line on Restorative Justice. We are also grateful for all the pleasant visits of Prof. Aertsen to Brazil for several conferences and debates on the big challenge of implementing restorative justice in a country marked by strong inequalities, urban violence and social injustice.

2 For a deeper analysis of such influences, see: Pallamolla (2009); Achutti 2017).

3 Restorative justice will be treated here as a *model* of justice to contrast it with the traditional criminal justice *model* (which is characterised by the use of the penal process to establish the offender's guilt and impose a punishment that is proportional to the seriousness of the crime and their culpability). However, despite strong opposition that arises from the use of the term *model*, it should be emphasized that the complexity of either of these models is not ignored, as well as the existence of features in common between them; however, due to the extensiveness of the topic, issues related to it will not be addressed in this chapter.

4 For detailed differences on the models, see: Pallamolla (2009).

Given these brief and cursory notions of restorative justice, it is worth mentioning the motives that drove its expansion in several countries. Notwithstanding those that are linked to the context of every country and which are then exclusive to each nation (or region), a number of motives can be identified that are present in the majority of countries, among them the crisis of the legitimacy of the criminal justice system (or at least acknowledgement of its inability to deal with social conflicts satisfactorily), the search for alternatives as to the manner of responding to the crime (or conflict), the victims' claims, etc.

In this regard, when discussing the expansion of restorative justice in Spain, Larrauri (2004: 461-462) refers to similar factors which arise from two sources: judicial and sociological. The first involves the existence of European legislation which encourages the use of restorative justice and the experiences of various countries that use it; while among the second is the crisis of the legitimacy of the criminal justice system, the impact on the victim, their claims and the new conception of a crime (as a conflict which harms someone and not only as a violation of the law), and the change in the role of the State.

Observing the Brazilian scenario and the sociological factors mentioned by the Spanish criminologist, it can be affirmed that the crisis of legitimacy of the criminal justice system takes centre stage in Brazil and is tied to the crisis in the forms of social regulation, manifest in the 'lack of credibility and efficiency of the legal system, the failure of public policies to restrain violence, the depletion of the repressive model of crime management, communication and participation deficits aggravated by the authoritarian practices of the legal agencies, etc.' (Sica, 2007:1).

When analysing one of the symptoms of contemporary culture of control pointed out by Garland (2005), Boutellier (2006: 27) states that the protection of citizens has become a dominant theme in criminal policy. Citizens no longer claim the guarantee of their rights against possible illegalities arising from state power but demand the state's protection from other citizens.

In the sphere of criminal justice, the old Leviathan State gives way to the state that protects its citizens from other (non-)citizens. Criminal law is relied upon to combat crime and defend society and legitimises its activity in one of the myths of modern society: 'the myth that the sovereign state is capable of producing "law and order" and control crime within its territorial boundaries' (Garland, 2005: 188).

As Carvalho (2004: 184) notes, the state becomes responsible for security and preventing risks, which also affect criminal law and which then need to be modified to meet these demands:

> By being called upon to operate preventive policies (...), criminal control (criminal law, criminal procedure, criminology, and criminal policy) was impelled to amplify its sphere of action, adapting to the new legal goods.

Crime then becomes another risk of the risk society. (Boutellier, 2006: 30). This first expansion of criminal law that absorbs the 'new' social legal assets in addition to the traditional individual legal assets serves, for criminal law, as the 'ideal ground for a crisis of legitimacy to flourish' (Carvalho, 2004: 186).

With the crisis of the welfare state in the central countries in the 1980s, the 'possibility of reaching some degree of social justice in the peripheral countries in which the social state was a simulacrum' was made impossible (Carvalho, 2004: 190). As a consequence, forms of exclusion spread, and citizens who have no value, according to market logic, became a problem. The 'solution' found was the 'maximisation of directly coercive police power' (Carvalho, 2004: 193).

In the peripheral countries – namely, Brazil – the inexpressive social state increasingly gave way to the penal state, which presents 'a policy of exacerbating and expanding the means of fighting crime as a solution to all social, political, and economic problems afflicting society' (Bitencourt, 1995: 118).

Zaffaroni et al., (2003) explain that during the 1960s, with labelling approach theory deeply influenced by strands of symbolic interactionism, phenomenology and ethnomethodology, the official purposes of the prison penalty and the asepsis of the penal system were demystified. There occurred then a 'severe de-legitimisation of the purpose that instrumental reason granted to punitive power, which put in crisis the instrumental arguments themselves' of preventing and curbing criminality (Zaffaroni et al., 2003: 641).

These findings, which exposed the dark figure of crime (as Edwin Sutherland had already done) and demonstrated the imbalances in the criminal justice system in relation to the discourse sustained, unveiling the selectivity of the system and the primary and secondary criminalisation processes, produced, according to Carvalho (2004: 203), the 'first narcissistic injury of criminal law' and shook 'the "efficiency discourse" that traditionally included the oppressive apparatuses able to control human conduct through the criminalisation of all social facts considered unacceptable'.

In this regard, Zaffaroni et al. (2003: 88) point out that 'state power grants *manifest functions* to its institutions, which are expressed, declared, and public'. This attribution arises from the republican need for power to have to justify its enforcement under penalty of not being able to be submitted to judgements of reason. However, normally, there is some disparity between these manifest functions and what is realised by the institution in society – that is, their latent or real functions. It so happens that 'state power with non-punitive manifest functions and latent punitive functions (one which does not discursively express its real functions) is much vaster than that which ostensibly has manifest punitive functions as its responsibility' (Zaffaroni et al., 2003: 88).

Thus, Zaffaroni (1991: 16) also points out that a criminal justice system would only be legitimate when this characteristic is granted to it by its rationality. He understands rationality as the 'internal coherence of the penal/legal discourse' and its 'truth value as to the new social operability'. To explain itself as an exercise of rationally planned power, the criminal justice system makes use of a theoretical or discursive construction: namely, the penal/legal discourse. Thus, the criminal justice system will be legitimate if its discourse is rational and its activities are in accordance with the discourse.

However, when analysing the Latin American criminal justice systems, Zaffaroni (1997: 26) notes that the 'discourse is schizophrenic in terms of the operating reality of the criminal justice systems' and that 'the rationality of the penal/legal discourse is absolutely unsustainable in a much more evident manner than in the central countries, and does not fulfill any of the requirements for legitimacy' (Zaffaroni, 1991: 19).

Particularly in the sphere of criminal justice, the 'paralysation' of the justice system and the inadequacy with which the conflict was handled resulted in a loss of legitimacy for the system. The selective and stigmatising operation of the criminal justice system, while exposing its inability to perform its (stated) function of preventing and curbing crime, demonstrates its success in fulfilling its (real) function of excluding and marginalising the most social and economically vulnerable part of the population.

On the other hand, also comprising the national scenario and closely connected to the crisis (or lack) of legitimacy of the criminal justice system is the growing social violence. Social disintegration and the destruction of community ties visible in Brazilian society can undoubtedly be seen as expressions of 'a system that elected the deprivation of liberty as the principal response to crime' (Sica 2007: 4).

Increased violence not only is a symbol of a society with weakened social ties but is also the result of various factors found in the recent Brazilian re-democratisation. Caldeira (2003), when analysing the increased violence in the city of São Paulo (at least in the last two decades), points out some of the factors that contributed to this increase and which clearly may be extended to the country's other large urban centres:

> The increased violence is the result of a complex cycle that involves factors such as the violent standard of police action; disbelief in the justice system as a legitimate public mediator of conflicts and provider of fair reparations; violent and private responses to crime; resistance to democratization; and the population's weak perception of individual rights and their support for violent forms of punishment. (Caldeira, 2003: 101)

Caldeira (2003: 55) explains that the universe of crime, comprised of the discourse of crime, fear, increased violence, the failure of institutions of order (mainly the police and the judiciary), the privatisation of security and justice, and the continued segregation of the cities, reveals the disjunctive character of Brazilian democracy – that is, the existence of contradictory development processes in society. The universe of crime, then, indicates this disjunctive character in two ways:

> firstly, because the increased violence in itself deteriorates citizens' rights; and secondly, because it offers a field in which the reactions to violence become not only violent and disrespectful of legal rights but help deteriorate the public space, segregate social groups, and destabilize the state of law. (Caldeira 2003: 56)

The challenge then is to restructure this system and seek for alternatives able to reduce the violence and harm caused by the criminal justice system. It can then be affirmed that the project of restorative justice is tied to the process of judicial reformulation that has been under development in Brazil with the aim of adapting both the legislation and the legal structures to the democratic context (Schuch, 2006).

According to Oxhorn & Slakmon (2005), restorative justice is an alternative to qualify the administration of justice, contributes to the growth of democracy and, consequently, makes justice more democratic, since it functions by means of civil society but is never independent of the state:

> by actively granting jurisdiction on some aspects of the justice system to social organizations, a state with low levels of social legitimacy and effectiveness will be able to strength civil society in ways that will help improve not only their ability to ensure fundamental civil rights but also, in a broader sense, the quality of democracy. (Oxhorn & Slakmon, 2005: 188)

These same authors correctly point out that 'in highly unequal democracies such as Brazil, the justice system tends to reflect and perpetuate existing socio-economic inequalities' (Oxhorn & Slakmon, 2005: 196). Reducing inequalities perpetuated and reproduced by the criminal justice system and making it more democratic and accessible to the socially and economically less favoured then becomes the project in which restorative justice emerges.

2 The risk of widening the net of penal control

One of the most frequent criminological critiques when discussing the use of restorative justice in the resolution of criminal conflicts must at least briefly be mentioned. This critique centres on the risk of extending the network of control (net-widening), which may result if restorative justice is not able to reduce the number of people who enter the traditional criminal justice system, such that it merely results in attracting more people to the new system (Larrauri, 2004: 455).

The use of restorative justice for the purpose of reducing the use of the criminal justice system may have a perverse effect, if its practices will be applied to situations and people that otherwise would not have entered the criminal justice system (Jaccoud, 2005: 178). Cases which normally would only have resulted in a police warning or redirection to other non-criminal sectors (Morris, 2005: 446) would, when referred to restorative justice, run the risk of entering the traditional criminal justice system and, consequently, of receiving a criminal sanction – this in the event that no agreement is reached in the restorative procedure or if the agreement is not met by the offender (Jaccoud, 2005: 178).

First, it should be noted that the critique against the net widening of formal control had previously been directed to alternative penalties and used similar grounds: with the intention of reducing the use of prison, the alternatives sought to be more 'benevolent' to the crime. However, what is perceived in practice is that they were not less rigorous, and they were not able to reduce the use of prison sentences, thus contributing to net-widening.

The importance of registering these critiques is in alerting restorative justice so that the same errors of the alternative penalties are not repeated, which would inflate the criminal justice system with new cases that would end in the imposition of penalties and not in a restorative agreement.

Larrauri (2004: 455) warns that the risk of net-widening, in the case of restorative justice, is linked to the idea that this justice represents a more lenient procedure that does not burden the offender, which would authorise it to handle only the smaller cases (those less serious). However, this idea ignores the fact that the restorative procedure is not simple and requires much effort on the part of both the victim and the offender.

The risk of net-widening may also be provoked by other factors: a) by the priority granted to the criminal justice system to decide which cases are eligible to go through a restorative procedure; b) due to agreements reached in restorative conferences not being valued by the judge when deciding the penalty; c) due to the fact that restorative procedures do not constitute an alternative to prison, if the sphere selected for its application is during the application of the prison penalty (Larrauri, 2004: 462) or if used only in less serious crimes, for which prison sentences do not apply.

However, there are ways to contain net-widening and the inappropriate use of restorative justice, such as by adopting clear criteria for sending cases to restorative programmes (Larrauri, 2004: 455) and avoiding the use of restorative justice in less serious cases (trifling cases) (Morris, 2005: 446-447).[5]

Although the problems pointed out by critics are avoidable, it is still necessary to carry out permanent assessments of restorative justice that highlight, among other things, its successful use by the number of people kept away from the criminal justice system (reducing the number of cases and the use of penal measures) (Larrauri, 2004: 455-456).

5 See Pallamolla (2009) for a more detailed analysis of the net widening of penal control with the use of restorative justice and strategies to avoid it. See Achutti (2014) for a critical model of restorative justice for the Brazilian case and the possibilities for avoiding the net in such a context.

3 RESTORATIVE JUSTICE AS A WAY FOR ACCESS TO JUSTICE: A FEW FINAL CONSIDERATIONS

Restorative justice emerges as another possible response to crime instead of the traditional criminal procedure; it does not intend to replace the punitive model but rather proposes to work with it, handling cases that before had little or no attention from the justice system or which received a response in the form of punishment (counterproductive for victim and offender).

The state is not alone in receiving demands of citizens who try to resolve a conflict. Both critical criminology and sociology have exposed this reality: first, by revealing the dark figure of crime (first with Sutherland and then with social reaction and critical criminology) and, second, by showing that there are alternative and informal means of resolving conflicts in contemporary societies (legal pluralism). In this respect, Santos (1995: 175-176) states:

> From a sociological point of view, the contemporary state does not have a monopoly over the production and distribution of law. Although state law is the dominant judicial modality, it coexists in society with other judicial modalities, other rights that with it are articulated in various ways.

In light of this plurality, conflict, when not resolved through formal channels (in the case of penal conflicts, through the criminal justice system) tends to be managed 'privately, which may give way to the use of illegal violence and suppression of the opponent' (Sinhoretto, 2006: 87).

Thus, through establishing the criteria of referring cases to its programmes, restorative justice can increase access to justice, in addition to developing mechanisms to avoid the danger of net-widening and preventing violent responses from becoming more pervasive – be they resulting from private ways to manage conflict or from the criminal justice system itself that responds violently to conflict.

In terms of illegal alternative justice practices, Oxhorn and Slakmon (2005: 202) state that real access to restorative justice – understood as a form of micro-justice – enables citizens to have 'a concrete option to private retribution'.

To then better evaluate the role of restorative justice in increasing access to justice, an analysis is necessary of what access to justice means in a democratic state of law and what the obstacles to this access are.

Like Arendt, Cappelletti and Garth (1998) also claim that access to justice may 'be seen as the fundamental requirement – the most basic of human rights – in a modern, egalitarian legal system that exists to ensure, and not only proclaim, the rights of all' (Cappelletti & Garth 1998: 12). Ensuring equal access to justice for all, however, implies materialising the rights guaranteed by the Constitution.

For these authors (Cappelletti & Garth 1998: 21-24), the main obstacles to access to justice and which may be related to criminal justice concern the 'possibilities of the parties' – that is, the advantages and disadvantages that some litigants have, such as (1) greater availability of financial resources, which allows the party the possibility of presenting their arguments more efficiently; (2) the ability to recognise a right and propose an action (which, in the case of the criminal justice system, would mean recognising oneself as victim of a crime and turning to the criminal justice system[6]); (3) the lack of psychological disposition to turn to legal processes, which may come about due to a shared distrust of lawyers – especially in the less favoured classes – or due to other reasons, such as complicated procedures, formalisms, intimidating environments (such as courts), figures considered oppressive (such as judges and lawyers) that have the individual who could or should seek out the justice system feeling lost, immersed in a strange world.

Cappelletti and Garth's study, in addition to identifying barriers in access to justice, also present the measures adopted by Western countries (since 1965) to overcome these obstacles, which occurred practically in chronological order: the first wave of reforms came about with the creation of free legal assistance for the poor; the second, with legal representation for the collective interests (especially in the environmental and consumer areas); the third and last proposes a new focus on access to justice, discussing the legal system more broadly. It is in this last wave that the question of informalisation of the justice system belongs (Cappelletti & Garth, 1998: 31). Thus, according to Cappelletti and Garth (1998: 71),

> this focus encourages the exploration of a wide variety of reforms, including changes in the forms of procedure; changes in the structure of the courts or the creation of new courts; the use of lay or paraprofessionals, both as judges and as defendants; changes in the substantial law intended to avoid litigation or facilitate its resolution; and the use of private or informal mechanisms of resolving litigations.

This third wave, as Sinhoretto (2006: 88-89) explains, was the first to concern itself with ensuring individual access to justice to the socially and economically less favoured social segments:

> this is the time to create alternatives to conflict resolution that are not only less costly and quicker, but that also are more understandable and closer to the daily reality of the social actors involved in the conflicts.

6 It is important to mention that, according to Santos (1995: 167), access to criminal justice takes place differently than access to civil justice, this because defendants are 'forced' to seek justice. However, it can still be said that there is social demand for criminal justice.

In terms of the Brazilian reality, the three waves mentioned did not occur as they did in the central countries. The third wave took place 'without the policy of individual legal assistance being universalized and without the postulation of collective demands having shown concrete effects, making the national experience a singular one' (Sinhoretto, 2006: 114). Sinhoretto (2006: 88-89) explains that

> Free legal assistance was, up until the 80s, practically the only compensatory public policy in this field. After the democratic opening and, most of all, after Law 9.099/05[7] was edited (...), initiatives for amplifying the offer of legal services have been multiplying in the spirit of the 'third wave'.

Thus, due to this crisis of legitimacy of the criminal justice system, the growth of violence in Brazilian society and the crisis of the administration of justice, alternative forms of managing conflicts have multiplied, seeking to increase access to justice and, thus, promote economic and social equality in a manner that strengthens democracy.

According to research conducted by Azevedo (2001) in the first two years of its implementation in the city of Porto Alegre (1996 and 1997), the Special Courts created by Law 9.099/95 tried to unburden the criminal courts of cases for lesser offences so that they could give greater attention to the more serious ones; however, this objective was not achieved. These courts were not able to reduce the number of processes in the common criminal courts. What did happen was that they 'began to deal with a type of crime that did not reach the criminal courts, that was resolved through informal "mediation" processes at the police stations or by pure and simple "shelving"' (Azevedo, 2001: 103).

Azevedo (2001) concluded, after extensive field research, that although cases were not redirected as intended, cases were included in the legal system that before never reached it. However, this increase in the number of cases should not be understood as increased formal control, since these before were 'resolved' in the stations. The Special Courts, though still precariously, were able to reduce the discretionary power of the police chiefs - who ended up acting as informal mediators and in practice decriminalising crimes - and increase access to justice for a portion of the population whose conflicts before were not considered by the legal system. Thus,

> While police mediation was informal, arbitrary and often combined with mechanisms to intimidate the victim (victimization) and the accused, legal mediation tends to widen the space for explaining the conflict and adopting a solution of consensus between the parties, reducing impunity. (Azevedo, 2001: 107)

7 The Law 9099/05 created the Special Criminal Courts, which comprise the adult criminal justice system and are responsible only for the judgement of minor offences (crimes whose maximum prison penalty does not exceed two years).

In this regard, restorative justice could be compared with the criminal courts at least in their intention stated in Law 9.099/95 of introducing informal mechanisms of conflict resolution in the criminal justice system. However, the differences between the two proposals are countless (and will not be analysed here). What is important is that restorative justice seeks to increase not the exercise of punitive power by the state but rather access to another model of justice. This is possible, according to Sica (2007: 153), by the splitting of the criminal justice system

> into a dual-entry framework (mediation and punishment), which could, in theory, reduce both the number of punishments imposed and the dark figure, offering a more accessible and feasible institutional response for a number of conflicts that were marginalized or did not find satisfactory answers within a one-way, closed, and inflexible system.

Although restorative justice does not deny the concept of crime (primary criminalisation) in its participation with the criminal justice system, it takes on greater importance by having an emphasis different from that of the traditional criminal justice system in its reaction to crime (Larrauri, 2004: 455), operating in the sphere of secondary criminalisation. Sica (2007) states that the de-judicialisation of access to justice with the use of restorative practices such as mediation – which could also result in 'de-criminalisation in practice', as it allows some cases to be resolved by restorative programmes without (re-) entering the criminal justice system – provides

> freer access to justice for marginalised social groups, for those who feel that the justice system is simply another way to provide services to the 'rich' and penalize the 'poor', and this 'informalisation' also enables a reduction in the level of stigmatisation and coercion inherent to formal justice. (Sica, 2007: 154-155)

Corroborating these ideas, a study (Sherman & Strang, 2007) conducted by the Smith Institute in England on restorative justice in various countries (including the United Kingdom, the United States and Australia) noted that this model is able to bring more crimes to justice, since its operation amplifies access to justice by providing an alternative way to deal with crime unlike that traditionally offered by the criminal justice system. According to the study, the greatest barrier is the reluctance of the victim and the witnesses, who fear retaliation, as well as the lack of time they have to involve themselves in legal formalities. There is also the issue of disbelief or fear of the system, resulting in a large number of crimes going unresolved (Sherman & Strang, 2007: 78), thus comprising the dark figure of crime. It can then be noted that the findings of this study do not differ from those previously mentioned and expose the true barriers in access to justice.

In light of the situation of the lack of legitimacy in which the Brazilian criminal justice system finds itself, the Brazilian violence figures and the consequent need for the justice system to make room for new forms of conflict resolution, restorative justice presents itself as a model able to (re)legitimise the criminal justice system by qualifying justice administration and introducing the possibility of resolving the conflict in a non-violent manner.

At the same time, restorative justice, as an alternative justice mechanism, not only allows the rights of citizenship and democracy to be strengthened but also contributes to the empowerment of civil society and provides less favoured groups with the skills that put their fundamental rights within reach.

REFERENCES

Achutti, D. (2014). Justiça restaurativa e abolicionismo penal [*Restorative justice and penal abolitionism*]. São Paulo: Saraiva Press.

Achutti, D. (2017). *Is a critical model of restorative justice possible? A penal abolitionist approach.* In I. Aertsen & B. Pali (eds.). *Critical restorative justice* (pp. 14-28). Oxford: Hart Publishing.

Azevedo, R. G. de (2001). Juizados Especiais Criminais. Uma abordagem sociológica sobre a informalização da justiça penal no Brasil [*Special Criminal Courts. A sociological approach to informalizing the Brazilian criminal justice system*]. *Revista Brasileira de Ciências Sociais* [*Brazilian Journal of Social Sciences*], 16 (47), pp. 97-110.

Bitencourt, C. R. (1995). Princípios garantistas e a delinqüência do colarinho branco [*Guaranteed Principles and White-Collar Crime*]. *Revista Brasileira de Ciências Criminais* [*Brazilian Journal of Criminal Sciences*], 3 (11), pp. 118-127.

Boutellier, H. (2006). The vital context of restorative justice. In I. Aertsen, T. Daems & L. Robert (eds.), *Institutionalising restorative justice* (pp. 25-43). Portland: Willan Publishing.

Caldeira, T. P. d. R. (2003). Cidade de muros: crime, segregação e cidadania em São Paulo [*City of Walls: Crime, Segregation, and Citizenship in São Paulo*]. São Paulo: Editora 34/Edusp.

Cappelletti, M. & Garth, B. (1998). Acesso à justiça [*Access to Justice*]. Porto Alegre: Sergio Antonio Fabris Press.

Carvalho, S. de (2004). A ferida Narcísica do Direito Penal (primeiras observações sobre as (dis)funções do controle penal na sociedade contemporânea) [*The Narcissistic Injury of Criminal Law (First Observations on the (Dis)Functions of Penal Control in Contemporary Society)*]. In R. M. C. Gauer (eds.). *A Qualidade do Tempo: Para Além das Aparências Históricas* [*The Quality of Time: Beyond Historic Appearances*] (pp. 179-211). Rio de Janeiro: Lumen Juris Press.

Garland, D. (2005). La cultura del control: crimen y orden social en la sociedad contemporánea [*The Culture of Control: Crime and Social Order in Contemporary Society*]. Barcelona: Editorial Gedisa.

Jaccoud, M. (2005). Princípios, Tendências e Procedimentos que cercam a Justiça Restaurativa [*Tendencies and Procedures in Restorative Justice*]. In C. Slakmon, R. De Vitto, R. Gomes Pinto (eds.), *Justiça Restaurativa* [*Restorative Justice*] (pp. 163-188). Brasília: Ministério da Justiça and PNUD.

Larrauri, E. (2004). Tendencias actuales en la justicia restauradora. In Álvares, Fernando Pérez (ed.). *SERTA in memoriam Alexandri Baratta*. Salamanca: Universidad de Salamanca.

Morris, A. (2005). Criticando os críticos: uma breve resposta aos críticos da justiça restauradora [*Criticizing the Critics: A Brief Response to the Critics of Restorative Justice*]. In C. Slakmon, R. De Vitto, R. Gomes Pinto (eds.). *Justiça Restauradora* (pp. 439-472). Brasília/DF: Ministério da Justiça e PNUD.

Oxhorn, P. & Slakmon, C. (2005). Micro-justiça, desigualdade e cidadania democrática. A construção da Sociedade Civil através da Justiça Restaurativa no Brasil [*Micro-Justice, Inequality, and Democratic Citizenship. The Construction of Civil Society through Restorative Justice in Brazil*]. In C. Slakmon, R. De Vitto & R. Gomes Pinto (eds.), *Justiça Restaurativa* (pp. 187-210). Brasília, Ministério da Justiça and Programa das Nações Unidas para o Desenvolvimento - PNUD.

Pallamolla, R. d. P. (2009). *Justiça restaurativa: da teoria à prática* [*Restorative Justice: From Theory to Practice*]. São Paulo: IBCCRIM.

Santos, B. d. S. (1995). *Pela mão de Alice. O social e o político na pós-modernidade* [*By the Hand of Alice. The Social and the Political in Postmodernity*]. São Paulo: Cortez.

Schuch, P. (2006). *Direitos e Afetos: Análise Etnográfica da "Justiça Restaurativa" no Brasil* [*Rights and Affectations: An Ethnographic Analysis of "Restorative Justice" in Brazil*]. Available at *30º Encontro Anual da ANPOCS*, 2006.

Sherman, L. W. & Strang, H. (2007). Restorative Justice: The Evidence. London, UK: The Smith Institute. Retrieved from www.iirp.edu/pdf/RJ_full_report.pdf (last accessed 7 May 2019).

Sica, L. (2007). *Justiça Restaurativa e Mediação Penal: o novo modelo de justiça criminal e de gestão do crime* [*Restorative Justice and Penal Mediation: The New Criminal Justice and Crime Management Model*]. Rio de Janeiro: Lumen Juris press.

Sinhoretto, J. (2006). *Ir aonde o povo está: etnografia de uma reforma da justiça* [*To Go Where the People Are: Ethnography of a Justice Reform*] (Doctoral Thesis). University of São Paulo.

Zaffaroni, E. R. (1991). *Em busca das penas perdidas: a perda da legitimidade do sistema penal* [*In Pursuit of Lost Penalties: The Loss of Legitimacy of the Criminal Justice System*]. Rio de Janeiro: Revan.

Zaffaroni, E. R. (1997). *Globalização e sistema penal na América Latina: da segurança nacional à urbana* [*Globalization and the Criminal Justice System in Latin American: From National to Urban Security*]. *Discursos Sediciosos: crime, direito e sociedade* [*Sedicious Discourses: Crime, Law, and Society*], 2(4), pp. 25-36.

Zaffaroni, E. R., Batista, N., Alagia, A. & Slokar, A. (2003). *Direito Penal Brasileiro: Teoria Geral do Direito Penal* [*Brazilian Criminal Law: General Theory of Criminal Law*]. Rio de Janeiro: Revan.

Populism, reconciliation and crime victims: the case of China

Xiaoyu Yuan

1 Introduction

The term *penal populism* or *populist punitiveness* has been used by criminologists to describe a defining trend in the field of penal policymaking in many Western countries. It generally refers to, in neo-liberal democracies, politicians tapping into and feeding on public expressions of anger, distrust and disenchantment with the criminal justice system (Pratt, 2007), in order to gain their electoral advantages. The crime victim has occupied a central symbolic position in this culture of control (Garland, 2001), which is often manifest in the claim of balancing victim's interests against the offender. As pointed out by scholars, however, victims are being used as a rhetoric device in the service of severity (Ashworth, 2000: 186; Hoyle & Zedner, 2007). Victimologists have also kept a distance from the political construction of crime victims, and they often demonstrate that the situation and experiences of actual victims do not correspond with the common notion of victimhood (Aertsen, 2010; Pemberton, 2011).

The discourse on penal populism has often focused on the 'penal' while tending to conflate populism with punitiveness (Hogg, 2013). The concept of populism has attracted much discussion in political arena, for example, populist politics. It essentially remains contested and receives quite different interpretations contingent on the different contexts (Mudde & Kaltwasser, 2017). A simplistic definition might be to equalise it with securing legitimacy through invigorating support from the public or the masses. In today's democratic politics, populism is tacitly understood as something negative, reactionary or dangerous (Hogg, 2013).

This chapter narrows the discussion of populism to the justice field, to be more specific, a penal practice in China's criminal justice system. It first situates the populist approach to justice within the grand agenda promoted by China's governing party. Secondly, it takes a close look at how and whether victims' needs have been met in a people-centred justice project called reconciliation, which takes 'justice for the people' as the desired goal. In so doing, it draws on the qualitative interviews with crime victims whose cases were processed by the justice authorities. Finally, it assesses the rhetoric of people-centred justice from the victim's perspective. It points out the necessity of further investigation into the construction of victimhood in contemporary China's justice practice.

2 Populism and reconciliation

It is believed that 'populism exists wherever there is an ideology of popular resentment against the order imposed on society by a long established, differential ruling class which is believed to have a monopoly of power, property, breeding and fortune' (Shils, 1956: 100-1 cf. Pratt, 2007: 9). A more popular understanding of populism tends to focus on the role of the media that shores up public sentiment and discussion. In recent years, scholars have noticed the phenomenon of penal populism in the handling of capital cases (Fu, 2016). While high-profile cases have constantly hit the headlines, public opinion around these cases reflected the public's resentment and anger at social evils, such as the declining moral cohesion, official corruption and injustice (Zhou, 2013). Fu (2016) went further to suggest that populism is a manifestation of the anger and frustration of the underdogs towards the more privileged class who manipulate the criminal justice. Pressed with the social discord that undoubtedly challenges the existing social order, the Chinese government and its justice authorities have not hesitated in addressing social realities. They adhere that simply stressing the legal effect by applying legal rules has not achieved satisfaction among the parties, thus bringing no good to social harmony. A populist approach, in contrary, is to ensure that both parties, in litigations of civil or criminal nature, have agreed on the outcome. It prioritises negotiation and agreement, while playing down confrontation or conflicts.

A 'populist turn' became salient (Fu & Cullen, 2011; Zhang, 2012) from 2006 onwards under the Hu era's catchphrase of building a harmonious socialist society. In line with the overall governing imperative, the Supreme People's Court (SPC) in 2007 issued the Opinion,[1] declaring 'mediate if possible' as a 'guiding agenda' of the Chinese judiciary and attached a strong emphasis to 'resolving cases and solving problems to promote social harmony' (Zhang, 2012). In 2009, the SPC's third five-year legal reform plan stressed the mass line as the central principle of judicial reform, requiring courts to fully listen to the opinion of the people and embody their will.[2] Some linked this populist turn with the Chinese Communist legal tradition and precedents as early as the prior-1978 era (Liebman, 2011). Others such as Minzner (2011) deemed this populist turn as a broader 'turn against law' that permeates the entire Chinese party-state. In the current rule-of-law-based governance, proposed in the New Era of socialism with Chinese characteristics, people-centredness came to prominence again. It urged the justice authorities to ensure people achieve a sense of gain and a sense of satisfaction in their conflict resolution.

---

1 Several Opinions on Further Enhancing the Positive Effect of Court-Directed Mediation in the Construction of a Harmonious Socialist Society (关于进一步发挥诉讼调解在构建社会主义和谐社会中积极作用的若干意见). www.globalchinalaw.com/zh/documents/a80a9885-c2bd-e5a3-3c02-d811d6321302/bilingual, visit on 12 May 2019.

2 The Third Five-Year Plan for People's Court 2009-2013《人民法院第三个五年改革纲要 (2009-2013)》, issued by the Supreme People's Court on 17 March 2009. www.court.gov.cn/shenpan-xiangqing-323.html, visit on 12 May 2019.

How does this populism work out in the penal field? A key mechanism in the Chinese criminal justice system is to achieve reconciliation between the governed – the offender and the victim and their respective supporters (Berti, 2011; Bian & Feng, 2008; Shi, 2007; Song & Yuan, 2009). Reconciliation departs from the traditional goal of the criminal justice system, which is sanctioning the crime and protecting the offender's rights, but adds another dimension, which is the pursuit of societal effects in the formal outcome. Thus, justice authorities should not only conclude the case but also resolve the conflict between the subjects, ensuring they readily accept the legal outcome. The ambiguities and uncertainties involved in 'societal effects' are not without criticisms from legal scholars. Some oppose using societal effects as the yardstick to evaluate justice activities on the grounds that the task for justice authorities is to strictly apply the law without allowing the public's opinion and assessment to influence the case's decision (Dai, 2005). However, the populist approach to justice has gained unmatched favour in legal practice, and this became particularly conspicuous with reconciliation being codified in the 2013 Criminal Procedure Law (CPL).

The top-down demand on the justice authority was to dissolve (*huajie*) the conflict peacefully and in a socially beneficial way. As dissatisfied victims can be a source of social discord, particularly by bringing appeals or petitions and letters to a higher authority or other government branches, reconciliation mechanism is believed to better cater to their interests and needs, thus reducing any negative events. However, is this the reality?

Criminal reconciliation has been subject to theoretical scrutiny and empirical investigation. The major focus in a range of studies has been on the defendants. Since the key to this mechanism is that the offender offered economic compensation to their victims in exchange for forgiveness, questions arise as to the fairness and equality before the law. Recently, scholars have examined institutional and cultural logics of the practice in an attempt to provide a framework for understanding the process and outcome of criminal reconciliation in China (Ng & He, 2017). Very rare studies so far have examined victim's perspective and experiences of criminal reconciliation in China. The current study draws upon empirical data to show how the populist approach has treated crime victims. Overall, populist rhetoric does not offer humane treatment to crime victims, but tends to depict them as a potential source of trouble.

3 SOURCE OF DATA

The current study draws on the empirical data I collected over a period of five months in 2014 for my PhD project, at X district in Y city. I visited a local police station, a prosecutor's office and a court and observed case handling that involved reconciliation as an option. I kept field notes that contained a detailed account of the working environment, the trials, the initiation and process of reconciliation, the interaction between the parties and the justice authority. An advantage of being in the field was that I could talk to various actors involved in criminal reconciliation, including judges, prosecutors, staff from the justice bureau, lawyers, victims and offenders or their supporters. The interviews provided a rich source for understanding criminal reconciliation as a complex issue embedded in institutional, individual, cultural and political dynamics.

The thematic analysis I did earlier on suggested that reconciliation could benefit crime victims in some way. The normative process, which only allowed material losses to be considered, failed to compensate the victim sufficiently. By contrast, reconciliation allowed the defendant to pay compensation directly to the victim in exchange for a forgiveness letter. As a result, the offender received a relatively lenient sentence, and the victim obtained a relatively higher amount of compensation. Thus, reconciliation seemed to be a better option for the crime victim. However, does this populist approach to justice cater to victim's actual needs? The current study suggests a striking and complicated picture.

4 Disentangling victims' actual needs

The fourteen victims included in the current study were mostly victims of theft (six cases) or assault crimes (five cases), with their perpetrators being captured and going through the criminal process. The assaults happened between strangers or acquaintances who had prior relationships, which was the same as in the theft cases. These crimes had differing effects on the victims, and the varying degrees of victimisation experiences were contingent on the losses and harm they suffered and their expectations of whether their losses could be recovered, etc. Psychological and emotional impact, such as anger, fear or helplessness, also affected some victims. Thus, they expected to receive reparation, have emotional closure and achieve psychological balance by getting rid of the matter. Despite the reconciliation project offering some 'benefits', they failed to fully address the crime victims' needs or to meet the victims' procedural expectations.

First, victims desired to be acknowledged and compensated regarding their losses. A victim-centred system revolves around reparation rather than punishment (Shapland, 1984). Comparatively speaking, China has not established a national victim support system nor is any national compensation scheme available to crime victims of serious injuries. The dominant practice of asking the offender to make direct compensation was contingent on whether the defendant was identified, as well as the capability to make financial compensation. Two collateral problems arose from this. On the one hand, inadequate compensation or less timely compensation rendered the victims dissatisfied and caused them to suffer pain. On the other hand, while direct compensation made by the offender was seen as an apology, lacking such an apologetic gesture when there was no financial capability caused the victim to have negative opinion of the offender. Hence, where the major work method was to urge the defendant to pay financial compensation to victims, one would question what else was available to serve the victim under this populist compensation-oriented reconciliation.

Second, meeting the victim's justice needs also means the system should effect to educate the offender, make them repent for their wrongdoing and promise not to do it again. The victims were generally concerned about whether their offenders were remorseful. If the offenders had repented, then the victims deemed a state-based punishment unnecessary. The victims believed a heavy punishment for the offenders would cause hatred and even revenge, while goodwill could end the vicious cycle. Obviously, the crime victims valued forgiveness, seeing the need to rehabilitate and reintegrate the offenders rather than antagonise them.

The paradox was that victims' opinion could not be fully considered, and the justice authorities exercised their own discretion when handling cases. While the reconciliation project concluded with an agreement between the subjects and with the victim's letter of forgiveness, in most cases, it simply had the effect of assuring that no further actions, such as petitions or appeals, would arise from the victim. Victims knew 'lenience' would be granted to the offender if they reconciled; however, they were not entirely aware of the final decision imposed on the offender in the aftermath of their 'reconciliation'. It happened that the mother of a victim visited the court and expressed concern upon knowing that the other defendants except the principal had also received custodial sentence, which to her was excessive. Other instances included despite the victims believing the offence was a trivial matter and granted total pardon to the offender, the juvenile offender was still prosecuted in court.

5 TREATING CRIME VICTIMS: SOME NOTES

Simplistically speaking, victims are witnesses of the crime, and they assist the system in investigating the crime and bringing the offender to justice. Peculiar to China's criminal justice system, however, the 'assembly line' of the system (Chen, 2016) indicated that convicting the offender is the goal commonly pursued by the police, the prosecutor and the judge. The prosecutor and the judge rely heavily on the investigation by the police, instead of questioning the evidence or supervising the police regarding the legality of the investigation process (Mou, 2017). In the conviction-oriented structure, having the victim agree on the compensation issue and sign the letter seems to seal the criminal process with some tacit recognition of legitimacy, with all parties consenting to the outcome. The populist approach to conflict resolution is essentially politically correct, catering to the needs of each party, which indicates the system and the people uphold the same interests (Nesossi & Trevaskes, 2018). The populist tactics included letting the victim surrender, persuading, appeasing or satisfying victims when they persist or pressuring them with an even less desirable option. Eventually, any potential 'troublemaker' is discouraged from making trouble again.

However, based on the actual needs expressed by crime victims, the populist approach seems not to prioritise the needs and interests of individual victims, and it fails to differentiate levels of victimisation and match victims to necessary services. This is not so dissimilar to the populist rhetoric in the West, in the sense that victims just became a symbol that urges the policymakers to act as well as justifies their action. In China's case, the populist approach may give the victims some power to negotiate, with the defendant or with the authority, but it does not change the fact that the structure and culture is not victim oriented. Such a rhetoric of people-centred justice becomes questionable in terms of its real purpose, when no other mechanisms are readily available to crime victims to use. This said, some suggestions for the victim-oriented reform seem naturally to follow. The first would be increased efforts to building victim services and victim support. Although crime victims are synonymous with the masses in socialist tradition, it is important to recognise differentiated victimisation in the contemporary era. However, due to the limits in the data regarding the demographic information of victims, the level of marginalisation they had experienced in society prior to their victimisation was unknown. Second, an alternative process to solve the conflict should be available at the community level, which has the effect of educating the offender and restoring the victim. Criminal justice system is a source of distress for many crime victims. Populist approach appears to 'help' the victim, but it does not couple with procedural respect and tends to perceive crime victims as trouble. Further, the formal criminal justice system is often a source of secondary victimisation.

6 Concluding remarks

This study tested the populist rhetoric, which claims to serve the people, including victims. The current study throws light on ordinary crimes where practitioners within the system prioritise populist strategies to reconcile the interests between the victim, the offender and the system itself. Assessed from the victim's point of view, this form of populism sustained by the system is devoid of genuine concern for their needs, which has generated populist pressure when victims are dissatisfied with their procedural treatment and with the unavailable remedy due to them. The victim has been epitomised as needy, troublesome and has been excluded from making any substantive input. While this observation may suffer from drawbacks posed by the limitation in the data, for example, a small sample of crime victims, one may wonder whether asking about the victims' experiences is a valid starting point. Perhaps, further research needs to shed light on how crime victims are constructed in Chinese society.

Historically, Chinese society has been embedded in a Confucian order that places group harmony over individuals. Victims are expected to be forgiving and ready to surrender their own interests for the sake of collective interests (Lin, 2002). Notably, there was a lack of strong tradition in protecting individual rights in Chinese legal history (Peerenboom, 1993). Restoring harmony is of utmost importance, and this is now conflated with the populist approach that requires achieving satisfaction from the masses in the handling of their conflicts. This approach accords some particularity in the circumstances of crime victims, but it risks simplifying the matter and pressurising victims into accepting an agreement. In the contemporary era, treating the masses' needs as uniform would cause some discord when there is rising demand for respect and rights protection. If it is reminded that the concept of victimhood 'is contingent, liable to various interpretations and susceptible to continuous evolution' (Aertsen 2010: 205), there could be more research about the dynamics that define and shape victimhood.

The position of crime victims in the reconciliation project is somewhat intriguing. While claiming to be people-centred, the populist approach tends to normalise or put down victims' demands for rights and better protection. Victims were largely subsumed in the top-down imperative towards social harmony. This departs from penal populism in neo-liberal democracies that not only demands longer and harsher prison sentences but also 'demands that the rights of victims, the rights of communities, must take precedence over the rights of individual criminals' (Pratt, 2007: 30). The current study raises some dissonance as to how the victim is situated in the penal power in the people-centred reconciliation project. Perhaps, further inquiry is needed, such as into the activism of the victim movement in China.

7 Afterword

This short piece of inquiry does not expand on many issues, but is a continuous reflection that leads from an earlier path where I pursued doctoral study at Leuven, a reflexive path that seeks to unravel the ideology and power that lies behind. Ivo Aertsen, an earnest promoter of penal reform, an action scholar who devotes his long-standing passion, wisdom and expertise to the cause of building a good and just society, is more than a supervisor of mine, but a mentor for anyone on the same path.

References

Aertsen, I. (2010). Punitivity from a victim's perspective. In S. Snacken & E. Dumortier (eds.), *Resisting punitiveness in Europe? Welfare, human rights and democracy* (pp. 202-224). London: Routledge.

Ashworth, A. (2000). Victims' rights, defendants' rights and criminal procedure. In A. Crawford & J. Goodey (eds.), *Integrating a victim perspective within criminal justice*. Aldershot: Ashgate Darmouth.

Berti, R. (2011). *The Xingshi Hejie: criminal concliation in Mainland China and in Taiwan*. Paper presented at the ACS (Asian Criminological Society) 3rd Annual Confernce, Taiwan.

Bian, J., & Feng, L.Q. (2008). Constructing Chinese model of criminal reconciliation: building on pardon. *Tribune of Political Science and Law*, 26(6), 3-21.

Chen, R. (2016). *The frontier issues of criminal process: volume 1 [xingshi susong de qianyan wenti]*. Peking: China Renmin University Press.

Dai, Q. (2005). Convergences and conflicts: what 'societal effects' as judicial standard means for justice [qihe yu chongtu: shehui xiaoguo sifa biaozhun zhiyu sifa gongzheng]. *Journal of Law Application*, 2005(5), 31-35.

Fu, H. (2016). Between deference and defiance: courts and penal populism in Chinese capital cases. In B. Liang & H. Lu (eds.), *The death penalty in China: policy, practice and reform* (pp. 274-299). New York: Columbia University Press.

Fu, H., & Cullen, R. (2011). From mediatory to adjudicatory justice: the limits of civil justice reform in China. In M. Y. K. Woo & M. E. Gallagher (eds.), *Chinese Justice: civil dispute resolution in contemporary China* (pp. 25-57). Cambridge: Cambridge University Press.

Garland, D. (2001). *The culture of control: crime and social order in contemporary society*. Oxford: Oxford University Press.

Hogg, R. (2013). Punishment and 'the people': Rescuing populism from its critics. In K. Carrington, M. Ball, E. O'Brien, & J. Tauri (eds.), *Crime, justice and social democracy: international perspectives* (pp. 105-119). New York: Palgrave Macmillan.

Hoyle, C., & Zedner, L. (2007). Victims, victimisation, and criminal justice. In M. Maguire, R. Morgan, & R. Reiner (Eds.), *The Oxford handbook of criminology* (pp. 461-495). Oxford: Oxford University Press.

Liebman, B.L. (2011). A populist threat to China's courts? In M. Y. K. Woo & M. E. Gallagher (eds.), *Chinese justice: civil dispute resolution in contemporary China* (pp. 269-313). New York: Cambridge University Press.

Lin, D. (2002). *Confucian ethics and legal culture: an exploration from sociological perspective [rujia lunli yu falv wenhua: shehuixue guandian de tansuo]*. Beijing: Press of China University of Polical Science and Law.

Minzner, C.F. (2011). China's turn against law. *The American Journal of Comparative Law*, 59(4), 935-984. doi:10.5131/ajcl.2011.0006.

Mou, Y. (2017). Overseeing criminal justice: the supervisory role of the public prosecution service in China. *Journal of Law and Society*, 44(4), 620-645. doi:10.1111/jols.12060

Mudde, C., & Kaltwasser, C.R. (2017). *Populism: a very short introduction*. Oxford: Oxford University Press.
Nesossi, E., & Trevaskes, S. (2018). *Procedural justice and the fair trial in contemporary Chinese criminal justice*. Leiden: Brill.
Ng, K.H., & He, X. (2017, January 31). The institutional and cultural logics of legal commensuration: blood money and negotiated justice in China. *Centre for Chinese & Comparative Law Research Paper No. 2017/003*.
Peerenboom, R.P. (1993). The victim in chinese criminal theory and practice: a historical survey. *Journal of Chinese Law*, 7, 63.
Pemberton, A. (2011). Too readily dismissed? A victimological perspective on penal populism. In C. Nelsen & V. Wersch (eds.), *Beyond the death penalty*. Antwerp, Belgium: Intersentia.
Pratt, J. (2007). *Penal populism*. London: Routledge.
Shapland, J. (1984). Victims, the criminal justice system and compensation. *British Journal of Criminology*, 24, 131.
Shi, L. (2007). Criminal reconciliation: the "Third Realm" of criminal dispute settlement [*xingshi hejie: xingshi jiufen jiejue de disan lingyu*]. *Tribune of Political Science and Law*, 25(6), 80-88.
Song, Y., & Yuan, J. (eds.). (2009). *Theory and practice of criminal reconciliation in China*. Peking: Peking University Press.
Zhang, T. (2012). The pragmatic court: reinterpreting the Supreme People's Court of China. *Columbia Journal of Asian Law*, 25, 1.
Zhou, A. (2013). The faces and bones of public opinion in public events: an analysis of ten classic legal cases [shesu yulun de mianxiang yu benxiang: shida jingdian anli fenxi]. *China Legal Science*, 2013(1), 160-174.

Challenges facing the development of restorative justice in Hong Kong

Dennis S.W. Wong

1 Introduction

A colony of the United Kingdom until 1997, Hong Kong maintained a youth justice system that was highly similar to that of England and Wales for many years. From the 1930s until 2003, the minimum age of criminal responsibility was kept at 7. It was only in July 2003 that the age was raised to 10. There are various statutory measures for handling youth offenders, such as police cautioning, community-based treatment and custodial sentencing options. Nevertheless, any statutory measure rooted in restorative justice is yet to be incorporated into Hong Kong's mainstream criminal justice system. Proponents of restorative justice have worked to develop innovative strategies for preventing misbehaved adolescents from becoming delinquents, and I am one such proponent who is willing to make use of restorative practices to help delinquents avoid a criminal career.

This chapter highlights my passion for restorative justice, a passion developed over 25 years. It begins with a brief review of preventive welfare services for children and young people and statutory formal measures for youth offenders in Hong Kong. It then introduces alternatives to prosecution, including several restorative initiatives that exist outside the criminal justice system. Finally, the chapter discusses an innovative project recently developed by a non-governmental organisation (NGO) that uses pre-trial diversion of juvenile delinquents to deter them from further criminality.

2 Preventive and remedial measures for handling delinquents

Approximately 40 years ago, the rate of juvenile delinquency was rather low in Hong Kong: in 1976, the juvenile delinquency[1] rate was 212 per 100,000 children aged 7 to 15. This rate increased rapidly and, by 1989, had increased to 962 per 100,000 children. Juvenile delinquency started to decline in the 1990s, falling to 800 per 100,000 by 1997, the year when Hong Kong was established as the Special Administrative Region of China. While juvenile delinquency increased as a proportion of total crime from 8.2 per cent in

1 Juvenile delinquency denotes number of persons arrested per 100,000 population of children aged between 7 and 15, whereas youth delinquency denotes number of persons arrested per 100,000 population of adolescents aged 16 to 20.

1976 to 17 per cent in 1989, this proportion also experienced a decline in the 1990s, falling to 14.3 per cent by 1997. Youth delinquency rates (regarding those aged 16 to 20) have risen since the early 1970s, but its momentum has not been as great as that of juvenile delinquency. Official statistics show that youth delinquency rates rose from 973 per 100,000 in 1976 to a peak of 2,203 in 1994. Youth delinquency rates fell to 1,579 in 1997, when the proportion of youth to total crime was approximately 16.4 per cent (Census and Statistics Department, 1996; 1998; also see Wong, 2000: 279-280).

In response to the upsurge of delinquency rates during the late 1970s, the government started to sponsor a number of NGOs to run social services for young people to reduce or prevent delinquent behaviour. From 1980 onwards, three major kinds of children and youth (CY) services had formed the basis for the preventive welfare model of crime control predominant in Hong Kong: CY centres, outreaching social work (OR) services and school social work (SSW) services. CY centres are neighbourhood venues where adolescents aged between 6 and 24 can obtain recreational services and the required guidance. These centres provide social work services and organise academic tuition classes or extracurricular activities for adolescents living in the same neighbourhood. By the late 1990s, there were approximately 230 different types of CY centres established in different public housing estates in Hong Kong to assist teenagers with their personal development.[2] OR workers are trained social work professionals who engage in street social work and counselling services to help vulnerable kids break free from undesirable peer influences. Street gangs are often the primary targets of an OR team. There were 32 OR teams with a total of about 220 professional OR workers in the late 1990s. SSW programmes provide services to secondary school pupils. Given that the social work staff-to-student ratio in schools during the 1980s was approximately 1 to 4,000 students, the primary objective of SSW has been to prioritise serving adolescents whose academic, social and emotional development is at risk. In view of SSW's popularity and usefulness, the government agreed to reduce the ratio to 1 staff member per 1,000 students beginning in September 2000 (Social Welfare Department, 2011; Wong, 2000). Nevertheless, SSW services are limited to secondary school students in a given district.

Despite the fact that a variety of services for young people had been developed between 1980 and the mid-1990s, these preventive services have been largely compartmentalised (Wong, 2000). Young people have to take on multiple roles derived from very different and often quite conflicting social values as they grow up in contemporary society. The different CY services available in Hong Kong until the mid-1990s were not well-integrated, creating difficulties for such programmes in responding to young people's diverse needs. In a report on the Review of CY Centre Services, the review team recommended that a holistic approach to CY services should be adopted to meet young people's multifarious needs. And that resources currently dispersed across different ser-

2 By January 2017, there were around 23 CY centres in Hong Kong (Social Welfare Department, 2017a).

vices for young people should be pooled together to set up Integrated Children and Youth (ICY) Services Centres (formerly called integrated teams) (Lo, Wong, Ma & Chan, 1997). I was one of the review team members at that time. Our team suggested that professional workers and personnel in ICY centres should be deployed flexibly to meet the particular needs faced by young people and to provide services in a diversity of settings such as schools, street neighbourhoods or CY centres (see Lo et al., 1997).

More and more ICY centres have been formed since 1995. Nearly all ICY centres pooled staff resources from both OR teams and CY centres that were already in operation. In addition, some ICY centres pooled resources from SSW and family life education services in the neighbourhoods that the former OR team and CY centre were supposed to serve (Wong, 2000). Today, there are very few independent CY or SSW[3] service units left in Hong Kong. Instead, different kinds of youth services are now integrated into ICY centres. By January 2017, there were 138 ICY centres running to serve all kinds of young people, including normal youth and misbehaved youth (Social Welfare Department, 2017d). Each ICY centre may have 20-30 professional staff serving local CY clienteles, depending on the number of service projects provided by the centre, such as drug prevention, anti-bullying or positive youth development. Interestingly, besides ICY centre services, due to the distinctive characteristics of high-risk youth and youth gangs, there are still nineteen district OR teams that independently operate to serve hardcore delinquents in Hong Kong (Social Welfare Department, 2017c).

The above review of welfare services for youth clearly suggests that the Hong Kong government has devoted much resource sponsoring NGOs for the development and provision of a variety of preventive, developmental and rehabilitative services to different kinds of young people over the past 30 years. Most of the services are geared towards preventing the onset and continuation of delinquency, with the overarching goal of reducing the rate of delinquency among CY. The juvenile delinquency rate decreased from 903 per 100,000 adolescents aged 10 to 15 in 2005 to 402 per 100,000 in 2015 (Census and Statistics Department, 2016). It is not easy to conclude whether such a preventive welfare approach alone has made significant impact on the decline in juvenile delinquency at this point in time. Nonetheless, these measures are definitely protective factors for assisting CY in instilling in them positive social values and enhancing their life skills, problem-solving abilities and overall potential.

Meanwhile, inherited from the traditional British correctional system, statutory measures such as detention centres, training centres, reformatory schools and probation homes have been running to deal with young convicted offenders in the period between

3 By September 2016, 34 NGOs were running SSW service for 465 secondary schools in Hong Kong (Social Welfare Department, 2017e). In primary schools, counselling or social work services are sponsored by the Education Bureau instead of Social Welfare. Each school shall have one full-time school guidance teacher or school guidance officer. September 2002 onwards, primary schools are allowed to employ school guidance personnel to replace school guidance teachers or officers under the comprehensive student guidance service scheme. School guidance personnel are mostly social workers instead of teachers (Education Bureau, 2016).

the late 1930s and 2010. Those who are found guilty of less serious offences but are not suitable for custodial sentences are put under community supervision by a probation or community service order. There are also opportunities for young offenders who have committed minor offences to be dealt with through police cautioning. With the exception of police cautioning, the Social Welfare Department (SWD) or the Correctional Services Department (CSD) runs all other services. The main objective of SWD services for juvenile offenders is to help them become law-abiding citizens and reintegrate them into the community. This is achieved through both community-based and residential services that adopt social work approaches. The SWD also runs residential institutes for juvenile offenders to help them change their behaviours and attitudes through the employment of social work methods. In addition to detention, such residential institutes provide academic, prevocational and character training programmes as well. Three different types of homes provide rehabilitation services for young offenders: reformatory schools, probation homes and remand homes.

CSD services aim to ensure a secure, safe and humane custodial environment for youth offenders and create rehabilitation opportunities that help them reintegrate into society. Under the different ordinances for various youth correctional institutions, including detention centres, rehabilitation centres, training centres, youth prisons and drug addiction treatment centres, the CSD operates institutions that provide different rehabilitation programmes for young offenders aged between 14 and 25 (Chui, 2005; Lo, 2017; Correctional Services Department, 2017).

3 Measures for diverting juveniles from the formal criminal justice system

There is only one formal alternative path to prosecution in Hong Kong. Juvenile offenders are not prosecuted if their crimes are minor (e.g. pilfering) and if both the victims' and the offenders' parents do not object. Instead of prosecution, juvenile offenders are dealt with under the police-cautioning scheme (formally known as the Police Superintendent's Discretionary Scheme or PSDS). The PSDS is generally seen as a formal path for diverting juvenile offenders away from early exposure to the formal criminal justice system by giving them a chance to receive a police caution (Hong Kong Police Force, 2017). The PSDS was introduced in 1963 when the then Attorney General authorised police officers of Superintendent rank and above the power to caution, rather than prosecute, young offenders under the age of 14. Over time, the PSDS has been extended to offenders aged under 16, 17 and 18 in 1966, 1987 and 1995, respectively (Security Bureau, 2002). Today, when a juvenile aged between 10 and 18 has committed an offence and there is sufficient evidence to lay a charge against him/her, police may prosecute the juvenile in court or deal with such matter by way of administering a caution under the PSDS. Issuing a police caution requires the juvenile to be put under police supervision for a period of two years or until he/she reaches the age of 18, whichever is earlier.

Table 1 shows the number of juveniles arrested and cautioned under PSDS. The juveniles cautioned are 37.1 per cent, 34.6 per cent and 31 per cent in 2011, 2012 and 2013, respectively. As compared to the highest of 44.4 per cent in 2005, the percentages of those cautioned in recent years are relatively lower. Based on the annual reports of the Fight Crime Committee, the most common reasons for not receiving PSDS are the serious nature of the offence and previous caution records of the offender (see Zhong, 2017). According to Zhong (2017), the average reconviction rate of cautioned juveniles was approximately 16 per cent between 1997 and 2011.

Table 1 Juveniles* arrested and cautioned under PSDS

Year	No. of arrested	No. of cautioned	% of those cautioned out of total arrested
2000	9,173	3,760	41.1
2001	8,732	3,585	41.0
2002	8,156	3,345	41.0
2003	7,918	3,012	38.0
2004	7,566	2,929	38.7
2005	6,821	3,026	44.4
2006	6,891	2,774	40.3
2007	6,875	2,736	39.8
2008	6,303	2,358	37.4
2009	6,049	2,220	36.7
2010	5,454	2,076	38.1
2011	5,355	1,987	37.1
2012	4,198	1,453	34.6
2013	3,413	1,059	31.0

*Remarks: *Juvenile offenders are delinquents aged 10 or above and under 16.*
Source: Data sourced from various annual reports of Fight Crime Committee; this table is extracted from Zhong (2017: 343).

In Hong Kong, all cautioned juveniles are referred to a Juvenile Protection Section of their respective police regions for regular supervision visits under normal circumstances (Security Bureau, 2002). In addition, if the police hold the view that additional aftercare service is necessary, they are referred to a Community Support Services Scheme (CSSS) for follow-up. The CSSS,[4] administered by NGOs, is sponsored by the SWD. The main purpose of the CSSS is to assist juveniles with reintegrating into the community, eliminating their deviant and unlawful behaviour and reducing the likelihood of criminal conduct. The services offer intensive social work-oriented programmes and activities including the following:

1. counselling, either on an individual or group basis, to assist PSDS juveniles in overcoming their difficulties in intrapersonal and social development, particularly as it relates to their offending behaviour;
2. educational or vocational guidance to reintegrate juveniles into the education system or workforce;
3. groups and activities to enhance social skills, interpersonal relationships and life aspirations, as well as modify undesirable attitudes and behaviour;
4. volunteer and community service activities designed to develop juveniles' sense of social responsibility and civic mindedness and provide them with opportunities for positive social recognition; and
5. work with relevant systems, such as parents/guardians and peers, to strengthen the supporting network for young people.

Between 2004 and 2013, over half of the cautioned juveniles each year were referred to CSSS for follow-up: 55.9 per cent, 52.0 per cent and 52.1 per cent were referred in 2004, 2008 and 2013, respectively (Zhong, 2017: 344).

4 RESTORATIVE PRACTICES AND OTHER INFORMAL DIVERSIONARY INITIATIVES

As the above discussion implies, there is no restorative justice option for treating juvenile offenders, neither as an alternative to prosecution nor as an alternative to sentencing. However, some NGOs have raised the idea of using restorative practices to assist delinquents in accounting for what they have done and learning to repair harm done to victims. In Hong Kong, I first introduced the concept of restorative justice to social work professionals (Wong, 1996). In the late 1990s, I contended that restorative justice pro-

4 At present, there are five NGOs running CSSS over the territory, and the five CSSS teams were attached to five existing ICY centres, namely 1) The Methodist Centre 'Project Phoenix'; 2) The Boys' and Girls' Clubs Association of Hong Kong 'Youth Action Network'; 3) The Hong Kong Playground Association 'New Horizon Community Supportive Services Scheme'; 4) The Hong Kong Federation of Youth Groups 'Youth Support Scheme'; and 5) Evangelical Lutheran Church Social Service 'Hong Kong Youth Enhancement Scheme' (Social Welfare Department, 2017b).

vides a balanced approach to holding delinquents accountable without simultaneously excluding them from mainstream education. Since 1996, I have suggested reforming the juvenile justice system to allow the Family Group Conference, a system introduced in New Zealand since 1989, to be adopted in Hong Kong (Wong, 1999, 2000, 2008). Although I have devoted much effort selling the ideas of restorative justice to the public, public interest towards it has been low over the years. It was only in 1999, when a detailed case example of youth service, which included a true case of a restorative conference, was televised by the Wednesday Report, a documentary programme produced by the Hong Kong Television Broadcasts Limited, that public awareness of the impact of restorative justice increased. As a result, more and more restorative practices have been tried in Hong Kong, with more people having heard of the term *restorative justice* since then (Wong, 2008).

In 2002, with increasing discussion on the use of restorative justice for handling juvenile offenders taking place in many parts of the world, the idea of whether to implement restorative justice in Hong Kong was eventually brought to the attention of the Hong Kong government (Lo, Wong & Maxwell, 2003). A research team was formed in that year to investigate alternative measures for treating juvenile offenders in Hong Kong. As a member of the research team, I helped identify six criminal justice systems using a variety of alternative practices in their juvenile justice system as cases for further study. In our report and recommendations provided to the Hong Kong government, we proposed a number of pre-trial restorative options including the use of family conferences to develop restorative plans to respond to juvenile offending (Lo, Wong & Maxwell, 2003). Despite this endeavour, our suggestions were not accepted by the Hong Kong government. Till date, a statutory restorative justice option has not been formally incorporated into the mainstream criminal justice system in Hong Kong.

In the past fifteen years, there have been a number of NGOs working hard to practice restorative justice outside the mainstream criminal justice system. For example, in the mid-2000s, two NGOs, namely the Evangelical Lutheran Church Social Service Hong Kong (ELCSSHK) and the Methodist Centre (MC), in Hong Kong experimented with restorative practices for cautioned juveniles. I acted as an honorary adviser for these two NGOs at that time. Learning from the restorative practices developed in Australia and Canada, social workers from the two organisations launched post-cautioning victim-offender mediation (VOM) meetings for the juveniles, victims, their family members and supporters.

The ELCSSHK focused on theft cases such as shoplifting and, in addition, extended its service to address other cases of criminality, including common assault after a few years of running the programmes. Between 2002 and 2004, ELCSSHK conducted 26 mediation meetings, with its evaluation showing very positive outcomes (ELCSSHK, 2004). In 2005, ELCSSHK extended such services to the East New Territories regions in Hong Kong. An evaluation report of the new services showed that 95 per cent of participants were satisfied with mediation results. Juveniles who went through VOM admitted that they understood more about their own faults and the victim's feelings. Furthermore, all offenders agreed to make reparation for victims voluntarily and were willing to restore relationships with victims as well. The report concluded that the juvenile offenders who participated in the VOMs were successfully reintegrated into the community and able to carry on a normal life (Ho et al., 2007). With the support of the police and the SWD, the agency continued its mediation services for offenders in five districts in Hong Kong (ELCSSHK, 2017). Similarly, the MC also provided mediation services for cautioned juvenile offenders since 2007. The MC conducted research to capture the service impacts of the programme, finding that nearly 70 per cent of the offenders were willing to take part in the mediation as well as show remorse and make apologies to those they harmed (The Methodist Centre, 2017).

Along with the review on whether restorative justice should be adopted in 2003 (Lo et al., 2003), the SWD did suggest implementing a new project called Family Conference to assist some police-cautioned delinquents who are in need of family support. Nevertheless, it is important to note that the suggested Family Conference is not a restorative measure. The Family Conference is in fact one of the enhanced support measures for unruly children and young offenders. The conference will be jointly run by the Hong Kong Police Force and the SWD (see Legislative Council, 2005). The objectives of the Family Conference are to bring together cautioned juveniles, their family members as well as professionals from relevant government departments and NGOs to assess the juveniles' needs and develop follow-up plans to address these needs as necessary (Social Welfare Department, 2005). In contrast to the New Zealand model, the Hong Kong Family Conference is a joint meeting only for the most involved stakeholders, excluding participation by victims and their supporters (Social Welfare Department, 2005, 2009).

In Hong Kong, the Centre for Restoration of Human Relationships (CRHR), which I established in the year 2000, has been practising restorative practices since 2000. The CRHR is the most well-known NGO that openly advocated the use of restorative justice for juvenile delinquents in Hong Kong in the early 2000s. Between 2001 and 2006, the Centre had trained staff from more than 50 schools to adopt a Restorative Whole School Approach (RWSA) to tackle the problem of bullying in Hong Kong (Wong, 2006). The RWSA is a three-tier intervention model which aims at tackling school bullying with concerted efforts from school management, teachers, social workers, parents and students. The three-tier approach makes intervention at the universal level (tier one), targeted level (tier two) and intensive level (tier three). In addition, the CRHR has conducted at least 100 conferences since 2007, with most cases evaluated as successful in terms of high participation and high satisfaction rates (Wong & Lo, 2011).

5 PROJECT R

The Hong Kong Federation of Youth Groups (HKFYG), Youth Crime Prevention Centre and the Hong Kong Police Force New Territories South Region jointly launched 'Project R' in June 2012, the first project of its kind in Hong Kong, serving juveniles aged 10-24 who are under arrest and investigation. Project R provides specialised services including crisis intervention, counselling and family support services for the arrested person and their family members, as well as support for the victims of crimes. The scheme adopts a '3R' service principle which places emphasis on re-offending prevention by enhancing juveniles' (1) Rational thinking; (2) Rational behaviour; and (3) Re-connection. This approach nurtures healthy growth in juveniles and enables them to re-connect with their families, social life, studies and work, as well as become law-abiding.

From July 2015 to May 2017, I collaborated with HKFYG to develop a Risk Assessment Tool for adolescents who are receiving services from Project R and simultaneously conduct research to measure the effectiveness of the initiative. This Risk Assessment Tool consists of 70 items across 10 domains; examples of items include 'prior and current offence', 'substance abuse', 'personality/behaviour', 'history of adverse experience' and 'mental health'. The tool was used to assess a client's risk level at different points in time and served as a reference for social workers' further intervention. A pre-post analysis was conducted from January 2016 to May 2017, and a total of 94 pre-post data sets were collected. A comparison of pre-tests and post-tests found that the number of risk factors for re-offending dropped significantly from 6.74 to 4.82 ($m = 1.926$; $t = 5.087$; $p < 0.001$). Furthermore, clients' risk for re-offending significantly decreased from 1.22 to 1.06 ($m = 0.160$; $t = 3.904$; $p < 0.001$). After intervention by social workers, 76.2 per cent of clients assessed as medium risk during the pre-test were classified as low risk during the post-test; 98.6 per cent of those who were deemed low risk by the pre-test continued to be classified as low risk by the post-test ($X^2 = 13.743$; df = 4; $p < 0.001$).

The research team also conducted a correlational analysis of social worker involvement (in terms of duration of services and number of service hours) and the client's risk level. Social worker involvement (in terms of total number of service hours devoted) was found to be significantly correlated with positive changes in a client's risk level ($r = 0.227$; $p < 0.05$). A significant correlation was also found between social worker involvement (in terms of duration of services devoted) and positive changes in a client's risk level ($r = 0.267$; $p < 0.01$). These results suggest that the clients' risk of re-offending is more likely to be lower if they have received adequate support from social workers. This demonstrates that social worker intervention is useful in lowering a client's risk of re-offending.

6 Conclusion

With the comprehensive personal welfare services developed for CY over recent decades and the positive research evidence supporting community-based measures and diversionary practices for the treatment of juvenile offenders, it is evident that a new paradigm of youth crime control in Hong Kong has emerged. The new paradigm no longer relies on the disciplinary welfare approach (Gray, 1994) but, rather, emphasises a restorative approach that reflects an alternative view of relations among juveniles and their communities, and how conflicts involving juveniles may be resolved. Restorative justice has developed rapidly in the past few decades across the globe. It is considered a significant element of mainstream criminological practices, with the aim of holding offenders accountable for their actions, restoring human dignity, compensating material losses and reconciling relationships (Braithwaite, 1989; Johnstone, 2002; Maxwell & Morris, 1993; Zehr, 1990). Over the past 20 years, restorative justice has increasingly flourished in Asia too. Governments in China, Singapore, Taiwan and Thailand have incorporated restorative justice into their juvenile justice or criminal justice system to some extent (Wong, 2014, 2016).

Real gains can be made by adopting and extending social work approaches with delinquents based on a restorative philosophy to the youth criminal justice system. Such schemes can reduce the involvement of young people in the juvenile justice system, provide increased support to adolescents and families and redress to victims, reduce the probability of re-offending and reduce costs associated with the juvenile justice system. Restorative practices challenge traditional notions regarding the trial and punishment of juvenile and youth offenders. With the efforts made by various scholars and NGOs as a foundation, it is hoped that a road map for the development of diversionary initiatives including the use of restorative justice in Hong Kong can be created, which may lead to youth justice system reforms and the advancement of social work practices. For example, after conducting the programme evaluation for Project R, I advised the staff of Project R to adopt restorative practices to help offenders repair the harm done to their victims whenever they have an opportunity to do it. This suggestion could serve dual purposes. On the one hand, youth offenders are asked to take accountability to what they have done. On the other hand, victims' voices will be heard and reparation or restitution for victims might be sought. I have been trying to sow the seeds of restorative justice in the appropriate soil and, hopefully, it will grow and flourish some day in Hong Kong, China.

Nevertheless, challenges exist regarding the further development of restorative justice. One challenge is related to the type of approach to restorative justice often taken in Asian countries, an approach which has emphasised reducing crime and transforming the behaviour of offenders, rather than empowering victims and fostering healing. In contrast to Chinese or Asian mediation approaches to restorative justice, careful screening mechanisms are normally in place for restorative justice practices taking place in Western countries, with the safety and interest of victims regarded as a top priority in the selection procedure. If restorative justice is incorporated into the criminal justice system in Hong Kong, China or other parts of Asia, the most pressing task is to identify useful approaches that could not only integrate cultural values and indigenous practices, but at the same time protect human rights and respect victims across different Asian communities. A legal framework and adequate training for facilitators is definitely needed to fulfil this task. International cooperation should be geared towards supporting the development of restorative justice training programmes, assisting governments in developing a set of well-recognised standards for implementing restorative justice practices and conducting evaluative studies across Asian jurisdictions.

Acknowledgement

This work was supported by The Research Grants Council of Hong Kong [CityU/11613018].

References

Braithwaite, J. (1989). *Crime, shame and reintegration*. Cambridge: Cambridge University Press.

Census and Statistics Department. (1996). *Hong Kong annual digest of statistics 1995 edition*. Hong Kong: Government Printer.

Census and Statistics Department. (1998). *Hong Kong annual digest of statistics* 1997 *edition*. Hong Kong: Government Printer.

Census and Statistics Department. (2016). *Hong Kong annual digest of statistics 2016*. Hong Kong: Government Printer.

Chui, W. H. (2005). Detention center in Hong Kong: a young offender's narrative. *Journal of Offender Rehabilitation*, 41, 67-84. doi:10.1300/j076v41n01_03.

Correctional Services Department. (2017). *Hong Kong correctional services: 2016 annual review*. Hong Kong: Government Printer.

Education Bureau. (2016). *School administration guide (2016/17 school year)*. Hong Kong: Education Bureau.

Evangelical Lutheran Church Social Service Hong Kong. (2004). *Response to the report on alternative measures to prosecution for handling unruly children and young persons*. Hong Kong: Evangelical Lutheran Church Social Service Hong Kong.

Evangelical Lutheran Church Social Service Hong Kong. (2017). *Mission and vision of the project*. Retrieved from http://iscr.elchk.org.hk/center_aboutus.php (last accessed 15 June 2017).

Gray, P. (1994). *Inside the Hong Kong juvenile court: the decision-making process in action.* Resource paper Series, No 23. Department of Social Work and Social Administration. Hong Kong: University of Hong Kong.

Ho, H. M., Chuk, W. H., Leung, W. H., Lam, H. Y., Lai, L. C. & Law, W. M. (2007). *Research report on the mediation between victims and offenders.* Hong Kong: Social Service of the Evangelical Lutheran Church of Hong Kong.

Hong Kong Police Force. (2017). *About crime related information.* Retrieved from www.police.gov.hk/ppp_en/13_faqs/faq_cri.html (last accessed 15 June 2017).

Johnstone, G. (2002). *Restorative justice: ideas, values, debates.* Cullompton: Willan.

Legislative Council. (2005). *Juvenile justice system: enhance support measures for unruly children and young offenders.* Hong Kong: Legislative Council Secretariat.

Lo, T. W. (2017). Prison and correctional services. In W. H. Chui & T. W. Lo (eds.) *Understanding criminal justice in Hong Kong* (pp. 337-358). New York: Routledge.

Lo, T. W., Wong, D. S. W., Ma, K. & Chan, W. T. (1997). *Evaluation on the implementation of the review report on children and youth centre services.* Commission Report for Social Welfare Department. Hong Kong: Hong Kong Government Printer.

Lo, T. W., Wong, D. S. W. & Maxwell, G. M. (eds.) (2003). *Measures alternative to prosecution for handling unruly children and young persons: overseas experiences and options for Hong Kong.* Research report from Youth Studies Net at City University of Hong Kong to Security Bureau of Hong Kong Government of SAR. Hong Kong: Youth Studies Net at City University of Hong Kong.

Maxwell, G. M. & Morris, A. (1993) *Family victims and culture: youth justice in New Zealand.* Wellington: Institute of Criminology, Victoria University of Wellington.

Security Bureau. (2002). *The police superintendent's discretion scheme. LC Paper No. CB (2) 298/02-03(02).* Hong Kong: Security Bureau.

Social Welfare Department. (2005). *Summary of the review report on family conference.* Hong Kong: Social Welfare Department.

Social Welfare Department. (2009). *Protocol on conducting family conference for juveniles cautioned under the police superintendent's discretion scheme.* Hong Kong: Social Welfare Department.

Social Welfare Department. (2011). *Additional funding of $50 million to enhance school social work services.* Retrieved from www.swd.gov.hk/en/index/site_pubpress/page_press/sub_fullpress/topic_392/ (last accessed 15 June 2017).

Social Welfare Department. (2017a). *Children and youth centres.* Retrieved from www.swd.gov.hk/en/index/site_pubsvc/page_young/sub_centreserv/id_childrenan (last accessed 15 June 2017).

Social Welfare Department. (2017b). *Community support service scheme.* Retrieved from www.swd.gov.hk/en/index/site_pubsvc/page_young/sub_seryouthrisk/id_cssscheme/ (last accessed 15 June 2017).

Social Welfare Department. (2017c). *District youth outreaching social work service.* Retrieved from www.swd.gov.hk/en/index/site_pubsvc/page_young/sub_seryouthrisk/id_districtyo/ (last accessed 15 June 2017).

Social Welfare Department. (2017d). *Integrated children and youth services centres.* Retrieved from www.swd.gov.hk/en/index/site_pubsvc/page_young/sub_centreserv/id_integrated4 (last accessed 15 June 2017).

Social Welfare Department. (2017e). *School social work service.* Retrieved from www.swd.gov.hk/en/index/site_pubsvc/page_young/sub_schoolsoci/ (last accessed 15 June 2017).

The Methodist Centre. (2017). *Project concord.* Retrieved from www.methodist-centre.-com/concord/tc (last accessed 15 June 2017).

Wong, D. & Lo, T. (2011). The recent development of restorative social work practices in Hong Kong. *International Social Work*, 54(5), 701-716. doi:10.1177/00208728 10382528.

Wong, D. S. W. (1996). *Reintegrative shaming: new direction for counseling the deviant youth.* Hong Kong: City University of Hong Kong.

Wong, D. S. W. (1999). Culturally specific causes of delinquency: implication for juvenile justice in Hong Kong. *Asia Pacific Journal of Social Work*, 9(1), 98-113. doi:10.1080/21650993.1999.9755809.

Wong, D. S. W. (2000). Juvenile crime and responses to delinquency in Hong Kong. *International Journal of Offender Therapy and Comparative Criminology*, 44(3), 279-292. doi:10.1177/0306624x00443003.

Wong, D. S. W. (2006). Tackling the school bullying behavior by restorative justice. In Hunag, P. (ed.), *Restorative justice forum II* (pp. 84-98). Beijing: Qun Zhong Publisher.

Wong, D. S. W. (2008). Advocating the use of restorative justice for misbehaving students and juvenile delinquents in Hong Kong'. In K. Van Wormer (ed.), *Restorative justice across the east and the west* (pp. 11-31). Taoyuan: Casa Verde Publishing.

Wong, D. S. W. (2014). Harmony comes first: challenges facing the development of restorative justice in Asia. *Restorative Justice: An International Journal*, 2(1), 1-8. doi:10.5235/20504721.2.1.1.

Wong, D. S. W. (2016). Restorative justice at different levels of the criminal justice system in China: Challenges and paths forward. *Restorative Justice: An International Journal*, 4(1), 10-26. doi:10.1080/20504721.2016.1149370.

Zehr, H. (1990). *Changing lenses: a new focus of crime and justice.* Scottsdale: Herald Press.

Zhong, L. Y. (2017). Crime prevention. In W. H. Chui & T. W. Lo (eds.), *Understanding criminal justice in Hong Kong* (pp. 337-358). New York: Routledge.

Restorative justice with corporations: the idea and the practicality

Martin Wright

Never doubt that a small group of thoughtful, omitted citizens can change the world – indeed it's the only thing that ever has ...
Margaret Mead

1 Introduction

It is an honour and a pleasure to be asked to contribute to a book in honour of Ivo Aertsen. He will long be remembered for his immense contribution to the development of restorative justice and to the practical work, in the background, of building the European Forum for Restorative Justice and keeping it going. It is typical of him that at a late stage of his career he has branched out into a new field, the application of restorative justice to corporate and environmental crime, not only writing and speaking about it (Aertsen, 2018, 2019) but also promoting a network to take the initiative further. This chapter will focus on one aspect, namely the dumping of toxic wastes: the most serious and longest-running example is that of Bhopal, in India (described below), and it is a serious component of the damage caused by humans to life on earth.

The world is experiencing a corporate crime wave. Hardly a day goes by without a report of people and animals being deprived of their habitat, their well-being and even their lives by the actions of a transnational company. Land is used for the disposal of (often toxic) waste; rivers provide free drainage; gases and particles are discharged into the air. In many cases, technologies already exist to prevent this from happening in the first place; how can those responsible be persuaded or compelled to use that technology in future? Laws and regulations have to be first created and then enforced. Remedying the damage done in the past can be more difficult and costly.

Why do otherwise decent people engage in these damaging practices? The cynical answer is 'Because they can':

Tugend, das ist jederzeit
Mangel an Gelegenheit[1]

1 German proverb

> or 'Virtue is lack of opportunity'. In more detail, Schnatterly et al. (2018) suggest that it is a combination of pressure (especially to make a profit, and to conform to the prevailing business culture), opportunity (including thinking that they can 'get away with it') and rationalisation (various forms of justification, some of which border on racism: 'They are "only" indigenous people'; 'it was "only" uncultivated land'). Another might be added: distance. Often the site of the operation is 'out of sight, therefore out of mind', far from the headquarters of the company, and this is a factor in regard to restorative justice, as we shall see.

Let us consider how these conflicts could be tackled by conventional and restorative means.

2 CONVENTIONAL JUSTICE

Regulations and laws can be created, but big companies, especially transnational corporations (TNCs), are adept at persuading legislators to water these down: they are seen as a 'bureaucratic' restraint on trade, undermining the capitalist principle of minimising government and letting the market be in control. Where regulations exist, inspection and enforcement are often under-resourced and are seen as being based on conventional notions of punishment and deterrence. The shortcomings of these as a means of promoting good behaviour are well known. Punishment only works as a deterrent if the offender knows of the potential punishment, and believes that his offence is likely to be successfully prosecuted, and that the penalty will be severe and will be enforced. In the case of corporations there is the additional failing that because of legislation on limited liability, fines are usually imposed not on the individual responsible but on the company, which can well afford to pay.

Laws and regulations do have a value as a declaration of social standards and can be upheld by persuasion rather than coercion, for example by inspectors who use praise when improvements are achieved and have a philosophy of reintegrative shaming (Braithwaite, 2002: 17-18). A British report on making sanctions effective recommends restorative justice, carried out by trained experts, as a regulatory sanction (Macrory, 2006: 72), and William Ury advises negotiators to warn, not threaten, their opponent (Ury, 1993: 136-137).

Public pressure can often use Internet petitions and public protests as other ways of influencing company behaviour, but to influence a large TNC, both methods are probably needed on a large, sustained scale. There are examples which show that this can be done and also that cleaning up is technically feasible. Some individual companies have at least tried to do the right thing by cleaning up their pollution, although in some cases, there are arguments about whether they have done so completely.

At General Electric, for example, the CEO Jack Welch was embroiled in a scandal (contamination of the Hudson River with polychlorinated biphenyls (PCBs) from 1947 to 1977) and reacted by fighting it tooth and nail. A new CEO, Jeff Immelt, took over in 2001, and he decided to reverse the policy and turn the company 'green', because GE couldn't claim to be a market leader in sustainable products with that case hanging over its head. He is reported to have said, 'That was Jack's problem but it's not going to be my problem' and spent many millions of dollars to dredge the river. However, a U.S. senator has said that the job was not completed and the Environmental Protection Agency (EPA) should not have issued a Certification of Completion (Gillibrand, 2019).

Another example is Hindustan Unilever, which ran a thermometer plant at Kodaikanal, India. Many of the company's workers had been exposed to mercury and weren't provided with adequate protective gear; 30 ex-workers and 15 children have died. Mercury is very toxic to babies and young children and is known to cause deformities. After fourteen years of campaigning, Unilever paid compensation. But further effort was needed to ensure that Kodaikanal's environment is cleaned up. There is still a lot of mercury left on the ground (SumOfUs, 2018).

A report by the Blacksmith Institute and Green Cross Switzerland (2010: 6) has said that:

> tens of thousands of polluted sites contaminate local populations – as many as 500 million people are poisoned each day in the developing world. Only a few of these problems have been fixed. But it's a start and worth recognizing.

In 2010 Blacksmith possessed a database of over 1,000 polluted sites awaiting cleanup, but only 45 where innovative techniques or approaches were implemented, and many of these showed 'less than optimal' results (ibid.: 10). The report (2010: 19-74) lists twelve more cases of successful cleanups. One example is from Chile: the Compañia Contractual Minera Candelaria and Freeport McMoRan Copper and Gold. The disposal of mine tailings (waste, often toxic, from operations such as mining) caused water pollution by heavy metals and cyanide. Local people had to drink contaminated groundwater. Intervention enabled treatment and recirculation of 80 per cent of the waters and prevented contamination of groundwater. A comprehensive cut-off wall system prevents leakage and filters water contained in tailings. Industry groups support the adoption of best practices. This case is cited as an industry good practice to be emulated by others. These initiatives were carried out by various agencies, including NGOs, companies, banks and governments, as well as local communities. It is not clear from these reports where the initiative for the projects came from, but a number of companies and governments have considered it worth their while, and there is scope for restorative methods in bringing such agencies together to create more of them.

3 Restorative justice: the theory

One definition of restorative justice is, a way of responding to harm or damage, in which all those concerned are invited to come together to resolve the harm. Collectively, they decide how to deal with the aftermath and its implications for the future. The idea of applying restorative principles in cases of corporate wrongdoing was inspired by the Australian criminologist John Braithwaite, who summed it up in his book *Restorative Justice and Responsive Regulation* (2002). Earlier, he had made his name with the concept that if wrongdoers are shamed, it should be done in a reintegrative way. He started with coal mines: as a young man he wanted to write an angry book for friends killed in mining accidents, but his research found that when workers and unions (representing the victims) were involved in deliberative regulatory processes (which could be described as restorative), leading to persuasion, it worked better than the threat of punishment. Braithwaite wrote a book called *To Punish or Persuade* (1985), in which he says:

> I shocked myself by concluding that after mine disasters … so long as there had been an open public dialogue among all those affected, the families of the miners cared for, and a credible plan to prevent recurrence put in place, criminal punishment served little purpose.

Likewise in Britain, during the first 50 years of mine safety enforcement, there was a shift from punitive to restorative enforcement, and the number of fatalities decreased from 1484 in 1866 to 44 in 1982-1983 (Braithwaite, 2002: 63).

4 Examples of the use of restorative justice in corporate crime

In recent years restorative justice has been applied in the criminal justice systems in many countries. However, this has almost always been in the context of the individual offender and his or her victim(s); it has yet to be applied extensively in cases of corporate crime. Restorative justice is based on the principle that offenders are more likely to recognise the harm they have done and want to put it right, where they have met the victim and heard directly the effects of their actions, rather than been reprimanded by a judge. This is called a 'fully restorative' process; it is 'partly restorative' if no actual meeting or dialogue takes place but the aim is a reparative outcome rather than a solely punitive one.

Attempts to use restorative principles in cases of corporate wrongdoing have been inspired by a case that John Braithwaite describes: A number of Australian insurance companies systematically ripped off consumers through misrepresentations about policies that in some cases were totally useless. The worst abuses were in 22 Aboriginal communities. Top management from the insurance company visited these communities for days on end at meetings with the victims. Some of those executives went back to the city deeply ashamed of what their company had done. Compensation was paid and a consumer education fund was set up. Later a police union realised that some of its own members were being ripped off by another company and again problem-solving was accomplished without going to court except with a couple of individuals who refused to cooperate (Braithwaite, 2002: 22-24).

Another example given by Braithwaite (2002: 110) concerns false advertising. A carpet company announced that the prices of its goods were reduced, when in fact they were not. The Trade Practices Commission tried without success to persuade the CEO to take corrective action. The standard next step would have been to take the company to court, where the likely penalty was light and there would be a problem with proving the case. As its final attempt, the Commission turned to Mr Solomon, the chairman of the board; he was ashamed that his company was flouting its legal obligations and put in place a compensation scheme for customers, which probably cost more than the likely fine. What Braithwaite's cases have in common and what sets them apart from the GE and Hindustan cases described above is a shaming component: somebody high ranking is ashamed, and in the case of the Aboriginals, it is personal contact with the victims that brings this about.

5 Combining conventional and restorative justice

A restorative approach may be used in conjunction with a conventional trial. Firstly, it could encourage the company not to resist a trial and indeed to attend it if it is held in another country. The court would then be the forum for deciding the outcome, such as compensation in a civil case, or the sentence in a criminal one. Advocates of restorative principles would hope that in the latter case the sentence would be a reparative one. There could still be a place for it in addition to a sentence, especially if the trial is held in another country: the directors of the company could choose whether to comply with the sentence or resist it, and a restorative discussion may help them to see that paying up with good grace may be in the best long-term interests of the company as well as the victims.

According to Land Conflict Watch, for example, there are 585 land-related conflicts in India, with investments totalling 13 trillion rupees and affecting 6.7 million people. One example involving both a court and local residents concerned Vedanta Resources Ltd, which wanted an open-pit aluminium ore mine in Niyamgiri Hills, Andhra Pradesh. A landmark Supreme Court verdict on 18 April 2013 said that forest clearance for the mining project, which had been withdrawn by the Environment Ministry in 2010, could be given only after taking the consent of the gram *sabhas*, or village councils, in the region. The villagers decided against giving permission (Seetharaman, 2018).

A case with an environmental aspect took place in Minamata Bay in Japan, which was heavily polluted in the 1950s and 1960s by wastewater, mixed with mercury, and particularly methylmercury, dumped into Hyakken Harbour and Shiranui Sea from the Chisso Corporation's factory. A neurological syndrome caused by severe mercury poisoning was called Minamata disease. Symptoms include ataxia, numbness in the hands and feet, general muscle weakness, narrowing of the field of vision and damage to hearing and speech. In extreme cases, insanity, paralysis, coma and death follow within weeks of the onset of symptoms. A congenital form of the disease can also affect foetuses (Boston University, 2017). In 1959 Minamata disease compensation agreements were made between the polluting Chisso company and representative groups of fishermen and Minamata disease patients who had been affected by mercury pollution. The agreements were formulated outside the legal system, by ad-hoc mediation committees specially established for the purpose. Membership of the committees was weighted in favour of Chisso, and this influenced the final agreements; they all included punitive clauses so that the groups could make no future claims for compensation against the company. Protesters were kept out of shareholders' meetings. Another group of victims chose direct negotiations: they sat in front of the Chisso building for one and a half years, and on some occasions occupied the building. Some met with the president of Chisso directly and they talked about responsibility, guilt and religious belief in everyday language. This made victims feel that they had been listened to. Although at first the company refused to accept liability, the two groups of victims then came together and won a lawsuit for compensation in 1973. There have been further lawsuits, and most Japanese know about them because they are taught about them in elementary schools. Instead of prosecution and fines which would have ruined the company, it was allowed to continue so that compensation could be paid to the victims. The burden of paying compensation soon pushed Chisso into financial difficulty. On 20 June 1978, the government convened a cabinet meeting 'Concerning Minamata Disease Countermeasures'. Stipulating that any financial aid to Chisso must adhere to the 'polluter pays' principle, but mindful of the need to ensure that there is no disruption of the compensation payments to Minamata disease victims, and also as a means of contributing to the economic and social stability of the region, Cabinet recommended Kumamoto Prefecture to issue prefectural bonds, the funds from which would be lent to Chisso to fund the payment of compensation. By 2004, Chisso Corporation had paid $86 million in compensation, and, in the same year, the company was ordered to clean up its contamination (Minamata Disease Municipal Museum, 2007; Boston University, 2017; Komatsubara, 2019).

This suggests that it would be possible to proceed directly to a restorative process, provided goodwill existed, but the court's involvement would enhance the settlement by demonstrating the state's endorsement. There are, however, some obstacles and objections.

6 Objections

If a group of survivors wish to open the restorative process, the company may consider it prudent to enter a dialogue; but if the initiative comes from external well-wishers, they will first have to discuss with the survivors which approach offers a better prospect of success. They have to establish their credibility; despite Margaret Mead's optimistic statement at the head of this chapter, a lone voice crying in the wilderness is not always heard. The survivors may feel that nothing less than the decision of a court, or even a criminal conviction, can adequately signal the seriousness of the harm they have suffered. As for deterrence, they may not share the abovementioned views of criminologists, and it would be inappropriate for outsiders to engage in a discussion implying that they know better than those who have endured the actual pain and suffering. Survivors may be sceptical of 'soft power', although, as we have seen in relation to the Chisso case, that may be at least as effective as state power in implementing a reparative solution. They may want what they regard as 'justice', meaning official condemnation of the wrongdoing by the state. A common wish of victims is that no one else should be subjected to the same trauma, and they may see punishment and deterrence as the means of inducing other companies to behave better. Unfortunately, deterrence is something of a mirage. A potential offender is only deterred by the threat of punishment if several conditions are fulfilled, as we have seen above. A large TNC can absorb substantial punishment, and it is the company, not the individuals responsible, that has to pay fines. In the case of a TNC that has caused environmental damage and human suffering, the cost of remediation and compensation could be considerable, in addition to the reputational damage. The deterrent effect of this cost can be as great or greater than the probable fine, especially when added to stigma. On the other hand, victims may be reluctant to see the company restore its reputation, too easily as they might see it, by carrying out the cleanup.

Survivors may justifiably have doubts as to whether any agreement will be kept. A robust procedure for monitoring implementation should be built into the agreement. It may be pointed out that, especially in international cases, even an order of a court is not necessarily enforceable; the directors of the company may choose to drag out the procedure with legal arguments and appeals, and even if the decision finally goes against them, they may refuse to comply.

Braithwaite argues that shame is a more powerful deterrent, but it should be 'reintegrative'; in other words, it should offer the offender a means of making amends to the victim and/or the community. Ironically, a process of persuasion, which might be called *restorative*, may offer the best chance of securing compliance with a judicial decision.

There is reason to believe that individuals, and even companies, comply better with an agreement reached voluntarily than with an order imposed by a court. Thus, the answer to the question, Whether to prefer conventional or restorative justice, may not be 'Either/ Or' but 'Both'.

7 OBSTACLES

Apart from theoretical objections, there are also practical obstacles. If the would-be mediators are not in either of the countries where the company and the survivors are located, there are the problems of making contact and of distance and travel costs (video links are not always a substitute for face-to-face contact). While a company that has been subject to criticism may be willing to give assurances about its future behaviour, persuading it to clean up toxic wastes which it dumped years or even decades ago can be more difficult. Changes of company ownership and restructuring can make it even harder to apportion responsibility on a strictly legal basis; for example the pesticide factory in Bhopal, India, was operated by Union Carbide India Ltd, in which the American company Union Carbide Corporation (UCC) held a controlling 50.9 per cent stake (Hanna, Morehouse & Sarangi, 2005: 101). The UCC (2019) states that

> In 1994, UCC sold its entire interest in UCIL to Mcleod Russel India Limited, which renamed the company Eveready Industries India Limited (EIIL). In 1998, the MPSG [Madhya Pradesh State Government], which owns and had been leasing the property to EIIL, cancelled the lease; took over the facility; and assumed all accountability for the site, including the completion of any additional remediation.

Their reasons for accepting responsibility for cleaning up someone else's detritus are not clear. In 2001 UCC was taken over by the Dow Chemical Company. This in turn merged with E.I.DuPont de Nemours in 2017, and in 2019 it is dividing into three companies using the names Dow, DuPont and Corteva Agriscience. The UN's special rapporteur on hazardous substances and wastes, Baskut Tuncak, has said that he is 'deeply concerned' that the merger between Dow Chemical and DuPont may erase any remaining possibility that the victims of the Bhopal disaster will see an 'effective remedy', more than three decades on from the tragedy. Joe Westby, a campaigner on business and human rights at Amnesty International, echoed Mr Tuncak's sentiments, saying it will now be even more difficult for victims to 'pin down' who is responsible (Goddard, 2017). These arrangements are variously called *hurdles* or *corporate veils*. Thus, it may be the case that persuasion based on restorative principles offers as good a chance of securing the desired result. Whatever the legal ownership and liability, it can reasonably be said that the restructured companies are the successors of the original one.

8 What can be done?

A group of people can promote public awareness, especially with the help of social media and the books and films that have been produced during the years that the situation has not been resolved (e.g. in the case of Bhopal, see Bhopal Medical Appeal, 2012). It may be noted that this is not only an environmental problem but involves basic human rights: the Swedish Consumer Association (2018) considers that in the case of Bhopal, human rights at stake include the rights to life, health, water, safe environment, to earn a living through work and to an effective remedy.

For the dialogue to have credibility, the support of an organisation, preferably a well-known one, or a prominent figurehead is needed. This person or organisation could invite all stakeholders to a facilitated discussion. Preparation of participants would be needed, to ensure that the discussion was carried on in a suitably problem-solving way. Until then, the way forward has to be through numbers: as many people as possible are invited to write to the decision-makers of the company. Letter writers may be tempted to tell the company what they think of its behaviour, but that is likely to be counterproductive:

> Cet animal est très méchant
> Quand on l'attaque, il se défend.[2]

It is likely to be more effective if each director is addressed acknowledging that they probably are uneasy about the situation and want to find a solution which meets the needs of survivors as well as being acceptable to shareholders; one may imagine him or her looking for facts, figures and arguments that will help to persuade other members of the board. If there is a personal contact with a senior figure in the company or among its shareholders, that could of course be very helpful.

Shareholders may be approached similarly, inviting them to put pressure on the company (e.g. at an annual general meeting) to remedy the situation. As we have seen, Ury advises 'Warn, don't threaten': in other words, do not threaten to try to reduce the value of its shares, but point out the risk assessment that this will happen if action is not taken to salvage the company's reputation by remedying the damage caused by, for example, cleaning up toxic wastes, providing medical treatment for health problems and paying adequate compensation to those whose well-being and livelihood have been harmed.

2 French saying, translated by Vladimir Nabokov (1966): This beast is very mean: in fact/It will fight back, when it's attacked.

There is growing concern about the need to observe environmental, social and governance principles. To adapt a phrase of Ernst Schumacher, we may be moving toward 'capitalism as if people matter'.

Meanwhile efforts can be made to maintain the legal pressure: even if a favourable verdict is not reached, or is not enforced, it provides a basis for a dialogue.

An indirect approach could be to focus on the technical aspects of remediating the site, for example, by finding antidotes to toxic substances, and leaving till later the question of who will carry out the work and pay for it.

9 Conclusion

This may become a broader movement as part of the urgent effort to prevent and if possible remedy damage caused by humans to the planet and human and animal life. Although the dumping of toxic waste does not affect everyone, as climate change does, it has devastating consequences for its victims, as well as many living creatures. Companies could be invited to sign a pledge on these lines:

> This company undertakes to conduct its work, and dispose of any waste products (both past and future), in a way that does not damage the health, livelihoods or environment of local people.

If that promise appeared to be broken, the primary response could be a facilitated circle of stakeholders, focused on the questions familiar to restorative justice advocates: what happened, who was affected and what needs to be done (and by whom) to put it right. In this case a further question could be added: What is needed to prevent it from happening again? Only when there was failure to agree and fulfil a satisfactory outcome, or to cooperate at all, would the power of the state need to be used, and it should be directed to the responsible individuals as well as the company.

I am grateful to Helen Curtis, Orika Komatsubara and Ulrike Tabbert for helpful comments and suggestions. Responsibility for any errors is of course mine.

References

Aertsen, I. (2018). Restorative justice for victims of corporate violence. In: G. Forti (ed.), *Victims and corporations: legal challenges and empirical findings*. Milano: Wolters Kluwer.

Aertsen, I. (2019). Re-shaping restorative justice to environmental crime. Paper to seminar *Restorative justice responses to environmental crime and ecocide*. KU Leuven, 26 April 2019.

Bhopal Medical Appeal. (2012). *The Bhopal marathon: an ordeal of pain measured not in miles but in years.* Brighton: The BMA. Retrieved from www.bhopalmarathon.org.

Blacksmith Institute & Green Cross Switzerland. (2010). *The world's worst polluted places: report 2009. 12 cases of cleanup and success.* New York: Blacksmith Institute and Zurich: Green Cross Switzerland. Retrieved from www.worstpolluted.org.

Boston University (2017). Minamata disease. In *The encyclopedia of earth.* Retrieved from www.bu.edu/sustainability/minamata-disease/ (last accessed 6 June 2019).

Braithwaite, J. (1985). *To punish or persuade: enforcement of coal mine safety.* Albany NY: State University of New York Press.

Braithwaite, J. (2002). *Restorative justice and responsive regulation.* New York: Oxford University Press.

Gillibrand, K. (2019). *Senator Gillibrand statement on EPA 'Certification of Completion' for GE's unfinished Hudson River PCB cleanup job.* Retrieved from www.gillibrand.senate.gov/news/press/release/senator-gillibrand-statement-on-epa-certification-of-completion-for-ges-unfinished-hudson-river-pcb-cleanup-job (last accessed 5 June 2019).

Goddard, E. (2017, 14 September). Bhopal disaster victims may never get compensation following Dow-DuPont merger, fears UN official. *The Independent.* Retrieved from www.independent.co.uk/news/business/news/bhopal-disaster-victims-dow-dupont-merger-un-india-official-gas-leak-chemical-industrial-a7946346.html (last accessed 23 May 2019).

Hanna, B., Morehouse, W. & Sarangi, S. (2005). *The Bhopal reader.* New York: Apex Press.

Komatsubara, O. (2019). Personal communication.

Macrory, R. B. (2006). *Regulatory justice: making sanctions effective.* Final report. London: Better Regulation Executive, Cabinet Office.

Minamata Disease Municipal Museum (ed.), (2007). *Minamata disease: its history and lessons.* Retrieved from www.minamata195651.jp/pdf/kyoukun_en/kyoukun_eng08.pdf (last accessed 29 December 2018).

Nabokov, V. (1966, 20 February). *Letter to New York review of books.* Retrieved from www.nybooks com/articles/1966/01/20/translation/ (last accessed 7 June 2019).

Schnatterly, K., Gangloff, K.A. & Tuschke, A. (2018). CEO wrongdoing: a review of pressure, opportunity, and rationalization. *Journal of Management*, 44(6), 2405-2432. doi:10.1177/0149206318771177.

Seetharaman, G. (2018, 18 April). *The story of one of the biggest land conflicts: No mine now, but is it all fine in Niyamgiri?* Retrieved from https://economictimes.indiatimes.com/industry/indl-goods/svs/metals-mining/theres-no-mine-but-is-it-all-fine-on-niyam-hills/articleshow/63763978.cms (last accessed 31 May 2019).

SumOfUs. (2018). *Victory! Unilever settles but must clean up its mercury mess.* Retrieved from https://actions.sumofus.org/avictory-unileversettles-but-must-clean-up-its-mercury-mess (last accessed 31 December 2018).

Swedish Consumer Association in collaboration with Swedish Section of Amnesty International. (2018). *Still irresponsible investments: a study of Swedish banks' investments in companies linked to human rights abuses.* Retrieved from https://fairfinanceguide.se/media/494410/report_stil_irresponsible_investments_180924.pdf (last accessed 5 June 2019).

Union Carbide Corporation. (2019). *Bhopal plant history and ownership.* Retrieved from www.bhopal.com/Bhopal-Plant-History-and-Ownership (last accessed 23 May 2019).

Ury, W. (1993). *Getting past no: negotiating your way from confrontation to cooperation* (Rev. ed.). New York: Bantam Books.

Betrayal of spiritual trust in victims of sexual abuse in the Spanish Catholic Church: some heuristics for victimological *praxis*

Gema Varona

Reflexive analysis is never innocent of context but situates itself on the boundaries between the seemingly possible and the impossible with the desire to shift these boundaries.
(Clegg, Flyvbjerg & Haugaard, 2014: 30)

1 Introduction

This contribution explores the intersection between three central concepts of classical virtue ethics (*eudaemonia*, *phronesis* and *praxis*), in relation to the sexual victimisation processes in the Spanish Catholic Church. Drawing from previous and current own research on the matter (Varona, 2019), within a qualitative methodology aiming at understanding the processes of victimisation and reparation, the ultimate purpose of this chapter is to discuss the implications of what is true or evident in this field and what still needs to be known in critical victimological terms. Finally, a heuristic model of accountability with an eye towards victim policy implications will be proposed.

This text is dedicated to Prof. Ivo Aertsen, with deep gratitude, for being a pioneer and collaborating with us in this topic and for teaching us to be aware and to be sensitive to what passes in front of us. We consider this a lesson not only for the academic research but also for the *praxis* of life, constantly adapting our approach to accommodate transforming ideas beyond inertias and isomorphism. As the photographer Anthony Hernandez states: 'Being aware is more important than the evidence of the awareness on a piece of paper' (O'Toole, 2019). Reflexive awareness is needed to walk from secondary victimisation as an iatrogenic effect (Illich, 1976) towards a more responsive justice.

2 The emerging social concern for sexual abuse cases in the Spanish Church: a new threshold of visibility

In recent years, child sexual abuse in the Church, like in some other institutional settings (Sköld, 2013), has become a more visible and global social concern (Böhm et al., 2014; Gallen, 2016; Dressing et al., 2017). However, unlike in other countries, in Spain the Catholic Church has neither carried out enquiries nor collaborated in investigations on sexual abuse in its different institutions (Varona & Martínez, 2015). Despite the cases brought to the attention of the media (Bastante, 2017; Beltrán, 2018), it has not established a central specific service for victims either (Varona, 2015; Tamarit, 2018). Some reasons for this lack of action can be found in power relationships together with the experiences of accumulated victimisation. By studying victims' testimonies in Spain (Pérez, 2018), even within its great diversity, we find similarities to those of victims in other countries. We contend that these testimonies are an adequate source to understand the complex dimensions of this kind of victimisation, as well as the starting point to react from a human rights perspective.

Despite the passive reaction by the Spanish Church, things seem to be changing in the last year. Responses provided by several institutions are promoting some initiatives by the Spanish Church itself. However, according to the victims interviewed in our research, they render those initiatives insufficient. It should be considered that many cases are under the statute of limitations and refer to historical abuses. At the end of 2018, the Spanish Episcopal Conference decided to create a committee to revise the protocols against abuses – criticised for not counting with a representation of victims, for protecting the Church rather than the victims and for not being very collaborative with the criminal justice system. It is obvious that the Church cannot investigate independently, particularly in cases of institutional cover-up. Like in other countries, in Spain the abuser was transferred to other Church or monastery without informing the police, without opening a canonical procedure or without informing the Vatican. In some cases, the Church offered money to keep the victims in silence.

Partly, in 2018, the public alarm (Malagón, 2019) has been fuelled by the investigations of the newspaper *El País* covering multiple testimonies of victims, many referring to processes of hiding or covering up by bishops or superiors of religious orders. It should be noted that the journalistic research had been previously initiated in Spain by the work of Cortés (2018), who compared the Spanish situation with other countries.

Just before the end of the Socialist legislature in 2019, by means of a letter by the Ministry of Justice, the Spanish government asked the Episcopal Conference of Spain for information on the cases of abuse of minors, including those currently under investigation and those investigated in the past. The objective of this request was 'to throw some light on facts that our society cannot allow to keep them hidden if it wishes to face its future with some dignity'. The inquiry of this data was already done, without success and with quite contradictions in the answers obtained, by the Basque Institute of Criminology of the University of the Basque Country in 2014 (Varona & Martínez, 2015).

In 2019, the Minister of Justice Dolores Delgado underlined that the cases of abuse 'being within the Church or in any other institution can neither be hidden nor considered a private matter'. According to her, this kind of acts deserves a clear answer from the criminal justice system due to 'an important public alarm' and a 'strong demand towards the government to tackle this phenomenon'.

The Ministry of Justice requested the General Prosecutor to deliver a report on the open investigations for aggressions and sexual abuse to minors within the Church, including schools or other religious institutions. It was reminded of the numerous news on this kind of victimisation and the perception of the Church 'protecting victimisers'. This request is legally based on Article 9.2 of the Organic Statute of the Prosecutor, which states that the government will be informed, when requested, and if there is no legal obstacle for it, on whatever matter in which the General Prosecutor can intervene, as well as on the general functioning of the administration of justice. The Minister of Justice indicated that a bill on the integral protection of children and adolescence against violence was approved in December 2018. One of the changes foreseen by this bill was that the statute of limitations could start counting when the victim would turn 30 years (20minutos, 2019).

Besides the role of the press and the government, in 2018, victims started to mobilise nationally. Thus it could be mentioned the pioneer work of the Asociación Nacional de Infancias Robadas (National Association of Stolen Childhoods) (ANIR), founded by the victim and activist Miguel Hurtado. Due to the lack of resources, its goal is not to offer assistance but to mobilise society about this topic. What is more interesting is that it belongs to the global organisation Ending Clergy Abuse. ANIR is trying to make different institutions react to get to know the extent of the problem. According to ANIR we are only seeing the top of the iceberg. Victims of this association are pressing for similar actions taken in other countries by proposing: (a) That the government creates a parliamentary inquiry commission (like in Australia or Belgium); (b) That the General Prosecutor investigates every case even if it is under the statute of limitations, as it has happened in Pennsylvania[1] and Chile (González, 2018); (c) That the Church itself commissions an independent research, as in the United States (Terry, 2008, 2015) and Germany (Rassenhofer et al., 2015), followed by reparation schemes.

Additionally, representatives of ANIR were also present to protest in the summit on pederasty in Rome in February 2019. Before, some members of this association appeared in the 2019 documentary film titled *Examen de conciencia* (*Exam of conscience*), directed by Albert Solé, for Netflix. According to Miguel Hurtado, the film showed well that: 'They

1 See the official report and testimonies of victims at www.attorneygeneral.gov/report/.

are not four rotten apples', but that the Church is a power structure protecting the responsible ones.

Meanwhile, following the example of *Towards Healing* in Ireland (Darmody, 2015; Gleeson, 2015), some specialised and independent centres for victim support, without limited financing, have been created by some Catholic experts (Núñez, 2019).[2]

3 *EUDAEMONIA* AS THE SEARCH OF INSTITUTIONAL COHERENCE FOR PERSONAL AND COLLECTIVE WELL-BEING

After the previous introduction to the state of affairs in Spain, in this section I concentrate on the incoherent organisational culture that makes secondary victimisation possible by the Church in this kind of victimisation. Organisational culture is defined as a set of understandings (including assumptions, values and behaviours), often unconscious, shared by its members. In order to get sustainable organisational change towards awareness and due diligence in preventing hidden victimisation in cases of sexual abuse of children in institutional settings, like the Church, multi-sectorial and multi-disciplinary cooperation structures are needed to enable relevant professionals to effectively collaborate among them. This is precisely what the Spanish Church is lacking today. It is crucial to understand that social problems need a collaborative or concerted action 'as the performance of an orchestra' like a 'joint enterprise in which understandings and interpretations of the music must be appreciated by all, even if the practitioners, the musicians, do different things' (Ison, Grant & Waden, 2014).

The Greek term *eudaemonia*, beyond its Aristotelian sense as a life of activity governed by reason, refers to well-being or the fulfilment of one person's true potential in the process of making sense of life. In this chapter this notion is important in relation to the coherence in responding to victims. It also relates to the developmental character of this victimisation across life, as well as the diversity of experiences. Although *eudaemonia* is usually identified with happiness or vital satisfaction, this translation is not really accurate (Ryff, 1989), as *eudaemonia* is more related to personal growth and openness to others and their experiences.

Already in the 17th century, the Dutch philosopher of Sephardic origins, Baruch Spinoza, defended the diversity for personal fulfilment in relation to good, truth and common good where harming passions, such as fear (of victims) or resentment (towards victimisers), should be controlled under what can be understood as Spinoza's theory of affects as a framework for humanising justice without denying accountability.

2 See the centre *Betania* at https://acogidabetania.es/.

4 Contextualised, reflexive and responsive knowledge: towards *phronesis*

Within that horizon of full development of capabilities (including the ones of those harmed), all *praxis* is contextual and dynamic (Ison et al., 2014). According to different authors (Burger, White & Yearworth, 2019), researching *praxis* produces situated and applied *phronetic* knowledge, in contrast to abstract and universalistic theory (*episteme*) or the technological (*techne*). In victimology, Anthony Pemberton (2018) has referred to the potentialities of the *phronetic* approach in the understanding of the processes of victimisation, recovery and restoration.

By analysing concrete practices, it is possible to make asymmetries of power transparent and, perhaps, open to change (Keenan, 2011; Palmer, 2016). Thus problematising taken-for-granted concrete reality allows transformation. Contextualism can be identified with situational ethics that departs from universalism or relativism in order to consider contested viewpoints to create grounded knowledge, admitting its limitations. In *phronetic praxis* researchers should question their own knowledge (including its process of production). Finally, as Clegg et al. (2014: 30) contend: 'truth claims are managed contextually through discourses, time and space as well as through agency in terms of identity, capital and practices, conjoined through power relations'.

Following the proposals of Prof. Bent Flyvbjerg,[3] analytical and instrumental rationality is balanced with the rationality of values to be clarified and contextualised for *praxis*. From a *phronetic* approach we should ask ourselves what is being done; what impact it is having, how (involving what power) and upon whom; if this is desirable; and what we should do. By answering these questions, we can have a map of possibilities, problems and risks in specific fields of social action.

A contextual framework can offer better conditions for responding to the vicissitudes of listening and engaging with human suffering. Coming back to the topic of this chapter, we are not really in front of a 'moral scandal' (Cencini, 2016), but in front of lines of thought that see victims as waste or discarded lives in a devastating secondary victimisation, to be thought as a social, cultural and political problem that is neither natural nor inevitable (Verdú, 2019b).

In this scenario perceptive paradoxes emerge: victims seem not to exist for the Church despite the media or advocate groups. Yet victims are feared by the Church (Verdú, 2019a) by attributing them some characteristics that don't match reality, according to the few studies done in Spain: they are not particularly revengeful or anticlerical. At the end, by arranging victims in the space of fear, an oppressive semantic system is created by institutional settings, where the abuse was produced. This is a hiding and discarding system, particularly for that majority of non 'ideal victims' (Christie, 1986).

---

3 See his web page at http://flyvberg.plan.auu.dk.

5 INCEST AS ALLEGORY

Some of the victims interviewed in our research have referred to the victimisation suffered as 'a spiritual incest'. Incest is usually defined as sexual intercourse between people who are very closely related. However, in the victims' words, incest can be conceived as an allegory: a symbol or expression that stands for something not explicitly stated, that is, the betrayal[4] of spiritual trust by someone who is called Father or Mother (Crisp, 2010; McLaughlin, 1994; Plante & Daniels, 2004). The matter is not mainly about sexual intercourse in a relationship of supposed trust, but about abuse of power by one person called Father or Mother who consciously puts the other (a minor) under conditions of vulnerability for his or her own satisfaction, taking advantage of the previous trust created.

By talking about spiritual incest, victims underline the paradox of a familiar relationship in a contextual setting. This means a simultaneous betrayal of spiritual and institutional trust with devastating consequences for the victim in three spheres: (a) loss of self-esteem and self-efficacy ('I deserve it, I cannot do anything'), (b) loss of trust in others ('I have to protect myself from further suffering'; 'See what the one close to God has done to me', 'See how their superiors reacted') and (c) loss of hope in the future ('I am confused', 'I cannot integrate or make any sense of the suffering to keep going in life').

Fractured by their idea of God represented by the aggressor and their feelings of shame and guilt, the institution responds to them with more alienation through imposing silence (Smith & Freyd, 2013, 2014). Most victims do not want to speak out and be exposed to the courts or the media, but they refer their interest to be listened and understood in different forums (Kelland, 2012), adapting the listening to their passing of time (Holder & Daly, 2017). Victims' words and gestures are signs and traces that make visible the harm, and thus the accountability, for the abuse of power produced. Many, no matter the time elapsed and consistently with studies of developmental victimology (Finkelhor, 2003; Gómez Zapiain, 2018), still feel like ruins of what they could have been without the abuse (Easton, Leone-Sheehan & O'Leary, 2019).

6 SOME HEURISTICS FOR A BETTER VICTIMOLOGICAL *PRAXIS*

To conclude, some methods of understanding the art of exercising a critical victimology will be commented upon, in order to foster further debate. I have learned some of these heuristics from Prof. Ivo Aertsen and they could be applied to any kind of victimisation, even though, in Spain, we need the Catholic Church to consider them in agonistic dialogues (Bull & Hansen, 2016) for recognising the slow violence provoked in the form of

4 The term *betrayal* was used in the title of the influential work published by the Boston Globe Investigative Staff (2002).

suffering added with the lack of an adequate response to the sexual victimisation within in.

According to Ison et al. (2014: 630):

> A heuristic model in the sense reported here is an epistemological device that captures the key conceptual outcomes of an inquiry process and which can be used to guide others in processes of context-sensitive process designing.

Heuristics can be defined as principles to generate new ideas and orientate decision making. It can be conceived as a way to orient decision making in research and policy considering values as a point of departure for *praxis* and for opening alternative outcomes generating new ideas. The proposed heuristics are the following:

1. Victims (persons who have been harmed) and offenders (responsible persons) are not natural antagonists. Notwithstanding normal tensions and difficulties in times of polarisation, their claims can be reframed in a common understanding of social goods, beyond private and adversarial interests (Holder, 2018).
2. Don't be afraid of the victims. They are human beings in pain showing the need for solidarity facing the unequal distribution of injustices, as well as the precarious human condition (Kirchhoff et al., 2013).
3. Listen actively to the victims. They are full of reasoned emotion and emotional reason, as neuroscientists discovering the making of affects show us. Victims see and suffer things; experts or general people do not (Bisschops, 2015). On this blindness, think about how much time it took for jurists and criminologists (experts in crime) to see (and study) victims' suffering. Think about how victims might offer a revolutionary vision of time as a gift to an accelerated society (Sobrino, 2001; Köhler, 2018).
4. 'Victim' is more of a dynamic adjective rather than an encapsulating or essentialist noun.
5. Some victims prefer to call themselves harmed persons or survivors to avoid being patronised or to circumvent a passive vision of what they are capable of. In any case, relational autonomy does not mean individualistic self-sufficiency.
6. Sometimes, victim is a role that can be played subsequently, successively or simultaneously as the offender's or responsible person's role.
7. Victimisation is not a pathology but a social process that can be understood in its micro-, meso- and macro-interdependent dimensions.
8. Part of secondary victimisation can be avoided with a human and professional response in coordination with other intervening agencies.
9. Institutional betrayal can be identified with secondary victimisation: the institutions or agencies in charge of protecting or repairing the victims should aim, at least, at not causing further harm.

10. Institutional betrayal in contexts of spiritual trust provokes a profound harm in the understanding of the self, the others and the future.
11. Restorative justice, as the art of the encounter with the harmed other, can provide personal, interpersonal and social reparation by means of accountability and interpellation on the causes and consequences of victimisation, transcending justice as therapy towards a critical justice as transformation of the injustice individually and collectively experienced (Aertsen & Pali, 2017). For this restorative justice must consider the particular context of child sexual abuse (Bolitho & Freeman, 2016; Byrne, 2018; Cossins, 2008; Gal, 2011).

In any case, as Goethe expressed it: 'All theory is gray, my friend. But forever green is the tree of life.' Dear Ivo, thank you for remaining endlessly curious no matter the passing of time, and thank you for challenging our own assumptions towards a more coherent and un-walling *praxis* that shifts boundaries.

REFERENCES

20minutos. (2019). El Gobierno pide a la Fiscalía datos sobre los abusos sexuales en la Iglesia. Retrieved from www.20minutos.es/noticia/3554821/0/justicia-pide-fiscalia-datos-abusos-sexuales-iglesia/#xtor=AD-15&xts=467263#xtor=AD-15&xts=467263 (last accessed 1 April 2019).

Aertsen, I. & Pali, B. (eds.). (2017). *Critical restorative justice*. Oxford: Hart Publishing.

Bastante, J. (2017, 6 March). *Las claves del 'caso Romanones', el mayor juicio contra la pederastia eclesial en España*. Retrieved from www.periodistadigital.com/religion/espana/2017/03/06/las-claves-del-caso-romanones-el-mayor-juicio-contra-la-pederastia-eclesial-en-espana-religion-iglesia-abusos-daniel-arzobispo-granada-papa-francisco.shtml (last accessed 1 March 2019).

Beltrán, J. (2018). La redención de Román: el Papa recibe y pide perdón al sacerdote absuelto por abusos. *Vida Nueva Digital*. Retrieved from www.vidanuevadigital.com/2018/07/27/la-redencion-de-roman-el-papa-recibe-y-pide-perdon-al-sacerdote-absuelto-por-abusos/ (last accessed 1 March 2019).

Bisschops, A. (2015). Procedimientos de queja en la iglesia católica y de víctimas de abuso sexual histórico: en busca de justicia. *Eguzkilore. Cuaderno del Instituto Vasco de Criminología*, 29, 93-108.

Böhm, B., Zollner, H., Fegert, J. M. & Liebhardt, J. (2014). Child sexual abuse in the context of the Roman Catholic Church: a review of literature from 1981-2013. *Journal of Child Sexual Abuse*, 23, 635-656. doi:10.1080/10538712.2014.929607.

Bolitho, J. & Freeman, K. (2016). *The use and effectiveness of restorative justice in criminal justice systems following child sexual abuse or comparable harms*. Sydney: Royal Commission into Institutional Responses to Child Sexual Abuse.

Boston Globe Investigative Staff. (2002). *Betrayal: the crisis in the Catholic Church*. New York: Little Brown.

Bull, A. & Hansen, H. (2016). On agonistic memory. *Memory Studies*, 9(4), 390-404. doi:10.1177/1750698015615935.

Burger, K., White, L. & Yearworth, M. (2019). Understanding front-end project workshops with social practice theory. *International Journal of Project Management*, 37(1), 161-175. doi:10.1016/j.ijproman.2018.11.003.

Byrne, D. (2018). *Meeting the monsters: a restorative response to the crisis of sexual abuse in the Roman Catholic Church*. Retrieved from https://orthodoxyindialogue.com/2018/08/24/meeting-the-monsters-a-restorative-response-to-the-crisis-of-sexual-abuse-in-the-roman-catholic-church-by-david-byrne/ (last accessed 1 March 2019).

Cencini, A. (2016). ¿Ha *cambiado algo en la Iglesia después de los escándalos sexuales? Análisis y propuestas para la formación*. Salamanca: Sígueme.

Christie, N. (1986). The ideal victim. In E. A. Fattah (ed.), *From crime policy to victim policy* (pp. 17-30). London: Palgrave Macmillan.

Clegg, S., Flyvbjerg, B. & Haugaard, M. (2014). Reflections on phronetic social science: a dialogue between Stewart Clegg, Bent Flyvbjerg, and Mark Haugaard. *Journal of Political Power*, 7, 275-306. doi:10.1080/2158379x.2014.929259.

Cortés, J. I. (2018). *Lobos con piel de pastor. Pederastía y crisis en la Iglesia católica*. Madrid: San Pablo.

Cossins, A. (2008). Restorative justice and child sex offences: the theory and the practice. *The British Journal of Criminology*, *48*(3), 359-378. doi:10.1093/bjc/azn013.

Crisp, B. R. (2010). Silence and silenced: implications for the spirituality of survivors of sexual abuse. *Feminist Theology*, 18, 277-293. doi:10.1177/0966735009360386.

Darmody, M. (2015). 'Towards healing': diecinueve años de escucha y aprendizaje. *Eguzkilore, Cuaderno del Instituto Vasco de Criminología*, 29, 77-92.

Dressing, H., Dolling, D., Hermann, D., Horten, B., Kruse, A., Schmitt, E., Bannenberg, B, Whittaker, K. & Salize, H. J. (2017). Sexual abuse of minors within the Catholic Church and other institutions. a literature review. *Neuropsychiatrie*, 31(2), 45-55. doi:10.1007/s40211-017-0223-4.

Easton, S. D., Leone-Sheehan, D. M., & O'Leary, P. J. (2019). 'I will never know the person who I could have become': perceived changes in self-identity among adult survivors of clergy-perpetrated sexual abuse. *Journal of Interpersonal Violence*, 34(6), 1139-1162. doi:10.1177/0886260516650966.

Finkelhor, D. (2003). The legacy of the clergy abuse scandal. *Child Abuse & Neglect*, 27, 1225-1229. doi:10.1016/j.chiabu.2003.09.011.

Gal, T. (2011). *Child victims and restorative justice: a needs-rights model.* Oxford: Oxford University Press.
Gallen, J. (2016). Jesus wept: the Roman Catholic Church, child sexual abuse and transitional justice. *International Journal of Transitional Justice*, 10(2), 332-349. doi:10.1093/ijtj/ijw003.
Gleeson, K. (2015). The money problem: reparation and restorative justice in the Catholic Church's towards healing program. *Current Issues in Criminal Justice*, 26 (3), 317-332. doi:10.1080/10345329.2015.12036024.
Gómez Zapiain, J. (2018). *Apego y teràpia sexual.* Madrid: Alianza.
González, M. (2018). Las cifras de los abusos en la Iglesia chilena: 267 víctimas en las últimas décadas, *Vida Nueva Digital.* Retrieved from www.vidanuevadigital.com/2018/07/23/las-cifras-de-los-abusos-en-la-iglesia-chilena-267-victimas-en-las-ul timas-cinco-decadas/ (last accessed 1 April 2019).
Holder, R. (2018). *Just interests: victims, citizens and the potential for justice.* Cheltenham: Edward Elgar Publishing.
Holder, R. & Daly, K. (2017). Sequencing justice: a longitudinal study of justice goals of domestic violence victims. *British Journal of Criminology*, 58(4), 787-804. doi:10.1093/bjc/azx046.
Illich, I. (1976). *Limits to medicine. Medical nemesis: the expropriation of health.* New York: Pantheon.
Ison, R., Grant, A. & Bawden, R. (2014). Scenario praxis for systemic governance: a critical framework. *Environment and Planning C: Government and Policy*, 32(4), 623-640. doi:10.1068/c11327.
Keenan, M. (2011). *Child sexual abuse and the Catholic Church: gender, power, and organizational culture.* Oxford: Oxford University Press.
Kelland, L. (2012). A narrative model of recovery. *South African Journal of Philosophy*, 31 (2), 290-300. doi:10.1080/02580136.2012.10751776.
Kirchhoff, J. Strackb, M. & Wagner, U. (2013). The needs of victims: an empirical categorization based on interpersonal conflicts. *Journal of Social and Political Psychology*, 1(1), 29-50. doi:10.5964/jspp.v1i1.44.
Köhler, A. (2018). *El tiempo regalado. Un ensayo sobre la espera.* Barcelona: Libros del Asteroide.
Malagón. (2019, 10 February). Pederastía en la Iglesia. *El País*, p. 8.
McLaughlin, B. R. (1994). Devastated spirituality: the impact of clergy sexual abuse on the survivor's relationship with God and the Church. *Sexual Addiction & Compulsivity*, 1(2), 145-158. doi:10.1080/10720169408400039.
Núñez, J. (2019, 19 Februrary). La Iglesia española crea el primer órgano para atender a víctimas de abusos. *El País.*
O'Toole, E. (2019). Anthony Hernandez. Madrid: Fundación MAPFRE.

Palmer, D. (2016). *The role of organisational culture in child sexual abuse in institutional contexts.* Sydney: Royal Commission into Institutional Responses to Child Sexual Abuse.

Pemberton, A. (2018). A world of struggle meets the faces of injustice (Judith Shklar and current affairs). *Tilburg Law Review*, 23, 125-129. doi:10.5334/tilr.132. Retrieved from https://tilburglawreview.com/articles/10.5334/tilr.132/ (last accessed 1 April 2019).

Pérez, E. (2018). *La experiencia de victimización en la agresión sexual durante la infancia* (Unpublished paper).

Plante, T. G. & Daniels, C. (2004). The sexual abuse crisis in the Roman Catholic Church: what psychologists and counselors should know. *Pastoral Psychology*, 52(5), 381-393. doi:10.1023/b:pasp.0000020686.94708.02.

Rassenhofer, M., Zimmer, A., Spröber, N. & Fegert, J. M. (2015). Child sexual abuse in the Roman Catholic Church in Germany: comparison of victim-impact data collected through church-sponsored and government-sponsored programs. *Child Abuse & Neglect*, 40, 60-67. doi:10.1016/j.chiabu.2014.11.013.

Ryff, C. D. (1989). Happiness is everything, or is it? Explorations on the meaning of psychological well-being. *Journal of Personality and Social Psychology*, 57(6), 1069-1081. doi:10.1037//0022-3514.57.6.1069.

Sköld, J. (2013). Historical abuse – a contemporary issue: compiling inquiries into abuse and neglect of children in out-of-home care worldwide. *Journal of Scandinavian Studies in Criminology and Crime Prevention*, 14(1), 5-23. doi:10.1080/14043858.2013.771907.

Smith, C. & Freyd, J. (2013). Dangerous safe havens: institutional betrayal exacerbates sexual trauma. *Journal of Traumatic Stress*, 26, 119-124. doi:10.1002/jts.21778.

Smith, C. & Freyd, J. (2014). The courage to study what we wish did not exist. *Journal of Trauma & Dissociation: The Official Journal of the International Society for the Study of Dissociation*, 15, 521-526. doi:10.1080/15299732.2014.947910.

Sobrino, J. (2001). Redención de la globalización. Las víctimas. *Concilium: Revista internacional de teología*, 5(129), 801-813.

Tamarit, J. M. (2018). Abusos sexuales en la Iglesia católica: ¿cómo responder a las demandas de justicia? *Nuevo Foro Penal*, 14(91), 11-42. doi:10.17230/nfp.14.91.1.

Terry, K. J. (2008). Stained glass: the nature and scope of child sexual abuse in the Catholic Church. *Criminal Justice and Behavior*, 35(5), 549-569. doi:10.1177/0093854808314339.

Terry, K. J. (2015). Child sexual abuse within the Catholic Church: a review of global perspectives. *International Journal of Comparative and Applied Criminal Justice*, 39 (2), 139-154. doi:10.1080/01924036.2015.1012703.

Varona, G. (2015). Reconocer a las víctimas para reparar y prevenir su sufrimiento: los abusos sexuales en la Iglesia y las posibilidades de la justicia restaurativa desde un enfoque victimológico. *Razón y Fe*, 272(1405), 383-395.

Varona, G. (2019). Los adultos víctimas de abusos sexuales en el seno de la Iglesia: ¿construcción de la memoria como forma de justicia restaurativa? In H. Soleto & A. Carrascosa (ed.), *Justicia restaurativa: Una justicia para las víctimas* (pp. 617-640). Valencia: Tirant lo Blanch.

Varona, G. & Martínez, A. (2015). Estudio exploratorio sobre los abusos sexuales en la Iglesia española y otros contextos institucionales. *Eguzkilore. Cuaderno del Instituto Vasco de Criminología*, 29, 7-76.

Verdú, D. (2019a, 17 February). Entrevista a Charles Scicluna. 'Es el momento de la verdad. Aunque dé miedo y nos huille'. *El País*, p. 32.

Verdú, D. (2019b, 23 February). Entrevista a Phil Saviano. 'El Papa nota la presión de las víctimas y de la ley'. *El País*, p. 24.

Two women's journeys: restorative justice after sexual violence

Marie Keenan (with Ailbhe Griffith)

1 Introduction

For more than 40 years I have worked in the field of sexual violence, and while not exclusively so for all of this time, it has nonetheless always been there. Sexual violence in all its multidimensions has always been part of my professional life – to a greater or lesser extent – and that does not seem to want to end any time soon. From my first child sexual abuse 'case' as a young Irish social worker in Brixton in 1976 to issues involving sexual harassment on campus and online child exploitation, with which I am concerned today, my professional life has involved almost every aspect of sexual violence – legal, social, therapeutic, organisational, research and policy – and for most of that time from all perspectives simultaneously. The work has also involved the full 360 degrees concerning multiple parties all together: victims, perpetrators, both sets of families, criminal justice systems and professionals, media, politicians, policy makers, communities, the Catholic Church (Keenan, 2012) and more latterly the film industry (www.themeeting.org). Sexual violence in its many dimensions seems to seek me out, and it is in this context too that I also first came to work with Ivo Aertsen when he supervised a Daphne-funded research project on *Integrated Approaches to Sexual Violence: the Role of Restorative Justice*, led by Estelle Zinsstag and myself (Zinsstag and Keenan, 2017).

In this tribute article to the work of Ivo Aertsen, we will begin by outlining Marie's work in the area of sexual violence and illustrate developments in Marie's thought over this time. We will conclude by offering the perspective of Ailbhe, a young woman who suffered a sexual assault and her journey towards restorative justice and getting her life back.

2 First-wave thinking: therapy and rehabilitation for victims and offenders

We all have our individual trajectories in how we come to know what we know and privileged what we do, and my professional journey in the sexual violence field was no different. When I first got involved in the work of responding to sexual violence, I believed that once the safety and protection of children was secured through the mechanism of state legislation and child protection procedures, what was next in the order of importance was to establish therapy and advocacy services for victims. In the 1970s and 1980s, this is where I focused my energy: helping victim survivors to heal (Bass and Davison, 1988; Herman, 1992). I offered individual, group and family therapy sessions for victims and ran bioenergetic workshops and residential healing weekends for them, in which all could be said and 'discharged' in the safety of a supportive group and all could be reclaimed. That was the theory. Gestalt techniques using 'the empty chair' to 'confront' offenders also formed part of the methodology.

In doing this work it didn't take long before I realised that most perpetrators of sexual violence and abuse have multiple victims, and it soon occurred to me that in order to avoid more victims, we needed to stop perpetrators from re-offending, and to stop potential perpetrators from becoming such in the first instance. It was clear that the best way to do this was through a combination of therapeutic interventions and criminal justice mechanisms, and I became an advocate for the 'Stop It Now' campaign (www.stopitnow.org.uk). In the late 1980s and 1990s this became the focus of my work.

In the late 1980s I worked in an Irish prison and developed interventions for sex offenders, based on the work of Groth and Birnbaum (1979) and Marshall, Anderson and Fernandez (2000). I did a study on men who rape and therapeutic conversations with them (Keenan, 1994, unpublished). In the early 1990s I was one of three people who developed a community-based treatment programme for sex offenders in Ireland (The Granada Institute), also influenced by the work of many researchers and practitioners in the sex offender field (Marshall et al., 2000; Ward & Stewart, 2003) but with a narrative and systemic overlay, influenced by the work of Michael White in Australia (White & Epston, 1990) and Art Fisher in Nova Scotia, both of whom helped with my narrative training (Keenan, 1998). I visited sex offender programmes in the United States, Canada, Australia, Nova Scotia and the UK and became an active member of the American Association for the Treatment of Sex Offenders (ATSA) and the International Association for the Treatment of Sex Offenders (IATSO), attending their annual conferences and learning from international colleagues. At 'The Granada', as it came to be known, we offered group and individual therapy for sex offenders as core, therapy for victims who wished for this, testimony and witness to courts as required, accountability meetings for the accused clients,[1] family therapy for families, victim meetings with the offender and support groups for family members and friends. We did residential workshops for clients and the women in their lives on multiple themes.

1 Accountability meetings were based on the idea that all members of a particular client system needed to be accountable; clients in treatment needed to be accountable to the people in their lives, their support people; in the case of clergy, their bishops needed to be accountable for the actions they were taking and therapists needed to be accountable to the client and client system. Accountability meetings took place every few months, in which all came together to 'be accountable' in dialogue and action.

As coordinator of the treatment programme, I took the position that therapists working with men who had perpetrated sexual violence and abuse had also to work with victims as part of their work too – to keep us 'honest' and 'grounded' – and lessen the risk of 'forgetting' or minimising the horrors of sexual violence when we were largely engaging with men who had sexually offended who were truly otherwise kind and ordinary men. When working with victims, the opposite did not apply, but I always ensured that therapists working with victims were fully knowledgeable of the strategies that sex offenders employ when sexually offending as well as the dynamics of sexual violence and the impact of trauma, in order to work effectively with victims. This is what I continue to teach students today (Keenan, 2018).

An interesting feature of the work of 'The Granada' was our work with Catholic clergy who had sexually offended. This work also involved therapeutic engagement with victims of clergy, Church leaders and hierarchy and a myriad of canonical lawyers and theologians, extending right to the Vatican. The work was both global and local, historical and contemporary and it was as long as it was broad. Sexual abuse by Catholic clergy was firmly on the social, political and moral agenda in Ireland in the mid-1990s, and we at 'The Granada' were in the thick of it. Historically while offending clergy had been moved to a new parish or sent out of the country to the United States or the United Kingdom for treatment, now they were sent to us. The 'cover-up' by Church leaders was also beginning to emerge, and they came to 'The Granada' too. The media camped outside the treatment centre, hoping to photograph accused clergy coming in and out. We were on every talk show in the country trying to make sense of what we knew and what we were learning. We wrote policy documents, best practice guides and gave workshops on everything from celibacy to secrecy. We walked a narrow cliff-edge of legal and ethical surveillance. I undertook a study on sexual abuse in the Catholic Church, a gender, power and organisational cultural perspective, and wrote everything I knew (Keenan, 2012). Tragically we buried clergy and victims who took their own lives as the intensity of the situation was unbearable for them. Today from Chile to Hungary as this problem reveals itself in these countries too, the work and research of the Irish girl in the land that was formerly referred to as the most Catholic Country in the world (Blanchard, 1954) continues to be called upon.

3 SECOND-WAVE REFLECTION: THE IMPORTANCE OF JUSTICE

In the early 2000s, as my work became primarily focused on research and teaching (with a small amount of continuing practice with victims and perpetrators of sexual violence and their families), the question of justice and how it is experienced by victims and offenders (Keenan, 2014) and how it can be measured by academics became a key concern. This theme of course was also on the minds of other theorists and practitioners (see for example Daly, 2017; Koss, 2006; McGlynn, Downes & Westmarland, 2017). Daly in particular argued for the need to build a body of evidence that could assess and compare different justice mechanisms in response to sexual violence and offered one way of doing this in the case of victims, using a Victimisation and Justice Model, which she had developed (Daly, 2011, 2017). She argued convincingly for me that different victims have differing justice needs and interests and no one approach will satisfy all. Thus, she suggested we needed to understand victims' justice interests more specifically so that we could develop tailor-made justice solutions for them rather than offering a one-size-fits-all justice remedy. The same could be considered in the case of offenders.

The Victimisation and Justice Model proposed by Daly comprises three components that must be analysed when trying to respond adequately to victims of sexual crime: (1) the context of the victimisation, (2) the possible range of justice mechanisms that could be made available to them and (3) victims' justice needs and interests. All three can be computated in a sophisticated template to arrive at the most suitable approach or approaches to justice for individual victims. A similar template could be applied to offenders. While the model is somewhat complex and requires a paper all on its own (Daly, 2017) here I will briefly summarise it in relation to victims.

First the context in which the sexual victimisation occurs needs to be specified and charted, on the assumption that the context of the crime may influence the victim's experience and the resultant needs that will arise. These contexts extend from a stranger offending alone to individuals using their position of authority in a family, or in an institution to offend, to offending by well organised groups or gangs. The second column of the Model identifies the range of justice mechanisms including those associated with *conventional* criminal justice (such as criminal prosecution, trial, sentencing, giving a victim impact statement) as well as those now with *innovative* criminal justice (such as victim offender mediation, restorative conferences, restorative circles or reparation agreements). Some victims will require access to a number of these justice mechanisms depending on the third column in the Model; their justice needs and interests of which Daly and others (Keenan, 2014, 2017, Koss, 2006) identify six: participation, voice, validation, vindication, offender accountability and child and adult protection. These terms and concepts need to be explicitly specified in detail in order to advance the evidence base for empirically comparing and demonstrating the potential of the different mechanisms in different circumstances and situations.

I was and am totally persuaded by this argument and have been working away in this vein for the past number of years. However, as the gulf between what the conventional criminal justice system seemed to promise and what it could actually deliver for victims continued to emerge, my interest in additional justice mechanisms for victims continued to grow.

I began to see that at its core, the criminal justice system was established to ensure a fair trial for an accused, to gather and test the state's evidence against an accused, to punish wrongdoing and to rehabilitate offenders (CIJ, 2014; Keenan, 2014). Like a slow dawning, I began to realise that the criminal justice system was not established to directly address the harm caused to victims. This became very clear the more cases I experienced. So did the realisation that the underlying concerns of the criminal justice system for due process and a fair trial for accused persons result in a criminal trial format that is highly adversarial, extremely strict on the kinds of evidence that can be adduced by the prosecution against the accused and the evidential threshold on the prosecution is to prove guilt 'beyond reasonable doubt'. It became increasingly clear that despite many improvements in the criminal justice system that were being applied in cases involving sexual violence, the fact remained that the criminal justice system was not directly about doing right by the victim, particularly victims of sexual crime, but rather about prosecuting the offender and protecting the community. The needs and views of victims were largely irrelevant to this core dynamic, and for many victims of sexual crime, the criminal process was an abstract, institutionalised and depersonalised procedure that failed to take their interests into account as they became a witness in the state's case and their role being limited to simply that (Christie, 1977: 5).

I wondered if the criminal trial format as we experienced it in Ireland was fit for purpose at all and I continue to wonder this. It leaves little space for the personal account of the victim's experience and his or her trauma as a result of the assault albeit that the victim impact statement offers victims some direct input into the process, if somewhat limited. With the hostile environment of courts, the gruelling cross examination of witnesses that occur and the myriad of rape myths that victims endure (see Gillen, 2018), it is little wonder that some scholars talk about 'secondary victimisation' by the criminal justice process itself (McDonald & Tinsley 2011: 63) and that some victims have described it as a form of 'secondary rape' (Parkinson, 2010: 3). Apart from the longer-term goal of campaigning for significant changes in how criminal justice applies in cases of sexual violence, something else had to be done. This is where restorative justice came on the horizon in earnest for me.

4 Third-wave commitment: restorative justice

In 2011 I began a research study on restorative justice after sexual violence in an Irish context (Keenan, 2014) and in 2012 I undertook a Daphne-funded project on restorative justice after sexual violence with Ivo Aertsen as supervisor and Estelle Zinsstag as co-principal investigator (Zinsstag & Keenan, 2017). I also began to get requests to facilitate restorative justice meetings and restorative circles during this time, and I continued to undertake additional specific training for this work. However, one extraordinary event also occurred about this time, which I will briefly share.

I received an email at the university on a day in 2013 from a young woman who requested a meeting with me. She told me that I didn't know her but that I had trained her sister as a social worker. She said when she told her sister what she wanted to do her sister suggested she contact me. Her name is Ailbhe Griffith. We met on the evening before I went to Leuven to begin the Daphne-funded restorative justice research with Ivo Aertsen and Estelle Zinsstag. I told them about this amazing woman when I arrived in Leuven. This is Ailbhe Griffith's story in her own words.

5 She didn't want an apology; she wanted her life back

There is one man alive in this world today that I have met only twice in my life in the most opposing of circumstances – once, when he violently sexually assaulted me and the other, when we sat on opposite sides of a round table wishing each other a successful future. This is why I am writing here – to tell you about this journey, to inform you of how I got from point A to point B. Above all, however, to let you know why it was so important for me to go back to where it all began, and it all began with him, in order to really gain the closure that I desired for so very long.

I would consider the journey that I have undertaken to be a cycle of healing. It began several years ago on one particularly fateful night when a man followed me, physically attacked me, sexually assaulted me, repeatedly choked me and threatened to kill me. Within those moments, that felt like an eternity, I believed that there was a significant chance my life was about to end. The following months and indeed years I was submerged in the depths of post-traumatic stress. I was deeply depressed, and I kept repeating and repeating and repeating the assault in my mind. I couldn't stop it. After all, what was the point of thinking about anything else? My mind couldn't process the information; my body couldn't process the sensations, so I was just stuck there. I cannot even begin to convey the hell what that is. I don't use the term *hell* lightly, but I couldn't imagine a more hellish place than post-traumatic stress disorder. Every aspect of my life, from my physical and mental health to my personal relationships, was affected. It had consumed me in my entirety.

Considering how the criminal justice system operates, certainly in Ireland, it would be fair to say that the outcome of this case in which I was the 'witness' was positive in terms of the sentence he received. Additionally, I found it therapeutic to read my victim impact statement out in court where I could say directly to him, as he was present in the courtroom, just how difficult it was for me to live with this experience. I recall feeling intensely satisfied that this man, who had taken away my power and personal autonomy would now, for the first time, hear my voice and what I had to say about his actions, regardless of whether he actually cared or not. As the sentence was passed, I felt that the state was acknowledging that I had been wronged by this man and I can certainly say that this was a good and a necessary feeling. It appeared to me that as far as the judge, the police, the barristers, the solicitors and even those close to me were concerned – justice had been done. For me however, the full extent of justice, in the manner I consider it to be, was a long way off – although I didn't know it then.

When I really reflect on it, my desire to speak to this man began even before he was sentenced. I attended every court appearance there was prior to the actual sentencing much to the surprise of the police involved who didn't think I needed to be there, and they told me this. For me, it was essential to be there as my mind and life was consumed by what had taken place and I needed to witness something happening that would validate this. At one particular court appearance, I recall seeing him afterwards in the carpark as I sat in my car. He was standing on the road speaking to his solicitor. I honestly couldn't believe that he was able to do this – speak to another human being. But I then realised something quite important, the reason he could do this was because he was actually a human. I began to think that if he was capable of speaking to another human being, then why could I not speak to him?

Although my life progressed and I had new life experiences totally unrelated to this one, the desire I felt to confront this man did not diminish; in fact, it grew and became more prevalent in my mind. When I moved back to Ireland following a period of living abroad, it was approaching the time when I knew he was going to be released from prison. Although I had a young child to look after, which occupied much of my time and energy, I would still imagine encountering him somewhere outside when he was going to be released. I pictured running up to him and letting him see how I was, to show him that I was not defeated and that

I understood now what he was, and to tell him that I want to hear an explanation from his own mouth. When he was released from prison, I tried to cover up this desire by playing the fearful victim. I wasn't completely playing the role, as I did still have fear but I wasn't being authentic. I knew then that this hadn't ended for me, although he was out of prison; I needed for something to manifest. I needed for something additional to happen.

Slowly, I began to imagine sitting face-to-face with him, the human that had impacted so enormously on my life and my perception of reality. Could I ever accept that he was a human? I began to think that I just might. An interesting thing about humans is that they are much less scary than monsters. Monsters are things that we fear greatly from a very young age. Fear of monsters can control us; fear of humans is much less likely to.

To say that most of my family were confused by and dismissive of this fantasy that I had of meeting this man when I very occasionally 'confessed' it would be a vast understatement. However, I was very fortunate to have one sister who confessed to understanding why I might be talking about doing such a thing. My sister studied to become a social worker and one day during one of my 'moments of fantasy' she mentioned that she had attended a few lectures of Marie Keenan's in University College Dublin. At one of these lectures she recalled seeing a documentary of a woman in England who had been raped by a man and this woman had discussed her motivations for engaging in a restorative justice programme with him. My sister was somewhat surprised that our feelings and motivations overlapped quite significantly. This was the first time I had considered that perhaps it was, after all, restorative justice that I was seeking. She suggested that I contact Marie to see if I could potentially attend some counselling sessions with her on the basis that she may understand why I would wish to meet with him. At that stage, I didn't believe that it would be in any way possible for me to engage in such a process, as I had never heard, or considered, that it was even on the agenda of any of the state agencies involved in criminal justice for victims of sexual violence. Back then, the best I hoped for was that I would finally meet a therapist with an understanding ear, who perhaps would be able to assist me more than by suggesting that I imagine this man in the room with me and talk to 'an empty chair'. For me, that was never enough.

It was a very interesting experience meeting Marie for the first time as I recall that she was attending an international meeting on restorative justice for victims of sexual violence the very next day. She said to me the purpose of the meeting was to raise questions about whether even after a conviction and a prison sentence there is something else that a victim might need or look for in order to heal. I indicated that I was living proof that in some instances the answer is most definitely yes. I told her about my own situation and I felt, for the first time, very comfortable in disclosing my motivations with another person. To my ultimate surprise, we ended the meeting by her indicating that she would assist me in seeking a meeting with this man. I recall having a physical reaction to what she said, as I felt something heavy on top of me suddenly begin to lift.

To summarise the next year and a half of my life is somewhat challenging as it entailed much effort to even initiate a process with the offender in my case before any actual preparation work took place. There was no dedicated restorative justice organisation or agency that we could approach so Marie contacted the Probation Service as it seemed to be the most logical step to take due to the fact that we thought he might under their post-release supervision, which he was. They agreed to take this process forward and after several months the offender was finally asked whether he was willing to participate. There is no doubt that this period was a rollercoaster of emotions for me as he had initially agreed and then retracted his agreement. By sheer luck, this man had another change of heart and agreed to hear more about the process. My case was then passed on to an organisation that the Probation Service use to outsource their restorative justice cases to. Before the facilitators met with the offender to explain this process to him, they of course, wanted to hear about my motivations. It would be fair to say that dealing with sexual crimes in the context of a restorative justice meeting was new even to them, so I explained what was motivating me to seek a meeting as the following:

The point for me in meeting with this man was to seek an end to my suffering, to seek an end to my perpetual state of disempowerment and to seek closure from all of the negativity that had blighted my life for many years.

I wanted to see and experience this man as a human, simply because I knew at a mental level that he was one. How could I ever stop fearing him if he was this monster? How could I ever let go of my anger, my seething anger for him if I could not see his humanity? If I had permitted myself to live the rest of my life fearing a 'monster' who existed out there, ready to attack and kill me at any time, then I felt that I was just engaging in, what I deem to be, self-victimisation. Obviously, it didn't take much to identify at an intellectual level that, based on the crime he had committed, he must have been a deeply flawed or damaged human being, and if I could witness this myself then perhaps I would be able to match this cognitive understanding with my emotional state. In this way, I would be in a position to switch my feelings of fear and the residue of anger into something much more positive for me. Additionally I had come to the realisation that all of the negative feelings that I had for such a long time, when I thought back to what occurred, were completely useless and in fact a burden on me. I began to understand that if I retained these negative feelings then I could never have the closure that I wanted. I needed to see him as a human to let go of my negativity towards him because I know that it is impossible to forgive a monster.

I wanted him to see that I was a human too. I knew that if he sat opposite me, seeing me in this light would be unavoidable. I didn't believe that, in his mind, he had ever seen me as a human and in order to move on from this event, I needed him to acknowledge that I am not just a representation of something that he hates or that angers him, but a real live person with a past and future. It was also vital for me that he knew that I was not permitting my fear to control me any longer – and therefore he would realise, at some level, that he had no control any longer.

Thirdly, I wanted to let this man know how I had experienced his assault on me and the full implications of this event on my life. I knew he had been physically present when I described the effects in the courtroom less than one year after the incident, but I knew he had not heard the overarching impacts and, as he was staring at the floor for the whole duration of that court session, he wasn't seeing me, the human, saying it. I wanted him to hear about the fear and shock I felt as he assaulted me; I needed him to know how confused I was about his rage towards me; I felt it was necessary for him to know that he never succeeded in humiliating me – not for one second, by his sexual assault of me. I wanted him to be aware of how a victim of sexual violence becomes a piece of physical evidence after such an assault and how de-humanising that experience is. I wanted him to hear me speak about the post-traumatic stress disorder, the depression, the eating disorders, the shift in my perception of reality – all of it. I was never concerned about whether he empathised with me in terms of this impact; all I wanted was for him to hear me say those words and that the knowledge of this impact was stored somewhere within his brain, even if he was emotionally unaffected by it. For me, this was vital, as I truly believed that I could only let go if I honoured my suffering in this way, by ensuring that the person who triggered it, at the very least, knew what he had done.

Fourthly, I felt compelled to let this man know how I had made a decision some time back to take the most positive out of this experience. This is not because I wanted him to feel that he had helped me in some way, but rather I hoped that he would see that I had chosen not to be defeated. For me, it was just as important to convey these positives to him as it was to describe the negatives.

Finally, I had an acute need to complete that fragmented picture in my mind with the remaining jigsaw-pieces of understanding. If I could place these final bits of understanding down and see the full picture, I knew that only then could I really move on from this event because I would be in a position to see it for what it was. On that basis, I needed to ask him some questions. These were questions that only this man could answer.

First, I needed to know, truthfully, whether he did intend to kill me, and second, I wished to ask him the question that I believe a victim of any crime would ask the person that offended against them – why did you do it, and why did you do it to me?

The preparation work involved in these meetings was vital. I met with the facilitators numerous times and Marie, my support person, was present. We discussed in depth what I might be able to expect from the meeting. I was very fortunate with the facilitators in my case, who I truly feel managed to balance being incredibly warm, understanding and considerate at one level with being highly professional at another. They were very truthful and honest about the reality of meeting with the offender from the outset while still being able to maintain the confidential nature of each of their meetings with him. At no point, right up until the very day that I met him, did the offender explicitly agree to meeting me, but my hope grew each time I found out that he had shown up for the next meeting. As time went on, it became clear to me that the man I was hoping to meet had very little empathy for me, if any at all. Additionally, it became clear that an apology from him was out of the question. Finally, I was made aware that he was willing to answer my questions about why he did it, but that he would only speak the full truth and would only be 'real' about it. All of this was acceptable for me, because I knew that I wasn't looking for empathy from him; I didn't need an apology and all I wanted was the truth – in whatever form it came. Finally the date was set, the 31st of October – Halloween, which is as good a day as any I suppose!

On the morning of the meeting I was anxious, as I expected to be. However, I was incredibly fortunate to have Marie as my support person and her encouragement and steadfast nature proved to be invaluable to me.

As I walked into that room I was met with a sheepish, and a very human half-smile. I can't deny that I was deeply surprised by this awkward smile from a man who had occupied so much space, in the recesses of my mind and memory, as a person choking me and threatening to kill me. My fear of this man suddenly began to evaporate. I sat down and tried to calm my nerves. As I was given my opportunity to speak, he commented that I was brave to be doing this. I told him I was just about to say the same thing to him. I thanked him for agreeing to participate, because even if he was doing it only to gain something for himself, I was also benefitting from it. I told him that he was courageous – because I will honestly always believe that he was, to be able to listen to what I was about to tell him. I told him that I knew it was all a long time ago but I explained that this was why it was so important to do have this meeting now so that there can be closure – finally.

I did not hold back in telling this man what it felt like to me during his assault of me. I did not gloss over the aftermath or how it changed my perception of reality. I am not sure whether he understood all of what I said, but I do know that he has heard it. All the while I was able to look directly at him with no real fear. Sometimes he would look down but I knew he could hear me and for me that was enough.

As much as this crime has caused me to suffer, as I already mentioned, I have also managed to salvage some positives from the experience. Part of the positives that I disclosed to him, and as I have already described to you, was that I had identified a need to see him as a human so that I could let go of the remaining negativity that I felt towards him. I let him know that sitting in front of him, hearing him speak to me, in his own voice explaining his reasons to me was causing this to actually manifest. I told him that I hoped he was now in a position to see me as a human and that perhaps he might remember this moment in the future and realise that others are human like me too. I had planned to wish him success in building a new life for himself as I wanted to convey to him at some level that I had forgiven him so that I could let go of the past. However, as I sat there in that room listening to him speak, I began to feel that I really fully meant it.

Finally, I was given the opportunity to ask the remaining questions that had been lingering in my mind for all these years. I asked him whether he did intend to kill me. The answer I got I will always feel was very truthful. He told me 'no', but it could have happened accidentally when he was choking me. To conclude, I asked him the 'why' question. Again, the answer I received was truthful, forthright and as understandable as it could ever be coming from behaviour that is so deeply irrational. I thanked him and told him that it helped because I could now put all of those jig-saw pieces together and that left me with a full and clear picture of things. I believe that I could never have let go until I could see this for myself.

As the meeting came to an end, after 1 hour 20 minutes I believe, I said goodbye. The moment I stepped outside that room I couldn't help but smile. I felt physically lighter but above all, I felt good. Although I had not explicitly stated the words 'I forgive you' during the course of that meeting, it would be fair to say that it was implied. I have been conscious not to disclose too much of what this person said to me during the course of the meeting, as I would always honour the confidential nature of and context in which he said them. However, within a relatively short number of days following our meeting, I received a message through one of the facilitators indicating that this person wanted to say that he was very sorry for the pain he caused me. To be honest, I could never have imagined that happening, but because I have met him, I do believe that he means it.

I am continually processing the enormous impact that this meeting has had on me and as time goes on I am sure there are many more conclusions I will be able to draw from it. I can honestly say that I'm still just in awe of the powerful nature of restorative justice. But what I can say is that, to date, I have come to the following realisations:

I have concluded that the man I met in that room is more than just the person from my memories. The person I met is a human rather than a monster. The man I met is no angel, but he's also not a devil. The man I encountered did not really wish to be the way he was, and he had a strong desire to do something 'good' by meeting with me. If you asked me how I feel about him now, well I can say that I feel nothing but compassion and pity for him at a very human level and truly I wish him all the best in his future life. I can't deny that it is a very profound experience to be transported from intensely fearing a person to having a strong desire to help them.

For me, this experience has been invaluable. I know that I will not regret a second of it for the rest of my life because with such a simple act of sitting face-to-face with this person at a round table, it has single-handedly changed the reaction I have when I think of the violence of that night all those years ago. When I think back now I am automatically catapulted into my restorative justice meeting with him, and therefore when I think back to this event, it actually generates a feeling of contentment. This is a dynamic that I could never have imagined occurring. For me, before this meeting, the memories I had equalled emotional pain, a strong feeling of disempowerment, fear, de-humanisation and an intense hatred for the offender. But now, when I think back to that night, the memories of it generate a strong feeling of empowerment, fulfilment and compassion for this man. I know that for me, no amount of therapy could ever have achieved that.

Restorative justice for me was always about my quality of life, it was about my liberation from this crime, and it was about healing. I do feel that it did all that.

For this man, I can only hope that it may have impacted him even half as much as it has me. I'm not sure whether this impact will help to reduce the probability of him ever re-offending, but I do know that he was a man who didn't feel he could ever say sorry to me, and yet he did. If you have ever been to Dublin you will know what a small city it is. Although I won't be looking for this person everywhere I go now, I know that there is a chance I may pass him by on the street one day. After having this meeting I know that I will be able to hold my head high and without any fear pass by, because what I lost has now been restored.

6 Conclusion

Ailbhe and I have made a film of the meeting (see www.themeeting.org) and we are engaged in consciousness-raising work in relation to restorative justice. We benefit in doing this work from what Ivo Aertsen has brought to our lives through his compassionate mind and dogged determination to help the world become a better place. We are honoured to have been welcomed into his world and to have witnessed that awesome wisdom.

References

American Association for the Treatment of Sex Offenders (ATSA). Retrieved from www.atsa.com.

Bass, E. & Davison, L (1988). *The courage to heal. A guide for women survivors of child sexual abuse*. New York: Harper Collins.

Blanchard, P. (1954). *The Irish and Catholic Power*. London: Derek Verschoyle.

Centre for Innovative Justice. (2014). *Innovative justice responses to sexual offending: pathways to better outcomes for victims, offenders and the community*. Melbourne: Centre for Innovative Justice, RMIT University.

Christie, N. (1977). Conflict as property. *British Journal of Criminology*, 17, 1-15. doi:10.1093/oxfordjournals.bjc.a046783.

Daly, K. (2011). Conventional and innovative justice responses to sexual violence. *ACCS Issues*, 12, 1-35. Melbourne: Australian Centre for the Study of Sexual Assault, Australian Institute of Family Studies.

Daly, K. (2017). Sexual violence and victims. In E. Zinsstag & M. Keenan (eds), *Restorative responses to sexual violence: legal, social and therapeutic dimensions*. London: Routledge.

Fisher, A. Retrieved from www.fswns.org/?page_id=190.

Gillen, J. (2018). *Preliminary report into the law and procedures in serious sexual offences in Northern Ireland*. Retrieved from www.gillenreview.org.

Groth, N. & Birnbaum, J. (1979). *Men who rape: the psychology of the offender*. Switzerland: Springer.

Herman, J. (1992). *Trauma and recovery: from domestic abuse to political terror*. New York: Basic Books.

International Association for the Treatment of Sex Offenders (IATSO). Retrieved from www.iatso.org.

Keenan, M. (1994). *Knowing and not-knowing: therapists and men who rape in conversation* (Unpublished MSocSc Thesis). University College Dublin.

Keenan, M. (1998). Narrative therapy with men who have sexually abuse children. *Irish Journal of Psychology*, Special Issue 1, 136-151. doi:10.1080/03033910.1998.10558176.

Keenan, M. (2012). *Child sexual abuse and the Catholic Church: gender, power and organizational culture.* New York: Oxford University Press.

Keenan, M. (2014). *Sexual trauma and abuse: restorative and transformative possibilities?* Dublin: University College Dublin. Retrieved from http://hdl.handle.net/10197/6247.

Keenan, M. (2017). Criminal justice, restorative justice, sexual violence and the rule of law. In E. Zinsstag & M. Keenan (eds.), *Restorative responses to sexual violence: legal, social and therapeutic dimensions* (pp. 44-68). London: Routledge.

Keenan, M. (2018). Training for restorative justice work in sexual violence cases. *The International Journal of Restorative Justice*, 1(2), 291-302. doi:10.5553/ijrj/2589089 12018001002007.

Koss, M. (2006). Restoring rape survivors: justice, advocacy and a call to action. *Annals of the New York Academy of Sciences*, 1087, 206-234. doi:10.1196/annals.1385.025.

Marshall, W., Anderson, D. & Fernandez, Y. (2000). *Cognitive behavioural treatment of sex offenders.* London: Wiley and sons.

McDonald, E. & Tinsley, Y. (2011). *From real rape to real justice: prosecuting rape in New Zealand.* Wellington: Victoria University Press.

McGlynn, C., Downes, J. & Westmarland, N. (2017). Seeking justice for survivors of sexual violence: recognition, voice and consequence. In E. Zinsstag & M. Keenan (eds.), *Restorative responses to sexual violence: legal, social and therapeutic dimensions* (pp. 179-191). London: Routledge.

The Meeting (www.themeeting.org) 'Stop it Now' campaign (ref). Retrieved from www.-stopitnow.org.uk.

Parkinson, D. (2010). Supporting victims through the legal process: the role of sexual assault service providers. *ACSSA Wrap: Australian Institute of Family Studies*, 8, 1-16.

Ward, T. & Stewart, C. (2003). Good lives and the rehabilitation of sex offenders. In T. Ward, D. Laws & Hudson (eds.), *Sexual deviance, issues and controversies* (pp. 21-44). Thousand Oaks: Sage.

White, M. & Epston, D. (1990). *Narrative Means to Therapeutic Ends.* New York: Norton.

Zinsstag E. & Keenan, M. (eds.). (2017). *Restorative responses to sexual violence: legal, social and therapeutic dimensions* (pp. 108-139). London: Routledge.

About the Editors

Katrien Lauwaert currently works as policy coordinator of the non-governmental organisation Moderator - Forum for restorative justice and mediation. Moderator organises victim-offender mediation for adult offenders and their victims in Flanders, acts as a forum for public discussion about the development of more participatory and democratic ways of doing justice and initiates innovative practices in this field. Katrien is also Bianchi professor for restorative justice at VU Amsterdam and senior affiliated researcher at the KU Leuven. She is a founding member of the European Forum for Restorative Justice. Katrien studied law and criminology at KU Leuven, l'Université Catholique de Louvain (Louvain-la-Neuve), Rijksuniversiteit Leiden and the American University (Washington D.C.). She obtained a PhD from the University of Maastricht for her dissertation on Procedural Safeguards in Restorative Justice. She worked as an assistant professor at the criminal law and criminology departments of Maastricht University (the Netherlands) and the University of Liège (Belgium), where she conducted research and taught courses on restorative justice, victimology, youth delinquency, criminology and criminal procedure. Her recent work focuses on the link between restorative justice and community building, on restorative justice in cases of corporate violence and environmental crime and on working with dialogue groups in delicate restorative justice areas such as sexual violence in an institutional context, radicalisation and violent extremism.

Brunilda Pali is a Research Foundation - Flanders (FWO) funded postdoctoral researcher at the Leuven Institute of Criminology (LINC) working on the project 'Restorative utopias in dystopian times: The shaping of restorative justice in the European penal systems and policies' (see her blog www.restorotopias.com). She is currently a board member and Secretary of the European Forum for Restorative Justice (EFRJ). Together with Ivo Aertsen she has co-edited Critical Restorative Justice (Hart Publishing, 2017) and Restoring Justice and Security in Intercultural Europe (Routledge, 2018). Brunilda obtained a PhD in Criminology in 2016 from KU Leuven, and has studied Psychology at the University of Bosphorus in Istanbul, Gender Studies at the Central European University in Budapest and Cultural Studies at Bilgi University in Istanbul. Her areas of interest are gender, critical social theory, social justice, restorative justice, cultural and critical criminology, and arts.

Stefaan Pleysier is associate professor in youth criminology at the Faculty of Law at KU Leuven (Belgium). He is coordinator, together with his colleague Johan Put, of the Research line on Youth Criminology affiliated to the Leuven Institute of Criminology (LINC). Since October 2016, Stefaan Pleysier is the director of LINC. He teaches youth criminology and research methods in the Bachelor and Master in Criminology at KU Leuven. His main research interests include youth delinquency, juvenile justice and the criminalization of behaviour. Stefaan Pleysier was previously a MacCormick Fellow at Edinburgh Law School at the University of Edinburgh (2012), and 'chercheur invité' at the Centre International de Criminologie Comparée (CICC) at the Université de Montréal (2015).

About the Authors

Daniel Achutti is currently the head of the Law and Politics School at La Salle University (Brazil), and also works as a criminal attorney. He works and researches in the topic of restorative justice, criminal justice, penal reforms, alternatives to punishment and mass incarceration. He is a member of the Brazilian Group of Critical Criminology, and an associate member of the Brazilian Institute of Criminal Sciences and of the Transdisciplinary Institute of Criminal Studies. He also worked as penitentiary counsellor for the State of Rio Grande do Sul (2014-2017), in South Brazil. Author of articles and books on the topics of restorative justice, critical criminology and penal abolitionism, Daniel holds a PhD (2012) and a master's degree (2006) in Criminal Sciences, both obtained at Pontifical Catholic University of Rio Grande do Sul (PUCRS/Brazil). During his PhD (2010-2011), he had a study stay at the KU Leuven (Belgium).

Kristel Beyens is professor of Penology and Criminology at the Vrije Universiteit Brussel (Belgium), where she is the head of the Department of Criminology and leads the Research Group Crime & Society. Kristel is a critical academic observer of the penal system and studies evolutions in prison and community sanctions from a cultural, organizational and social perspective.

John Braithwaite is a Distinguished Professor and Founder of RegNet (the Regulatory Institutions Network) at the Australian National University. Since 2004 he has led a 25-year comparative project called Peacebuilding Compared (most recent book: *Networked Governance of Freedom and Tyranny* (ANU Press, 2012, with Hilary Charlesworth and Aderito Soares). He also works on business regulation and the crime problem. His best known research is on the ideas of responsive regulation (see *Regulatory Capitalism: How it works, ideas for making it work better,* Edward Edgar Publishing, 2008) and restorative justice (see *Restorative Justice and Responsive Regulation*, Oxford University Press, 2002). Reintegrative shaming has also been an important focus (see *Crime, Shame and Reintegration,* Cambridge University Press, 1989). John Braithwaite has been active in the peace movement, the politics of development, the social movement for restorative justice, the labour movement and the consumer movement, around these and other ideas for 50 years in Australia and internationally.

Kristel Buntinx studied Criminology and Law at KU Leuven. She works since almost nineteen years as a victim-offender mediator for the non-profit organisation Moderator - Forum for restorative justice and mediation in Belgium. Moderator is recognized and gets funding by the government as the umbrella and forum organisation for victim-offender mediation for adults in the Flemish part of Belgium. She started working in 2001 as a mediator in the stage of execution of punishment, in almost all prisons in the Flemish part of Belgium. Since 2008 she has also gained experience with mediation before trial. She has eighteen years of experience in serious cases as homicide, murder, armed robbery and sexual violence, and had done almost two hundred face-to-face meetings in those cases.

Dobrinka Chankova is professor of Criminal Procedure Law at South-West University, Blagoevgrad (Bulgaria). She also teaches Alternative Dispute Resolution at the same university. From 2004 until 2018 she lectured on Mediation in Penal and Civil Matters at the New Bulgarian University (Sofia). She has been guest-professor at many foreign universities. She is the chair of the Institute of Conflict Resolution in Sofia and has served as an expert of the National Assembly and Ministry of Justice of Bulgaria and of the Council of Europe Committees on Crime Problems and Mediation in Penal Matters. Professor Chankova has specialized in the USA, UK, Austria etc. During the year 2009 she was a Research Fellow at Tokiwa International Victimology Institute at Tokiwa University (Mito, Japan). Dobrinka Chankova has played a pioneering role in the introduction of mediation to Bulgaria's justice system and in increasing public awareness of the benefits of restorative justice. She has conducted a number of research projects at both national and international level and has published widely in the areas of restorative justice and victim-offender mediation.

Tim Chapman is a visiting lecturer at the University of Ulster in (Northern Ireland, UK), teaching in the Masters programme in Restorative Practices. He has contributed to the development of restorative justice practice in both the community and statutory sectors in Northern Ireland. He spent 25 years working in the probation service in Northern Ireland. He played an active part in developing effective probation practice in the UK particularly through the publication of *Evidence Based Practice* (Home Office, 1998, written jointly with Michael Hough). His 'Time to Grow'-model for the supervision of young people has influenced youth justice practices especially in Scotland. He has published widely on restorative justice and effective practice and has conducted significant research into restorative justice in Northern Ireland, including the ALTERNATIVE project which focused on restorative justice and intercultural conflict. Two books have been recently published on this research. In 2015 he wrote with Maija Gellin and Monique Anderson *A European Model of Restorative Justice with Children and Young People* (IJJO, 2015). He is chair of the Board of the European Forum for Restorative Justice.

Maia Chochua is a Georgian lawyer, with a master's degree in public administration, with over twenty years of experience in justice sector reform. She has held senior positions within USAID and European Union supporting justice sector reform projects, targeting the following areas: judicial reform, liberalization of criminal justice policy and capacity building of criminal justice institutions, strengthening of bar and legal aid service, reforming juvenile justice system, promoting restorative justice approaches, building resocialization and rehabilitation programs in the probation and penitentiary systems, sector management and interagency cooperation, legal education, etc. During the last ten years, Maia Chochua focused on introducing restorative justice mechanisms and reforming juvenile justice in Georgia. She supported the development and implementation of the Juvenile Justice Code of Georgia. Currently, she continues to work on promotion of restorative justice in Georgia that includes expansion of mediation for adults. She has done consultancy work in the region through providing expertise to Ukraine, Belorussia and Armenia on reforming juvenile justice system. Maia Chochua and Justice Renate Winter are founders of the non-profit organization 'New Page', which supports rehabilitation of children, who were diverted away from criminal prosecution through mediation or community work. She is a member of European Forum for Restorative Justice.

Sanja Ćopić is a senior research associate at the Institute of Criminological and Sociological Research in Belgrade and a researcher and the President of the Executive Board of the Victimology Society of Serbia. She currently serves as the editor-in-chief of *Temida*, a Serbian leading academic journal on victimisation, human rights and gender. After obtaining her PhD, she has participated in numerous research and action-oriented projects on victims of crime, domestic violence, human trafficking, gender-based discrimination, reconciliation, victim support and restorative justice, and has published extensively on these topics. Main focus of her recent work has been the use of restorative justice in criminal matters and victim's position in restorative justice programs, and applying restorative approaches in intercultural settings.

Beata Czarnecka-Dzialuk is Assistant Professor at the Department of Criminology, Institute of Law Studies, Polish Academy of Sciences. She has specialised in the problems of reacting to juvenile criminality and introducing restorative justice into the justice system, especially mediation. She carries research in juvenile criminality and justice, probation, restorative justice programs, lecturing restorative justice, mediation and victimology at universities in Gdańsk, Lublin and Warsaw. She is a founding member of the initiative group for 'Introducing mediation' in Poland, co-author of the Experimental VOM Program for Juveniles and its evaluation research, and ember of the Polish Society of Criminology and the European Forum for Restorative Justice.

Johan Deklerck has a PhD in criminology and studied orthopedagogics, criminology and anthropology. He works at KU Leuven (Belgium) and as an independent expert in criminological issues. He obtained extensive practical expertise in youth care, education, justice and prisons, and a research expertise in juvenile delinquency, restorative justice and mediation and prevention (since 1994). He was affiliated with the Master Européen en Médiation, IUKB, Sion (Switzerland) (2000-2010), and with the Master en Médiation, Université du Luxembourg since 2003. He integrated his expertise into his own, scientifically based existential-ecological approach to delinquency, which is visible in his own theoretical models and concepts such as the prevention pyramid, a scientific, highly disseminated model for an integral and positive prevention, the 'flow of life'- model, the restorative pyramid, a cyclical perspective on modernity.

Albert W. Dzur is Distinguished Research Professor in the Political Science and Philosophy departments at Bowling Green State University (USA). He has published widely on citizen participation and power-sharing innovations in criminal justice. He is the author of *Democracy Inside: Participatory Innovation in Unlikely Places* (Oxford University Press, 2018); *Rebuilding Public Institutions Together: Professionals and Citizens in a Participatory Democracy* (Cornell University Press, 2017); *Punishment, Participatory Democracy, and the Jury* (Oxford University Press, 2012); *Democratic Professionalism: Citizen Participation and the Reconstruction of Professional Ethics, Identity, and Practice* (The Pennsylvania State University Press, 2008); and a co-editor of *Democratic Theory and Mass Incarceration* (Oxford University Press, 2016). His conversations with restorative justice innovators regularly appear in the *International Journal of Restorative Justice*, where he serves on the editorial team.

Ezzat A. Fattah graduated from the Faculty of Law, Cairo University, in 1948. For the next twelve years he worked in the justice system in various Egyptian cities as a prosecutor and investigating judge. Fed up with the oppression of Nasser's regime and disillusioned with punitive criminal justice, he left Egypt and headed to Austria where he studied social sciences at the University of Vienna focusing on criminology and victimology. In 1964, seeking a degree in criminology he enrolled at the University of Montreal (Canada) where he obtained an MA in 1965 and a PhD in 1968. He taught at the School of Criminology until 1974 when he was invited by Simon Fraser University in Vancouver to set up the first School of Criminology in Western Canada where he currently is professor emeritus. He is the author, co-author, editor and co-editor of over a dozen books and has published over a hundred scholarly papers and book chapters in learned journals and edited collections. He is a staunch defender of human rights and civil liberties, a harsh critic of punishment and retribution and a strong advocate of restorative justice.

Leo Van Garsse was involved in starting up the first practices of victim-offender mediation in Flanders (Belgium). As a pedagogue, he acted as a mediator and promoter of restorative justice in national and international contexts. In 2000, he was a founding member of the European Forum for Restorative Justice. From 2002 onwards, he was closely involved in preparing a Belgian law on mediation in the criminal justice context, approved by Belgian Parliament in June 22th 2005. In 2015 Van Garsse obtained a degree of doctor in Social Pedagogy (Ghent University) with a research on the dynamics of social work developments in the Flemish forensic sphere. Currently Van Garsse works as a staff-member within Catholic Church administration for the region of Mechelen and Brussels. Ethical and political aspects of 'doing justice' are still at the centre of his interests.

Ailbhe Griffith is a restorative justice advocate. She lives in Dublin and works in the financial services industry. Ailbhe has a personal interest in advocating for the use of restorative justice in cases of violent and sexual crime following her own experience of a victim-offender restorative justice meeting. Alongside Marie Keenan, she has participated in a number of international restorative justice conferences by sharing her story and she has recently portrayed herself in the production of the film 'The Meeting', based upon her real-life experience of her restorative justice meeting. This film was directed by Alan Gilsenan and produced by Parzival Productions.

David L. Gustafson is executive director of Fraser Region Community Justice Initiatives Association (FRCJIA) in Langley, B.C. Canada, an adjunct professor in the School of Criminology at Simon Fraser University, an ordained pastor, and a registered clinical counsellor (psychotherapist). He has worked in the areas of crime, prisons, victimology, criminology and trauma recovery for over thirty years. He holds a PhD in Criminological sciences from KU Leuven (Belgium). His primary research interests continue to be in the fields of trauma and recovery, the related brain science and the impacts of facilitating therapeutic dialogue between victims and offenders in crimes of severe violence.

Marie Keenan is an associate professor at the School of Social Policy, Social Work and Social Justice, University College Dublin (2000-present) and a member of the Advisory Board of UCD's Criminology Institute. She was involved with the Australian Royal Commission into the abuse of children in an advisory capacity and was a member of an International Academic Board for review of the literature. Previously she worked as a forensic psychotherapist and social worker in child protection (1976-79), mental health (1979-1984), the Irish Probation service (1984-1987) and addiction treatment (1987-1992). She was instrumental in establishing the Granada Institute in Dublin for the treatment of sexual offenders (1995-2000). She has served on several statutory boards and professional bodies in Ireland and internationally in relation to sexual violence and abuse. She is an accredited psychotherapist and a restorative justice practitioner and a statutory registered social worker. Her publications include *Child Sexual Abuse in the Catholic Church: Gender, Power and Organizational Culture*, (Oxford University Press, 2012); *Restorative Responses to Sexual Violence: Legal Social and Therapeutic Dimensions*, (Routledge, 2017, with Estelle Zinsstag (Eds)); *Broken Faith: Why Hope Matters* (Lang, 2013, with Pat Claffey and Joe Egan (Eds)); *Sexual Trauma and Abuse: Restorative and Transformative Possibilities?* (UCD, 2014)).

Grazia Mannozzi is professor of Criminal Law and of Restorative Justice and Victim-offender Mediation at the University of Insubria (Como, Italy), where she is also the director of the Restorative Justice and Mediation Study Centre (CeSGReM) and of the master in Restorative Justice and Humanistic Mediation. For the year 2019 she is chair of Working Group on Restorative Cities established at the European Forum for Restorative Justice. In 2013 and 2017 she was member of two different Italian legislative commissions, the first one to reform the sanction system, the second one to reform the enforcement of punishment. In her research activity, she has mainly focused on sentencing system, restorative justice, economic crimes, corruption, corporate liability, law and language. Her publications have been translated in several languages. She published the first Italian handbook of restorative justice, titled *La giustizia riparativa. Formanti, parole e metodi*, (Giappichelli, 2017, with G. A. Lodigiani).

Vesna Nikolić-Ristanović is a full professor of criminology, victimology, juvenile delinquency and child abuse at the Faculty of Special Education and Rehabilitation, University of Belgrade (Serbia). She is a founder and the director of the Victimology Society of Serbia (VDS). She is also a member of the European Academy of Science and Arts, former president of the European Society of Criminology (ESC) and honorary member of the World Society of Victimology (WSV). She is a founder and served for years as an editor-in-chief of *Temida*, a Serbian leading academic journal on victimisation, human rights and gender. She is the initiator and coordinator of the Association Joint Action for Truth and Reconciliation in Serbia. She is also yoga instructor certified by the International Yoga Academy - Yoga alliance of Serbia. Her main fields of experience and research include: victims of crime, violence against women, victim support, women's crime, war and crime, reconciliation and inter-group communication, yoga, mindfulness and victims, and restorative justice.

George Pavlich obtained a PhD from the University of British Columbia, and is currently a Canada Research Chair in Social Theory, Culture and Law at the University of Alberta, where he is also a professor of Law and Sociology. He has published several academic articles in the fields of social theory, socio-legal studies, settler-colonial criminal law, restorative justice, critical criminology, and criminal accusation. His books include *Justice Fragmented: Mediating Community Disputes Under Postmodern Conditions* (Routledge, 1996), *Critique and Radical Discourses on Crime* (Ashgate, 2000), *Governing Paradoxes of Restorative Justice* (GlassHouse Press, 2005), *Law and Society Redefined* (Oxford University Press, 2010), and *Criminal Accusation: Political Rationales and Socio-legal Practices*

(Routledge, 2018). George Pavlich's co-edited collections include *Entryways to Criminal Justice: Accusation and Criminalization in Canada* (UofA Press, 2019), *Accusation: Creating Criminals* (UBC Press, 2016), *Rethinking Law, Society and Governance: Foucault's Bequest* (Hart Publishing, 2001), and *Sociology for the Asking* (Oxford University Press, 2003). He is currently working on a history of settler-colonial criminal law in Canada's west.

Christa Pelikan has been a researcher and a senior consultant with the Institute for the Sociology of Law and Criminology in Vienna. After obtaining her PhD, she has been mainly working in the field of criminal law, especially juvenile justice and in the field of family law. Starting in 1985, she has been doing accompanying research on the large Austrian pilot project on 'Victim-offender-mediation in juvenile justice' and later on a pilot project 'Victim-offender-mediation in general criminal law'. She has been chair of the 'Committee of experts on mediation in penal matters' within the European Committee on Crime Problems (CDPC) and member of the Criminological Scientific Council to the CDPC of the Council of Europe. She is a founding member of the European Forum for Restorative Justice and has been the chair of its 'communication committee', participating in various GROTIUS, AGIS, and COST projects at the EU-level. The last of her research activities was with the project 'ALTERNATIVE' within the EU Framework 7 Programme, which dealt with conflict resolution in intercultural settings taking place in Austria, Belgium, Hungary, Northern Ireland, Norway and Serbia.

Antony Pemberton is a master in Political Sciences at Radboud University Nijmegen. In 2010 he obtained a PhD in Victimology at Tilburg University (with professors Groenhuijsen and Winkel as promoters) entitled *The cross-over. An interdisciplinary approach to the study of victims of crime*. Previously he worked as a trainee researcher at the Central Bureau of Statistics Heerlen, researcher and project leader in the Research for Policy department in Leiden and senior staff member for the Victim Support Netherlands service in Utrecht. Between 2007 and 2011 he was a senior researcher at Tilburg University where he became a professor after his PhD. He is currently professor of Victimology at Tilburg University, where he has been the director of INTERVICT (International Victimology Institute) since 2016, and since 2019 professor of Restorative Justice and Victimology at KU Leuven, taking forward the legacy of Ivo Aertsen.

Raffaella da Porciuncula Pallamolla is currently assistant professor at the Law and Politics School at La Salle University (Brazil). She works and researches in the topic of restorative justice, critical criminology and gender issues. She is a member of the Brazilian Group of Critical Criminology, and an associate member of the Brazilian Institute of Criminal Sciences. Author of several articles and books on the topics of restorative justice and critical criminology, Raffaella holds a PhD in Social Sciences, obtained at Pontifical

Catholic University of Rio Grande do Sul (PUCRS/Brazil), with study stays at KU Leuven (Belgium) and at the University of Bologna (Italy). Raffaella also holds master's degrees in the criminal sciences field obtained at Autonomous University of Barcelona (Spain) and at Pontifical Catholic University of Rio Grande do Sul (Brazil).

Fernanda Fonseca Rosenblatt is professor of law at the Catholic University of Pernambuco (Brazil), and a faculty member at the International Institute for Restorative Practices (USA). In January 2014, she completed her DPhil in Criminology at the Centre for Criminology, University of Oxford. In 2005, she was awarded a Master's degree from KU Leuven (Belgium). She is currently an elected member of the executive committee of the *World Society of Victimology*, the book review editor for *The International Journal of Restorative Justice*, and a member of the research committee of the *European Forum for Restorative Justice*. She is also a member of the *Asa Branca Research Group of Criminology*. Her research interests include restorative justice, community (justice), youth justice, street children, critical criminology and victimology. She has published peer-reviewed articles and book chapters in these areas, both in Brazil and abroad, and is the author of *The Role of Community in Restorative Justice* (Routledge, 2015).

Joanna Shapland is the Edward Bramley Professor of Criminal Justice and Director of the Centre for Criminological Research at the University of Sheffield (UK). She has been at the University of Sheffield since 1988, previously working at Kings College London and the University of Oxford, where she obtained her MA and DPhil degrees. She has researched and published on victimology and restorative justice over a long period, and is currently the Chair of the Restorative Justice Forum (Scotland) and Executive Editor of the *International Review of Victimology*.

Kris Vanspauwen holds a master's degree in Criminology from the KU Leuven (Belgium). For eleven years he has worked as a senior mediator at Moderator - Forum for restorative justice and mediation in Belgium, where he has facilitated more than 250 cases, ranging from murder, fatal traffic accidents, and sexual violence. Between 2002-2007 Kris worked as a researcher at the Institute for Law and Society (KU Leuven) on transitional justice and the use of restorative justice in mass victimisation in South Africa and the Balkans. Currently, he is an associate researcher at the Leuven Institute for Criminology and a guest lecturer in the Masters Programme on Human Rights and Multiculturalism at the University College of South East Norway. Between 2013 and 2015 Kris was the executive director of European Forum for Restorative Justice.

Gema Varona is a senior researcher at the Basque Institute of Criminology, University of the Basque Country (Spain). She also teaches courses of victimology and criminal policy at both undergraduate and postgraduate levels. She has published on various aspects of human rights and restorative justice including the interests of victims of terrorism and sexual abuse. Her educational background includes a PhD in law degree from the University of the Basque Country, a master in criminology and a master in sociology of law. Former coordinator of the degree in criminology (2013-2017), current coordinator of the UPV/EHU MOOC on Victimology (2016-), and co-director of the master in victimology of that University (2014-), she is also the co-editor of the Journal of Victimology/*Revista de Victimología.*

Lode Walgrave is emeritus professor in Criminology at KU Leuven (Belgium), where he taught Youth Criminology and Theoretical Criminology, and directed the Research Group on Youth Criminology. He served as a member of the KU Leuven Research Council. Lode Walgrave chaired the International Network for Research on Restorative Justice. In 2008, he received the European Criminology Award. He was guest professor or a fellow at the Université de Montréal, the Australian National University Canberra and at the University of Pennsylvania Philadelphia. He has given key notes to congresses, guest lectures and conferences in almost all parts of the world, and in most European countries. He published about 400 titles in Dutch, which is his mother tongue, in English and in French. Translations are published in Chinese, German, Korean, Portuguese, Russian and Spanish.

Renate Winter has been a judge in Austria since 1981 until the start of her international carrier at the UNODC in Vienna. Her expertise covers juvenile justice, war crimes, crimes against humanity, gender issues, organized crime and restorative justice. She served as international judge of the Supreme Court of Kosovo, as part of the United Nations mission. She was appointed to the Special Court for Sierra Leone in 2002. She served as consultant in justice matters in more than forty countries. She was president of the International Association of Youth and Family Court Judges and Magistrates, president of both the Special Court as well as the Residual Special Court of Sierra Leone and president of the UN Committee of the Rights of the Child (now again vice-president) and is team-leader since eight years of an EU-project 'EU4Justice' in Georgia, where she received an honorary citizenship by the president of the country. She has published numerous articles in national and international press media and professional journals and contributed to books for children. She is bearer of three distinctions of Austria.

Pieter De Witte is a Catholic prison chaplain and a researcher at the Center for Religion, Ethics and Detention (KU Leuven, Belgium). He studied philosophy and theology and wrote his doctoral dissertation on the ecumenical dialogue between Lutherans and Roman Catholics. He taught exegesis, systematic theology and philosophy of religion at the Chishawasha Regional Seminary in Harare (Zimbabwe). His current research interests include the ethics of punishment, human rights in prison and communitarian ethics.

Together with Geertjan Zuijdwegt, he teaches a university course in prison on the ethics of punishment for a mixed group of university and prison-based students.

Dennis S.W. Wong is a professor of criminology and social work at Department of Social and Behavioural Sciences, City University of Hong Kong. His areas of expertise include juvenile delinquency, bullying studies and restorative justice. Professor Wong is honorary consultant on youth drugs abuse, school bullying and offenders' rehabilitation for governmental organisations. He serves as board member for a number of non-governmental organisations and academic societies. He is well-known criminologist in the Greater China region and a life member of the Asian Criminological Society. Apart from publishing articles in local and international journals, he has published books related to criminology, juvenile delinquency, school bullying, alternative to prosecution and restorative justice.

Martin Wright has been director of the Howard League for Penal Reform and policy officer for Victim Support. His PhD at the London School of Economics was on the development of restorative justice, published as *Justice for victims and offenders* (Waterside Press, 1996). He was a founding member of the European Forum for Restorative Justice, and the Restorative Justice Consortium (UK). He has been a volunteer mediator in Lambeth, South London, and with CALM Mediation Service in West London. He is joint editor (with David Cornwell and John Blad) of *Civilising criminal justice: an international agenda for penal reform* (Waterside Press, 2013). In 2012 he received the European Forum's European Restorative Justice Award.

Xiaoyu Yuan is currently an assistant professor at the School of Criminal Justice, Shanghai University of Political Science and Law (Shanghai, China). She holds a master's degree in Criminal Law from China University of Political Science and Law (Beijing, China) and bachelor's degree in Law from Southwest University of Political Science and Law (Chongqing, China). In 2016, she received a doctoral degree in Criminology from KU Leuven (Belgium). She has published a monograph with Springer as well as several articles in peer-reviewed journals. She has been visiting scholar at the University of Oxford, University of Queensland, and Queensland University of Technology.

Estelle Zinsstag is a senior researcher affiliated to the Leuven Institute of Criminology (KU Leuven, Belgium), an associate member of the Scottish Centre for Crime and Justice Research (UK) and co-chair of the Scottish Network of Restorative Justice Researchers. She is a founding member and the managing editor of *The International Journal of Restorative Justice* and joint-chief editor of the book series *Studies in Restorative Justice* both published by Eleven International Publishing (the Netherlands). She publishes mainly in the fields of sexual violence, restorative justice and transitional justice. Most recently she published an article with co-authors Lode Walgrave and Tony Ward in the *European*

Journal of Criminology entitled 'When restorative justice meets the Good Lives model: contributing to a criminology of trust' (2019) and edited with Marie Keenan *Restorative Responses to Sexual Violence: Legal Social and Therapeutic Dimensions* (Routledge, 2017). She has been a visiting fellow at Cornell Law School (USA) and been invited to present her work in the USA, Hong Kong, Iran, Brazil, Germany, Poland, Hungary, the UK, Belgium, France, Spain and Portugal.

Geertjan Zuijdwegt is a Catholic chaplain in Leuven Central prison and researcher at the Center for Religion, Ethics and Detention and the Faculty of Theology and Religious Studies (both KU Leuven, Belgium). His doctoral dissertation in theology was an intellectual biography of the nineteenth-century religious thinker John Henry Newman. His other research interests include the ethics of punishment, the intellectual history of the penal system, and theories of the moral subject. Together with Pieter De Witte, he teaches a university course in prison on the ethics of punishment for a mixed group of university and prison-based students.

9 789462 369696

Printed by Libri Plureos GmbH in Hamburg, Germany